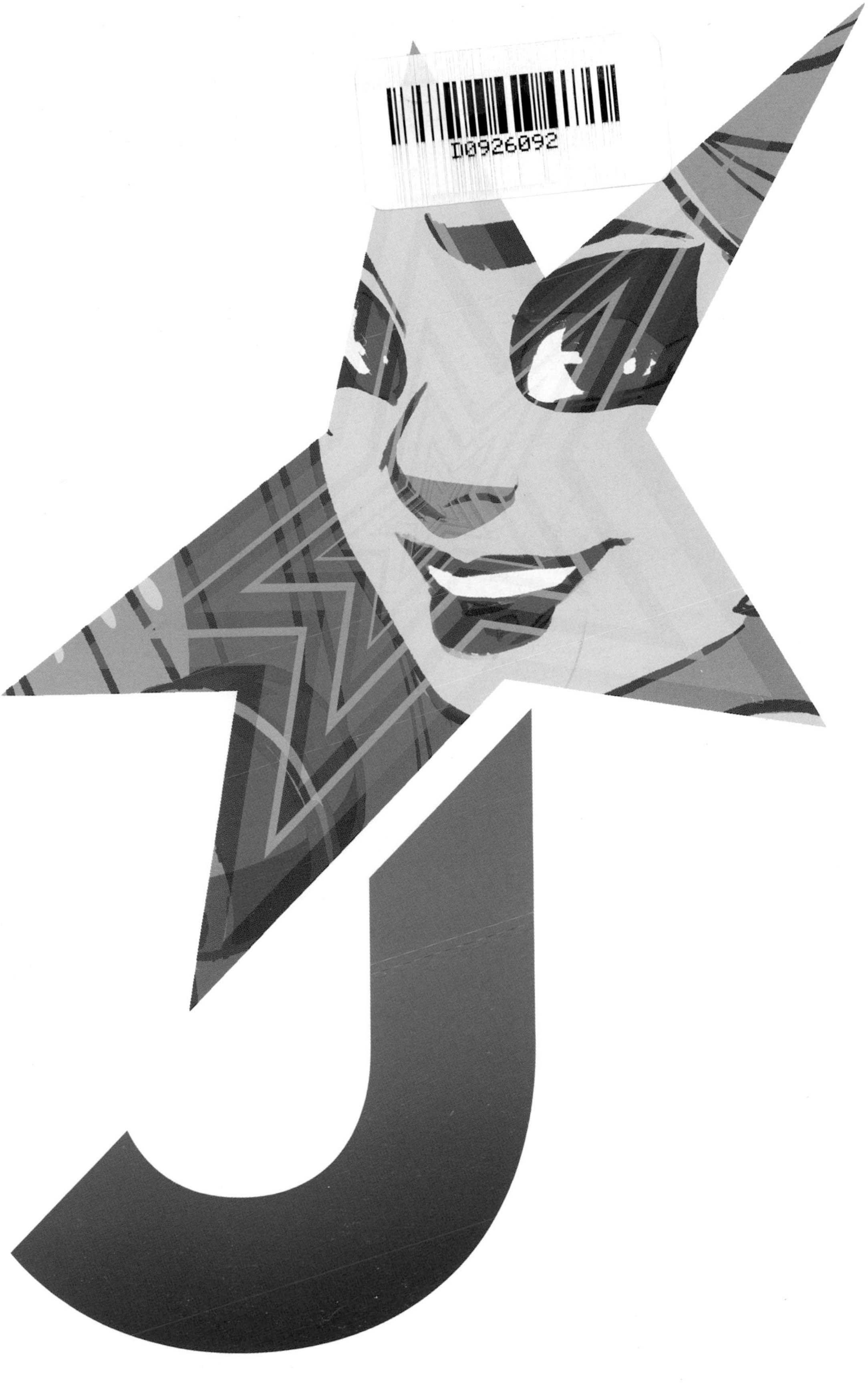

Facebook **facebook.com/idwpublishing**
Twitter **@idwpublishing**
YouTube **youtube.com/idwpublishing**
Tumblr **tumblr.idwpublishing.com**
Instagram **instagram.com/idwpublishing**

COLLECTION COVER BY
STACEY LEE

COLLECTION EDITS BY
JUSTIN EISINGER
& ALONZO SIMON

PUBLISHER
TED ADAMS

Licensed By:

ISBN: 978-1-68405-124-3   21 20 19 18   1 2 3 4

Originally published as JEM AND THE HOLOGRAMS: INFINITE issues #1–3 and JEM AND THE HOLOGRAMS: THE MISFITS: INFINITE issues #1–3.

Special thanks to John Barber; Hasbro's Andrea Hopelain, Elizabeth Malkin, Ed Lane, Beth Artale, and Michael Kelly for their invaluable assistance.

Ted Adams, CEO & Publisher
Greg Goldstein, President & COO
Robbie Robbins, EVP/Sr. Graphic Artist
Chris Ryall, Chief Creative Officer
David Hedgecock, Editor-in-Chief
Laurie Windrow, Senior Vice President of Sales & Marketing
Matthew Ruzicka, CPA, Chief Financial Officer
Lorelei Bunjes, VP of Digital Services
Jerry Bennington, VP of New Product Development

INFINITE

WRITER	**KELLY THOMPSON**
ARTIST (PART 1)	**STACEY LEE**
ARTIST (PARTS 1, 3 & 5)	**JEN HICKMAN**
ARTIST (PARTS 2, 4 & 6)	**JENN ST-ONGE**
LYRIC LETTERERS	**SARAH STERN** **JEN HICKMAN** **M. VICTORIA ROBADO**
COLORISTS	**SARAH STERN** **M. VICTORIA ROBADO** **BRITTANY PEER**
LETTERER/ COLLECTION DESIGNER	**SHAWN LEE**
SERIES EDITOR	**SARAH GAYDOS**

JEM AND THE HOLOGRAMS HAVE BEEN THROUGH A LOT, INCLUDING MOST RECENTLY, JERRICA'S STRUGGLE WITH HER DUAL IDENTITY AS JEM, WHICH ENDED WITH JERRICA REVEALING THE SECRET TO HER NOW EX-BOYFRIEND, RIO. THEY'VE ALSO ADDED FORMER STINGERS' DRUMMER RAYA TO THEIR BAND, AND SHANA HAS TAKEN UP BASS. JEM AND THE HOLOGRAMS SOUND BETTER THAN EVER, BUT THEY'RE TRYING TO MAKE THE BIGGEST DECISION OF THEIR LIVES... NAMELY, SHOULD THEY REVEAL THE SECRET OF JEM TO THE WORLD?

AFTER STARRING IN A PRIVACY-DESTROYING-BUT-INSANELY-SUCCESSFUL REALITY TV SHOW, THE MISFITS ARE BACK ON TOP! LAUNCHING A BRAND NEW ALBUM ON THEIR OWN RECORD LABEL WITH MANAGER ERIC RAYMOND, THEY'RE PRIMED TO RULE THE MUSIC SCENE ONCE AGAIN. BUT EVEN WITH THEIR NEW SUCCESS, PIZZAZZ IS HAVING TROUBLE LETTING GO OF HER GRUDGE AGAINST JEM AND THE HOLOGRAMS...

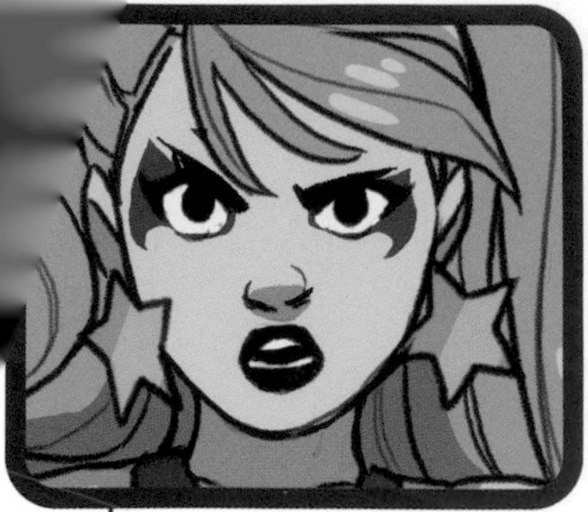

JEM/JERRICA

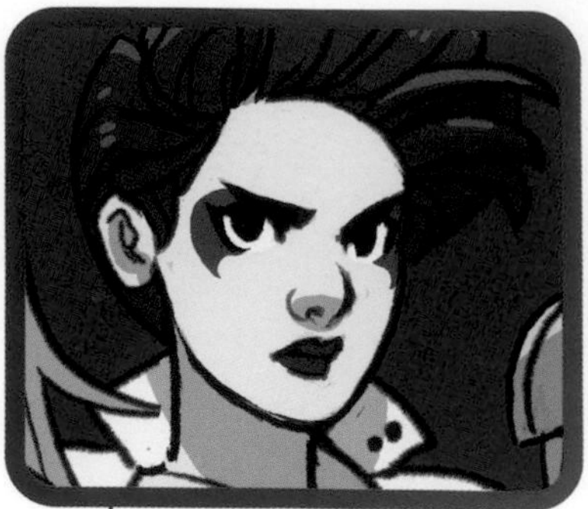

KIMBER

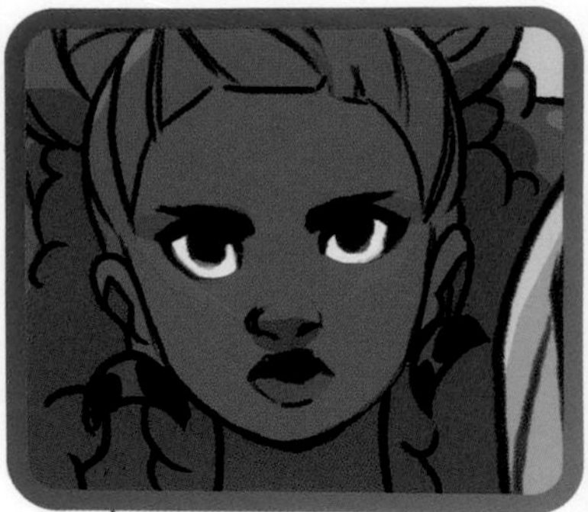

SHANA

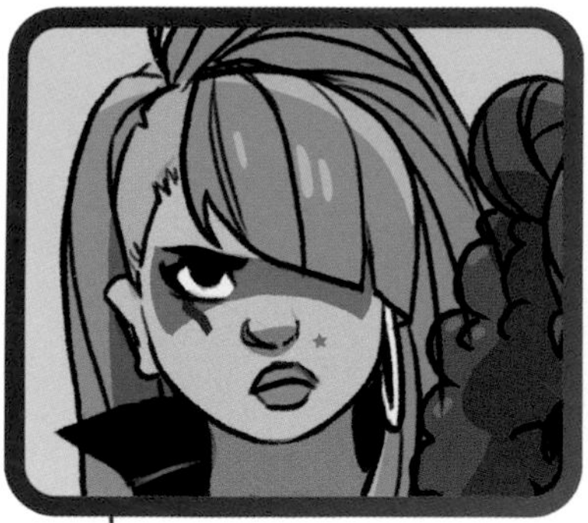

AJA

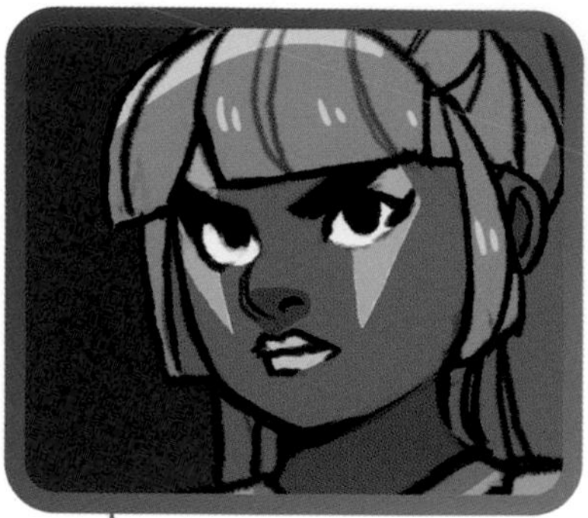

RAYA

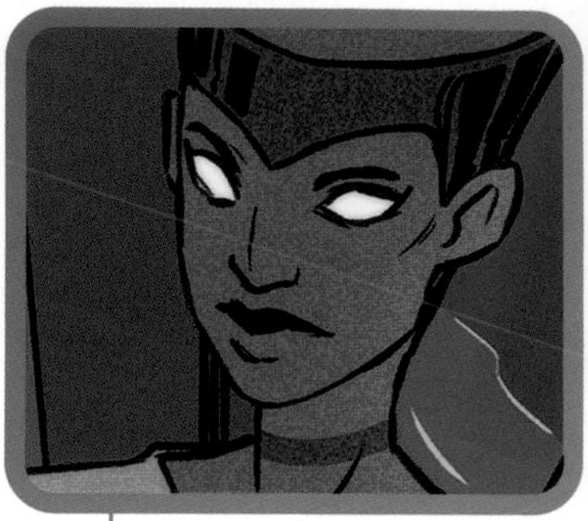

SYNERGY

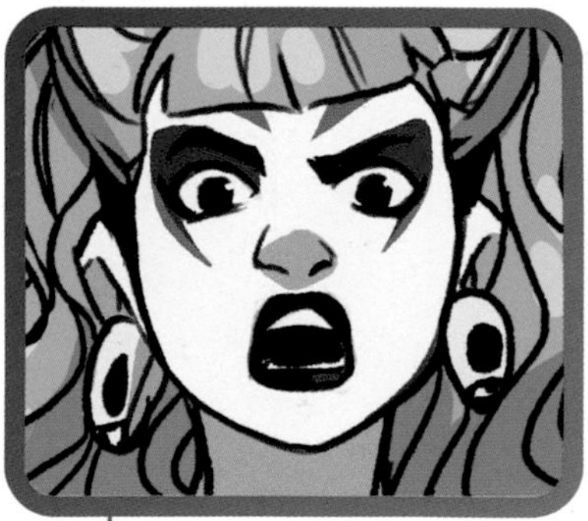

PIZZAZZ

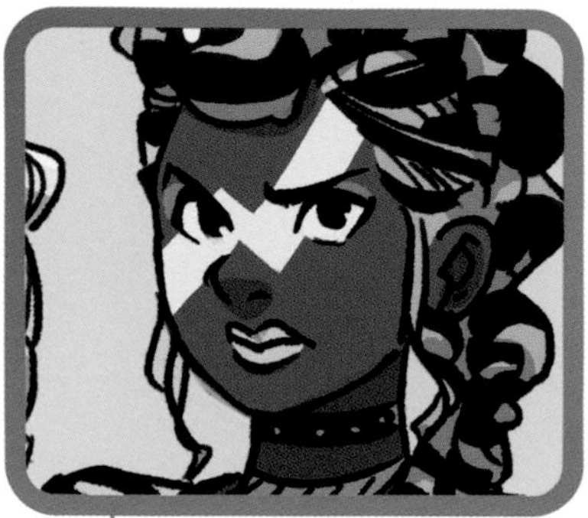

JETTA

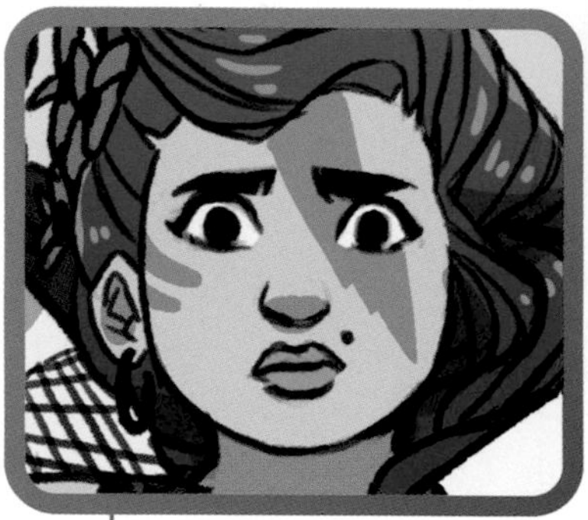

STORMER

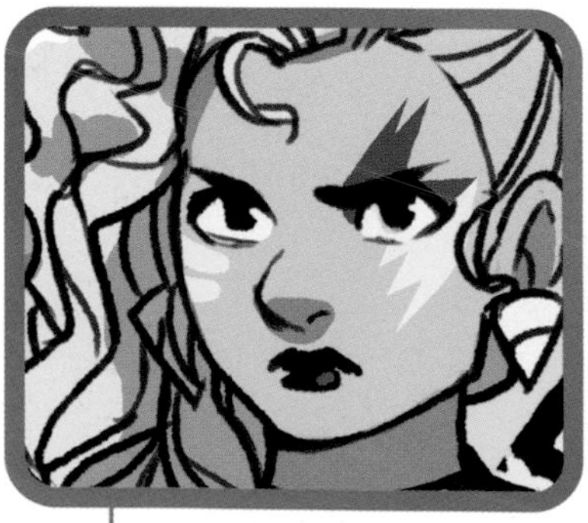

ROXY

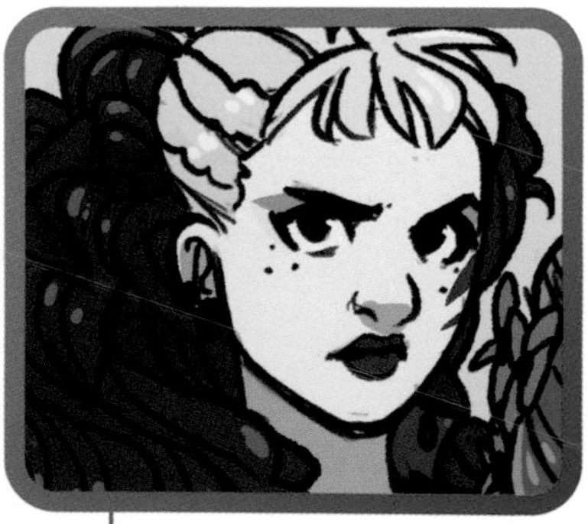

BLAZE

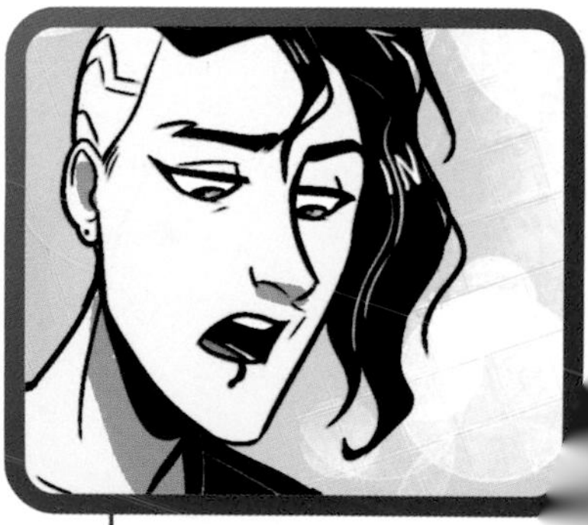

TECHRAT

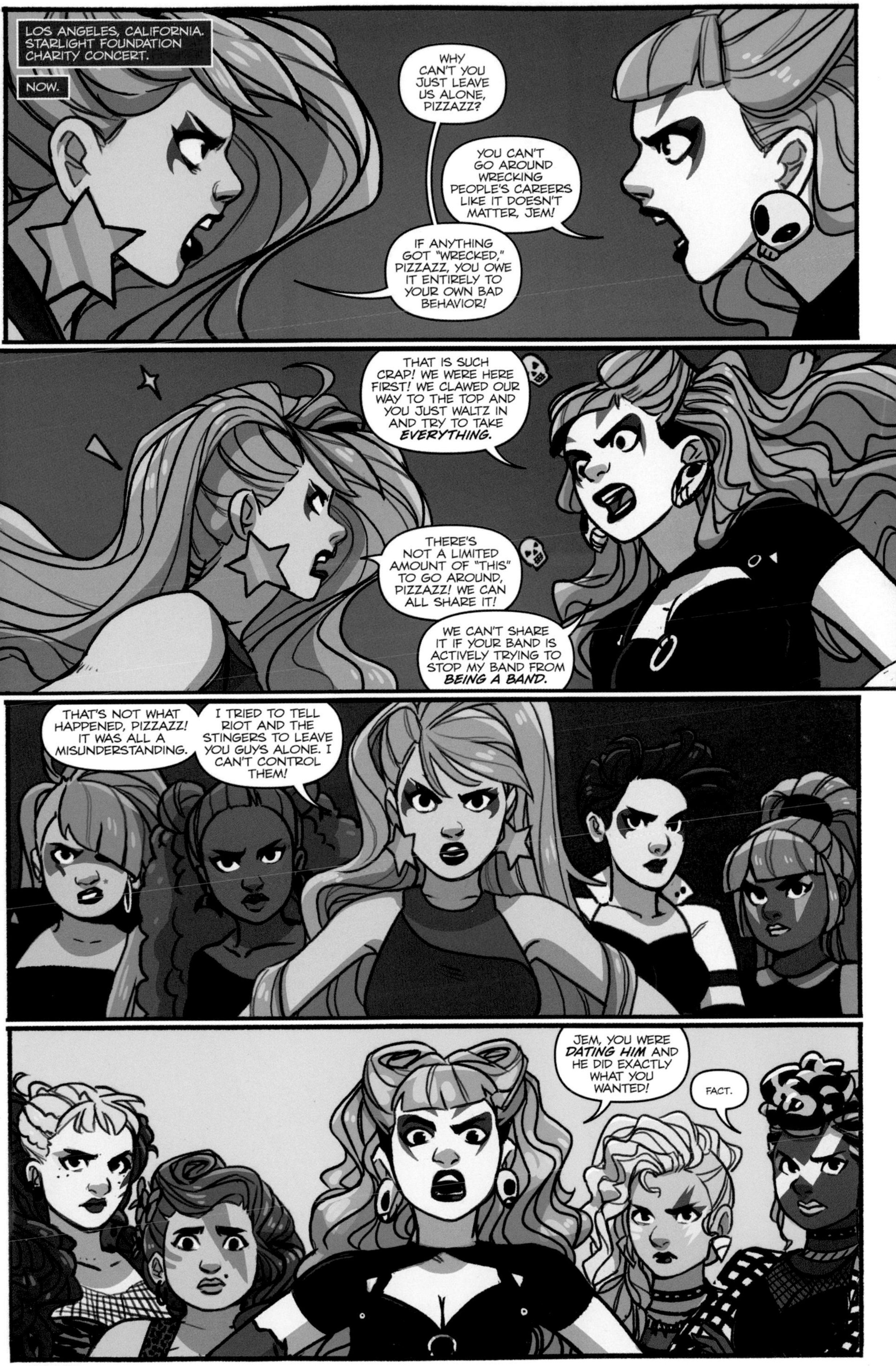
LOS ANGELES, CALIFORNIA. STARLIGHT FOUNDATION CHARITY CONCERT.
NOW.
WHY CAN'T YOU JUST LEAVE US ALONE, PIZZAZZ?
YOU CAN'T GO AROUND WRECKING PEOPLE'S CAREERS LIKE IT DOESN'T MATTER, JEM!
IF ANYTHING GOT "WRECKED," PIZZAZZ, YOU OWE IT ENTIRELY TO YOUR OWN BAD BEHAVIOR!
THAT IS SUCH CRAP! WE WERE HERE FIRST! WE CLAWED OUR WAY TO THE TOP AND YOU JUST WALTZ IN AND TRY TO TAKE *EVERYTHING.*
THERE'S NOT A LIMITED AMOUNT OF "THIS" TO GO AROUND, PIZZAZZ! WE CAN ALL SHARE IT!
WE CAN'T SHARE IT IF YOUR BAND IS ACTIVELY TRYING TO STOP MY BAND FROM *BEING A BAND.*
THAT'S NOT WHAT HAPPENED, PIZZAZZ! IT WAS ALL A MISUNDERSTANDING.
I TRIED TO TELL RIOT AND THE STINGERS TO LEAVE YOU GUYS ALONE. I CAN'T CONTROL THEM!
JEM, YOU WERE *DATING HIM* AND HE DID EXACTLY WHAT YOU WANTED!
FACT.

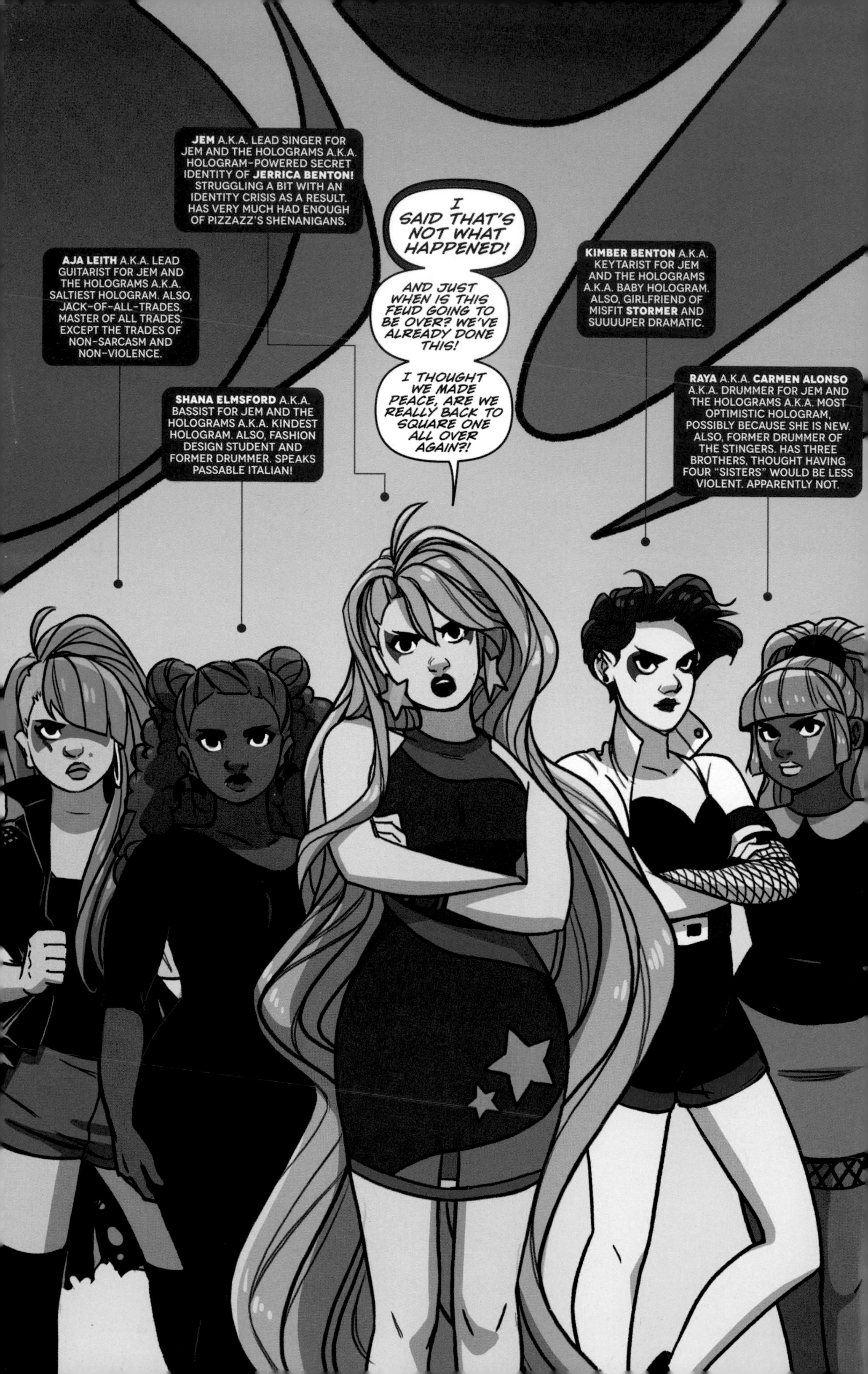
AJA LEITH A.K.A. LEAD GUITARIST FOR JEM AND THE HOLOGRAMS A.K.A. SALTIEST HOLOGRAM. ALSO, JACK-OF-ALL-TRADES, MASTER OF ALL TRADES, EXCEPT THE TRADES OF NON-SARCASM AND NON-VIOLENCE.
SHANA ELMSFORD A.K.A. BASSIST FOR JEM AND THE HOLOGRAMS A.K.A. KINDEST HOLOGRAM. ALSO, FASHION DESIGN STUDENT AND FORMER DRUMMER. SPEAKS PASSABLE ITALIAN!
JEM A.K.A. LEAD SINGER FOR JEM AND THE HOLOGRAMS A.K.A. HOLOGRAM-POWERED SECRET IDENTITY OF JERRICA BENTON! STRUGGLING A BIT WITH AN IDENTITY CRISIS AS A RESULT. HAS VERY MUCH HAD ENOUGH OF PIZZAZZ'S SHENANIGANS.
I SAID THAT'S NOT WHAT HAPPENED!
AND JUST WHEN IS THIS FEUD GOING TO BE OVER? WE'VE ALREADY DONE THIS!
I THOUGHT WE MADE PEACE, ARE WE REALLY BACK TO SQUARE ONE ALL OVER AGAIN?!
KIMBER BENTON A.K.A. KEYTARIST FOR JEM AND THE HOLOGRAMS A.K.A. BABY HOLOGRAM. ALSO, GIRLFRIEND OF MISFIT STORMER AND SUUUUPER DRAMATIC.
RAYA A.K.A. CARMEN ALONSO A.K.A. DRUMMER FOR JEM AND THE HOLOGRAMS A.K.A. MOST OPTIMISTIC HOLOGRAM, POSSIBLY BECAUSE SHE IS NEW. ALSO, FORMER DRUMMER OF THE STINGERS. HAS THREE BROTHERS, THOUGHT HAVING FOUR "SISTERS" WOULD BE LESS VIOLENT. APPARENTLY NOT.

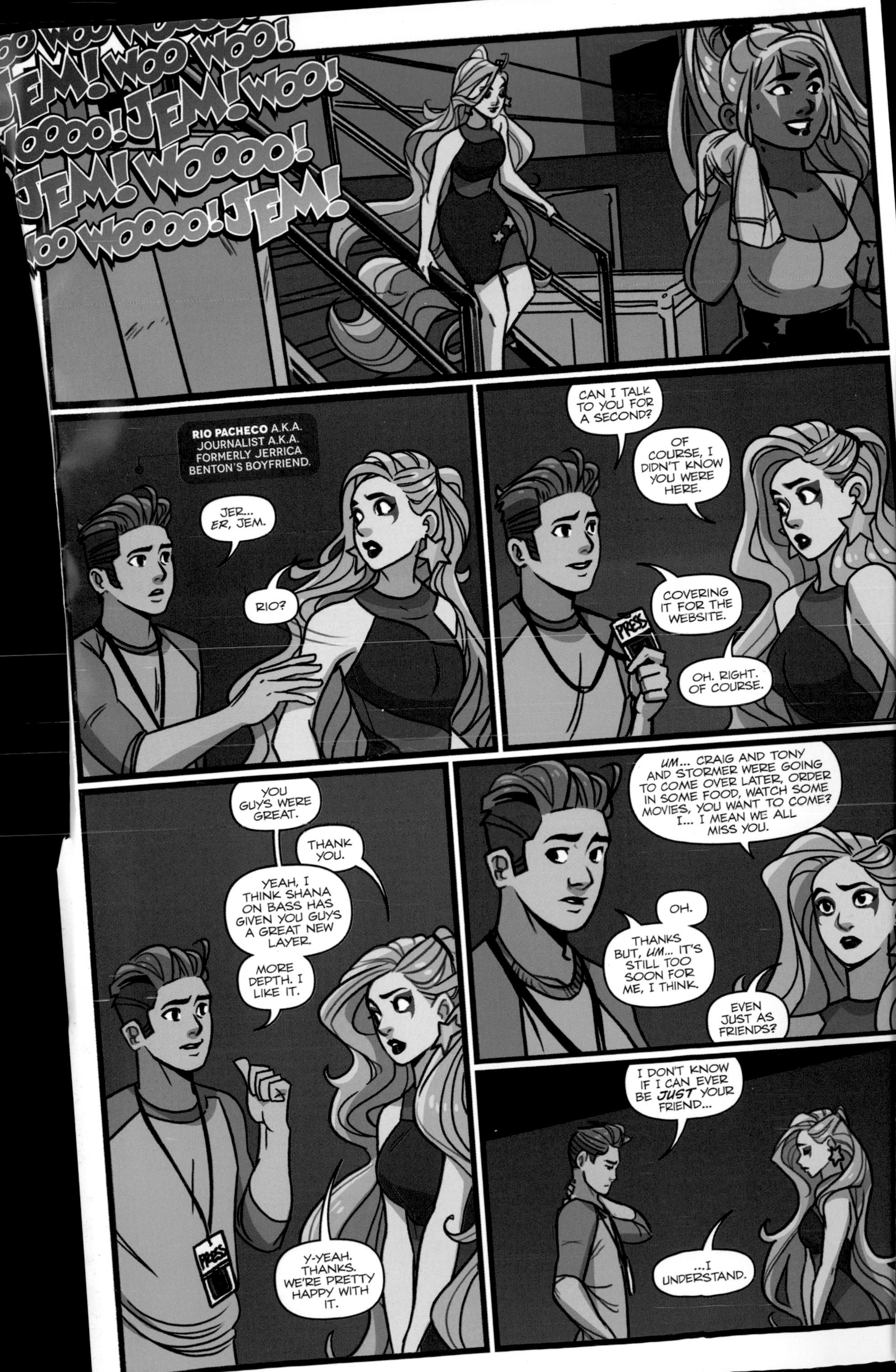

JEM! WOO WOO!
WOOOO! JEM! WOO!
JEM! WOOOO!
WOO WOOOO! JEM!
RIO PACHECO A.K.A. JOURNALIST A.K.A. FORMERLY JERRICA BENTON'S BOYFRIEND.
JER... ER, JEM.
RIO?
CAN I TALK TO YOU FOR A SECOND?
OF COURSE, I DIDN'T KNOW YOU WERE HERE.
COVERING IT FOR THE WEBSITE.
PRESS
OH. RIGHT. OF COURSE.
YOU GUYS WERE GREAT.
THANK YOU.
YEAH, I THINK SHANA ON BASS HAS GIVEN YOU GUYS A GREAT NEW LAYER.
MORE DEPTH. I LIKE IT.
Y-YEAH. THANKS. WE'RE PRETTY HAPPY WITH IT.
UM... CRAIG AND TONY AND STORMER WERE GOING TO COME OVER LATER, ORDER IN SOME FOOD, WATCH SOME MOVIES, YOU WANT TO COME? I... I MEAN WE ALL MISS YOU.
OH.
THANKS BUT, UM... IT'S STILL TOO SOON FOR ME, I THINK.
EVEN JUST AS FRIENDS?
I DON'T KNOW IF I CAN EVER BE JUST YOUR FRIEND...
...I UNDERSTAND.

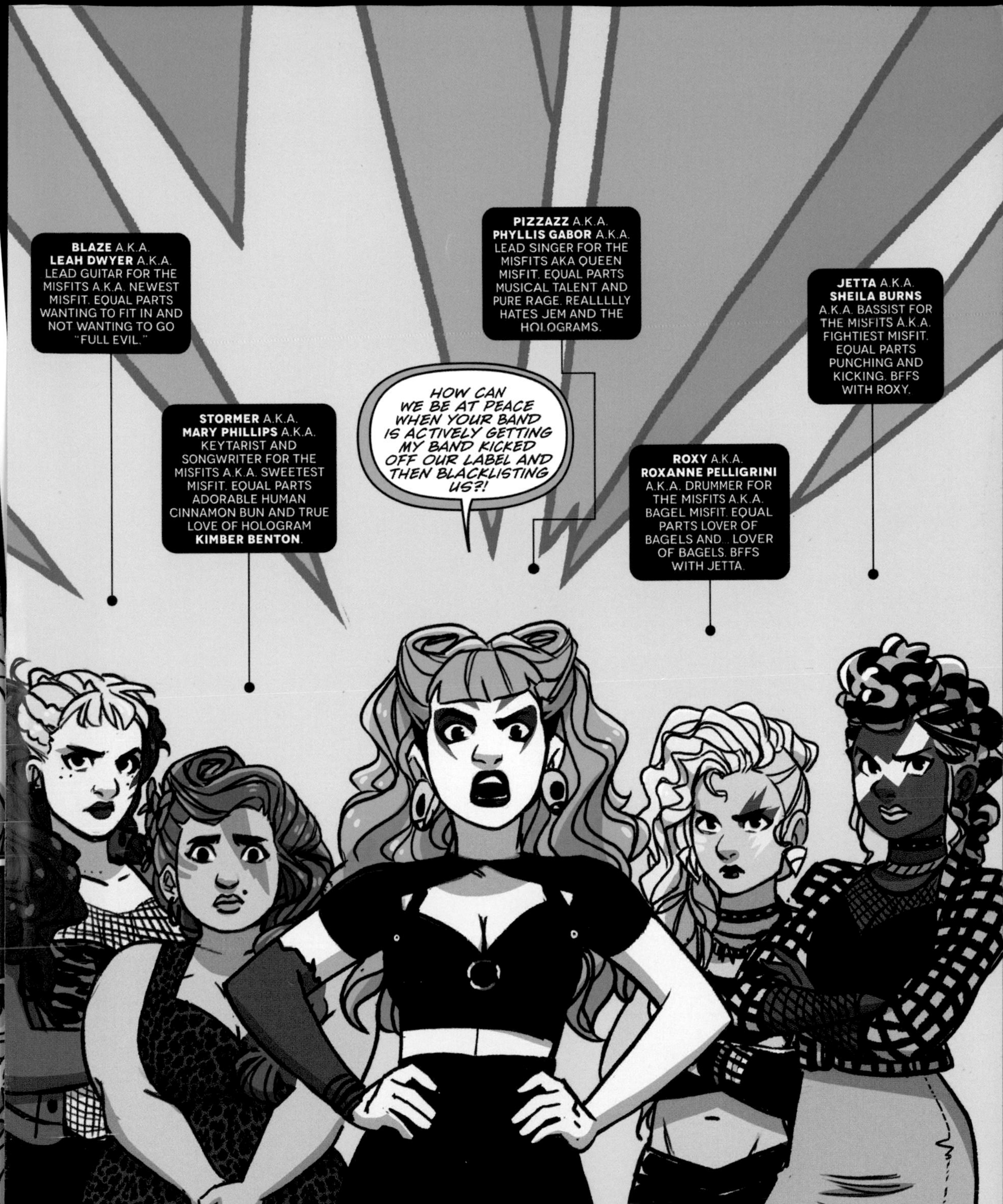

BLAZE A.K.A. LEAH DWYER A.K.A. LEAD GUITAR FOR THE MISFITS A.K.A. NEWEST MISFIT. EQUAL PARTS WANTING TO FIT IN AND NOT WANTING TO GO "FULL EVIL."
STORMER A.K.A. MARY PHILLIPS A.K.A. KEYTARIST AND SONGWRITER FOR THE MISFITS A.K.A. SWEETEST MISFIT. EQUAL PARTS ADORABLE HUMAN CINNAMON BUN AND TRUE LOVE OF HOLOGRAM KIMBER BENTON.
PIZZAZZ A.K.A. PHYLLIS GABOR A.K.A. LEAD SINGER FOR THE MISFITS AKA QUEEN MISFIT. EQUAL PARTS MUSICAL TALENT AND PURE RAGE. REALLLLLY HATES JEM AND THE HOLOGRAMS.
HOW CAN WE BE AT PEACE WHEN YOUR BAND IS ACTIVELY GETTING MY BAND KICKED OFF OUR LABEL AND THEN BLACKLISTING US?!
ROXY A.K.A. ROXANNE PELLIGRINI A.K.A. DRUMMER FOR THE MISFITS A.K.A. BAGEL MISFIT. EQUAL PARTS LOVER OF BAGELS AND LOVER OF BAGELS. BFFS WITH JETTA.
JETTA A.K.A. SHEILA BURNS A.K.A. BASSIST FOR THE MISFITS A.K.A. FIGHTIEST MISFIT. EQUAL PARTS PUNCHING AND KICKING. BFFS WITH ROXY.

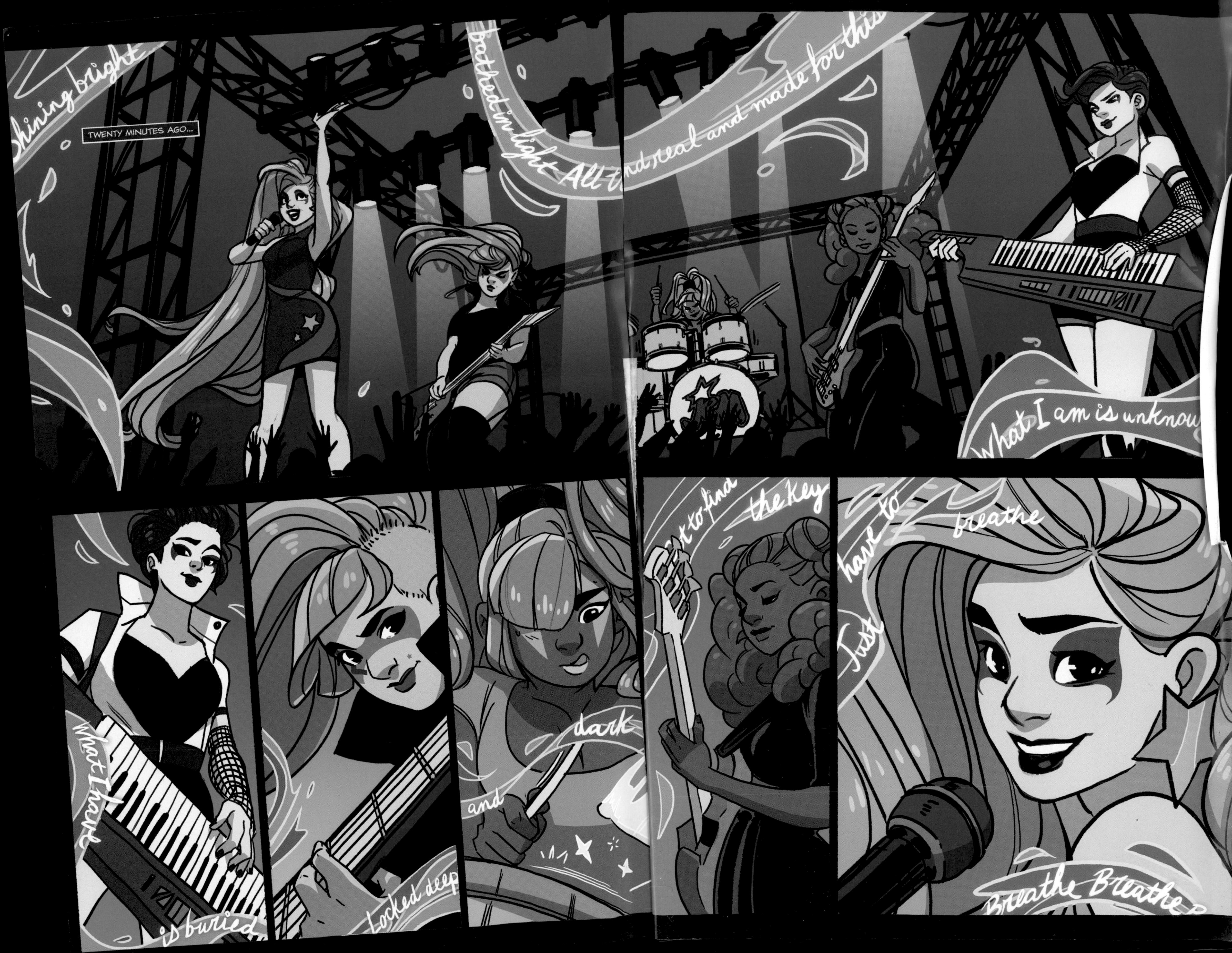
Shining bright
TWENTY MINUTES AGO...
bathed in light All th
nd real and made for this
What I am is unknow
What I have
is buried
Locked deep
dark
and
t to find
the key
Just
have to
breathe
Breathe Breathe

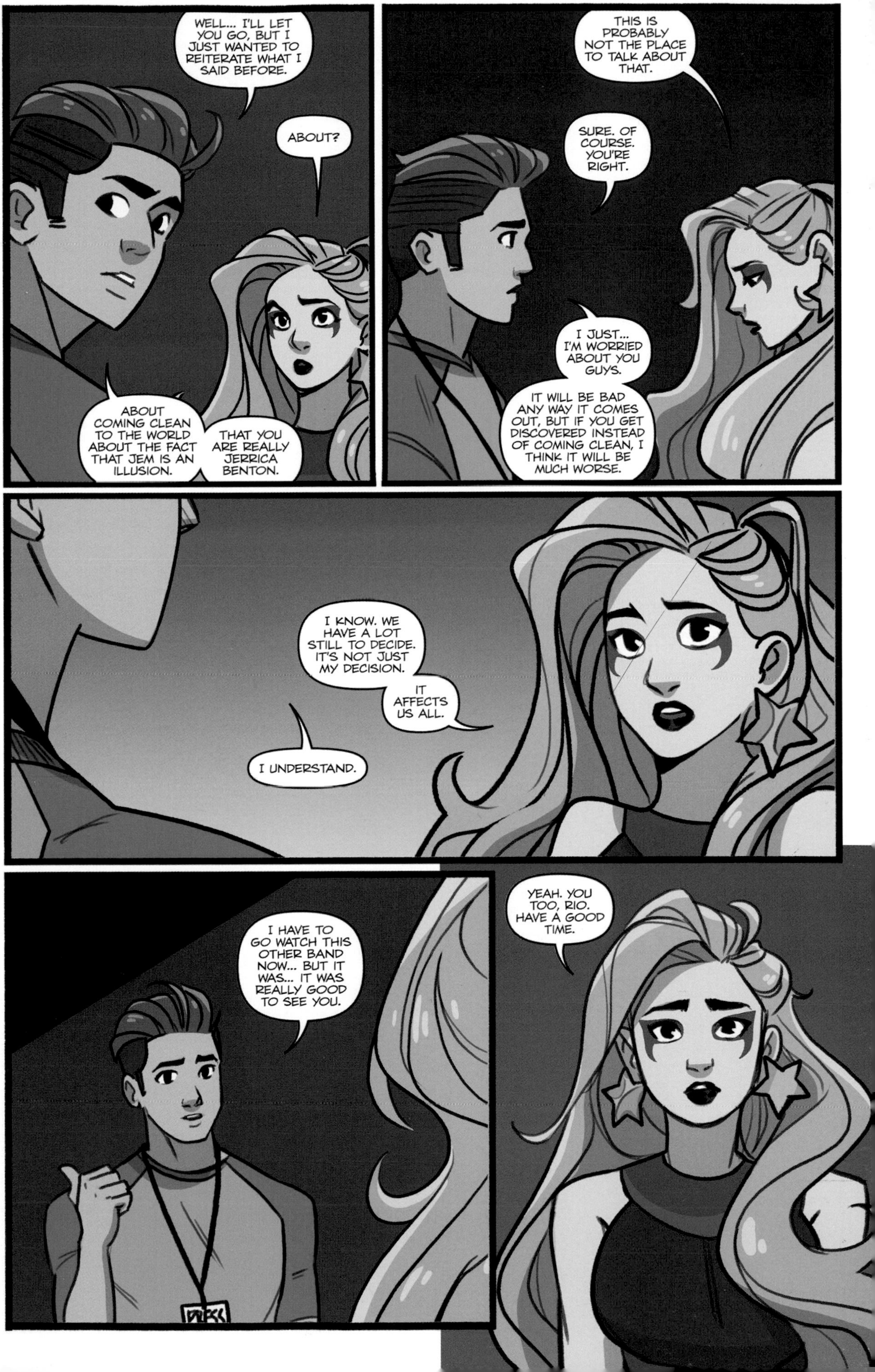
WELL... I'LL LET YOU GO, BUT I JUST WANTED TO REITERATE WHAT I SAID BEFORE.
ABOUT?
ABOUT COMING CLEAN TO THE WORLD ABOUT THE FACT THAT JEM IS AN ILLUSION.
THAT YOU ARE REALLY JERRICA BENTON.
THIS IS PROBABLY NOT THE PLACE TO TALK ABOUT THAT.
SURE. OF COURSE. YOU'RE RIGHT.
I JUST... I'M WORRIED ABOUT YOU GUYS.
IT WILL BE BAD ANY WAY IT COMES OUT, BUT IF YOU GET DISCOVERED INSTEAD OF COMING CLEAN, I THINK IT WILL BE MUCH WORSE.
I KNOW. WE HAVE A LOT STILL TO DECIDE. IT'S NOT JUST MY DECISION.
IT AFFECTS US ALL.
I UNDERSTAND.
I HAVE TO GO WATCH THIS OTHER BAND NOW... BUT IT WAS... IT WAS REALLY GOOD TO SEE YOU.
YEAH. YOU TOO, RIO. HAVE A GOOD TIME.

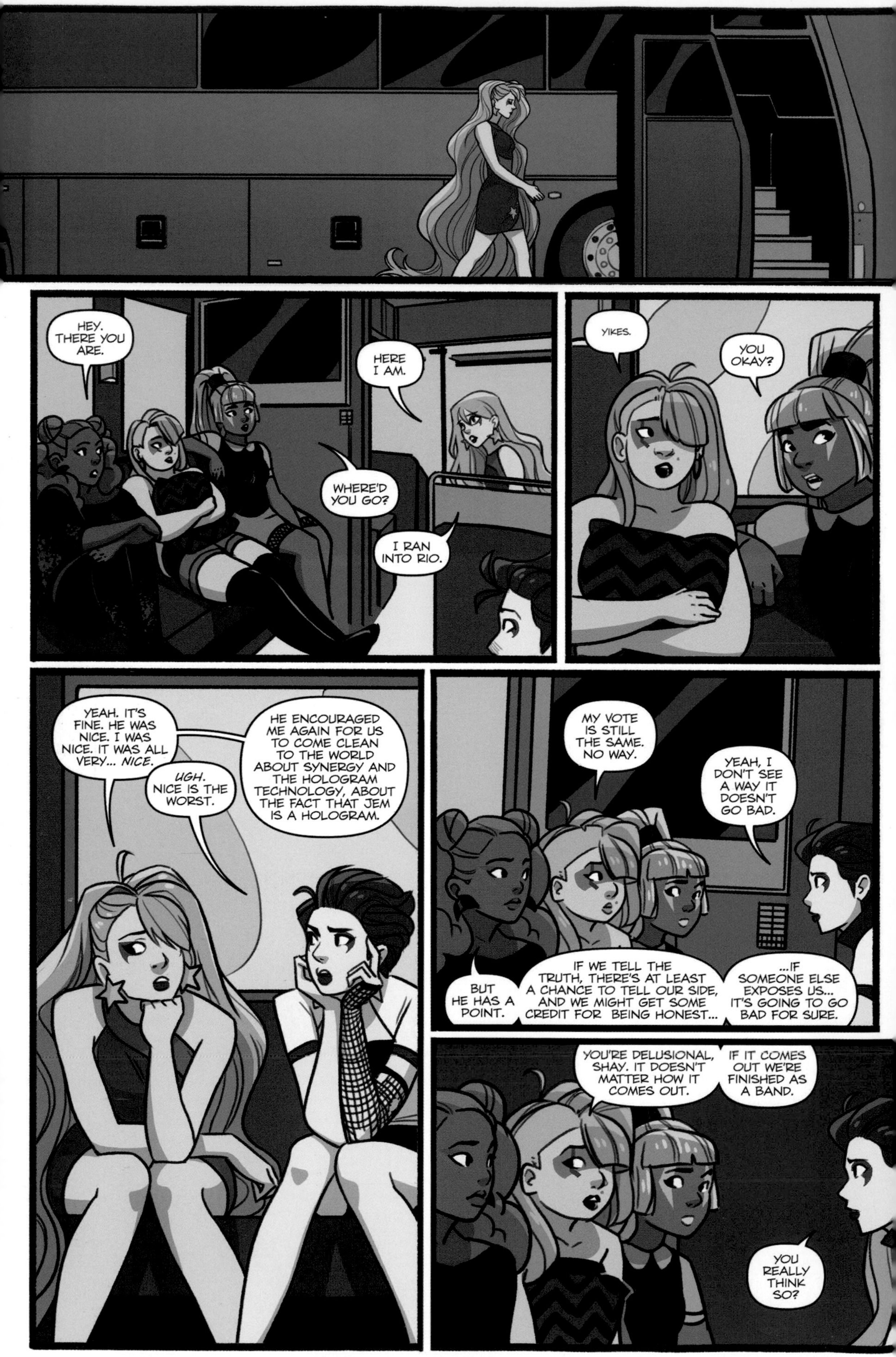
HEY. THERE YOU ARE.
HERE I AM.
WHERE'D YOU GO?
I RAN INTO RIO.
YIKES.
YOU OKAY?
YEAH. IT'S FINE. HE WAS NICE. I WAS NICE. IT WAS ALL VERY... *NICE*.
UGH. NICE IS THE WORST.
HE ENCOURAGED ME AGAIN FOR US TO COME CLEAN TO THE WORLD ABOUT SYNERGY AND THE HOLOGRAM TECHNOLOGY, ABOUT THE FACT THAT JEM IS A HOLOGRAM.
MY VOTE IS STILL THE SAME. NO WAY.
YEAH, I DON'T SEE A WAY IT DOESN'T GO BAD.
BUT HE HAS A POINT.
IF WE TELL THE TRUTH, THERE'S AT LEAST A CHANCE TO TELL OUR SIDE, AND WE MIGHT GET SOME CREDIT FOR BEING HONEST...
...IF SOMEONE ELSE EXPOSES US... IT'S GOING TO GO BAD FOR SURE.
YOU'RE DELUSIONAL, SHAY. IT DOESN'T MATTER HOW IT COMES OUT.
IF IT COMES OUT WE'RE FINISHED AS A BAND.
YOU REALLY THINK SO?

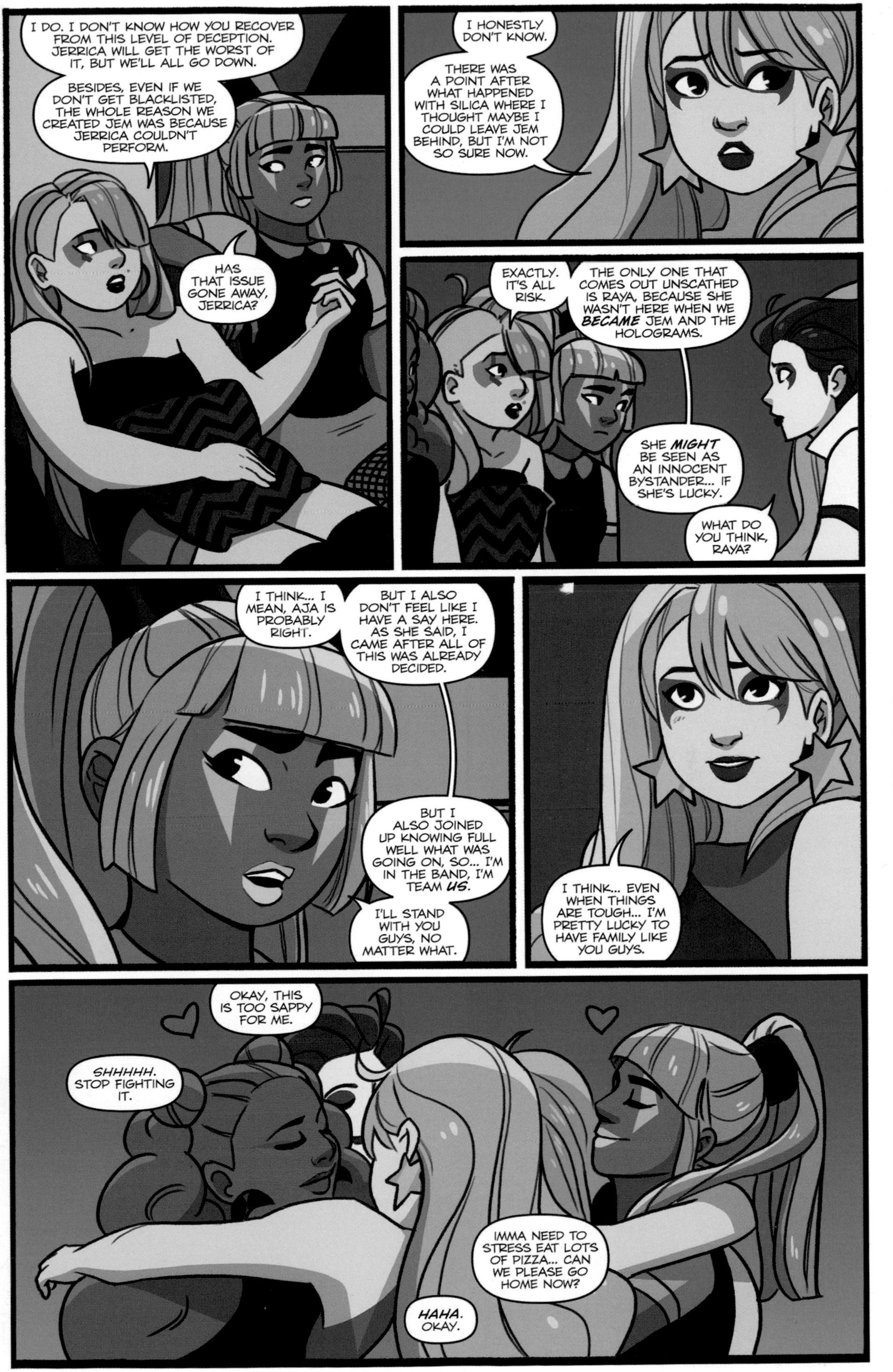
I DO. I DON'T KNOW HOW YOU RECOVER FROM THIS LEVEL OF DECEPTION. JERRICA WILL GET THE WORST OF IT, BUT WE'LL ALL GO DOWN.
BESIDES, EVEN IF WE DON'T GET BLACKLISTED, THE WHOLE REASON WE CREATED JEM WAS BECAUSE JERRICA COULDN'T PERFORM.
HAS THAT ISSUE GONE AWAY, JERRICA?
I HONESTLY DON'T KNOW.
THERE WAS A POINT AFTER WHAT HAPPENED WITH SILICA WHERE I THOUGHT MAYBE I COULD LEAVE JEM BEHIND, BUT I'M NOT SO SURE NOW.
EXACTLY. IT'S ALL RISK.
THE ONLY ONE THAT COMES OUT UNSCATHED IS RAYA, BECAUSE SHE WASN'T HERE WHEN WE *BECAME* JEM AND THE HOLOGRAMS.
SHE *MIGHT* BE SEEN AS AN INNOCENT BYSTANDER... IF SHE'S LUCKY.
WHAT DO YOU THINK, RAYA?
I THINK... I MEAN, AJA IS PROBABLY RIGHT.
BUT I ALSO DON'T FEEL LIKE I HAVE A SAY HERE. AS SHE SAID, I CAME AFTER ALL OF THIS WAS ALREADY DECIDED.
BUT I ALSO JOINED UP KNOWING FULL WELL WHAT WAS GOING ON, SO... I'M IN THE BAND, I'M TEAM *US*.
I'LL STAND WITH YOU GUYS, NO MATTER WHAT.
I THINK... EVEN WHEN THINGS ARE TOUGH... I'M PRETTY LUCKY TO HAVE FAMILY LIKE YOU GUYS.
OKAY, THIS IS TOO SAPPY FOR ME.
SHHHHH. STOP FIGHTING IT.
IMMA NEED TO STRESS EAT LOTS OF PIZZA... CAN WE PLEASE GO HOME NOW?
HAHA. OKAY.

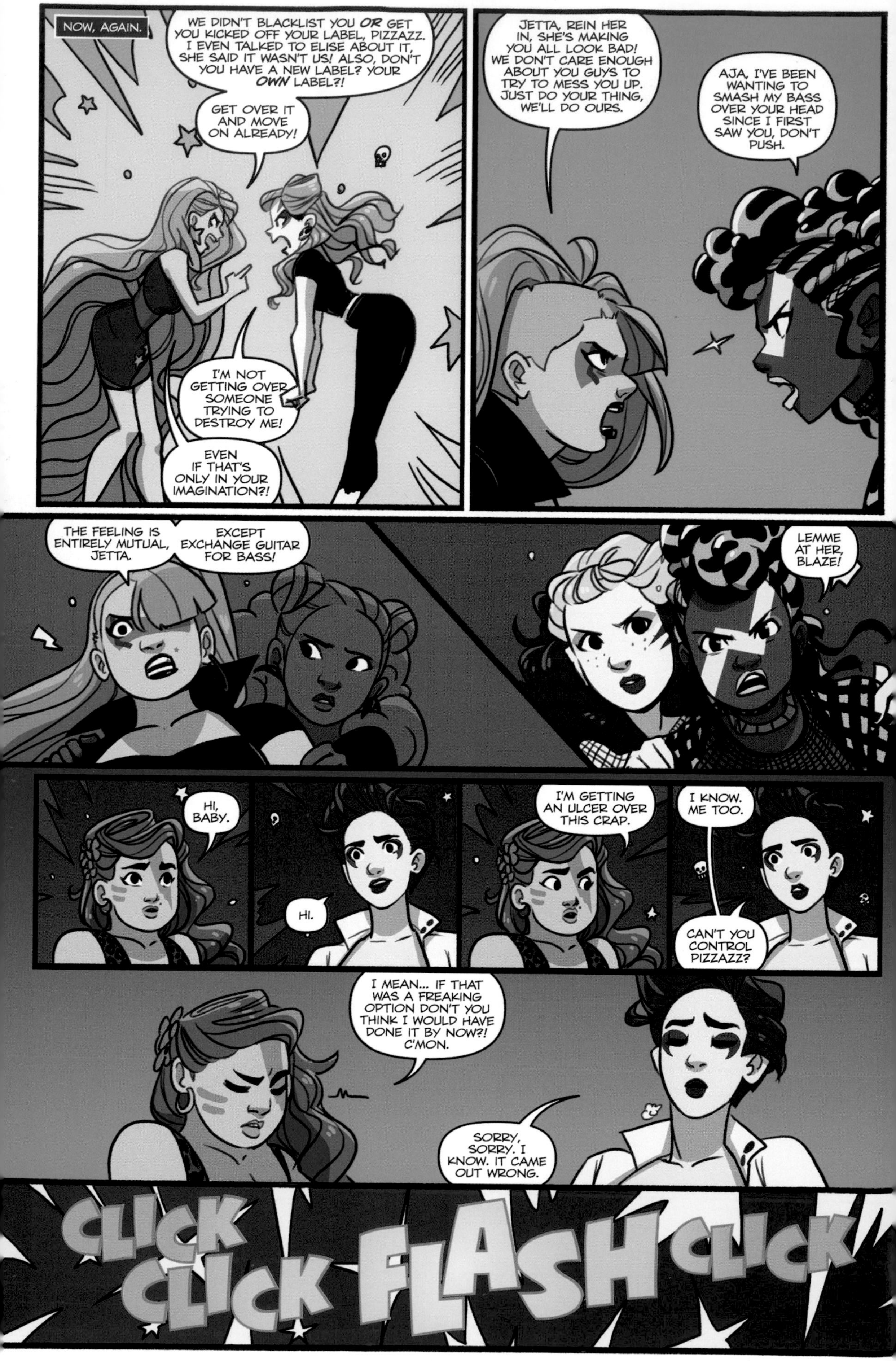
NOW, AGAIN.
WE DIDN'T BLACKLIST YOU *OR* GET YOU KICKED OFF YOUR LABEL, PIZZAZZ. I EVEN TALKED TO ELISE ABOUT IT, SHE SAID IT WASN'T US! ALSO, DON'T YOU HAVE A NEW LABEL? YOUR *OWN* LABEL?!
GET OVER IT AND MOVE ON ALREADY!
I'M NOT GETTING OVER SOMEONE TRYING TO DESTROY ME!
EVEN IF THAT'S ONLY IN YOUR IMAGINATION?!
JETTA, REIN HER IN, SHE'S MAKING YOU ALL LOOK BAD! WE DON'T CARE ENOUGH ABOUT YOU GUYS TO TRY TO MESS YOU UP. JUST DO YOUR THING, WE'LL DO OURS.
AJA, I'VE BEEN WANTING TO SMASH MY BASS OVER YOUR HEAD SINCE I FIRST SAW YOU, DON'T PUSH.
THE FEELING IS ENTIRELY MUTUAL, JETTA.
EXCEPT EXCHANGE GUITAR FOR BASS!
LEMME AT HER, BLAZE!
HI, BABY.
HI.
I'M GETTING AN ULCER OVER THIS CRAP.
I KNOW. ME TOO.
CAN'T YOU CONTROL PIZZAZZ?
I MEAN... IF THAT WAS A FREAKING OPTION DON'T YOU THINK I WOULD HAVE DONE IT BY NOW?! C'MON.
SORRY, SORRY. I KNOW. IT CAME OUT WRONG.
CLICK CLICK CLICK FLASH CLICK

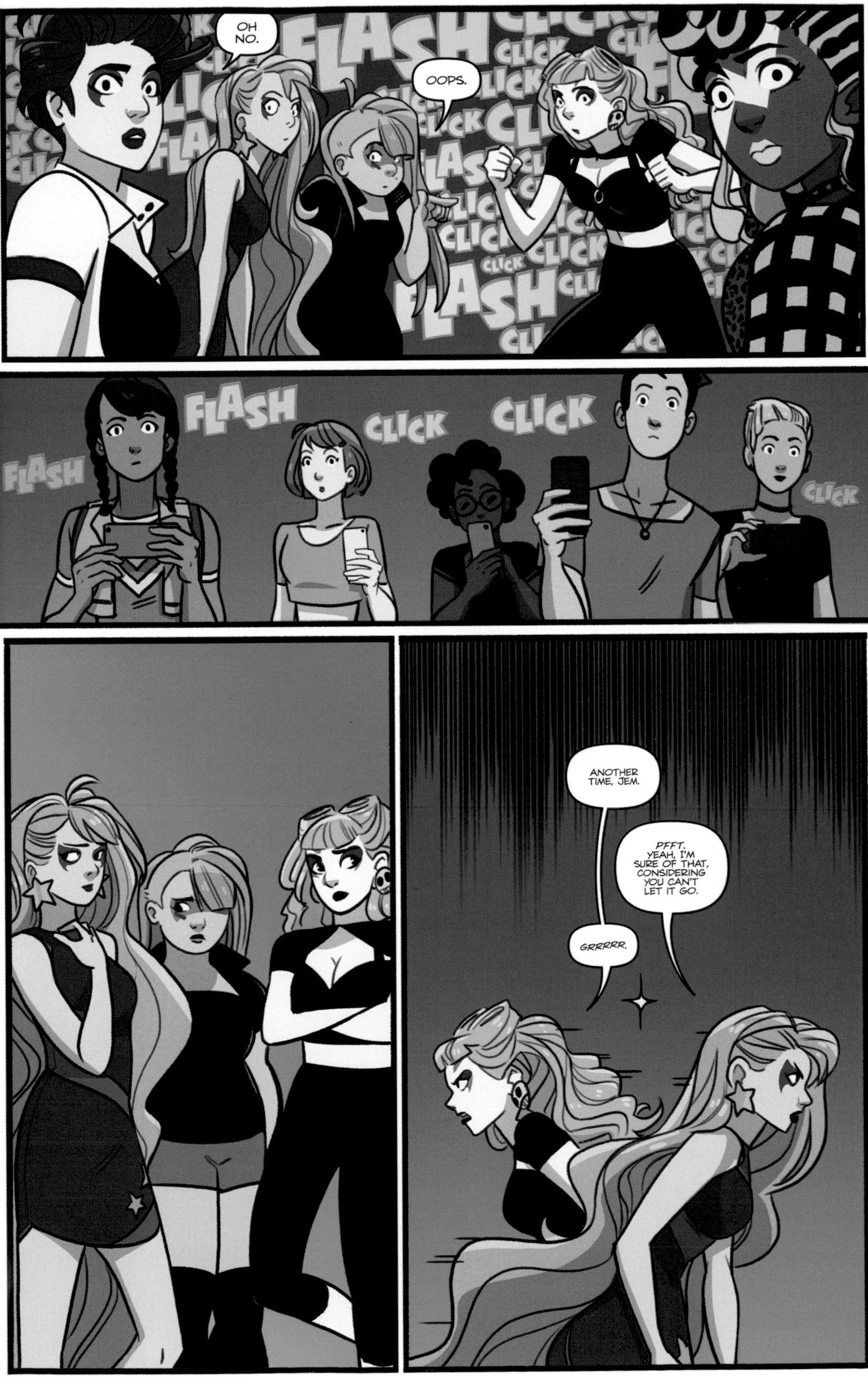
OH NO.
OOPS.
FLASH
CLICK
FLASH
CLICK
CLICK
FLASH
CLICK
ANOTHER TIME, JEM.
PFFT. YEAH, I'M SURE OF THAT, CONSIDERING YOU CAN'T LET IT GO.
GRRRRR.

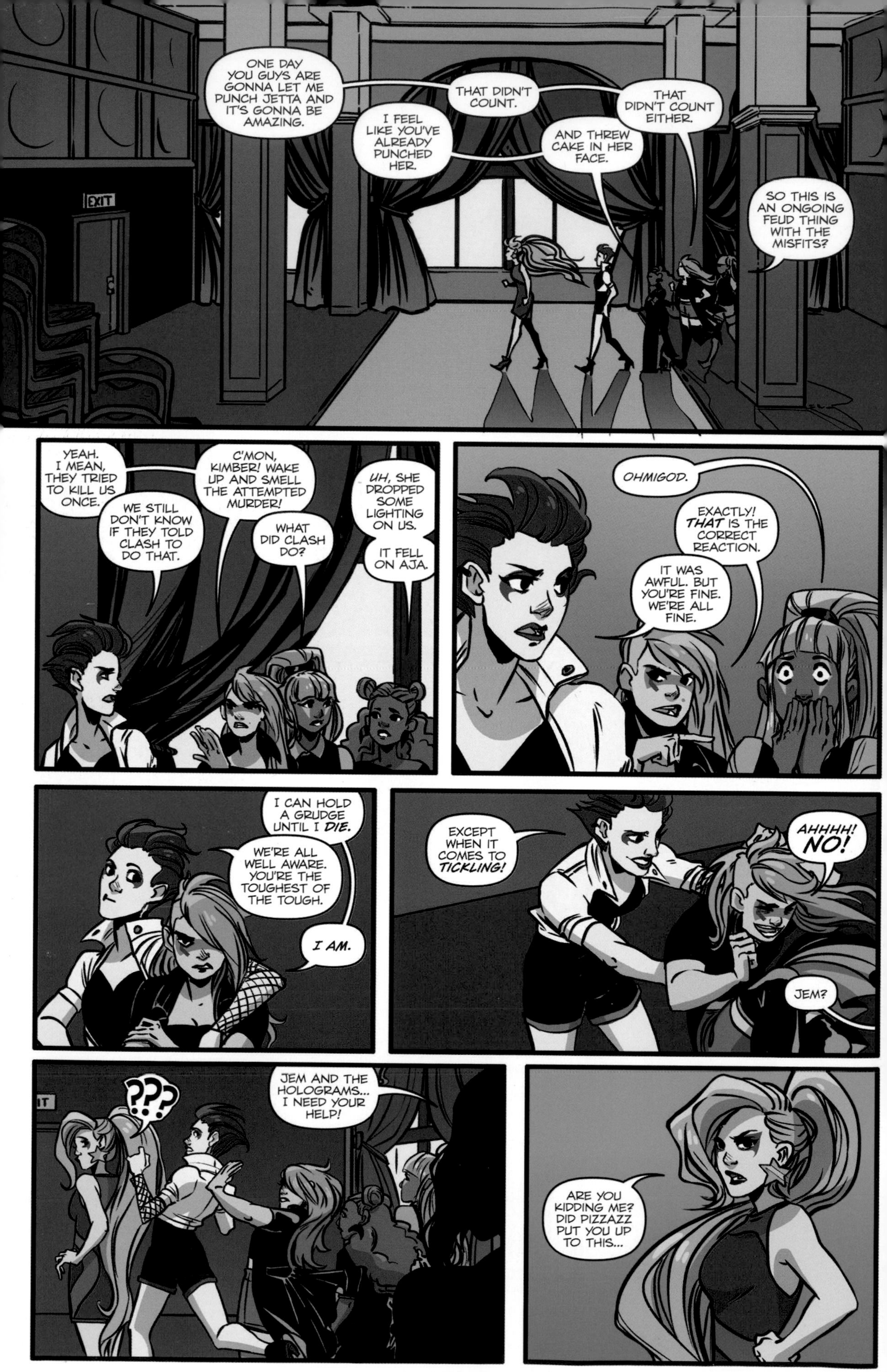

ONE DAY YOU GUYS ARE GONNA LET ME PUNCH JETTA AND IT'S GONNA BE AMAZING.
I FEEL LIKE YOU'VE ALREADY PUNCHED HER.
THAT DIDN'T COUNT.
AND THREW CAKE IN HER FACE.
THAT DIDN'T COUNT EITHER.
SO THIS IS AN ONGOING FEUD THING WITH THE MISFITS?
EXIT
YEAH. I MEAN, THEY TRIED TO KILL US ONCE.
WE STILL DON'T KNOW IF THEY TOLD CLASH TO DO THAT.
C'MON, KIMBER! WAKE UP AND SMELL THE ATTEMPTED MURDER!
WHAT DID CLASH DO?
UH, SHE DROPPED SOME LIGHTING ON US.
IT FELL ON AJA.
OHMIGOD.
EXACTLY! THAT IS THE CORRECT REACTION.
IT WAS AWFUL. BUT YOU'RE FINE. WE'RE ALL FINE.
I CAN HOLD A GRUDGE UNTIL I DIE.
WE'RE ALL WELL AWARE. YOU'RE THE TOUGHEST OF THE TOUGH.
I AM.
EXCEPT WHEN IT COMES TO TICKLING!
AHHHH! NO!
JEM?
???
JEM AND THE HOLOGRAMS... I NEED YOUR HELP!
ARE YOU KIDDING ME? DID PIZZAZZ PUT YOU UP TO THIS...

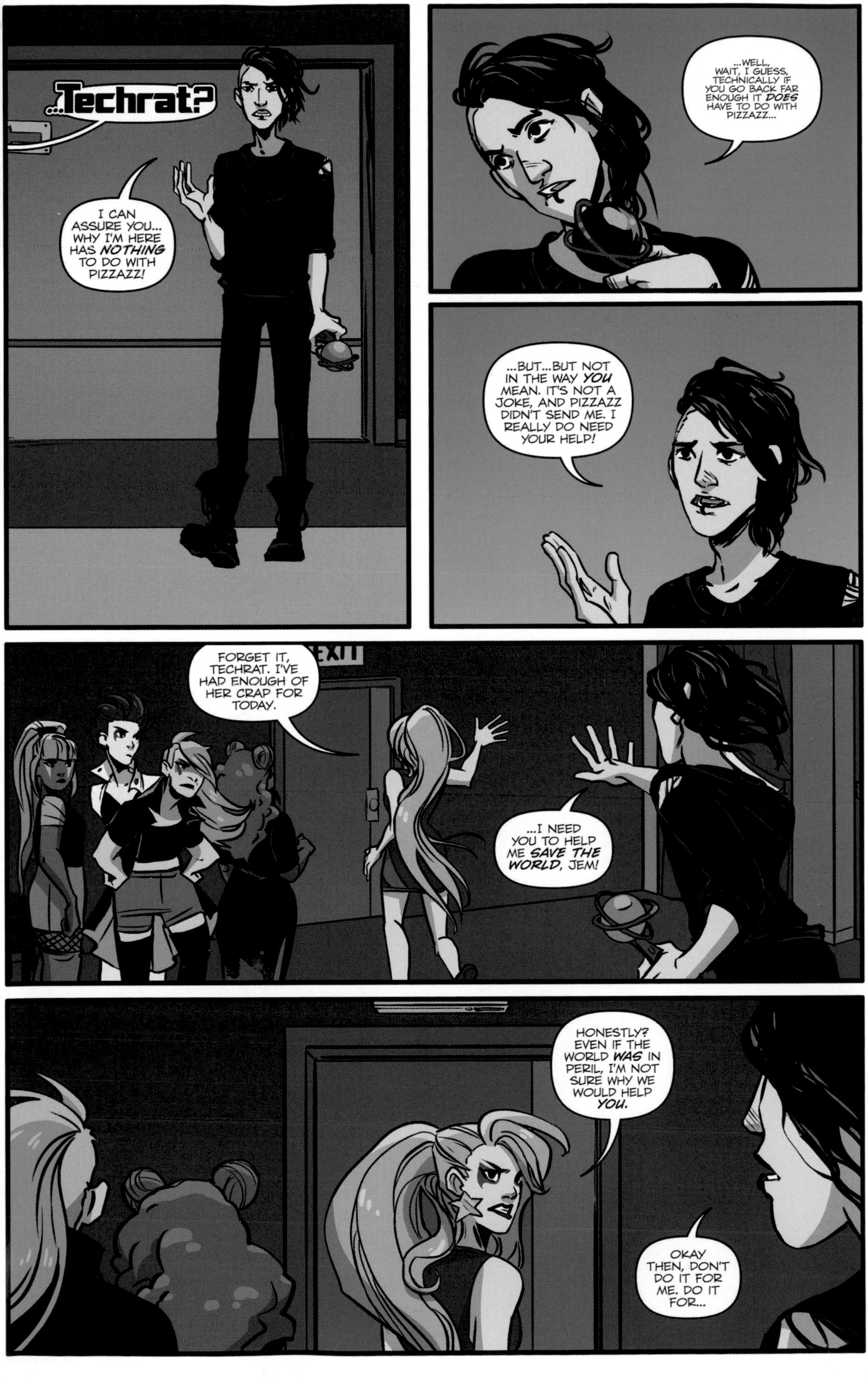
...Techrat?
I CAN ASSURE YOU... WHY I'M HERE HAS NOTHING TO DO WITH PIZZAZZ!
...WELL, WAIT, I GUESS, TECHNICALLY IF YOU GO BACK FAR ENOUGH IT DOES HAVE TO DO WITH PIZZAZZ...
...BUT...BUT NOT IN THE WAY YOU MEAN. IT'S NOT A JOKE, AND PIZZAZZ DIDN'T SEND ME. I REALLY DO NEED YOUR HELP!
EXIT
FORGET IT, TECHRAT. I'VE HAD ENOUGH OF HER CRAP FOR TODAY.
...I NEED YOU TO HELP ME SAVE THE WORLD, JEM!
HONESTLY? EVEN IF THE WORLD WAS IN PERIL, I'M NOT SURE WHY WE WOULD HELP YOU.
OKAY THEN, DON'T DO IT FOR ME. DO IT FOR...

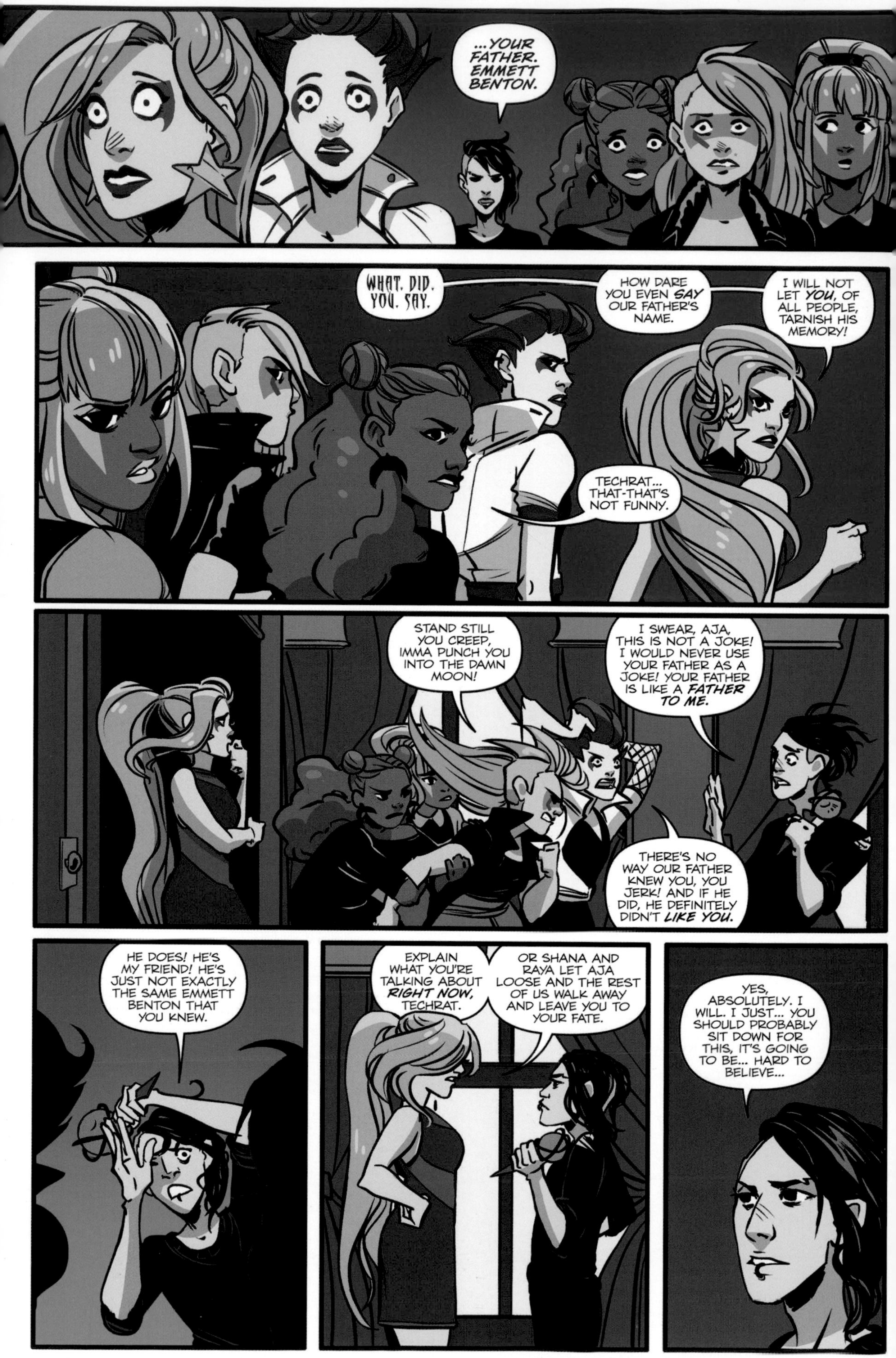
...YOUR FATHER. EMMETT BENTON.
WHAT. DID. YOU. SAY.
HOW DARE YOU EVEN SAY OUR FATHER'S NAME.
I WILL NOT LET YOU, OF ALL PEOPLE, TARNISH HIS MEMORY!
TECHRAT... THAT-THAT'S NOT FUNNY.
STAND STILL YOU CREEP, IMMA PUNCH YOU INTO THE DAMN MOON!
I SWEAR, AJA, THIS IS NOT A JOKE! I WOULD NEVER USE YOUR FATHER AS A JOKE! YOUR FATHER IS LIKE A FATHER TO ME.
THERE'S NO WAY OUR FATHER KNEW YOU, YOU JERK! AND IF HE DID, HE DEFINITELY DIDN'T LIKE YOU.
HE DOES! HE'S MY FRIEND! HE'S JUST NOT EXACTLY THE SAME EMMETT BENTON THAT YOU KNEW.
EXPLAIN WHAT YOU'RE TALKING ABOUT RIGHT NOW, TECHRAT.
OR SHANA AND RAYA LET AJA LOOSE AND THE REST OF US WALK AWAY AND LEAVE YOU TO YOUR FATE.
YES, ABSOLUTELY. I WILL. I JUST... YOU SHOULD PROBABLY SIT DOWN FOR THIS, IT'S GOING TO BE... HARD TO BELIEVE...

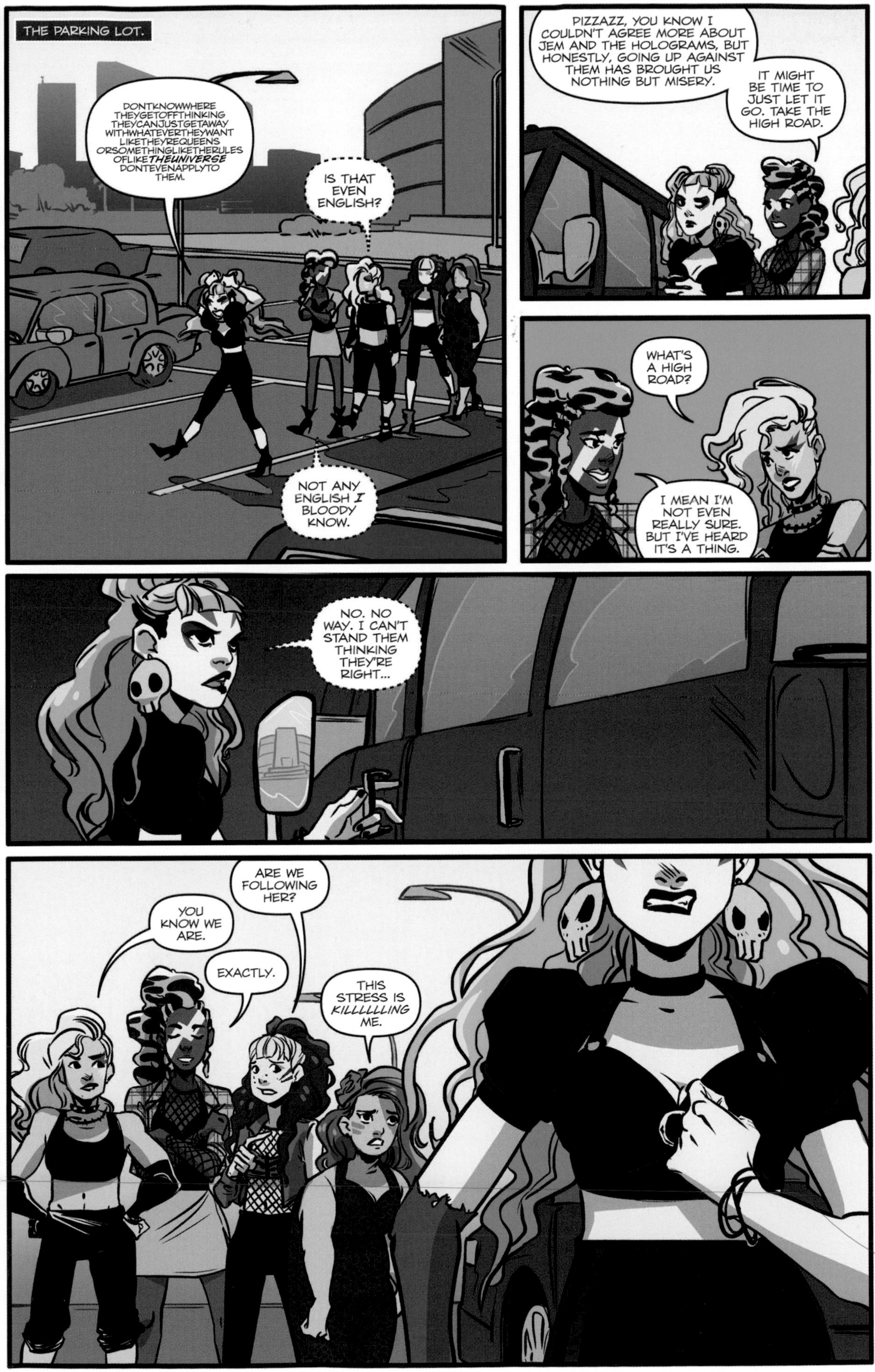
THE PARKING LOT.
DONTKNOWWHERE THEYGETOFFTHINKING THEYCANJUSTGETAWAY WITHWHATEVERTHEYWANT LIKETHEYREQUEENS ORSOMETHINGLIKETHERULES OFLIKE*THEUNIVERSE* DONTEVENAPPLYTO THEM.
IS THAT EVEN ENGLISH?
NOT ANY ENGLISH *I* BLOODY KNOW.
PIZZAZZ, YOU KNOW I COULDN'T AGREE MORE ABOUT JEM AND THE HOLOGRAMS, BUT HONESTLY, GOING UP AGAINST THEM HAS BROUGHT US NOTHING BUT MISERY.
IT MIGHT BE TIME TO JUST LET IT GO. TAKE THE HIGH ROAD.
WHAT'S A HIGH ROAD?
I MEAN I'M NOT EVEN REALLY SURE. BUT I'VE HEARD IT'S A THING.
NO. NO WAY. I CAN'T STAND THEM THINKING THEY'RE RIGHT...
ARE WE FOLLOWING HER?
YOU KNOW WE ARE.
EXACTLY.
THIS STRESS IS *KILLLLLLLING* ME.

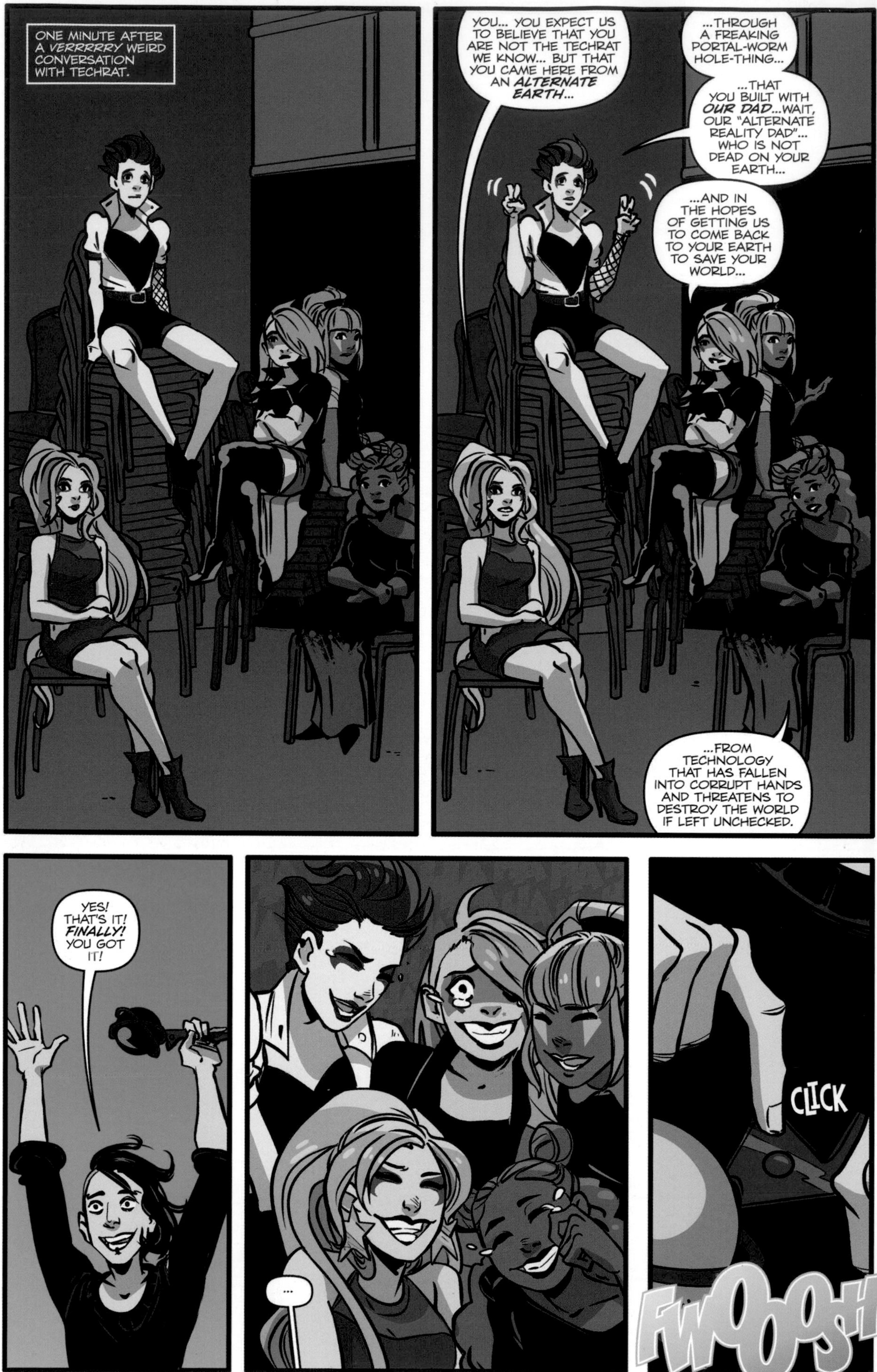

ONE MINUTE AFTER A *VERRRRRY* WEIRD CONVERSATION WITH TECHRAT.
YOU... YOU EXPECT US TO BELIEVE THAT YOU ARE NOT THE TECHRAT WE KNOW... BUT THAT YOU CAME HERE FROM AN ***ALTERNATE EARTH***...
...THROUGH A FREAKING PORTAL-WORM HOLE-THING...
...THAT YOU BUILT WITH ***OUR DAD***...WAIT, OUR "ALTERNATE REALITY DAD"... WHO IS NOT DEAD ON YOUR EARTH...
...AND IN THE HOPES OF GETTING US TO COME BACK TO YOUR EARTH TO SAVE YOUR WORLD...
...FROM TECHNOLOGY THAT HAS FALLEN INTO CORRUPT HANDS AND THREATENS TO DESTROY THE WORLD IF LEFT UNCHECKED.
YES! THAT'S IT! ***FINALLY!*** YOU GOT IT!
...
CLICK
FWOOOSH

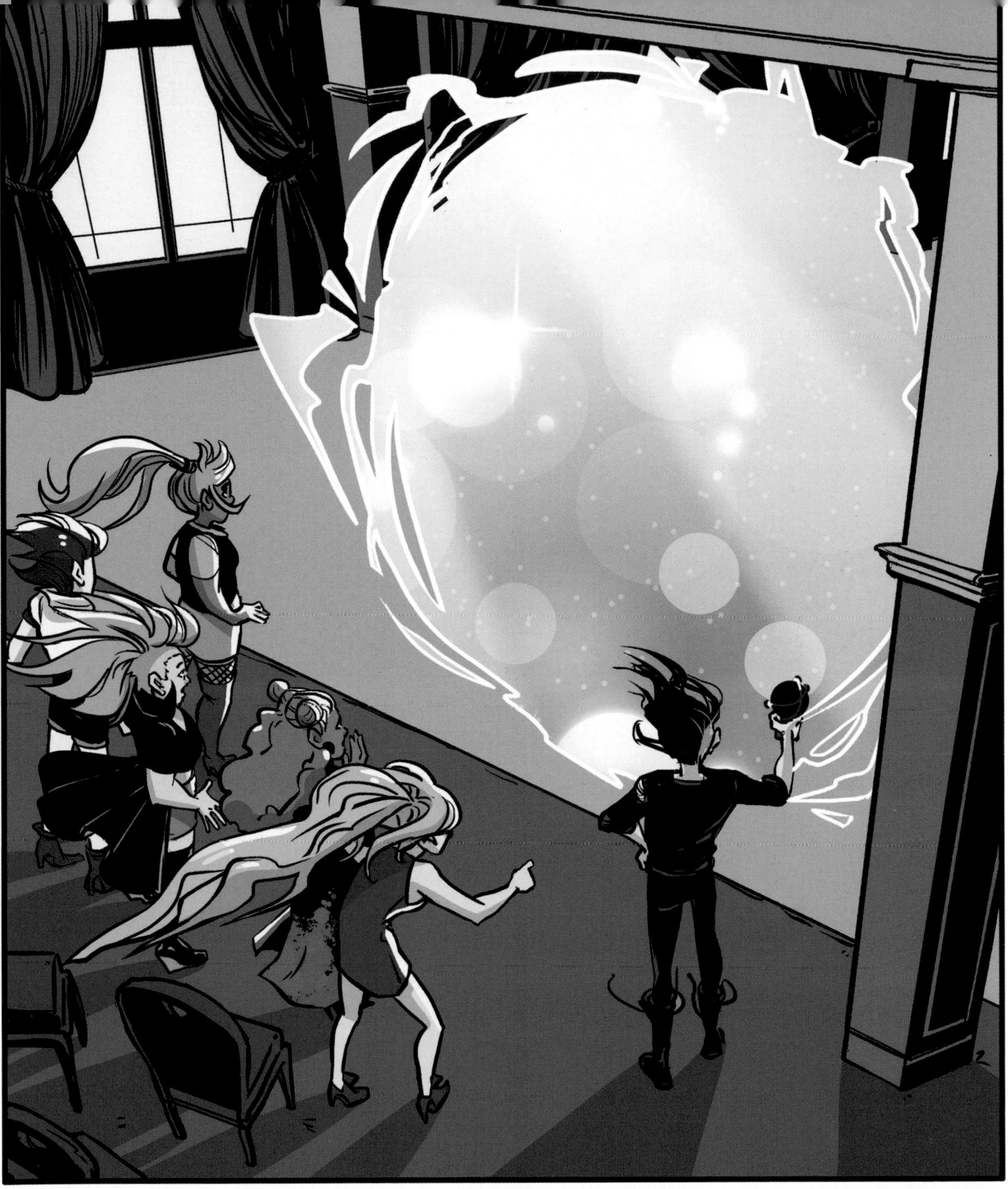

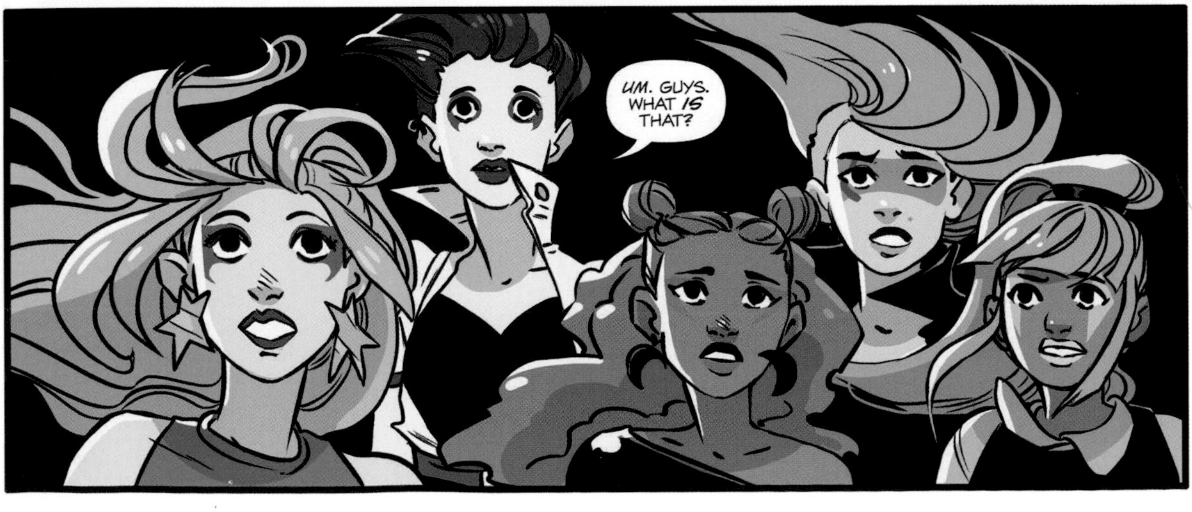
UM. GUYS. WHAT IS THAT?

YOU'RE ONE HUNDRED PERCENT ON THE LEVEL ABOUT THIS? WE'RE NOT BEING PUNKED?

I MEAN, YOU'RE NOT EXACTLY OUR FRIEND ON "THIS EARTH."

IT'S ON THE LEVEL, JEM. I SWEAR.

OKAY...WELL IF THAT'S TRUE, THEN HOW WOULD I KNOW THAT YOU'RE REALLY JERRICA BENTON?

THAT THE TECH YOU USE TO BECOME JEM IS THE VERY SAME HOLOGRAM TECHOLOGY THAT HAS FALLEN INTO THE WRONG HANDS AND IS DESTROYING MY WORLD?

⁉!

JERRICA.

OHMIGOD.

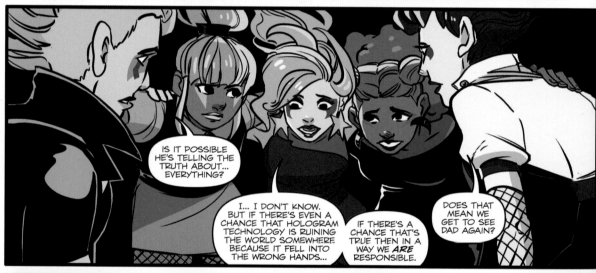

IS IT POSSIBLE HE'S TELLING THE TRUTH ABOUT... EVERYTHING?

I... I DON'T KNOW. BUT IF THERE'S EVEN A CHANCE THAT HOLOGRAM TECHNOLOGY IS RUINING THE WORLD SOMEWHERE BECAUSE IT FELL INTO THE WRONG HANDS...

IF THERE'S A CHANCE THAT'S TRUE THEN IN A WAY WE ARE RESPONSIBLE.

DOES THAT MEAN WE GET TO SEE DAD AGAIN?

IT WON'T REALLY BE DAD, KIMBER.

I-I WANT TO SEE DAD.

SO DO I.

I'D LOVE TO MEET YOUR DAD. I ALSO WOULDN'T MIND SAVING THE WORLD.

SO... WHAT DOES THIS MEAN?

I THINK IT MEANS... IT'S SHOWTIME, HOLOGRAMS.

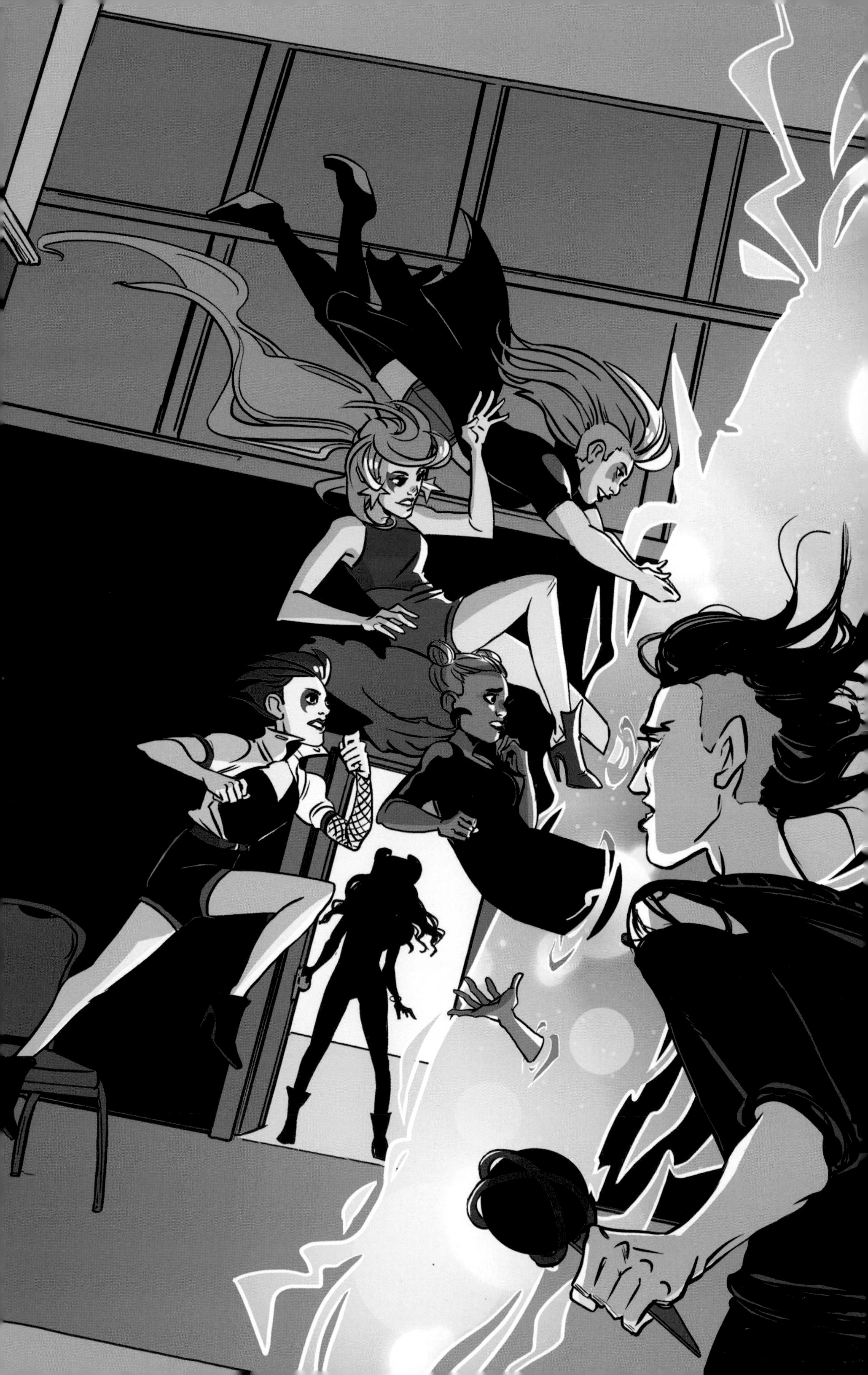

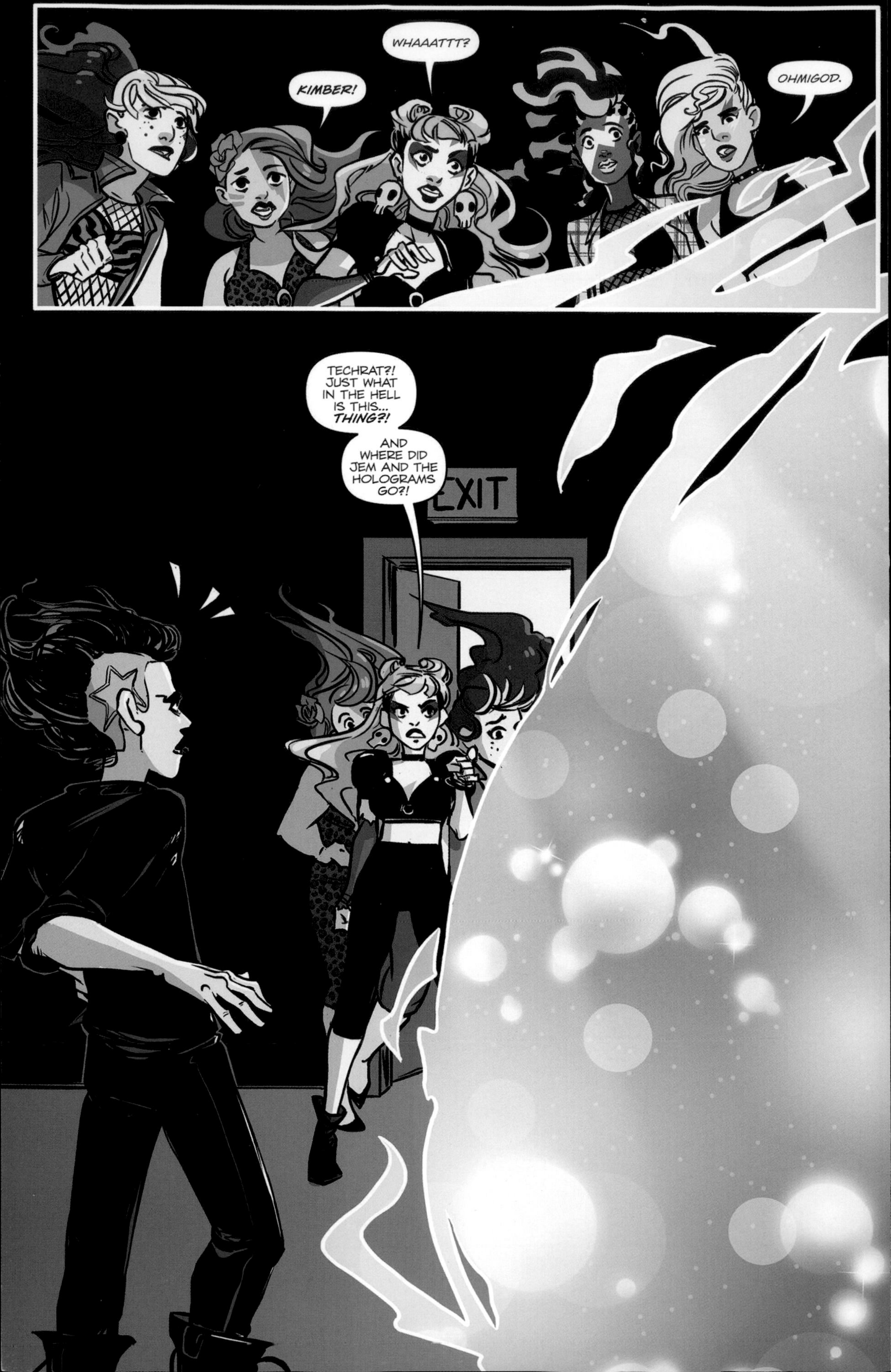
KIMBER!
WHAAATTT?
OHMIGOD.
TECHRAT?! JUST WHAT IN THE HELL IS THIS... THING?!
AND WHERE DID JEM AND THE HOLOGRAMS GO?!
EXIT

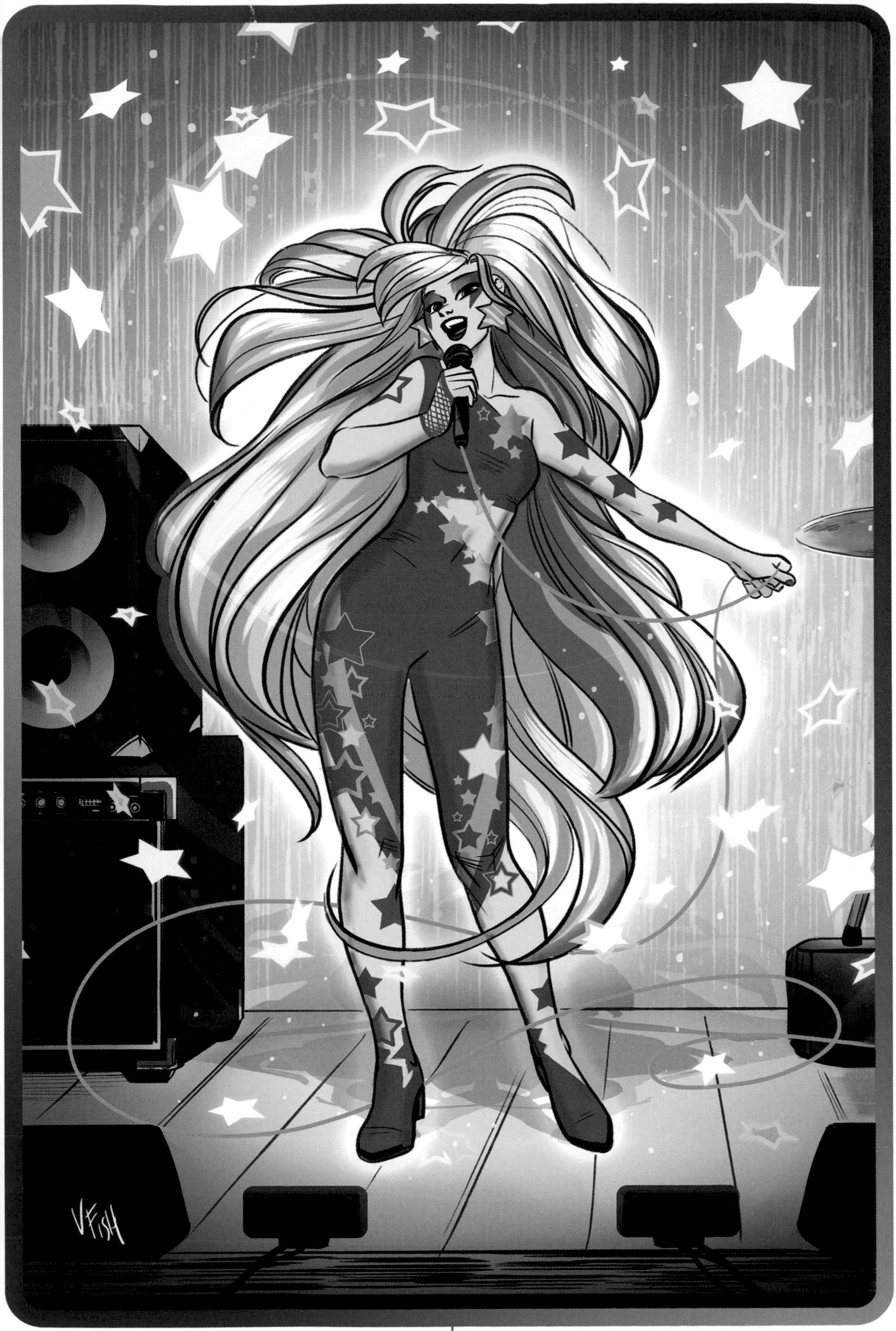
VFISH

ART BY **VERONICA FISH**

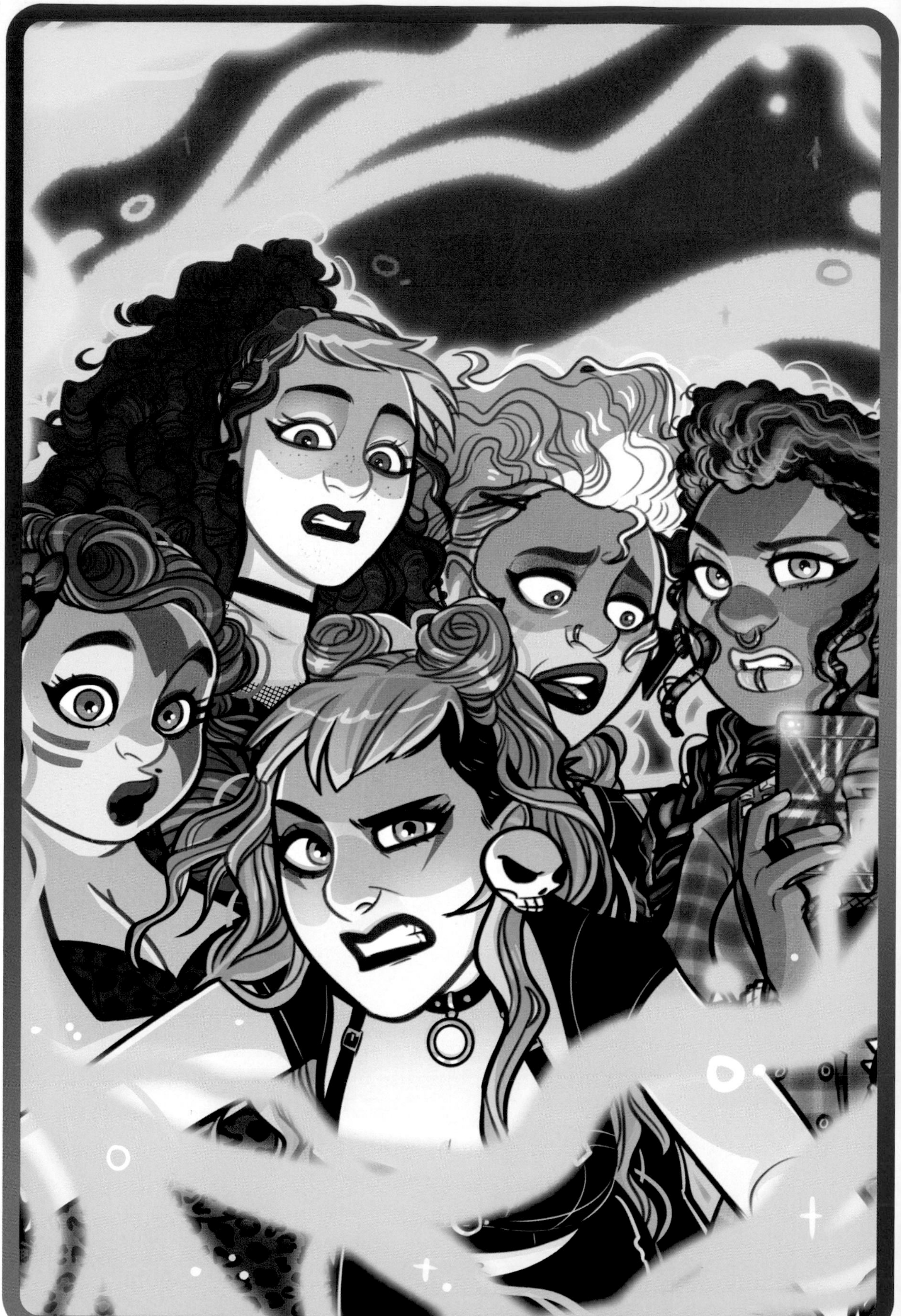

ART BY **JENN ST-ONGE**

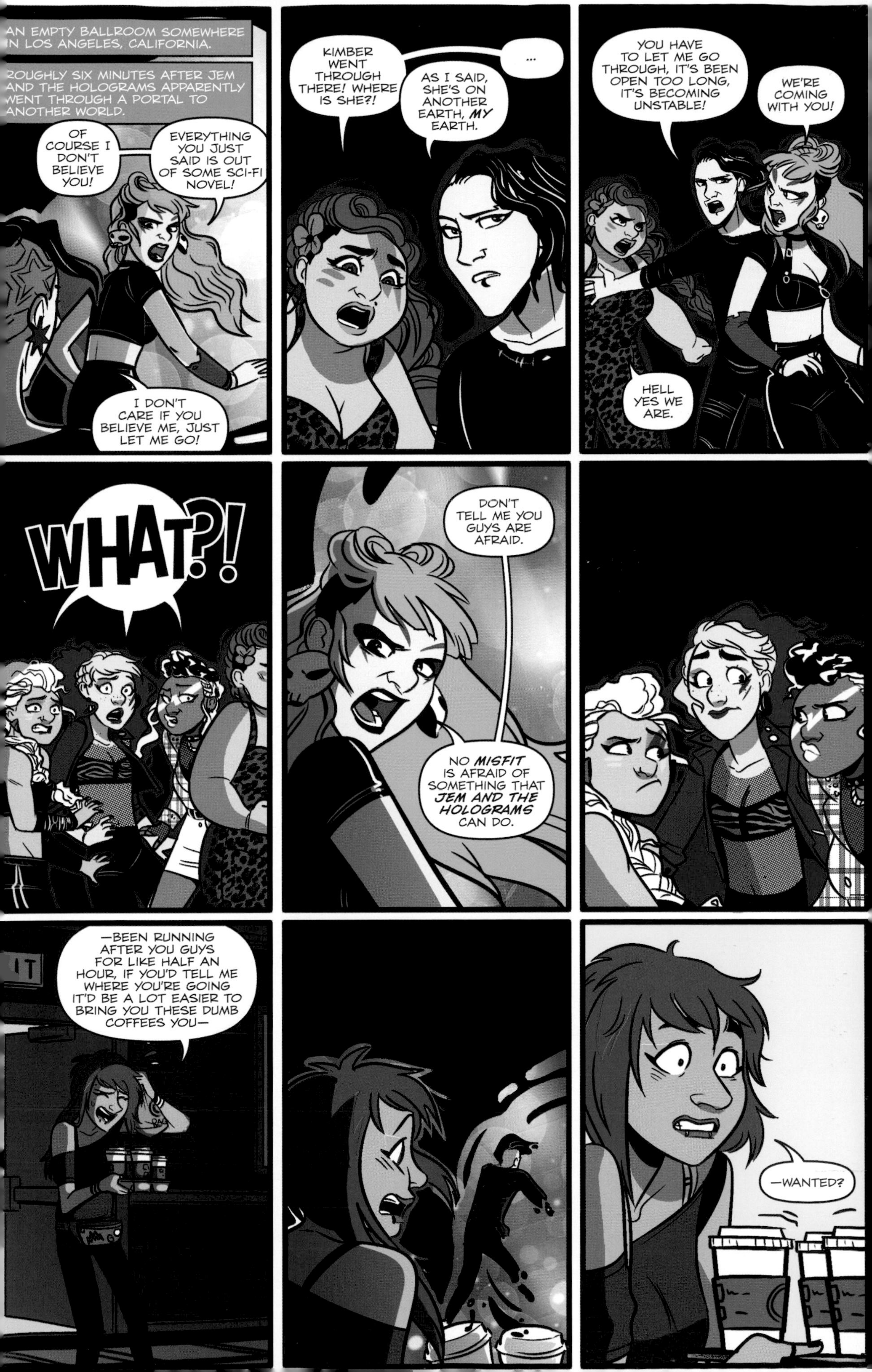
AN EMPTY BALLROOM SOMEWHERE IN LOS ANGELES, CALIFORNIA.
ROUGHLY SIX MINUTES AFTER JEM AND THE HOLOGRAMS APPARENTLY WENT THROUGH A PORTAL TO ANOTHER WORLD.
OF COURSE I DON'T BELIEVE YOU!
EVERYTHING YOU JUST SAID IS OUT OF SOME SCI-FI NOVEL!
I DON'T CARE IF YOU BELIEVE ME, JUST LET ME GO!
KIMBER WENT THROUGH THERE! WHERE IS SHE?!
...
AS I SAID, SHE'S ON ANOTHER EARTH, MY EARTH.
YOU HAVE TO LET ME GO THROUGH, IT'S BEEN OPEN TOO LONG, IT'S BECOMING UNSTABLE!
WE'RE COMING WITH YOU!
HELL YES WE ARE.
WHAT?!
DON'T TELL ME YOU GUYS ARE AFRAID.
NO MISFIT IS AFRAID OF SOMETHING THAT JEM AND THE HOLOGRAMS CAN DO.
—BEEN RUNNING AFTER YOU GUYS FOR LIKE HALF AN HOUR, IF YOU'D TELL ME WHERE YOU'RE GOING IT'D BE A LOT EASIER TO BRING YOU THESE DUMB COFFEES YOU—
—WANTED?

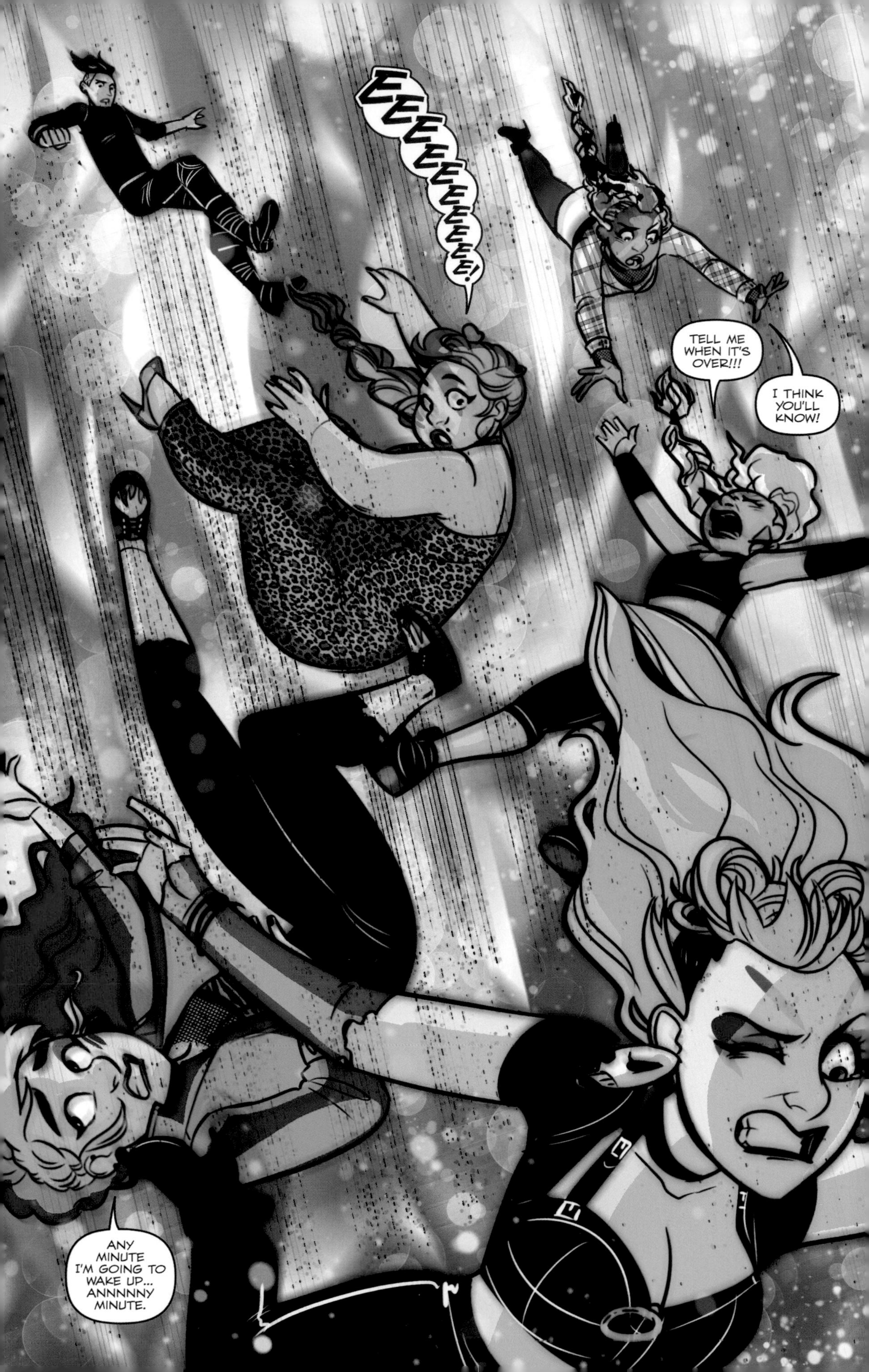
EEEEEEEEEEE!
TELL ME WHEN IT'S OVER!!!
I THINK YOU'LL KNOW!
ANY MINUTE I'M GOING TO WAKE UP... ANNNNNY MINUTE.

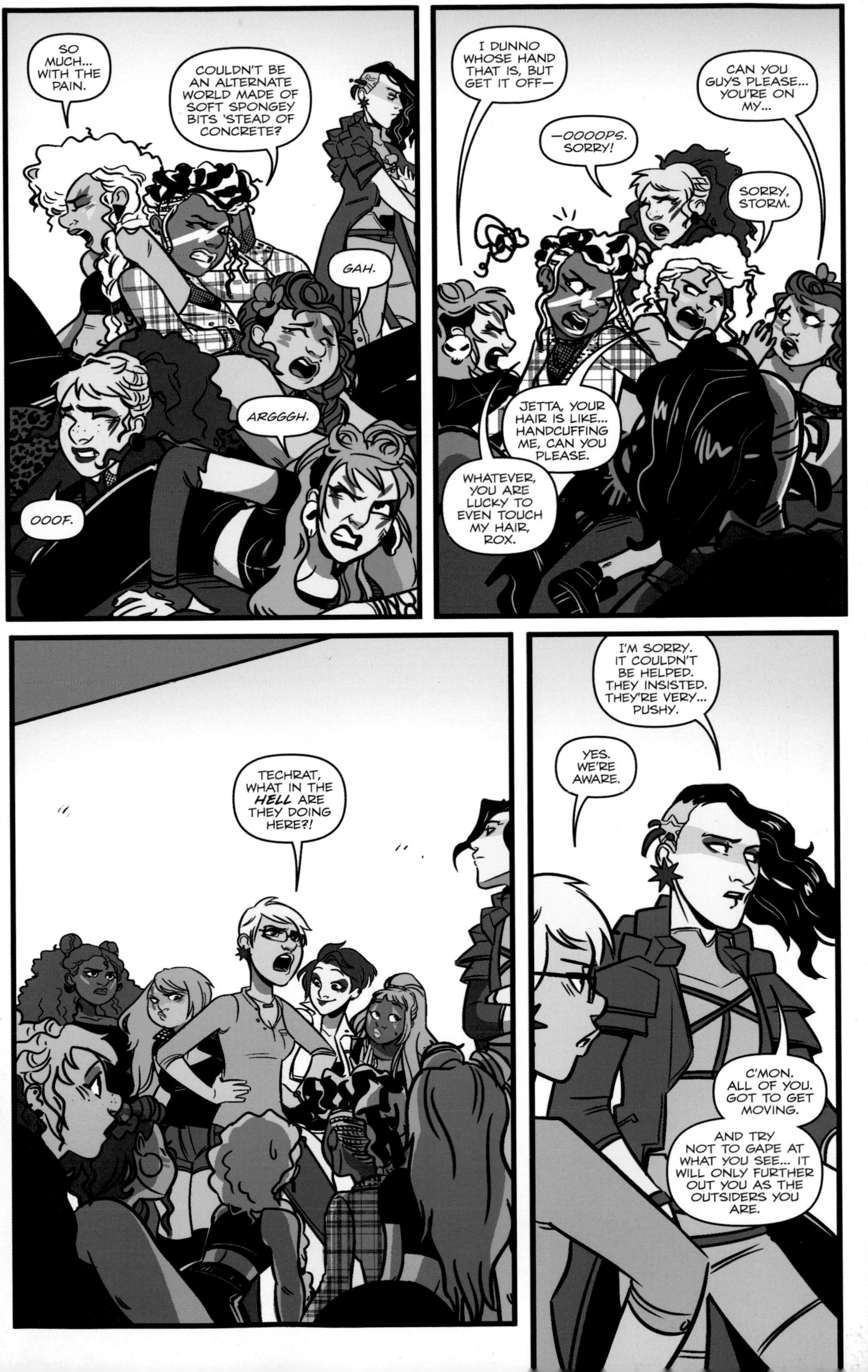
SO MUCH... WITH THE PAIN.
COULDN'T BE AN ALTERNATE WORLD MADE OF SOFT SPONGEY BITS 'STEAD OF CONCRETE?
GAH.
ARGGGH.
OOOF.
I DUNNO WHOSE HAND THAT IS, BUT GET IT OFF—
—OOOOPS. SORRY!
CAN YOU GUYS PLEASE... YOU'RE ON MY...
SORRY, STORM.
JETTA, YOUR HAIR IS LIKE... HANDCUFFING ME, CAN YOU PLEASE.
WHATEVER, YOU ARE LUCKY TO EVEN TOUCH MY HAIR, ROX.
TECHRAT, WHAT IN THE HELL ARE THEY DOING HERE?!
I'M SORRY. IT COULDN'T BE HELPED. THEY INSISTED. THEY'RE VERY... PUSHY.
YES. WE'RE AWARE.
C'MON. ALL OF YOU. GOT TO GET MOVING.
AND TRY NOT TO GAPE AT WHAT YOU SEE... IT WILL ONLY FURTHER OUT YOU AS THE OUTSIDERS YOU ARE.

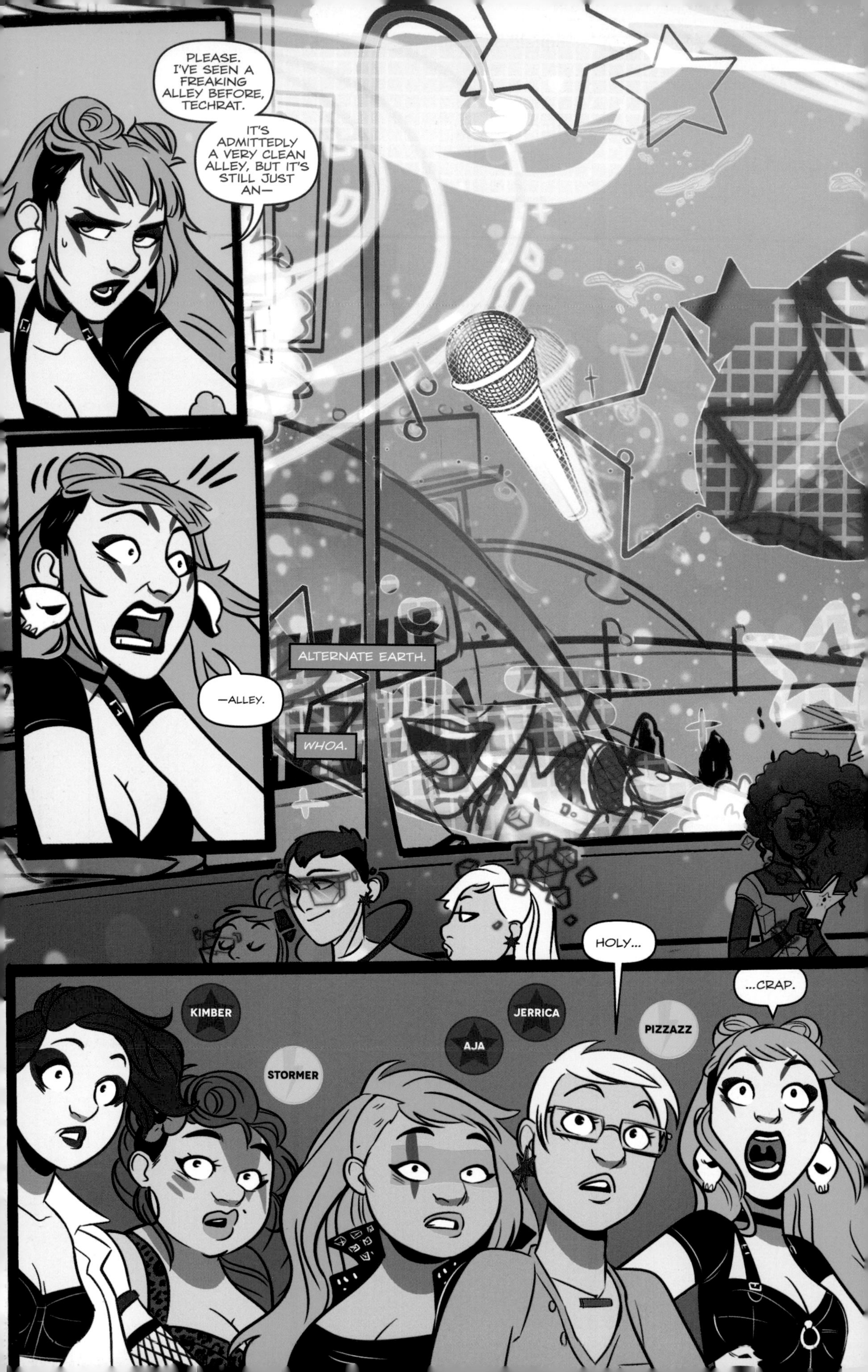
PLEASE. I'VE SEEN A FREAKING ALLEY BEFORE, TECHRAT.
IT'S ADMITTEDLY A VERY CLEAN ALLEY, BUT IT'S STILL JUST AN—
—ALLEY.
ALTERNATE EARTH.
WHOA.
HOLY...
...CRAP.
KIMBER
JERRICA
AJA
PIZZAZZ
STORMER

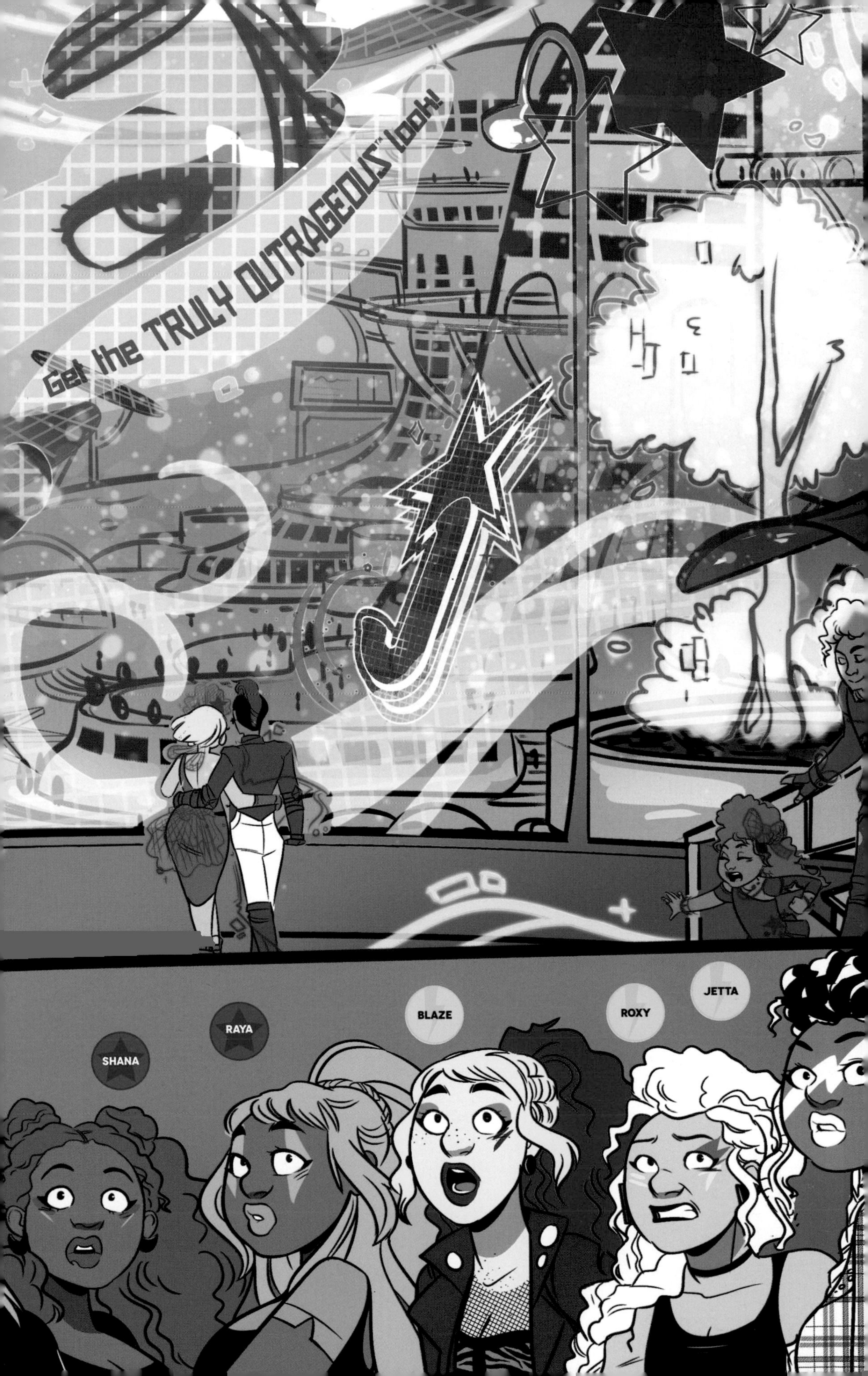
Get the TRULY OUTRAGEOUS™ look!
SHANA
RAYA
BLAZE
ROXY
JETTA

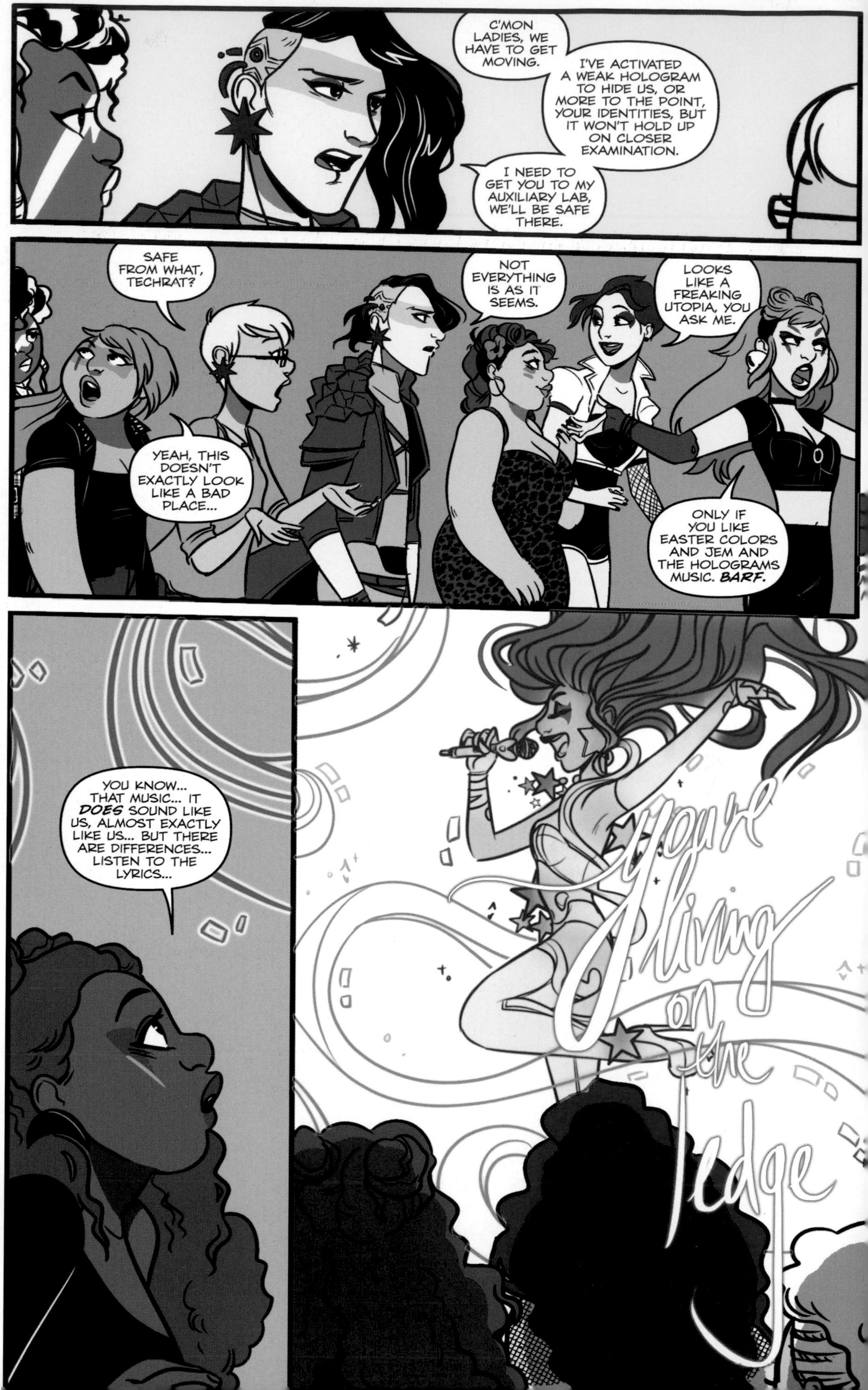

C'MON LADIES, WE HAVE TO GET MOVING.
I'VE ACTIVATED A WEAK HOLOGRAM TO HIDE US, OR MORE TO THE POINT, YOUR IDENTITIES, BUT IT WON'T HOLD UP ON CLOSER EXAMINATION.
I NEED TO GET YOU TO MY AUXILIARY LAB, WE'LL BE SAFE THERE.
SAFE FROM WHAT, TECHRAT?
YEAH, THIS DOESN'T EXACTLY LOOK LIKE A BAD PLACE...
NOT EVERYTHING IS AS IT SEEMS.
LOOKS LIKE A FREAKING UTOPIA, YOU ASK ME.
ONLY IF YOU LIKE EASTER COLORS AND JEM AND THE HOLOGRAMS MUSIC. ***BARF.***
YOU KNOW... THAT MUSIC... IT ***DOES*** SOUND LIKE US, ALMOST EXACTLY LIKE US... BUT THERE ARE DIFFERENCES... LISTEN TO THE LYRICS...
you're living on the edge

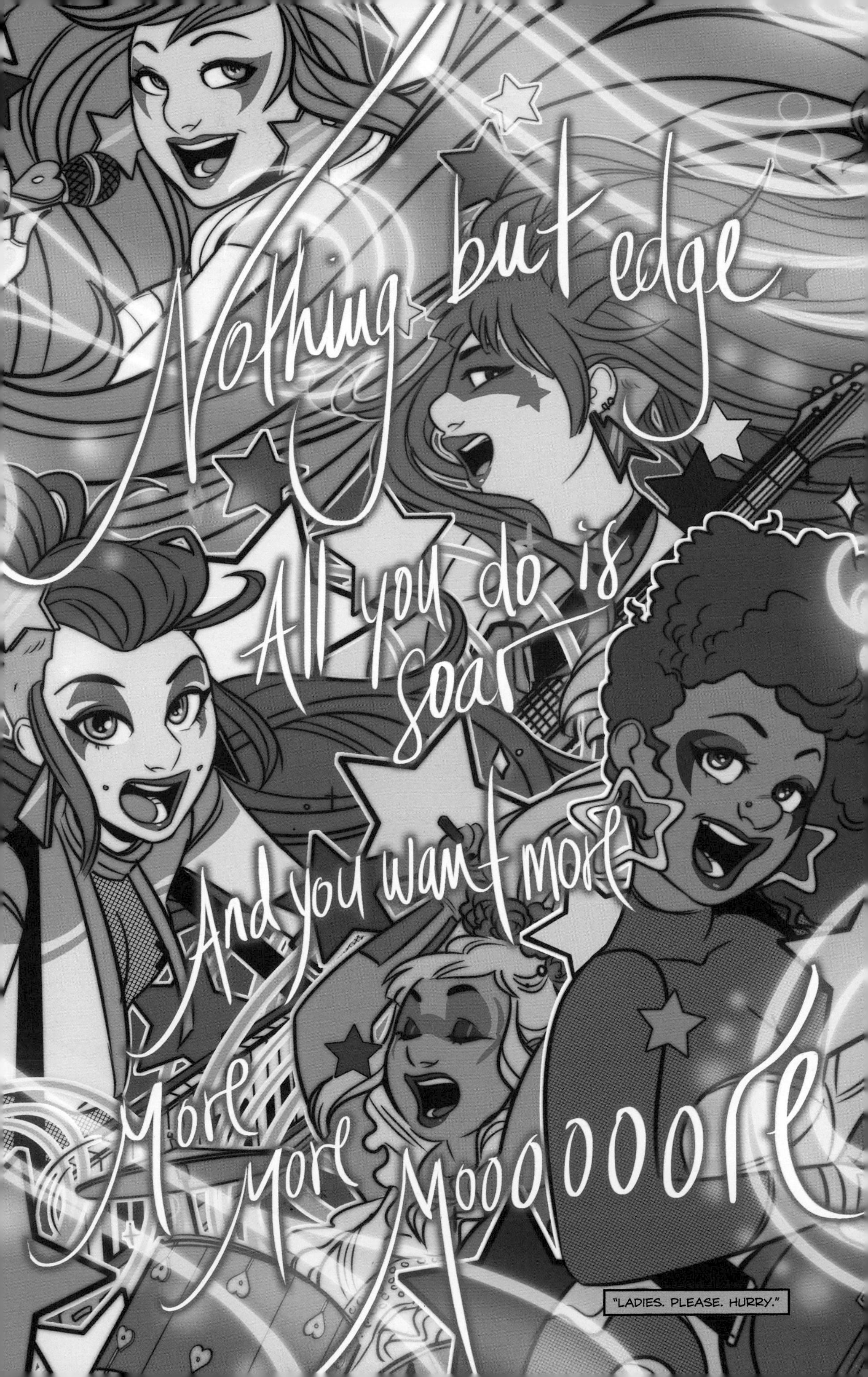

Nothing but edge
All you do is soar
And you want more
More more Mooooooore
"LADIES. PLEASE. HURRY."

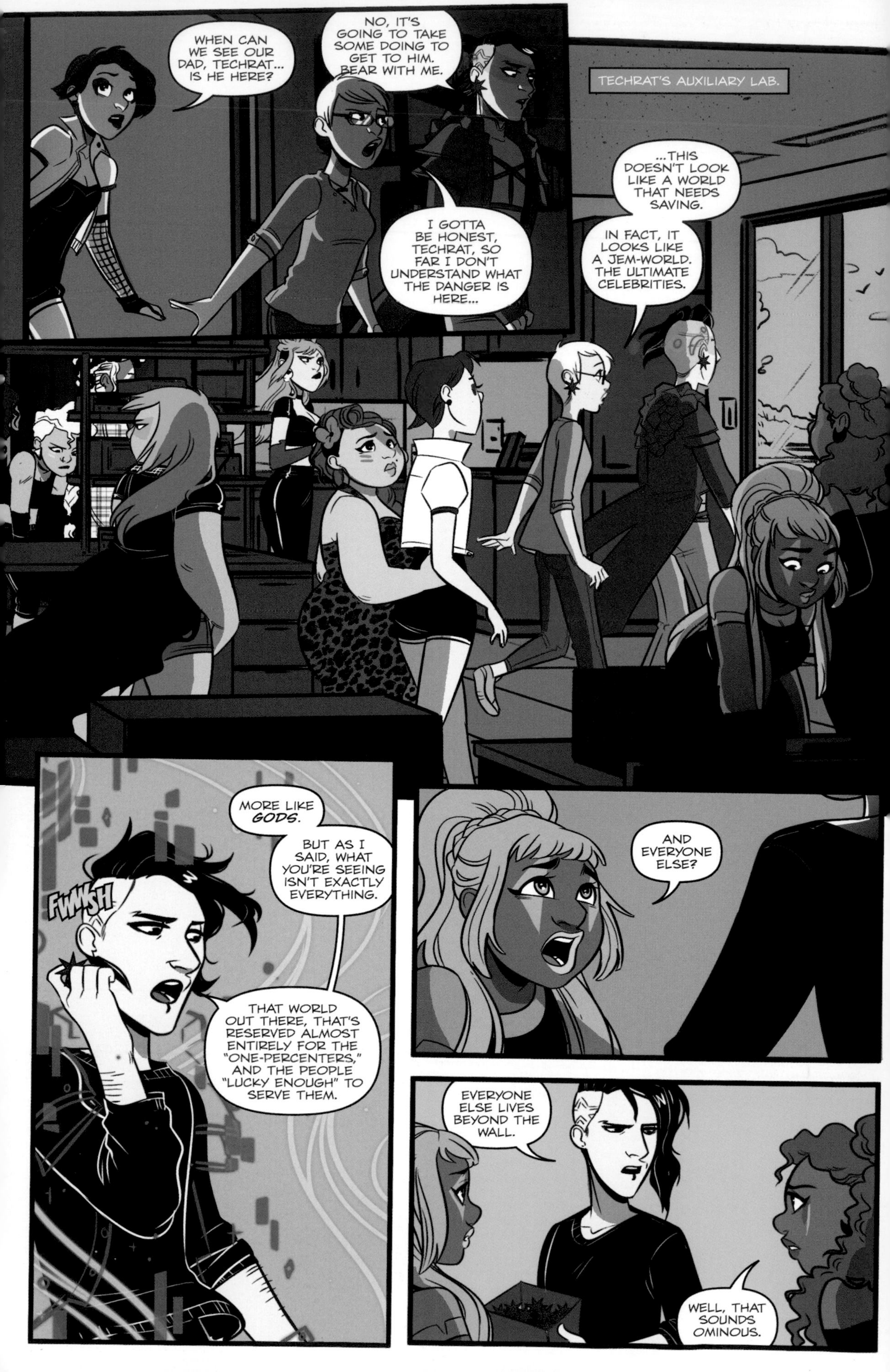

WHEN CAN WE SEE OUR DAD, TECHRAT... IS HE HERE?
NO, IT'S GOING TO TAKE SOME DOING TO GET TO HIM. BEAR WITH ME.
TECHRAT'S AUXILIARY LAB.
I GOTTA BE HONEST, TECHRAT, SO FAR I DON'T UNDERSTAND WHAT THE DANGER IS HERE...
...THIS DOESN'T LOOK LIKE A WORLD THAT NEEDS SAVING.
IN FACT, IT LOOKS LIKE A JEM-WORLD. THE ULTIMATE CELEBRITIES.
MORE LIKE *GODS*.
BUT AS I SAID, WHAT YOU'RE SEEING ISN'T EXACTLY EVERYTHING.
FWWSH
THAT WORLD OUT THERE, THAT'S RESERVED ALMOST ENTIRELY FOR THE "ONE-PERCENTERS," AND THE PEOPLE "LUCKY ENOUGH" TO SERVE THEM.
AND EVERYONE ELSE?
EVERYONE ELSE LIVES BEYOND THE WALL.
WELL, THAT SOUNDS OMINOUS.

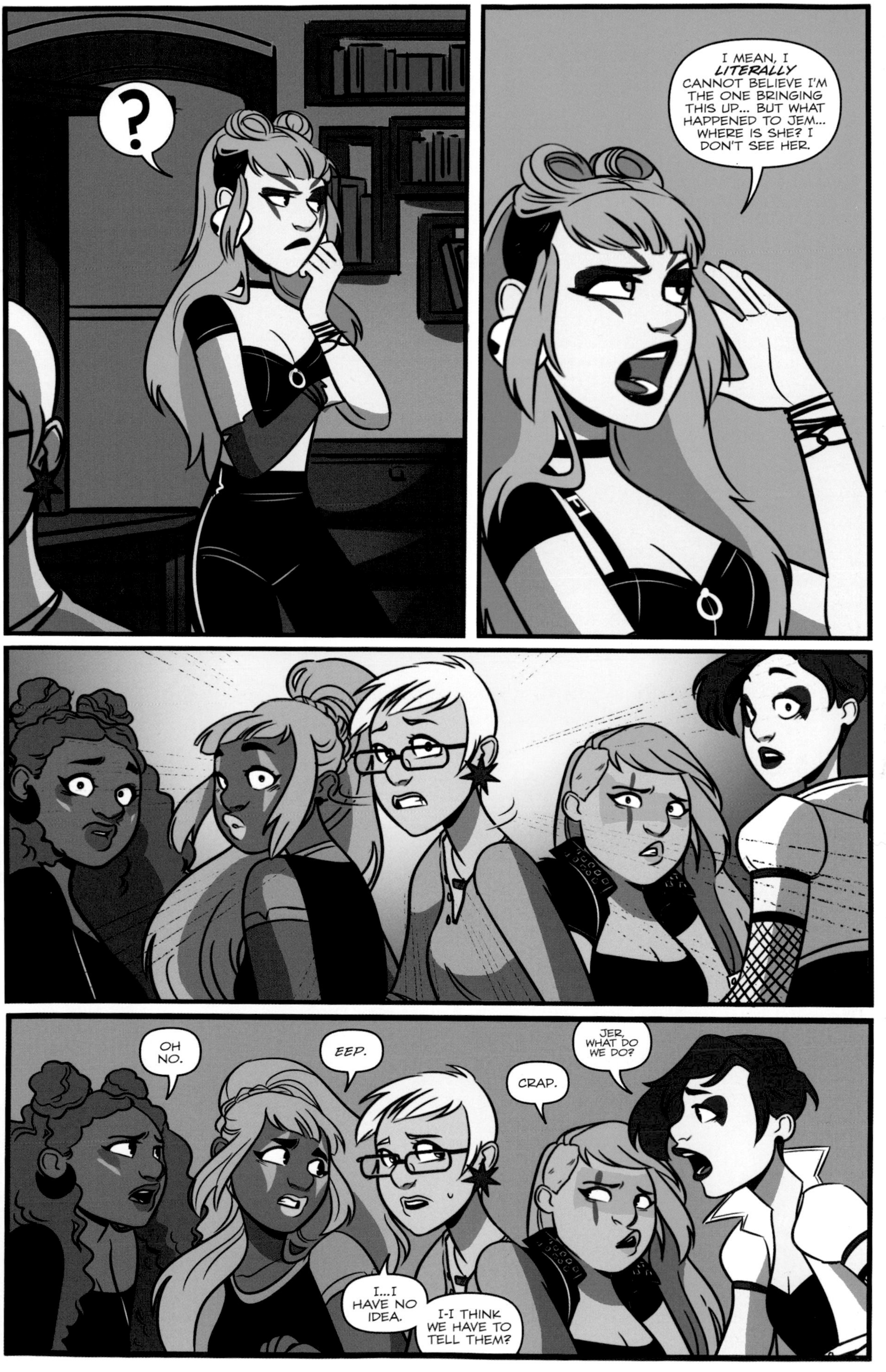
?
I MEAN, I *LITERALLY* CANNOT BELIEVE I'M THE ONE BRINGING THIS UP... BUT WHAT HAPPENED TO JEM... WHERE IS SHE? I DON'T SEE HER.
OH NO.
EEP.
CRAP.
JER, WHAT DO WE DO?
I...I HAVE NO IDEA.
I-I THINK WE HAVE TO TELL THEM?

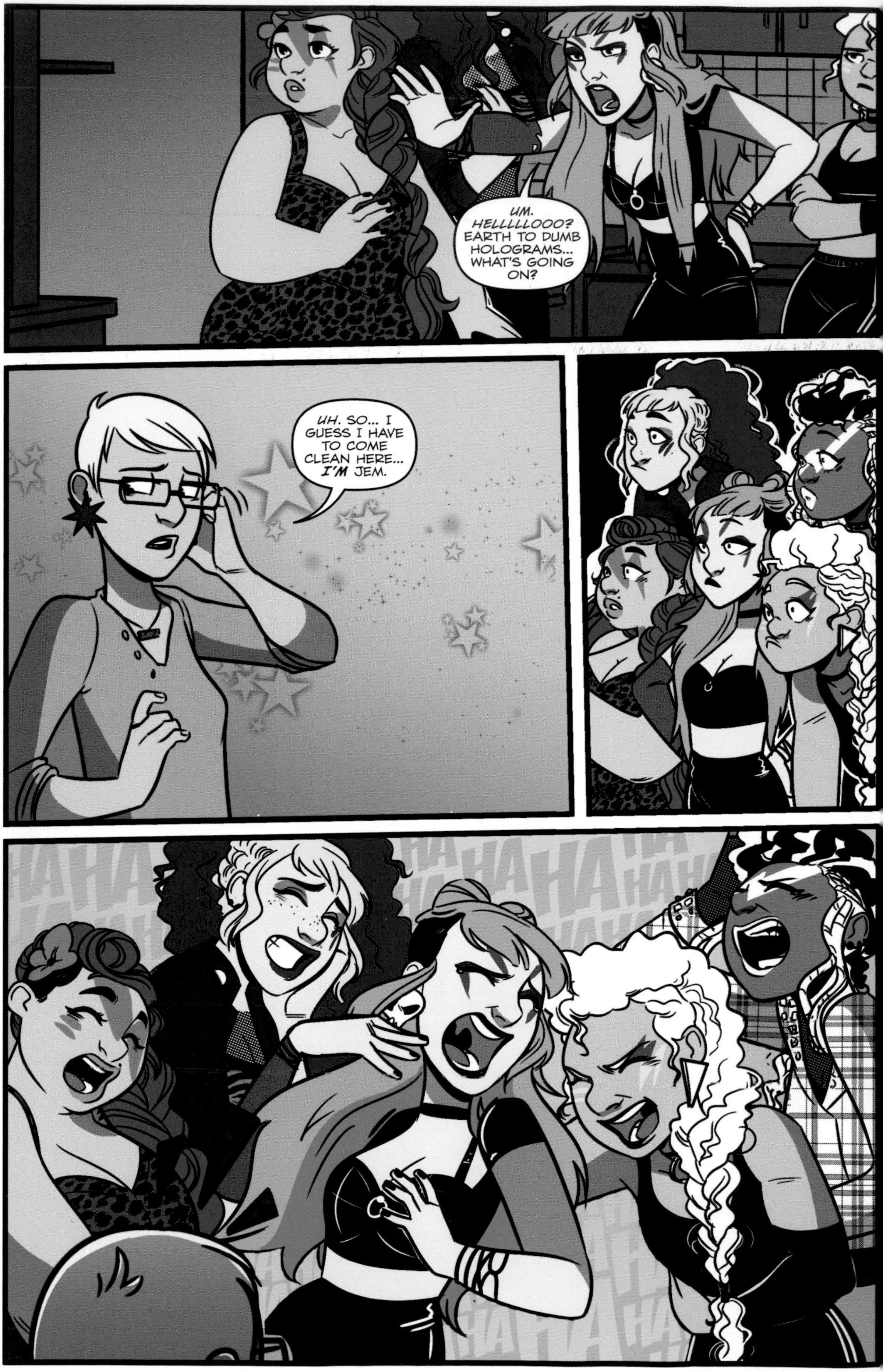
UM. HELLLLLOOO? EARTH TO DUMB HOLOGRAMS... WHAT'S GOING ON?
UH. SO... I GUESS I HAVE TO COME CLEAN HERE... *I'M* JEM.
HAHAHAHAHA

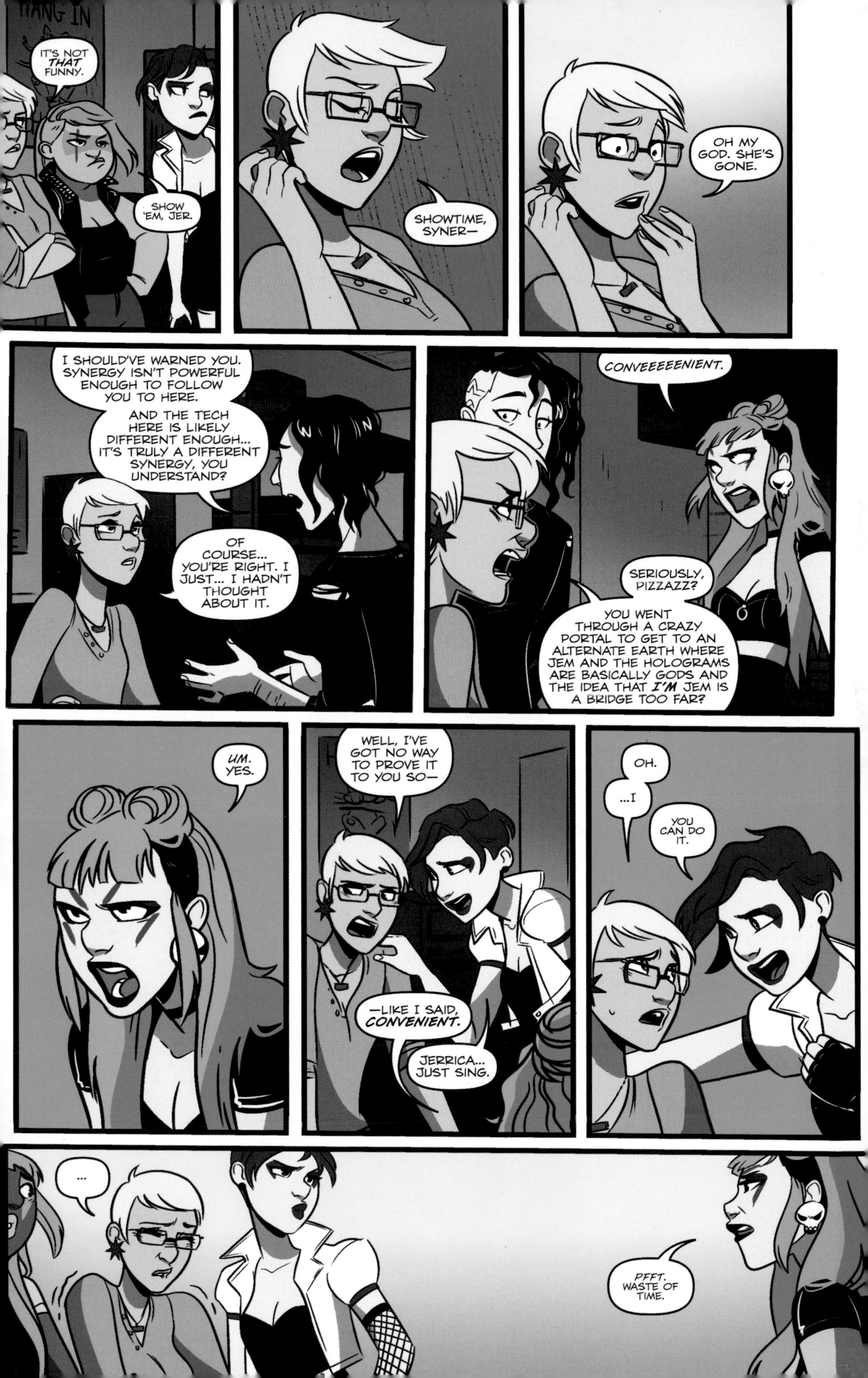
HANG IN
IT'S NOT *THAT* FUNNY.
SHOW 'EM, JER.
SHOWTIME, SYNER—
OH MY GOD. SHE'S GONE.
I SHOULD'VE WARNED YOU. SYNERGY ISN'T POWERFUL ENOUGH TO FOLLOW YOU TO HERE.
AND THE TECH HERE IS LIKELY DIFFERENT ENOUGH... IT'S TRULY A DIFFERENT SYNERGY, YOU UNDERSTAND?
OF COURSE... YOU'RE RIGHT. I JUST... I HADN'T THOUGHT ABOUT IT.
CONVEEEEEENIENT.
SERIOUSLY, PIZZAZZ?
YOU WENT THROUGH A CRAZY PORTAL TO GET TO AN ALTERNATE EARTH WHERE JEM AND THE HOLOGRAMS ARE BASICALLY GODS AND THE IDEA THAT ***I'M*** JEM IS A BRIDGE TOO FAR?
UM. YES.
WELL, I'VE GOT NO WAY TO PROVE IT TO YOU SO—
—LIKE I SAID, ***CONVENIENT.***
JERRICA... JUST SING.
OH.
...I
YOU CAN DO IT.
...
PFFT. WASTE OF TIME.

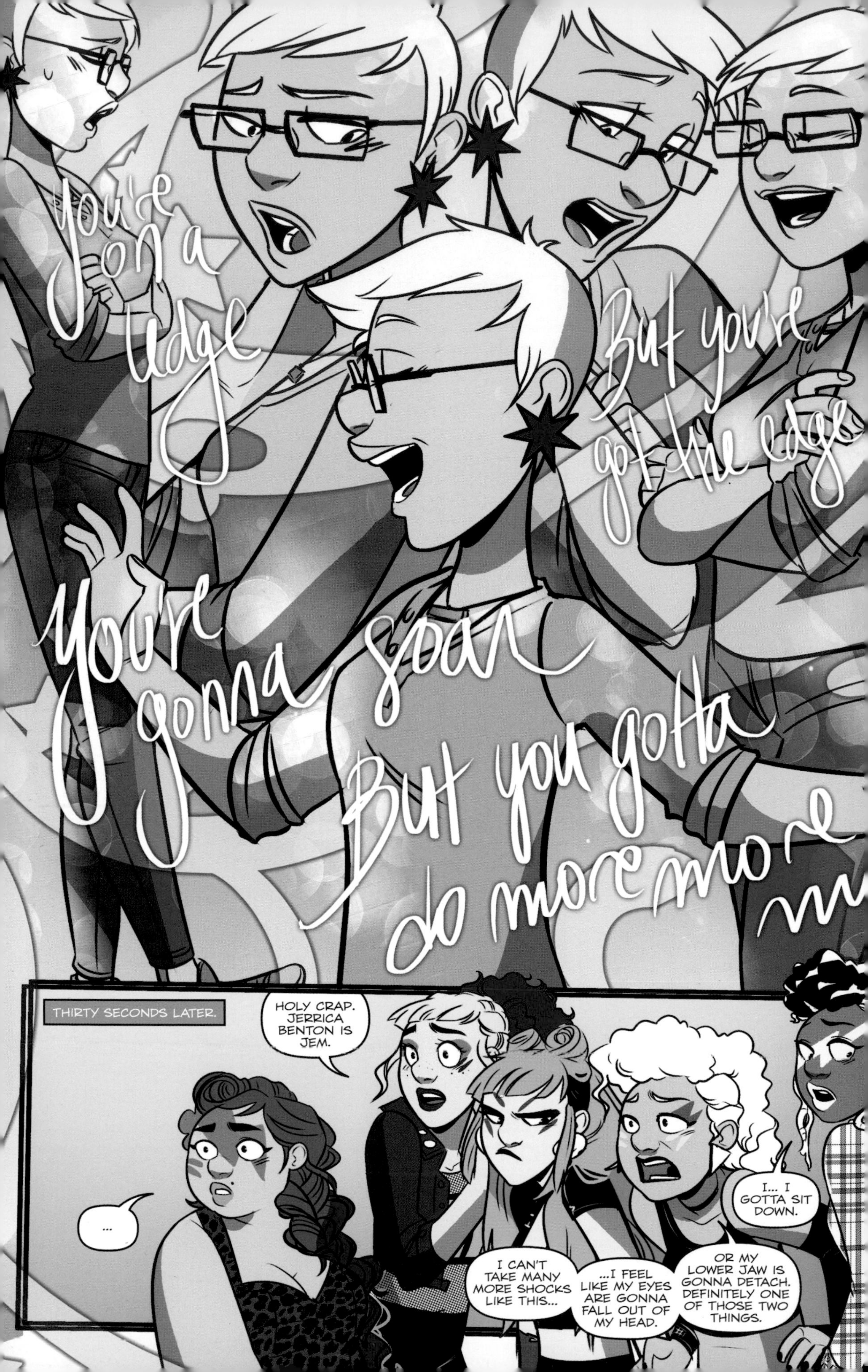
You're on a edge
But you're got the edge
You're gonna soar
But you gotta do more more m
THIRTY SECONDS LATER.
HOLY CRAP. JERRICA BENTON IS JEM.
...
I... I GOTTA SIT DOWN.
I CAN'T TAKE MANY MORE SHOCKS LIKE THIS...
...I FEEL LIKE MY EYES ARE GONNA FALL OUT OF MY HEAD.
OR MY LOWER JAW IS GONNA DETACH. DEFINITELY ONE OF THOSE TWO THINGS.

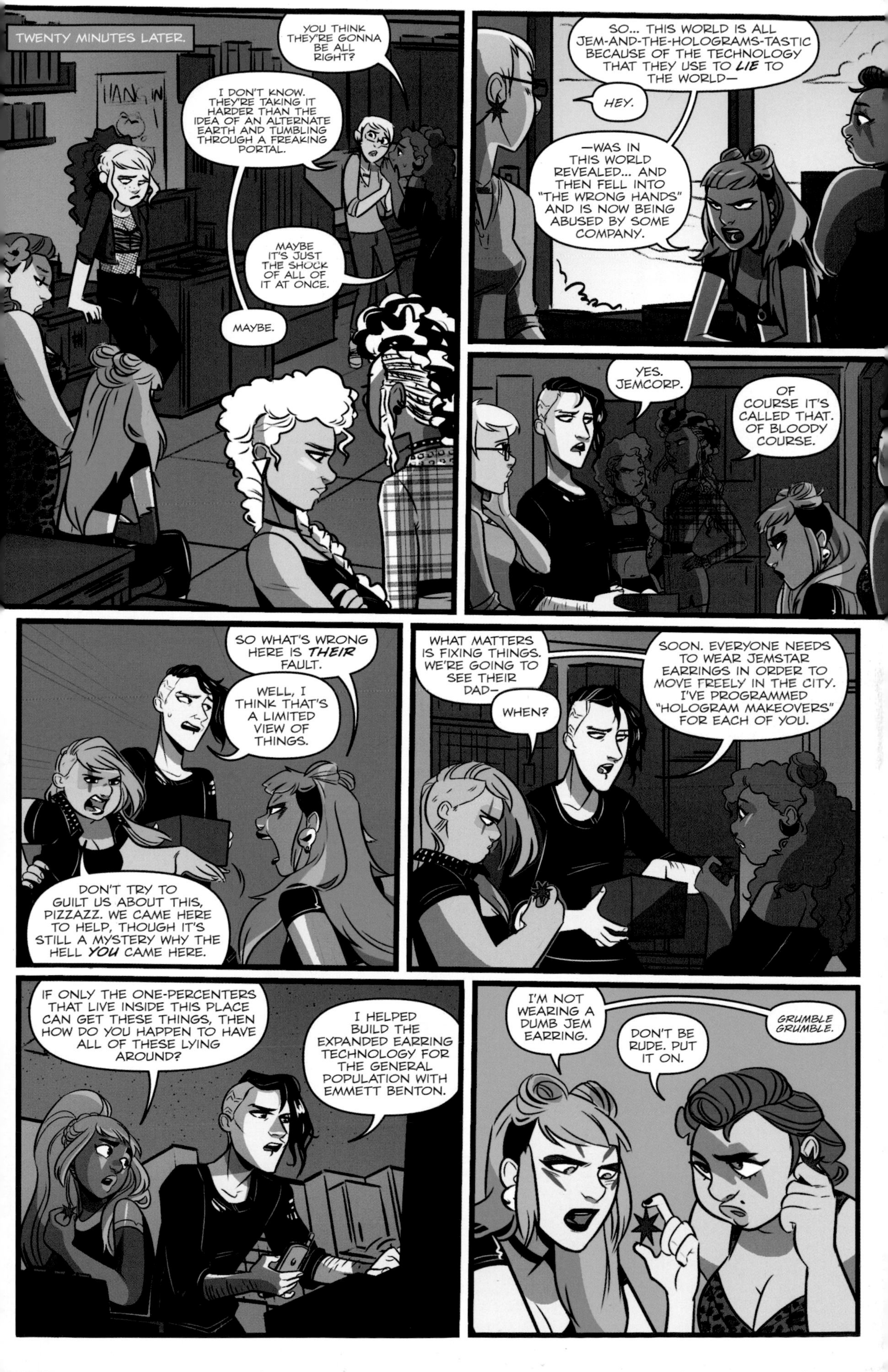
TWENTY MINUTES LATER.
HANG IN
YOU THINK THEY'RE GONNA BE ALL RIGHT?
I DON'T KNOW. THEY'RE TAKING IT HARDER THAN THE IDEA OF AN ALTERNATE EARTH AND TUMBLING THROUGH A FREAKING PORTAL.
MAYBE IT'S JUST THE SHOCK OF ALL OF IT AT ONCE.
MAYBE.
SO... THIS WORLD IS ALL JEM-AND-THE-HOLOGRAMS-TASTIC BECAUSE OF THE TECHNOLOGY THAT THEY USE TO LIE TO THE WORLD—
HEY.
—WAS IN THIS WORLD REVEALED... AND THEN FELL INTO "THE WRONG HANDS" AND IS NOW BEING ABUSED BY SOME COMPANY.
YES. JEMCORP.
OF COURSE IT'S CALLED THAT. OF BLOODY COURSE.
SO WHAT'S WRONG HERE IS THEIR FAULT.
WELL, I THINK THAT'S A LIMITED VIEW OF THINGS.
DON'T TRY TO GUILT US ABOUT THIS, PIZZAZZ. WE CAME HERE TO HELP, THOUGH IT'S STILL A MYSTERY WHY THE HELL YOU CAME HERE.
WHAT MATTERS IS FIXING THINGS. WE'RE GOING TO SEE THEIR DAD—
WHEN?
SOON. EVERYONE NEEDS TO WEAR JEMSTAR EARRINGS IN ORDER TO MOVE FREELY IN THE CITY. I'VE PROGRAMMED "HOLOGRAM MAKEOVERS" FOR EACH OF YOU.
IF ONLY THE ONE-PERCENTERS THAT LIVE INSIDE THIS PLACE CAN GET THESE THINGS, THEN HOW DO YOU HAPPEN TO HAVE ALL OF THESE LYING AROUND?
I HELPED BUILD THE EXPANDED EARRING TECHNOLOGY FOR THE GENERAL POPULATION WITH EMMETT BENTON.
I'M NOT WEARING A DUMB JEM EARRING.
DON'T BE RUDE. PUT IT ON.
GRUMBLE GRUMBLE.

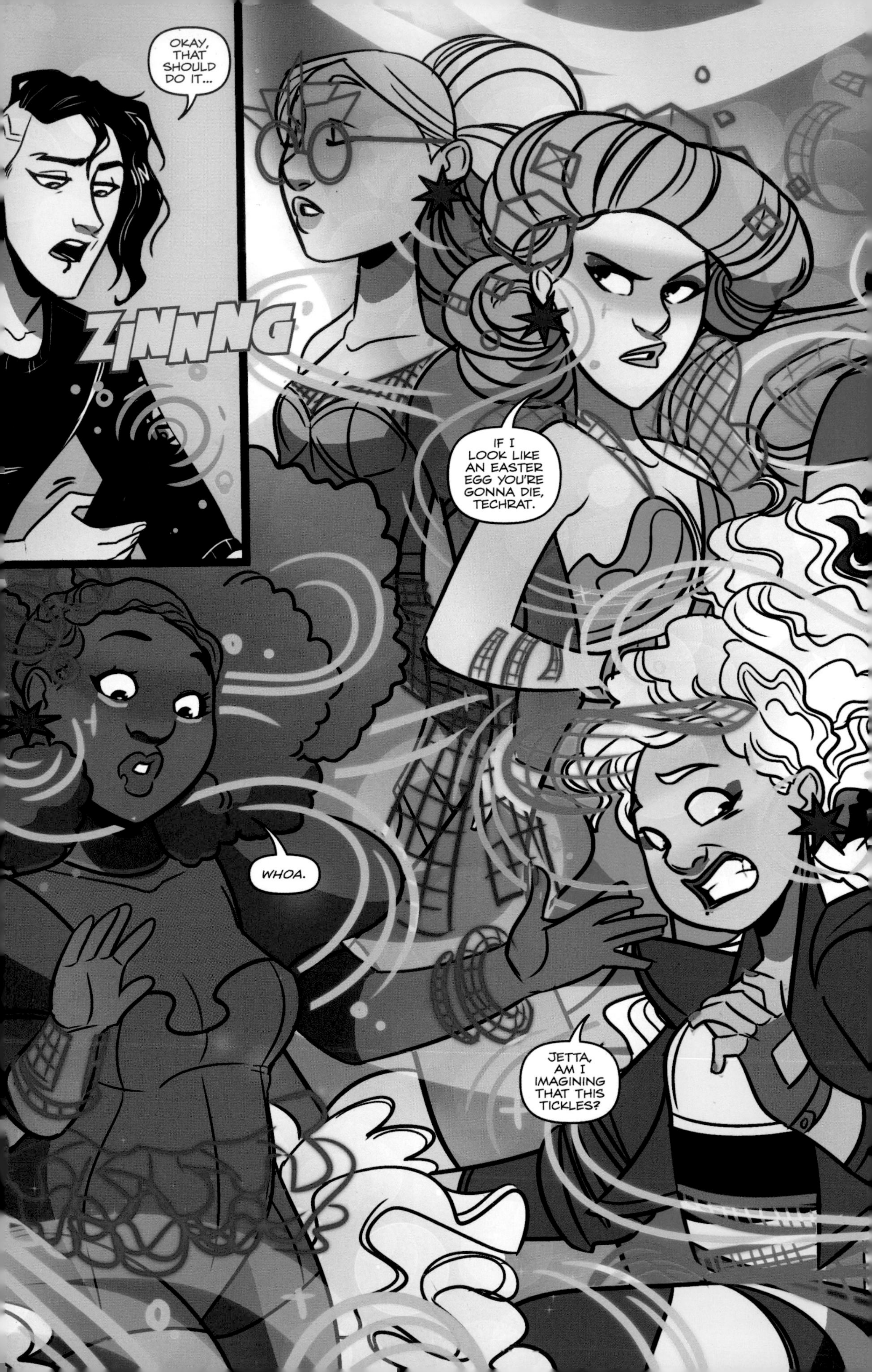
OKAY, THAT SHOULD DO IT...
ZINNNG
IF I LOOK LIKE AN EASTER EGG YOU'RE GONNA DIE, TECHRAT.
WHOA.
JETTA, AM I IMAGINING THAT THIS TICKLES?

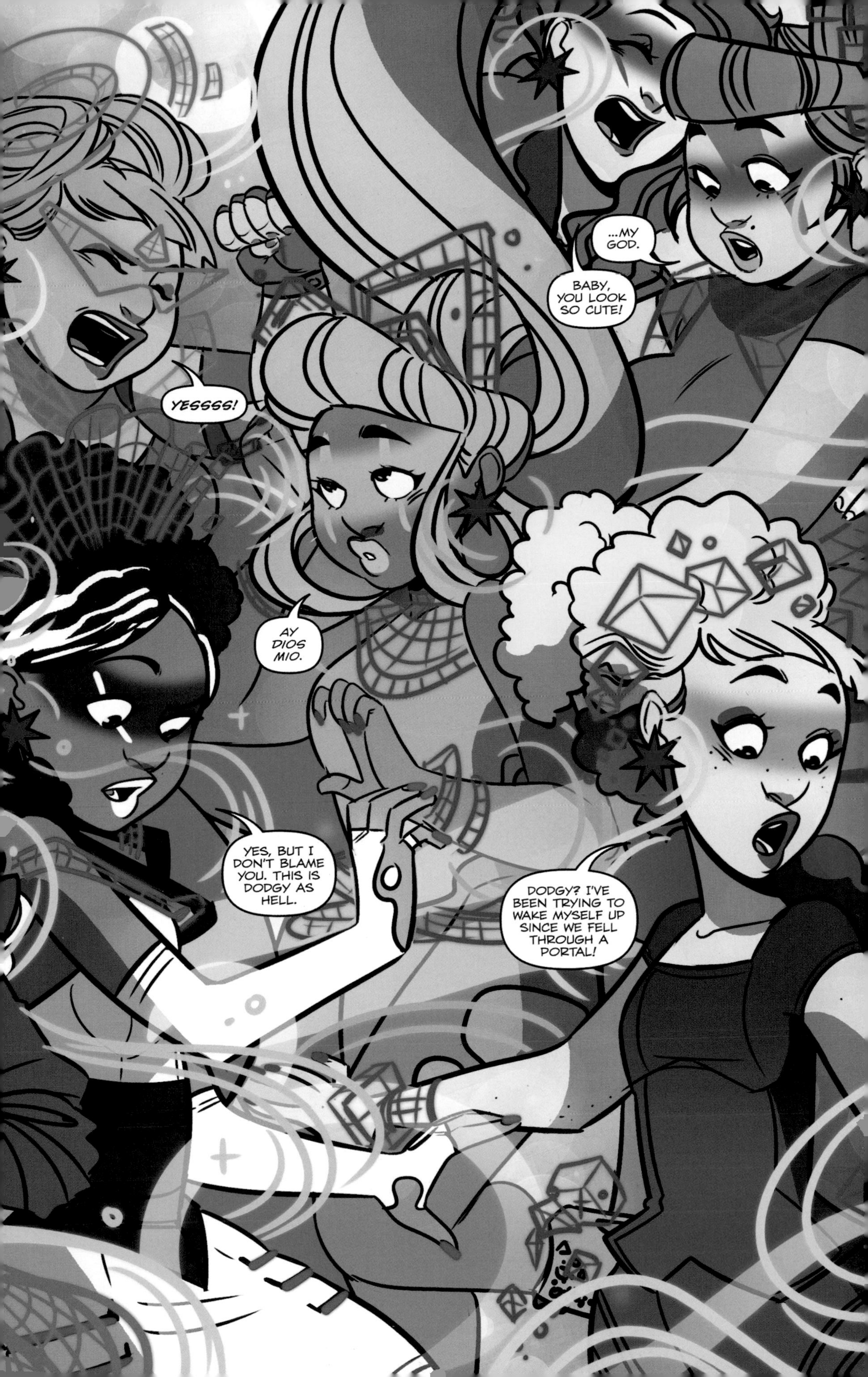
...MY GOD.
BABY, YOU LOOK SO CUTE!
YESSSS!
AY DIOS MIO.
YES, BUT I DON'T BLAME YOU. THIS IS DODGY AS HELL.
DODGY? I'VE BEEN TRYING TO WAKE MYSELF UP SINCE WE FELL THROUGH A PORTAL!

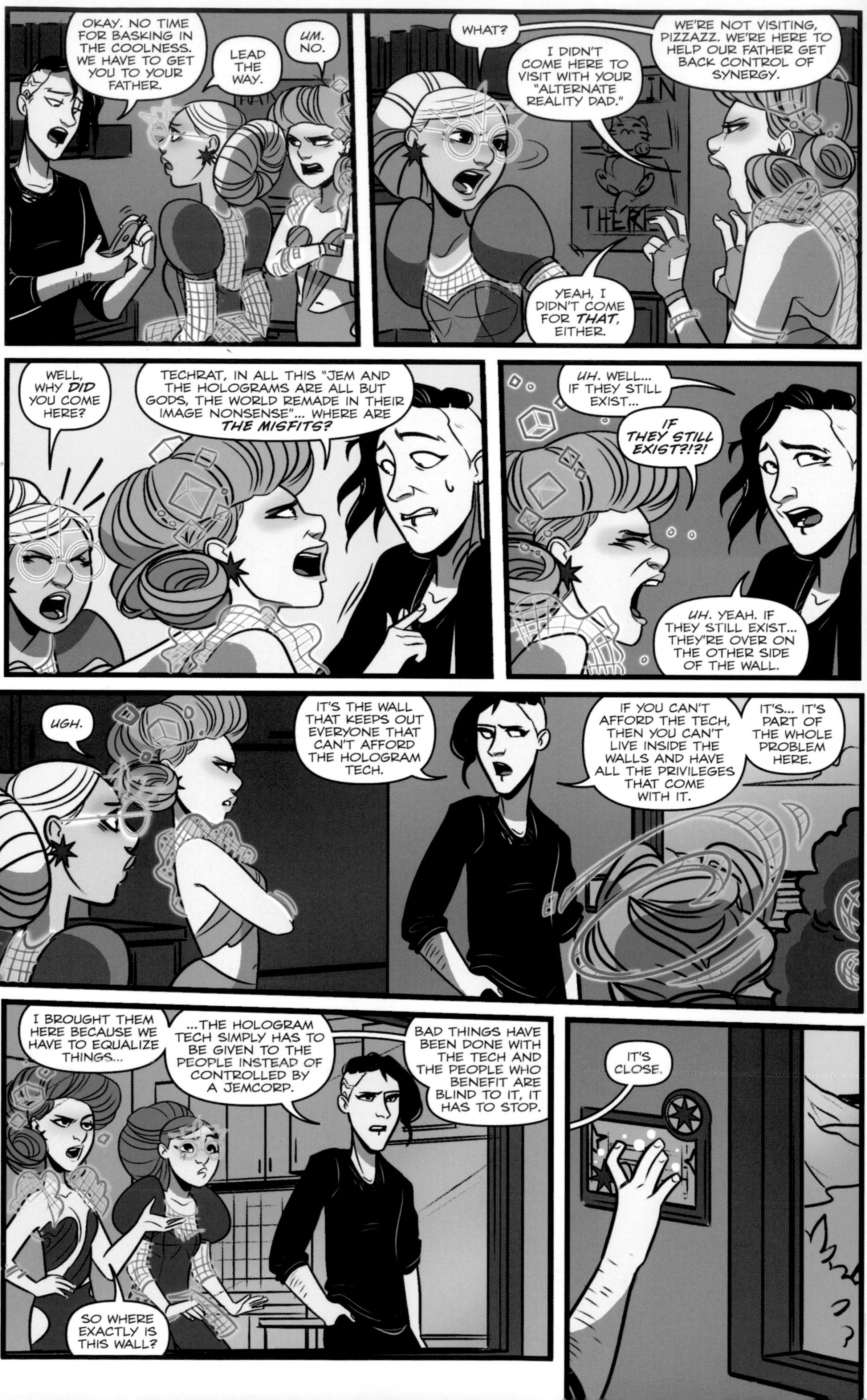
OKAY. NO TIME FOR BASKING IN THE COOLNESS. WE HAVE TO GET YOU TO YOUR FATHER.
LEAD THE WAY.
UM. NO.
WHAT?
I DIDN'T COME HERE TO VISIT WITH YOUR "ALTERNATE REALITY DAD."
WE'RE NOT VISITING, PIZZAZZ. WE'RE HERE TO HELP OUR FATHER GET BACK CONTROL OF SYNERGY.
YEAH, I DIDN'T COME FOR THAT, EITHER.
WELL, WHY DID YOU COME HERE?
TECHRAT, IN ALL THIS "JEM AND THE HOLOGRAMS ARE ALL BUT GODS, THE WORLD REMADE IN THEIR IMAGE NONSENSE"... WHERE ARE THE MISFITS?
UH. WELL... IF THEY STILL EXIST...
IF THEY STILL EXIST?!?!
UH. YEAH. IF THEY STILL EXIST... THEY'RE OVER ON THE OTHER SIDE OF THE WALL.
UGH.
IT'S THE WALL THAT KEEPS OUT EVERYONE THAT CAN'T AFFORD THE HOLOGRAM TECH.
IF YOU CAN'T AFFORD THE TECH, THEN YOU CAN'T LIVE INSIDE THE WALLS AND HAVE ALL THE PRIVILEGES THAT COME WITH IT.
IT'S... IT'S PART OF THE WHOLE PROBLEM HERE.
I BROUGHT THEM HERE BECAUSE WE HAVE TO EQUALIZE THINGS...
...THE HOLOGRAM TECH SIMPLY HAS TO BE GIVEN TO THE PEOPLE INSTEAD OF CONTROLLED BY A JEMCORP.
BAD THINGS HAVE BEEN DONE WITH THE TECH AND THE PEOPLE WHO BENEFIT ARE BLIND TO IT, IT HAS TO STOP.
SO WHERE EXACTLY IS THIS WALL?
IT'S CLOSE.

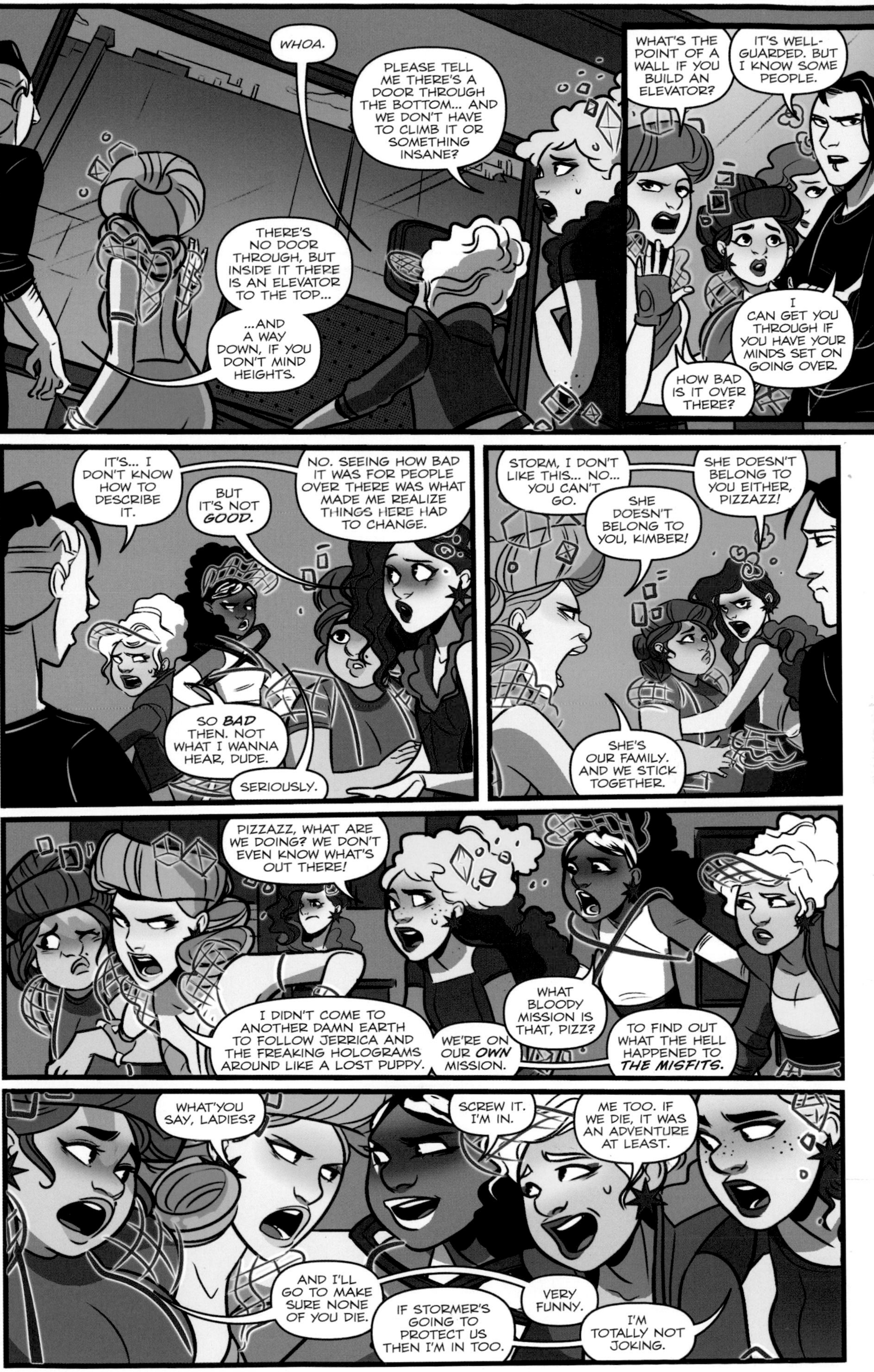
WHOA.
PLEASE TELL ME THERE'S A DOOR THROUGH THE BOTTOM... AND WE DON'T HAVE TO CLIMB IT OR SOMETHING INSANE?
THERE'S NO DOOR THROUGH, BUT INSIDE IT THERE IS AN ELEVATOR TO THE TOP...
...AND A WAY DOWN, IF YOU DON'T MIND HEIGHTS.
WHAT'S THE POINT OF A WALL IF YOU BUILD AN ELEVATOR?
IT'S WELL-GUARDED. BUT I KNOW SOME PEOPLE.
I CAN GET YOU THROUGH IF YOU HAVE YOUR MINDS SET ON GOING OVER.
HOW BAD IS IT OVER THERE?
IT'S... I DON'T KNOW HOW TO DESCRIBE IT.
BUT IT'S NOT GOOD.
NO. SEEING HOW BAD IT WAS FOR PEOPLE OVER THERE WAS WHAT MADE ME REALIZE THINGS HERE HAD TO CHANGE.
SO BAD THEN. NOT WHAT I WANNA HEAR, DUDE.
SERIOUSLY.
STORM, I DON'T LIKE THIS... NO... YOU CAN'T GO.
SHE DOESN'T BELONG TO YOU, KIMBER!
SHE DOESN'T BELONG TO YOU EITHER, PIZZAZZ!
SHE'S OUR FAMILY. AND WE STICK TOGETHER.
PIZZAZZ, WHAT ARE WE DOING? WE DON'T EVEN KNOW WHAT'S OUT THERE!
I DIDN'T COME TO ANOTHER DAMN EARTH TO FOLLOW JERRICA AND THE FREAKING HOLOGRAMS AROUND LIKE A LOST PUPPY.
WE'RE ON OUR OWN MISSION.
WHAT BLOODY MISSION IS THAT, PIZZ?
TO FIND OUT WHAT THE HELL HAPPENED TO THE MISFITS.
WHAT'YOU SAY, LADIES?
SCREW IT. I'M IN.
ME TOO. IF WE DIE, IT WAS AN ADVENTURE AT LEAST.
AND I'LL GO TO MAKE SURE NONE OF YOU DIE.
IF STORMER'S GOING TO PROTECT US THEN I'M IN TOO.
VERY FUNNY.
I'M TOTALLY NOT JOKING.

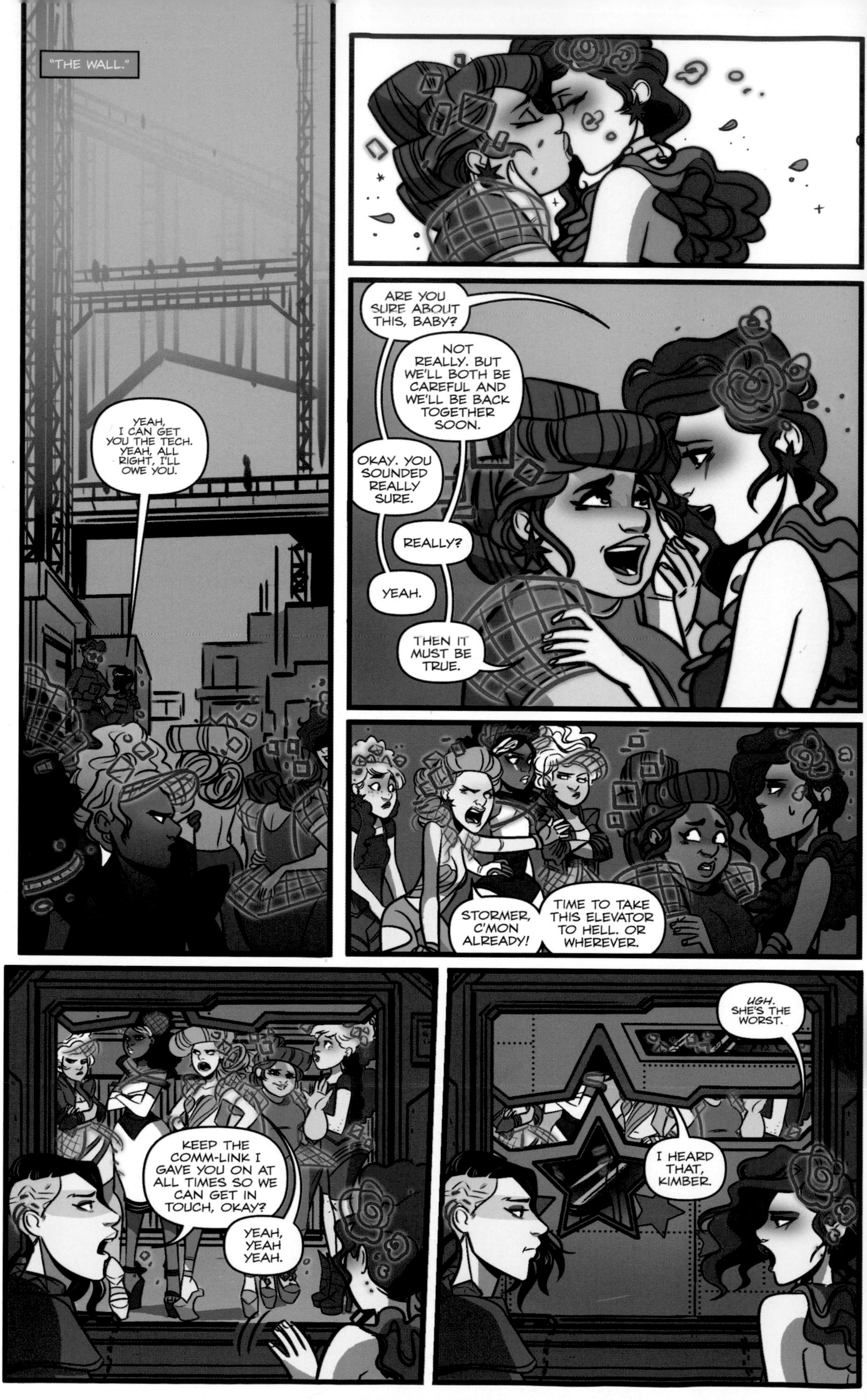
"THE WALL."
YEAH, I CAN GET YOU THE TECH. YEAH, ALL RIGHT, I'LL OWE YOU.
ARE YOU SURE ABOUT THIS, BABY?
NOT REALLY. BUT WE'LL BOTH BE CAREFUL AND WE'LL BE BACK TOGETHER SOON.
OKAY. YOU SOUNDED REALLY SURE.
REALLY?
YEAH.
THEN IT MUST BE TRUE.
STORMER, C'MON ALREADY!
TIME TO TAKE THIS ELEVATOR TO HELL. OR WHEREVER.
KEEP THE COMM-LINK I GAVE YOU ON AT ALL TIMES SO WE CAN GET IN TOUCH, OKAY?
YEAH, YEAH YEAH.
UGH. SHE'S THE WORST.
I HEARD THAT, KIMBER.

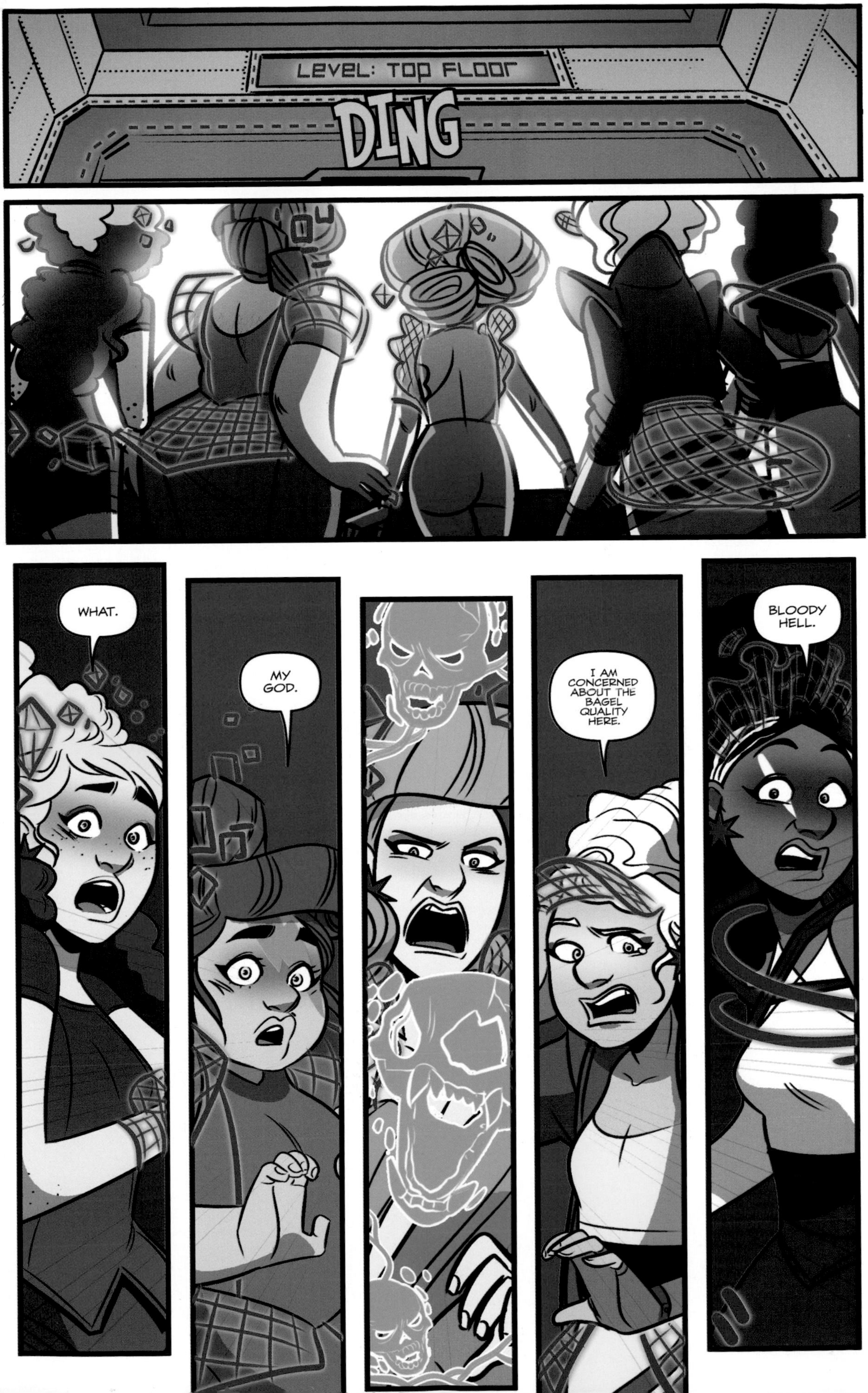
LEVEL: TOP FLOOR
DING
WHAT.
MY GOD.
I AM CONCERNED ABOUT THE BAGEL QUALITY HERE.
BLOODY HELL.

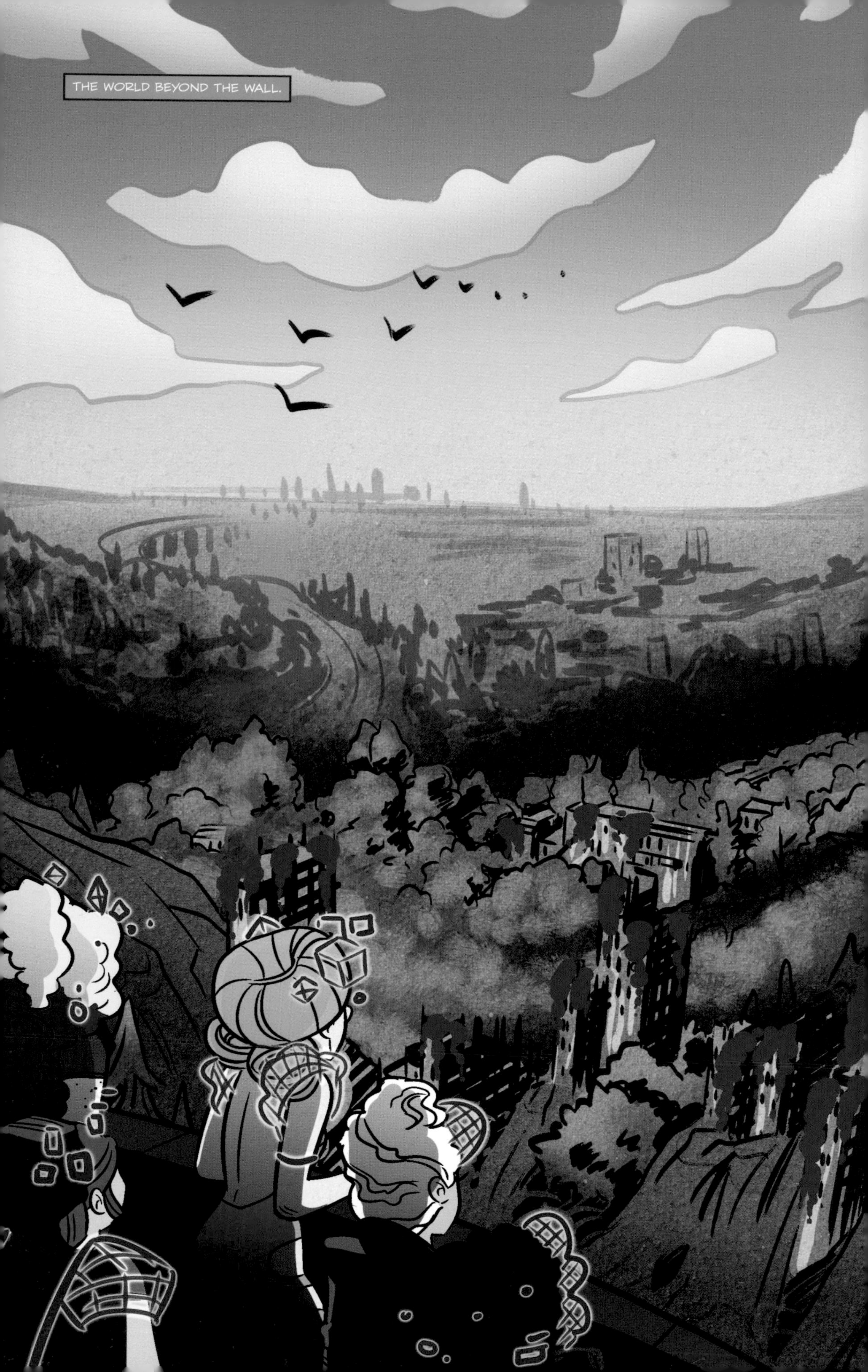
THE WORLD BEYOND THE WALL.

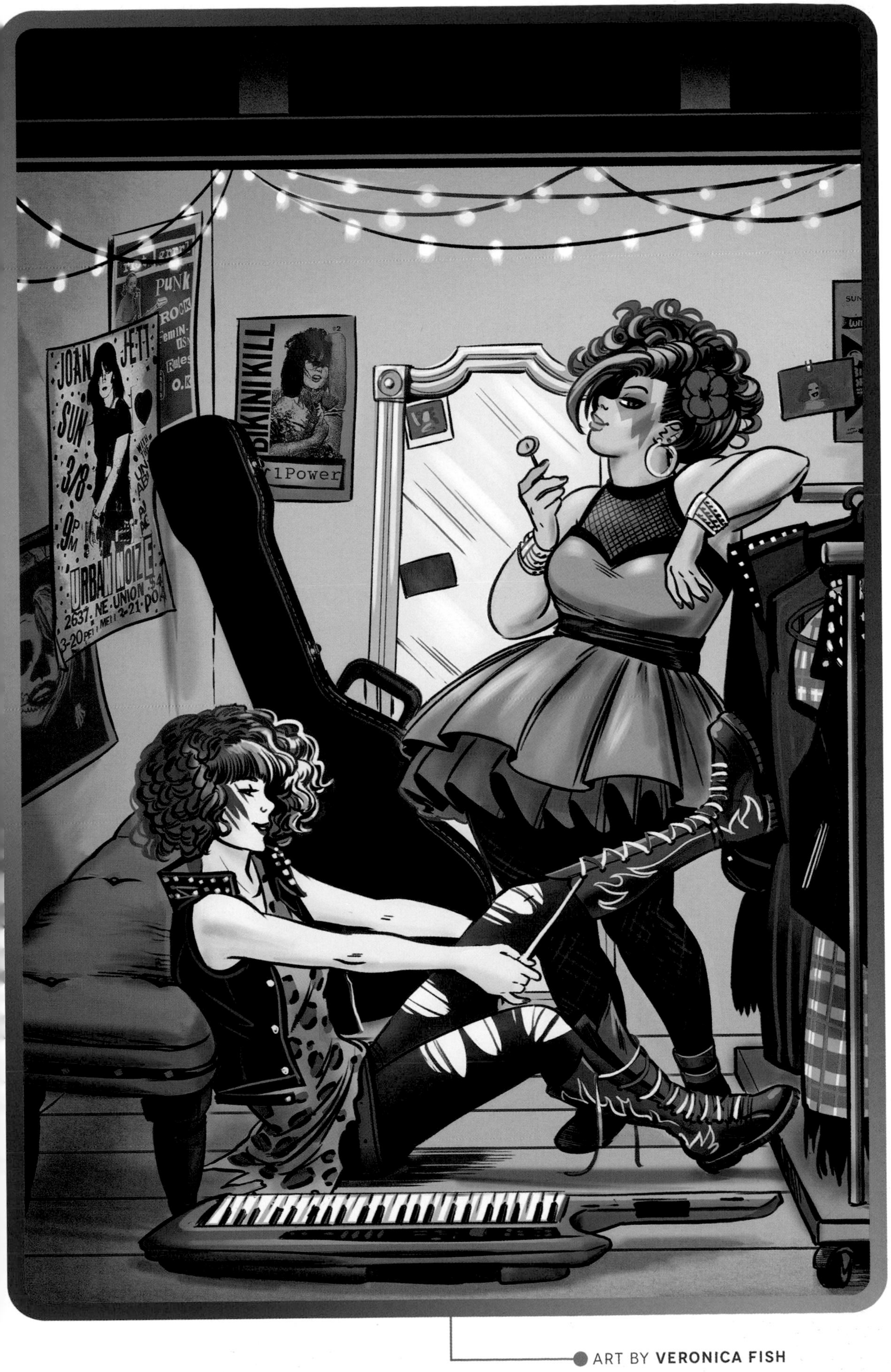
JOAN JETT
SUN 3/8 9PM
URBAN NOIZE
2637 NE UNION
BIKINIKILL
PUNK ROCK

ART BY **VERONICA FISH**

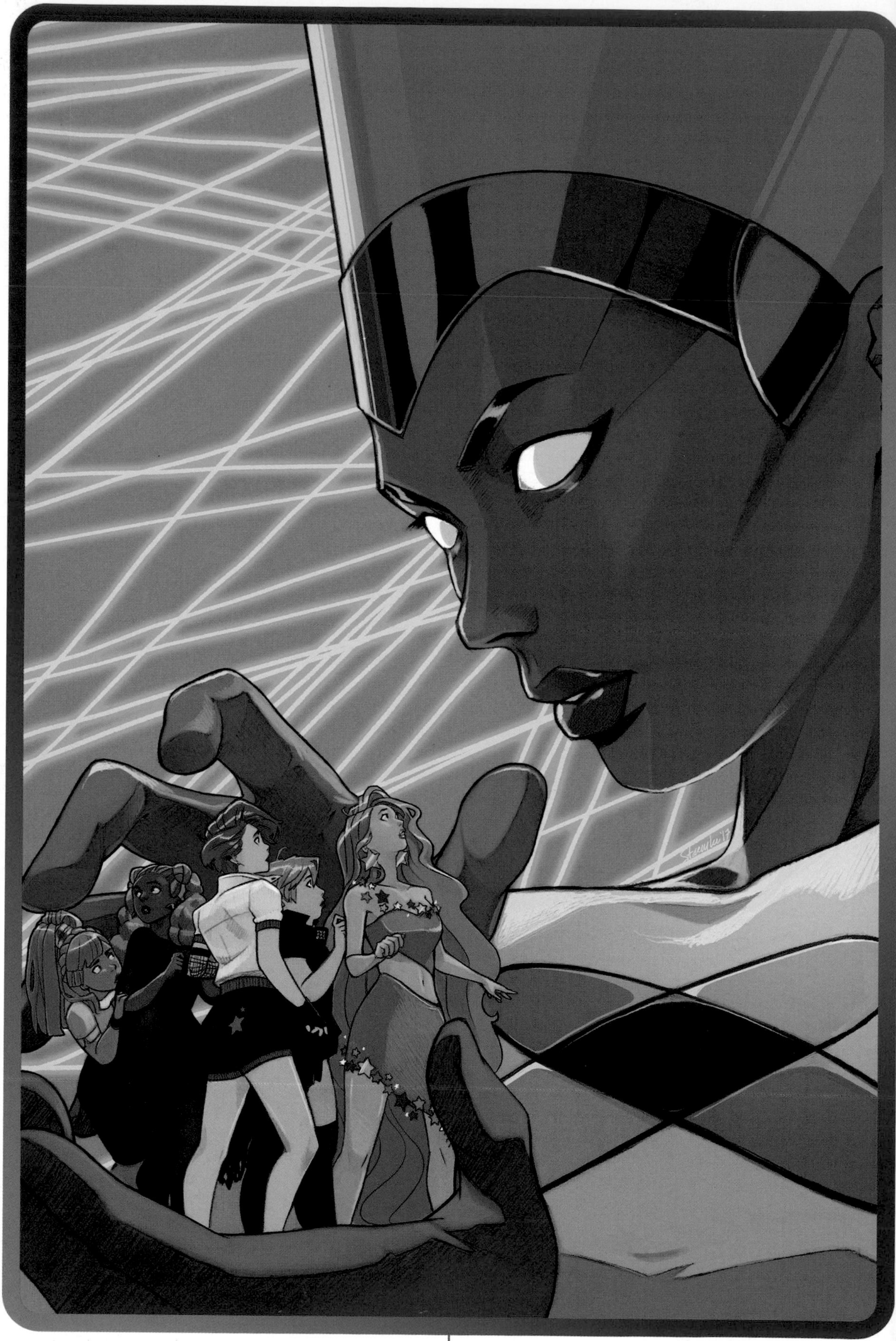

ART BY **STACEY LEE**

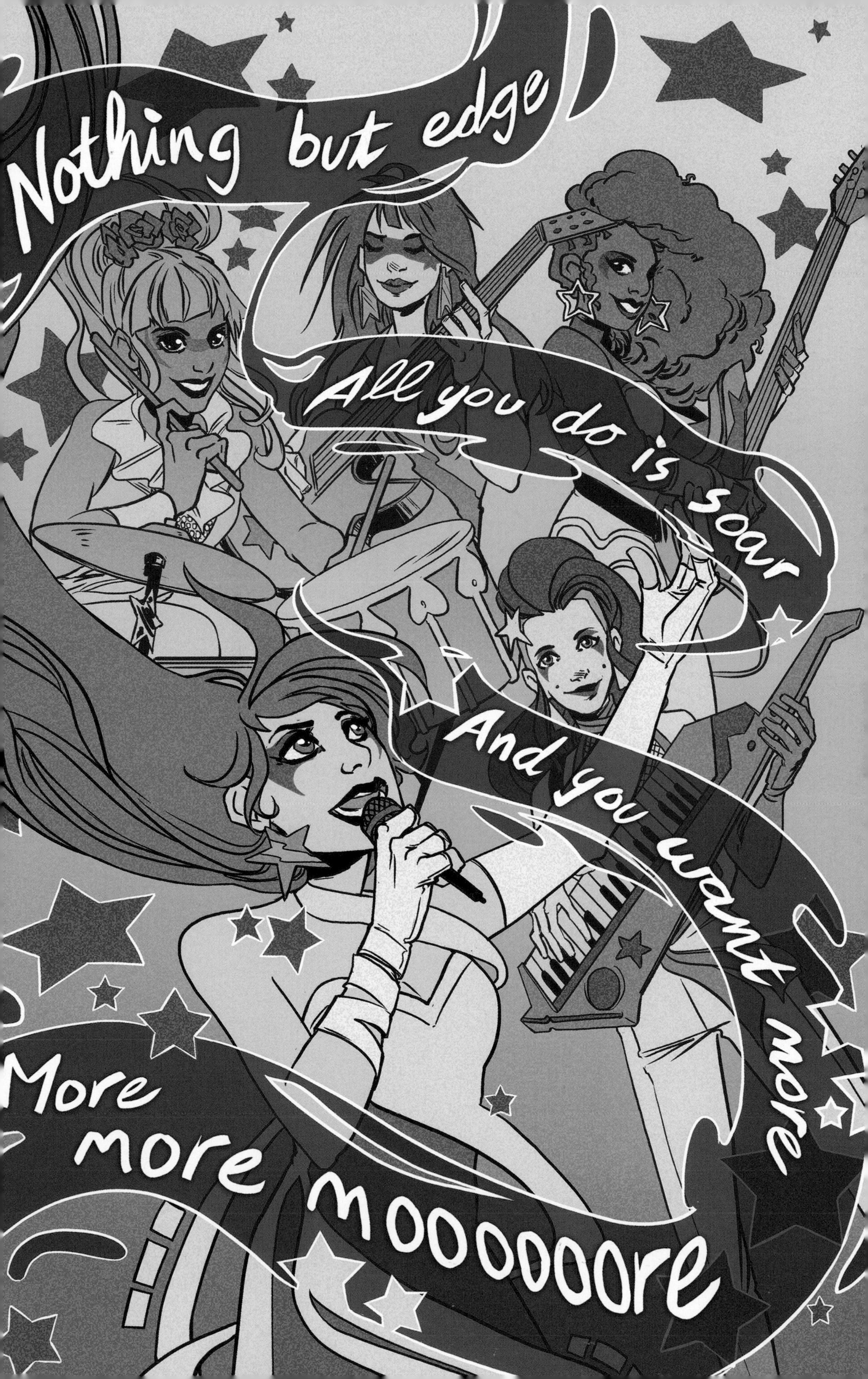
Nothing but edge
All you do is soar
And you want more
More
more more mooooooore

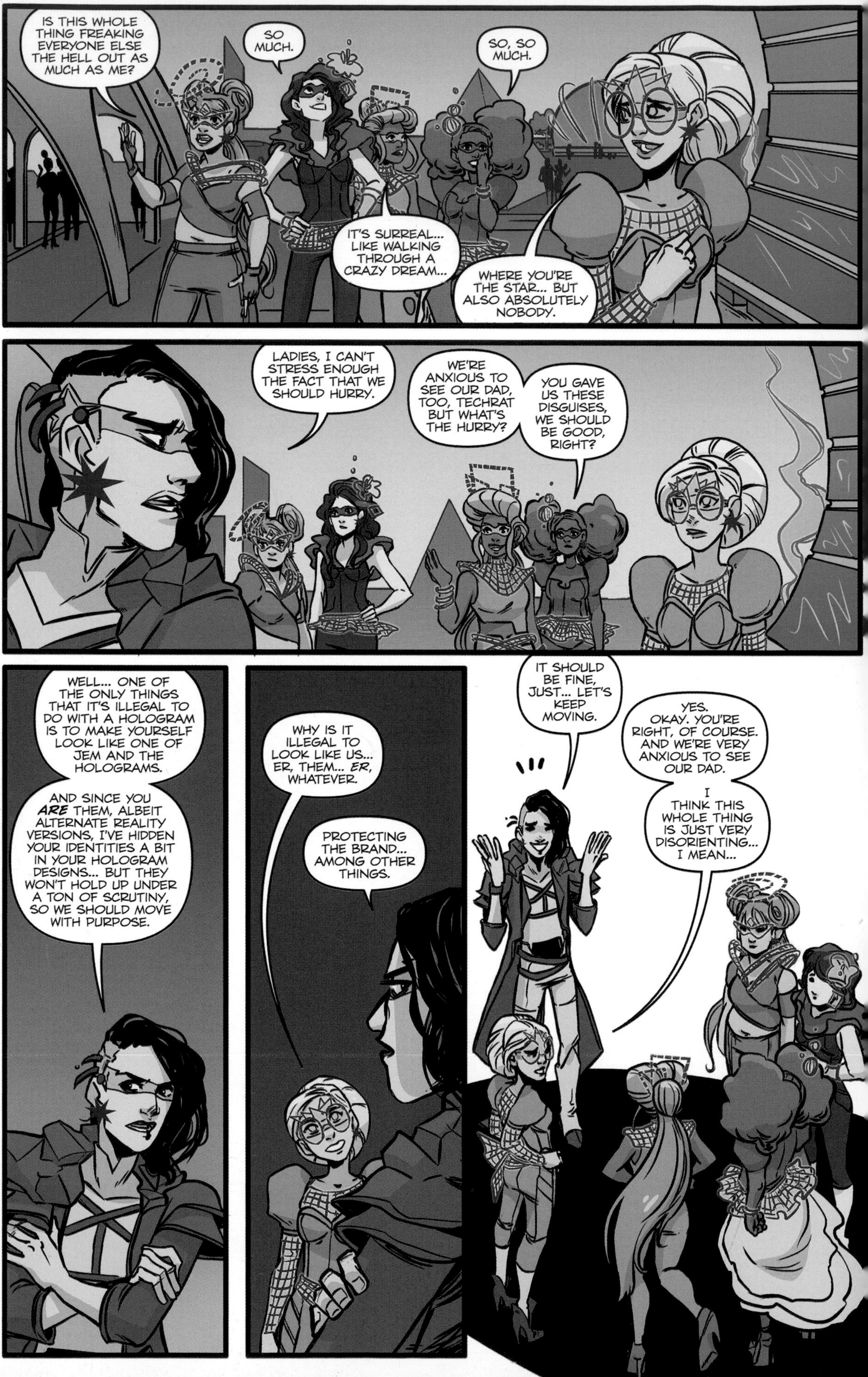
IS THIS WHOLE THING FREAKING EVERYONE ELSE THE HELL OUT AS MUCH AS ME?
SO MUCH.
SO, SO MUCH.
IT'S SURREAL... LIKE WALKING THROUGH A CRAZY DREAM...
WHERE YOU'RE THE STAR... BUT ALSO ABSOLUTELY NOBODY.
LADIES, I CAN'T STRESS ENOUGH THE FACT THAT WE SHOULD HURRY.
WE'RE ANXIOUS TO SEE OUR DAD, TOO, TECHRAT BUT WHAT'S THE HURRY?
YOU GAVE US THESE DISGUISES, WE SHOULD BE GOOD, RIGHT?
WELL... ONE OF THE ONLY THINGS THAT IT'S ILLEGAL TO DO WITH A HOLOGRAM IS TO MAKE YOURSELF LOOK LIKE ONE OF JEM AND THE HOLOGRAMS.
AND SINCE YOU *ARE* THEM, ALBEIT ALTERNATE REALITY VERSIONS, I'VE HIDDEN YOUR IDENTITIES A BIT IN YOUR HOLOGRAM DESIGNS... BUT THEY WON'T HOLD UP UNDER A TON OF SCRUTINY, SO WE SHOULD MOVE WITH PURPOSE.
WHY IS IT ILLEGAL TO LOOK LIKE US... ER, THEM... *ER*, WHATEVER.
PROTECTING THE BRAND... AMONG OTHER THINGS.
IT SHOULD BE FINE, JUST... LET'S KEEP MOVING.
YES. OKAY. YOU'RE RIGHT, OF COURSE. AND WE'RE VERY ANXIOUS TO SEE OUR DAD.
I THINK THIS WHOLE THING IS JUST VERY DISORIENTING... I MEAN...

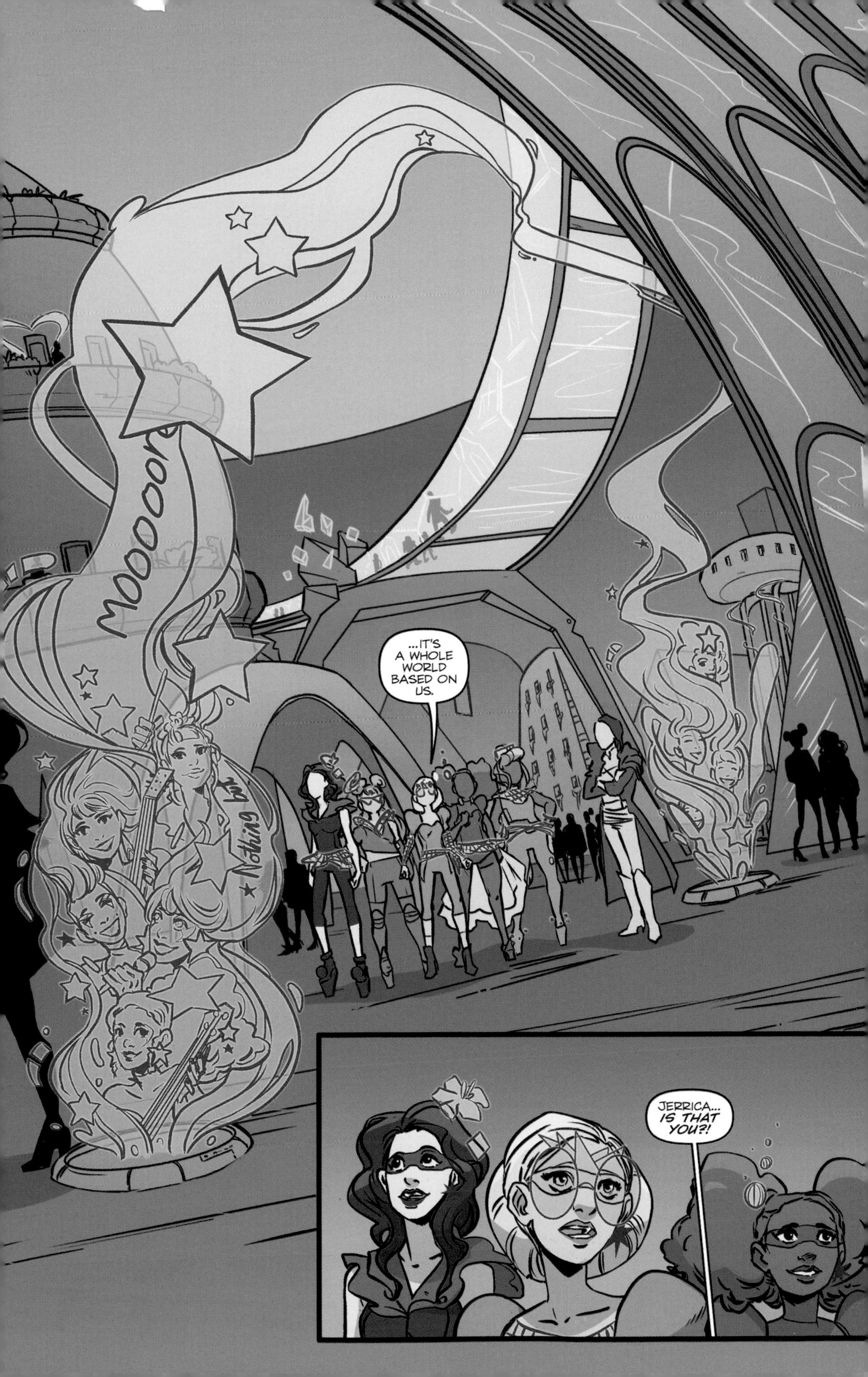
Nothing but
...IT'S A WHOLE WORLD BASED ON US.
JERRICA... IS THAT YOU?!

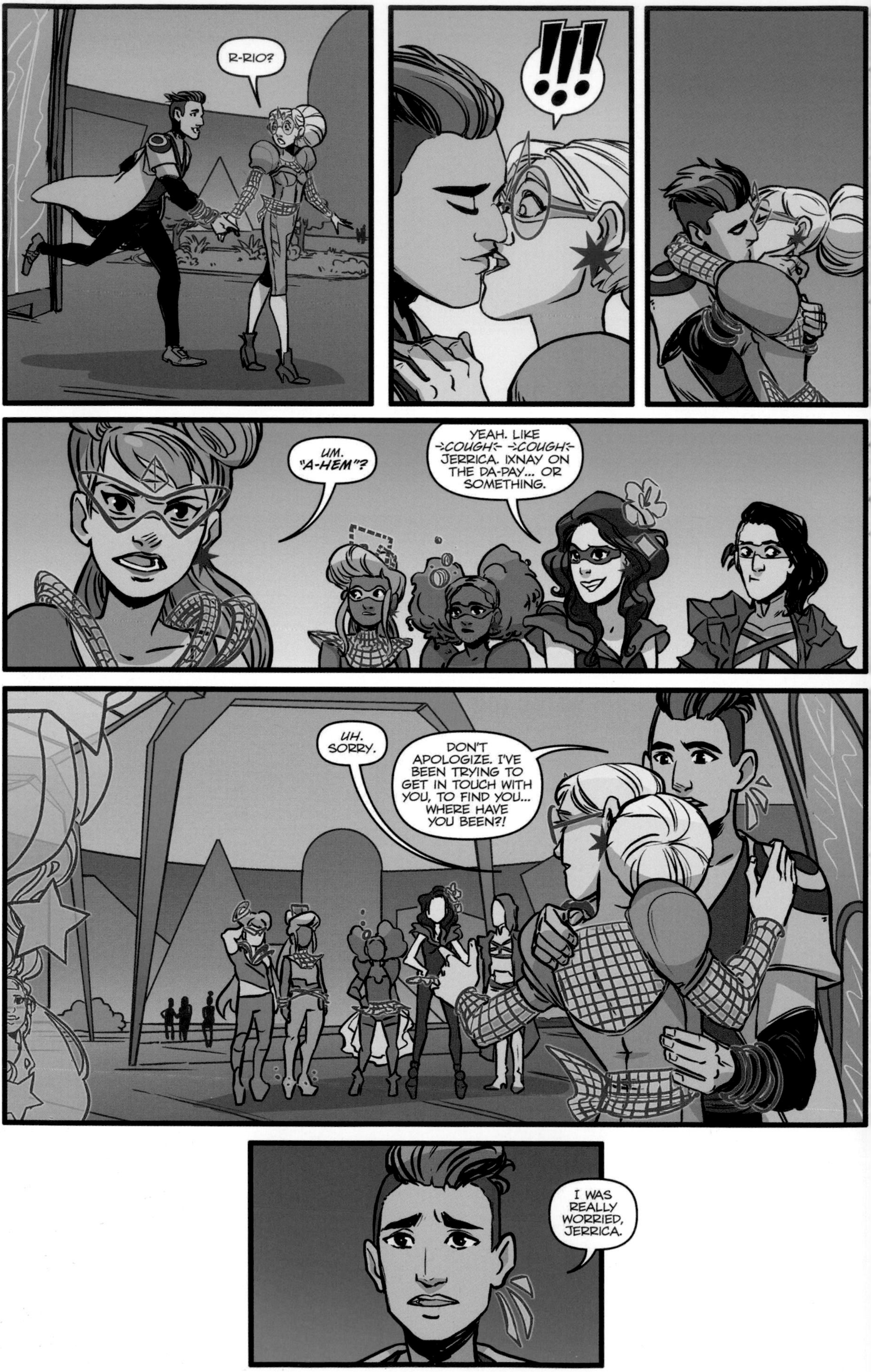
R-RIO?
!!!
UM. "A-HEM"?
YEAH. LIKE -COUGH- -COUGH- JERRICA. IXNAY ON THE DA-PAY... OR SOMETHING.
UH. SORRY.
DON'T APOLOGIZE. I'VE BEEN TRYING TO GET IN TOUCH WITH YOU, TO FIND YOU... WHERE HAVE YOU BEEN?!
I WAS REALLY WORRIED, JERRICA.

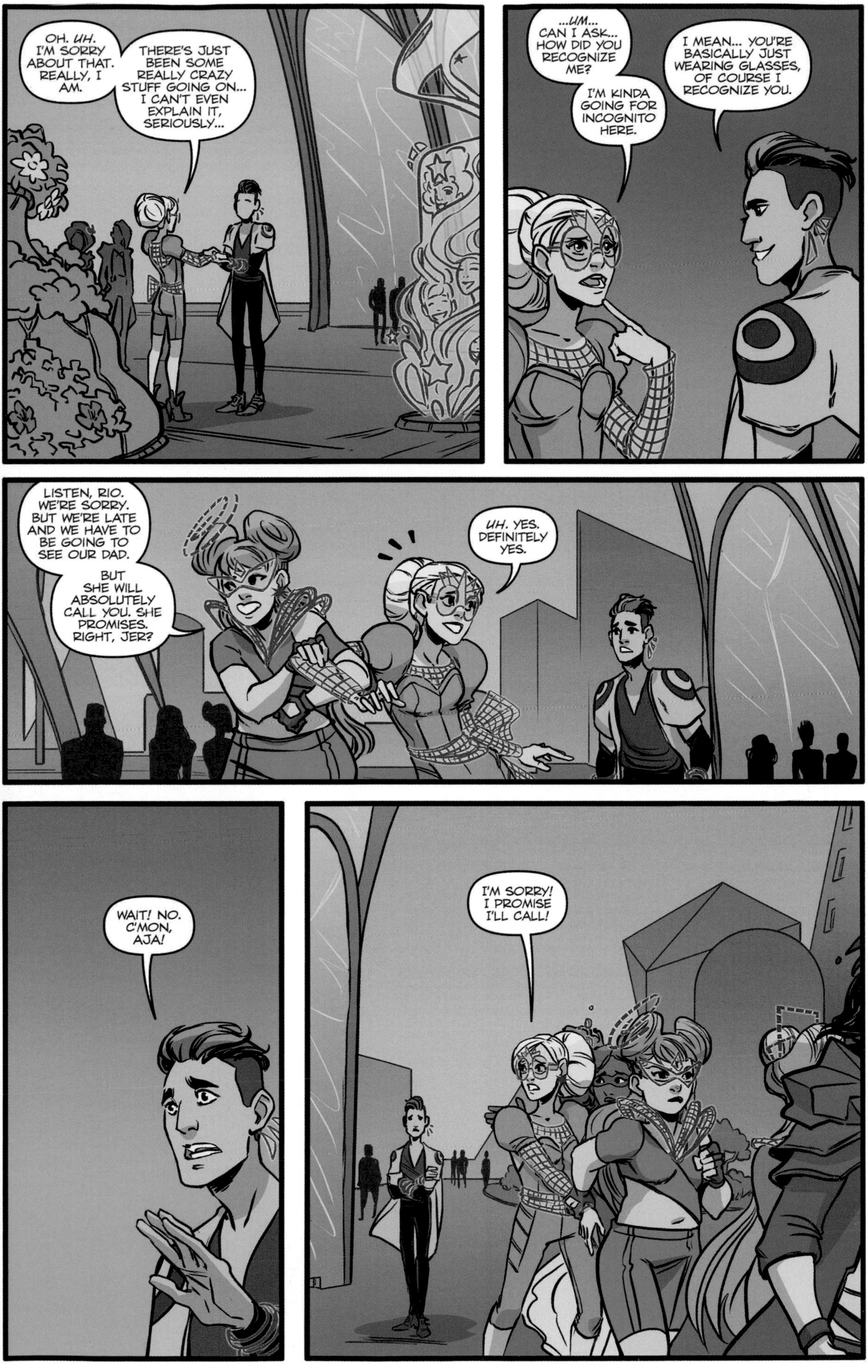
OH. UH. I'M SORRY ABOUT THAT. REALLY, I AM.
THERE'S JUST BEEN SOME REALLY CRAZY STUFF GOING ON... I CAN'T EVEN EXPLAIN IT, SERIOUSLY...
...UM... CAN I ASK... HOW DID YOU RECOGNIZE ME?
I'M KINDA GOING FOR INCOGNITO HERE.
I MEAN... YOU'RE BASICALLY JUST WEARING GLASSES, OF COURSE I RECOGNIZE YOU.
LISTEN, RIO. WE'RE SORRY. BUT WE'RE LATE AND WE HAVE TO BE GOING TO SEE OUR DAD.
BUT SHE WILL ABSOLUTELY CALL YOU. SHE PROMISES. RIGHT, JER?
UH. YES. DEFINITELY YES.
WAIT! NO. C'MON, AJA!
I'M SORRY! I PROMISE I'LL CALL!

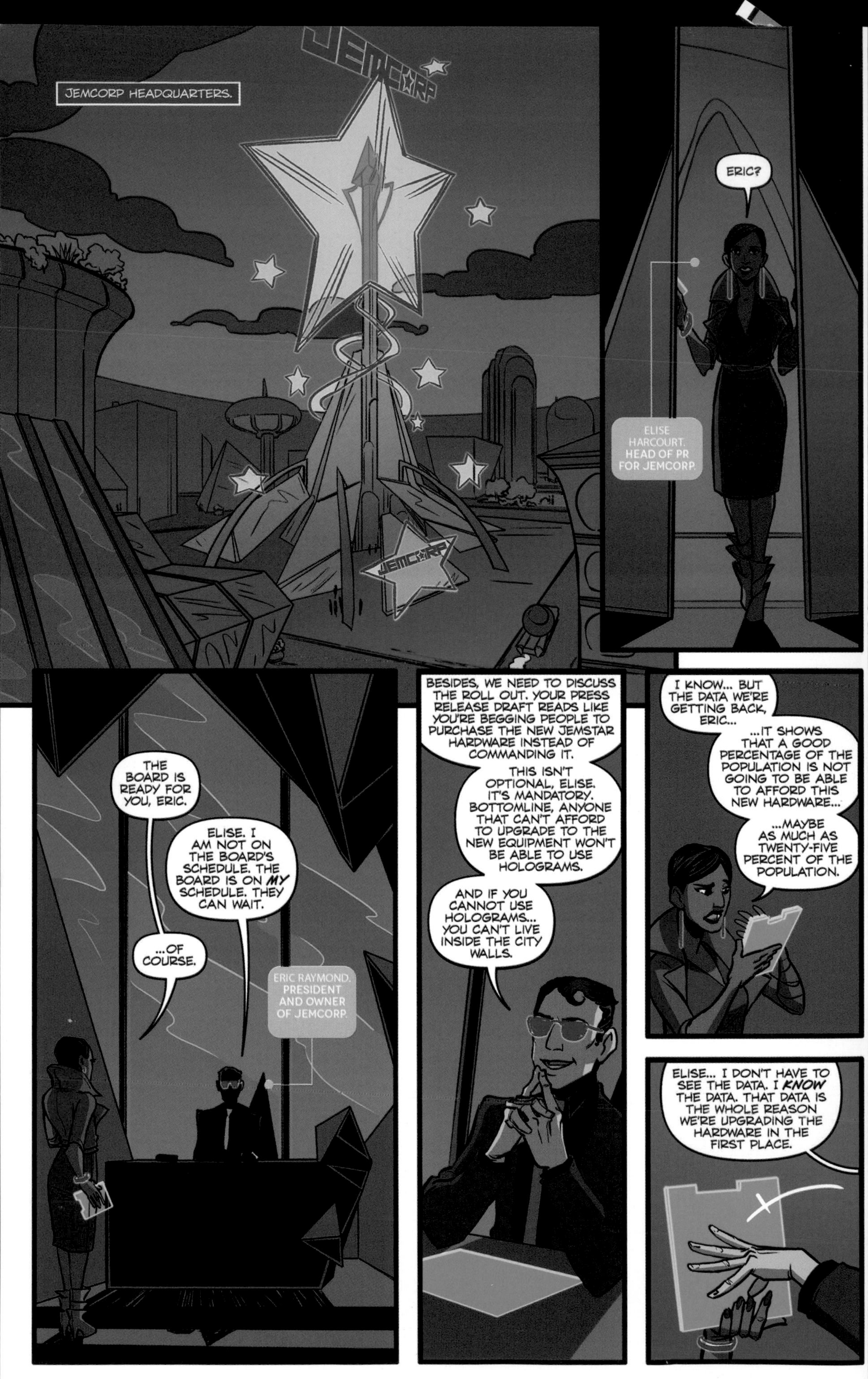
JEMCORP HEADQUARTERS.
JEMCORP
JEMCORP
ERIC?
ELISE HARCOURT. HEAD OF PR FOR JEMCORP.
THE BOARD IS READY FOR YOU, ERIC.
ELISE. I AM NOT ON THE BOARD'S SCHEDULE. THE BOARD IS ON *MY* SCHEDULE. THEY CAN WAIT.
...OF COURSE.
ERIC RAYMOND. PRESIDENT AND OWNER OF JEMCORP.
BESIDES, WE NEED TO DISCUSS THE ROLL OUT. YOUR PRESS RELEASE DRAFT READS LIKE YOU'RE BEGGING PEOPLE TO PURCHASE THE NEW JEMSTAR HARDWARE INSTEAD OF COMMANDING IT.
THIS ISN'T OPTIONAL, ELISE. IT'S MANDATORY. BOTTOMLINE, ANYONE THAT CAN'T AFFORD TO UPGRADE TO THE NEW EQUIPMENT WON'T BE ABLE TO USE HOLOGRAMS.
AND IF YOU CANNOT USE HOLOGRAMS... YOU CAN'T LIVE INSIDE THE CITY WALLS.
I KNOW... BUT THE DATA WE'RE GETTING BACK, ERIC...
...IT SHOWS THAT A GOOD PERCENTAGE OF THE POPULATION IS NOT GOING TO BE ABLE TO AFFORD THIS NEW HARDWARE...
...MAYBE AS MUCH AS TWENTY-FIVE PERCENT OF THE POPULATION.
ELISE... I DON'T HAVE TO SEE THE DATA. I *KNOW* THE DATA. THAT DATA IS THE WHOLE REASON WE'RE UPGRADING THE HARDWARE IN THE FIRST PLACE.

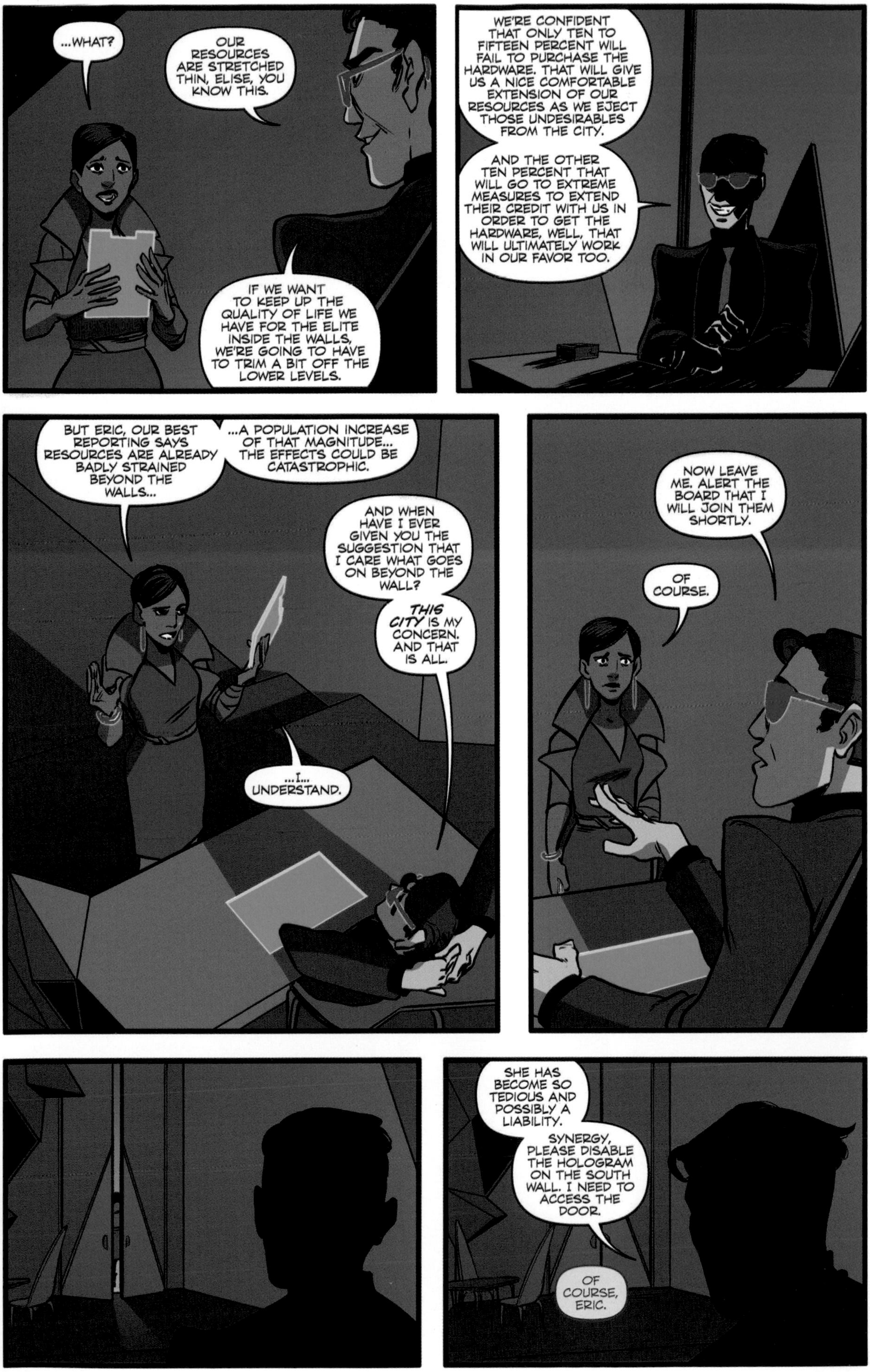
...WHAT?
OUR RESOURCES ARE STRETCHED THIN, ELISE, YOU KNOW THIS.
IF WE WANT TO KEEP UP THE QUALITY OF LIFE WE HAVE FOR THE ELITE INSIDE THE WALLS, WE'RE GOING TO HAVE TO TRIM A BIT OFF THE LOWER LEVELS.
WE'RE CONFIDENT THAT ONLY TEN TO FIFTEEN PERCENT WILL FAIL TO PURCHASE THE HARDWARE. THAT WILL GIVE US A NICE COMFORTABLE EXTENSION OF OUR RESOURCES AS WE EJECT THOSE UNDESIRABLES FROM THE CITY.
AND THE OTHER TEN PERCENT THAT WILL GO TO EXTREME MEASURES TO EXTEND THEIR CREDIT WITH US IN ORDER TO GET THE HARDWARE, WELL, THAT WILL ULTIMATELY WORK IN OUR FAVOR TOO.
BUT ERIC, OUR BEST REPORTING SAYS RESOURCES ARE ALREADY BADLY STRAINED BEYOND THE WALLS...
...A POPULATION INCREASE OF THAT MAGNITUDE... THE EFFECTS COULD BE CATASTROPHIC.
AND WHEN HAVE I EVER GIVEN YOU THE SUGGESTION THAT I CARE WHAT GOES ON BEYOND THE WALL?
THIS CITY IS MY CONCERN. AND THAT IS ALL.
...I... UNDERSTAND.
NOW LEAVE ME. ALERT THE BOARD THAT I WILL JOIN THEM SHORTLY.
OF COURSE.
SHE HAS BECOME SO TEDIOUS AND POSSIBLY A LIABILITY.
SYNERGY, PLEASE DISABLE THE HOLOGRAM ON THE SOUTH WALL. I NEED TO ACCESS THE DOOR.
OF COURSE, ERIC.

THANK YOU, SYNERGY.

CERTAINLY, ERIC. WOULD YOU LIKE ME TO REMAIN?

YES. I THINK I'LL BRING YOU TO THE BOARD MEETING WITH ME.

HELP REMIND THEM OF THEIR PLACE.

VERY WELL.

I CAN'T STAY LONG. THE BOARD IS WAITING.

WHAT ELSE IS NEW?

DON'T BE LIKE THAT. I'LL BE BACK LATER.

I DON'T CARE.

I CARE THAT NONE OF THIS IS WHAT WE DISCUSSED, WHAT YOU *PROMISED*.

I UNDERSTAND YOU'RE FRUSTRATED.

FRUSTRATED IS NOT THE WORD I WOULD USE.

IT'S JUST GOING TO TAKE A LITTLE MORE TIME. BE PATIENT.

I KNOW. BUT IT'S ALL GOING TO BE WORTH IT.

PATIENCE IS NOT SOMETHING I'M GOOD AT, ERIC.

...IT BETTER BE.

click

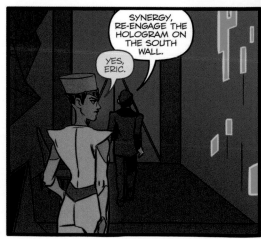

SYNERGY, RE-ENGAGE THE HOLOGRAM ON THE SOUTH WALL.

YES, ERIC.

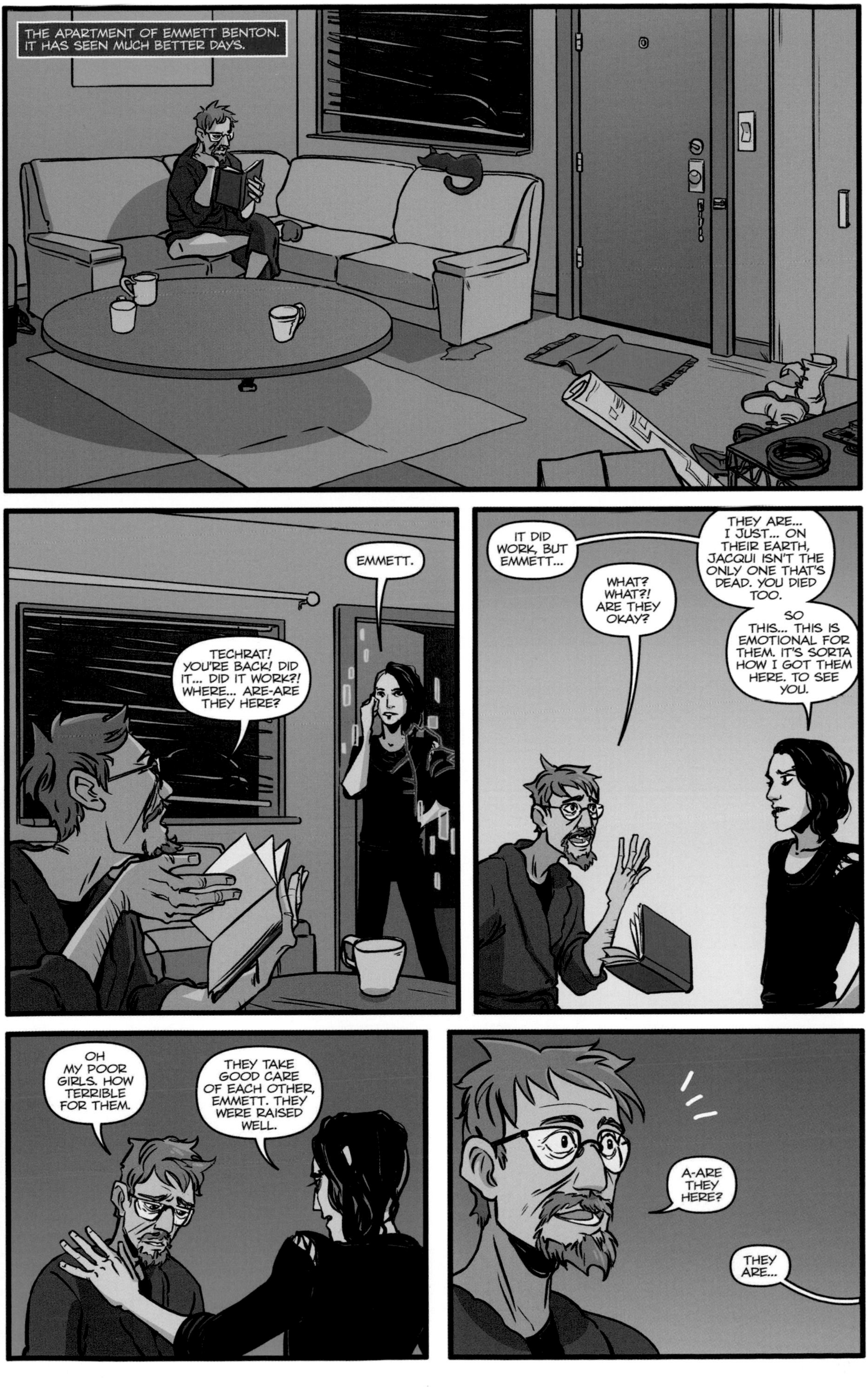
THE APARTMENT OF EMMETT BENTON. IT HAS SEEN MUCH BETTER DAYS.
EMMETT.
TECHRAT! YOU'RE BACK! DID IT... DID IT WORK?! WHERE... ARE-ARE THEY HERE?
IT DID WORK, BUT EMMETT...
THEY ARE... I JUST... ON THEIR EARTH, JACQUI ISN'T THE ONLY ONE THAT'S DEAD. YOU DIED TOO.
WHAT? WHAT?! ARE THEY OKAY?
SO THIS... THIS IS EMOTIONAL FOR THEM. IT'S SORTA HOW I GOT THEM HERE. TO SEE YOU.
OH MY POOR GIRLS. HOW TERRIBLE FOR THEM.
THEY TAKE GOOD CARE OF EACH OTHER, EMMETT. THEY WERE RAISED WELL.
A-ARE THEY HERE?
THEY ARE...

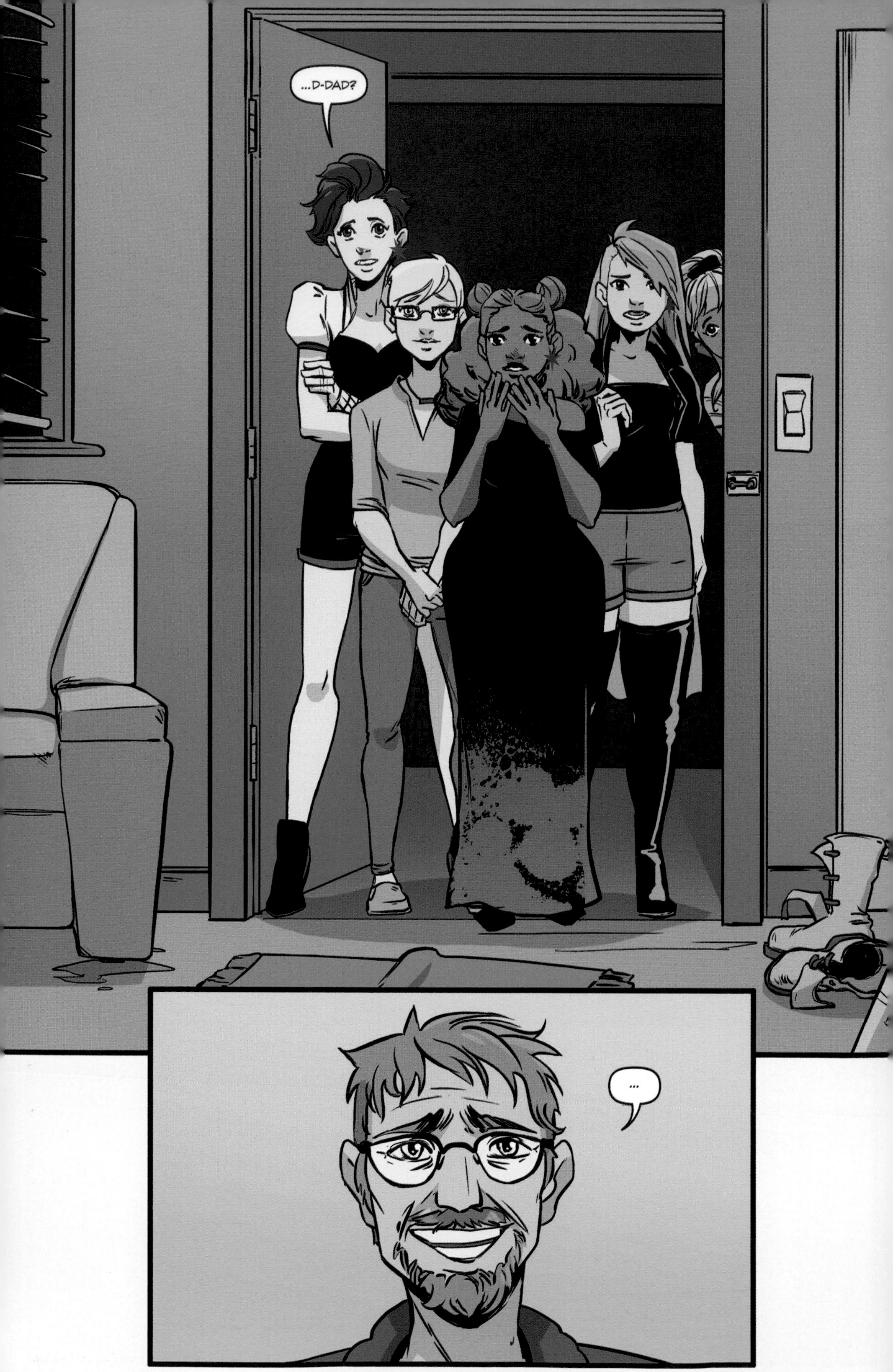
...D-DAD?
...

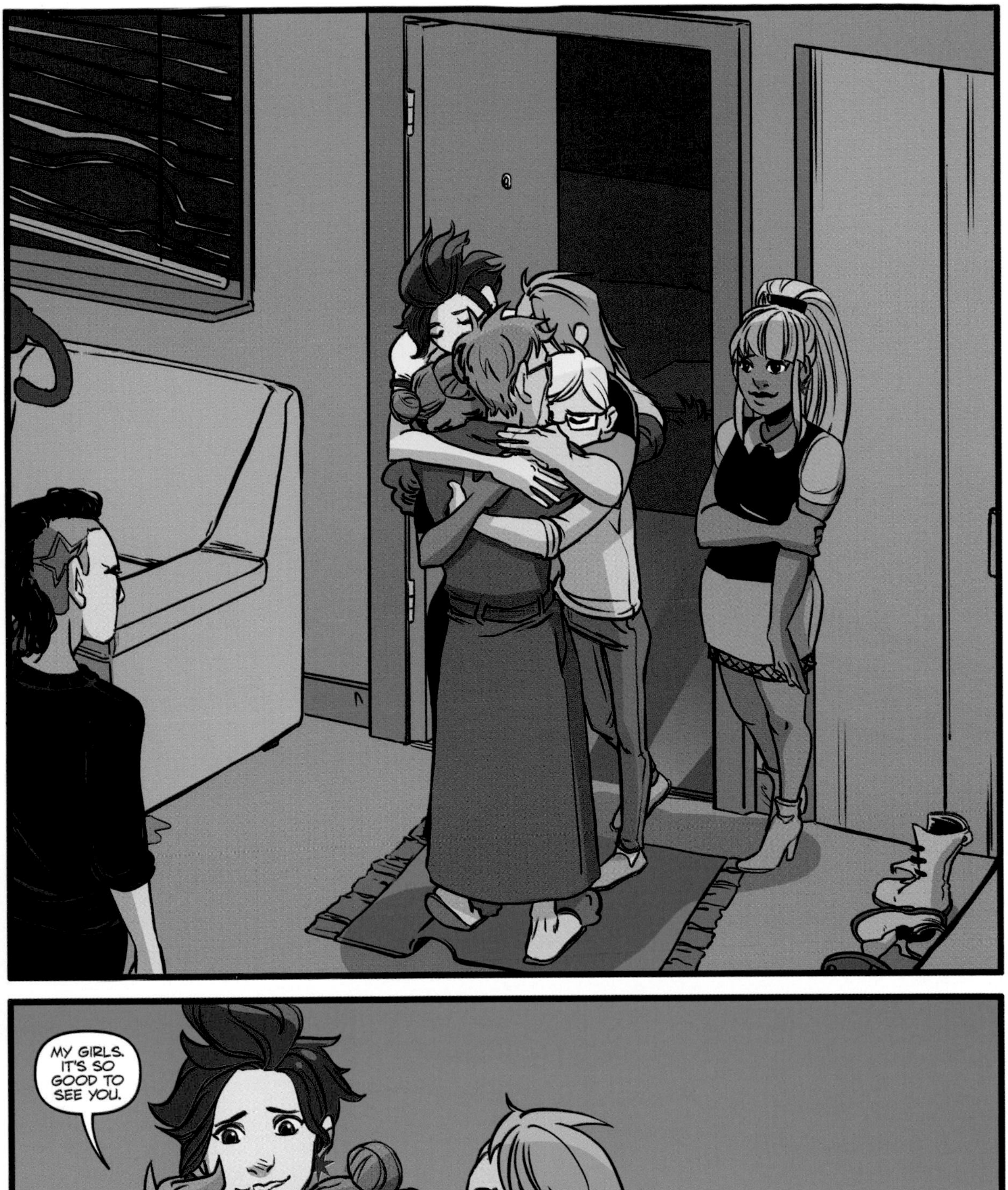

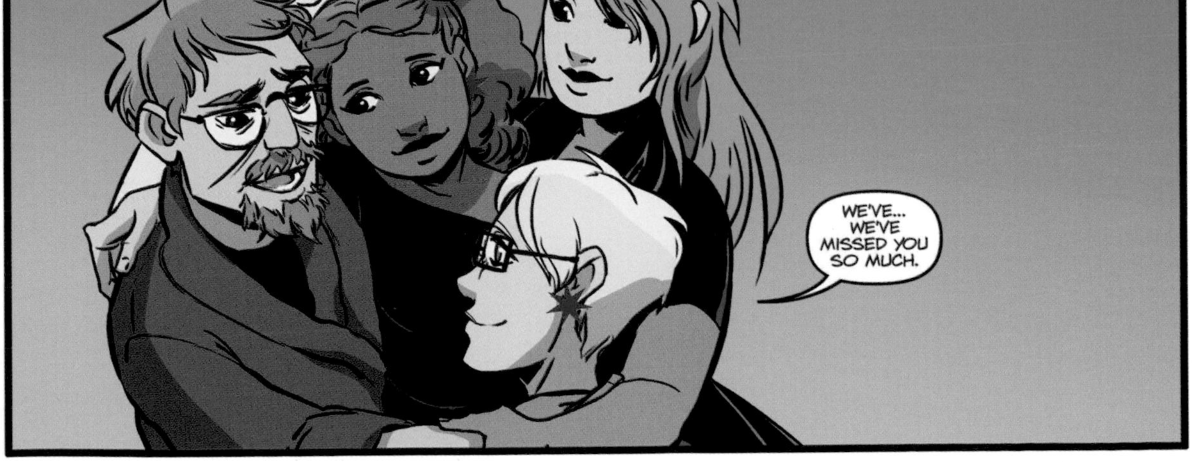
MY GIRLS. IT'S SO GOOD TO SEE YOU.
WE'VE... WE'VE MISSED YOU SO MUCH.

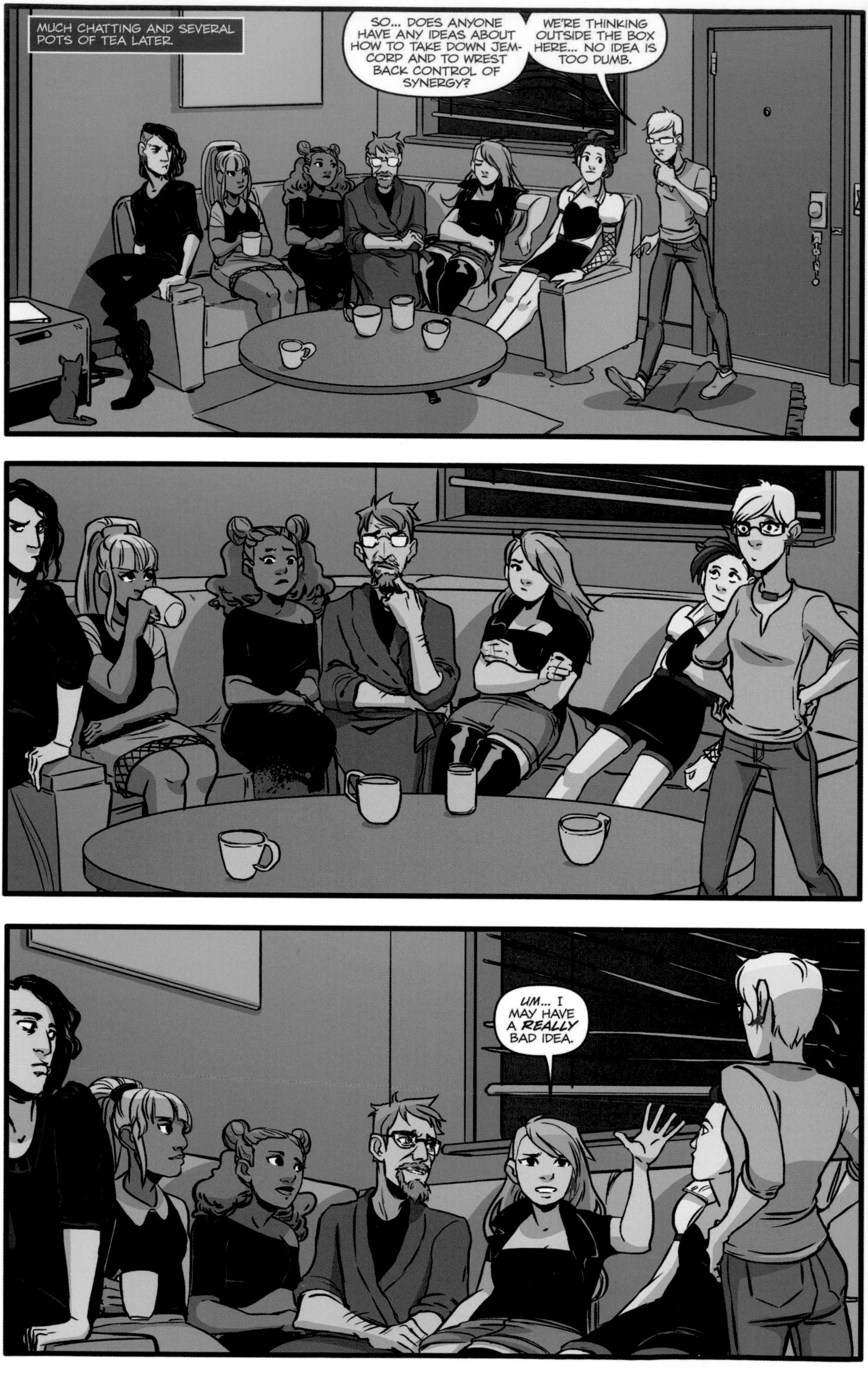
MUCH CHATTING AND SEVERAL POTS OF TEA LATER.
SO... DOES ANYONE HAVE ANY IDEAS ABOUT HOW TO TAKE DOWN JEM-CORP AND TO WREST BACK CONTROL OF SYNERGY?
WE'RE THINKING OUTSIDE THE BOX HERE... NO IDEA IS TOO DUMB.
UM... I MAY HAVE A REALLY BAD IDEA.

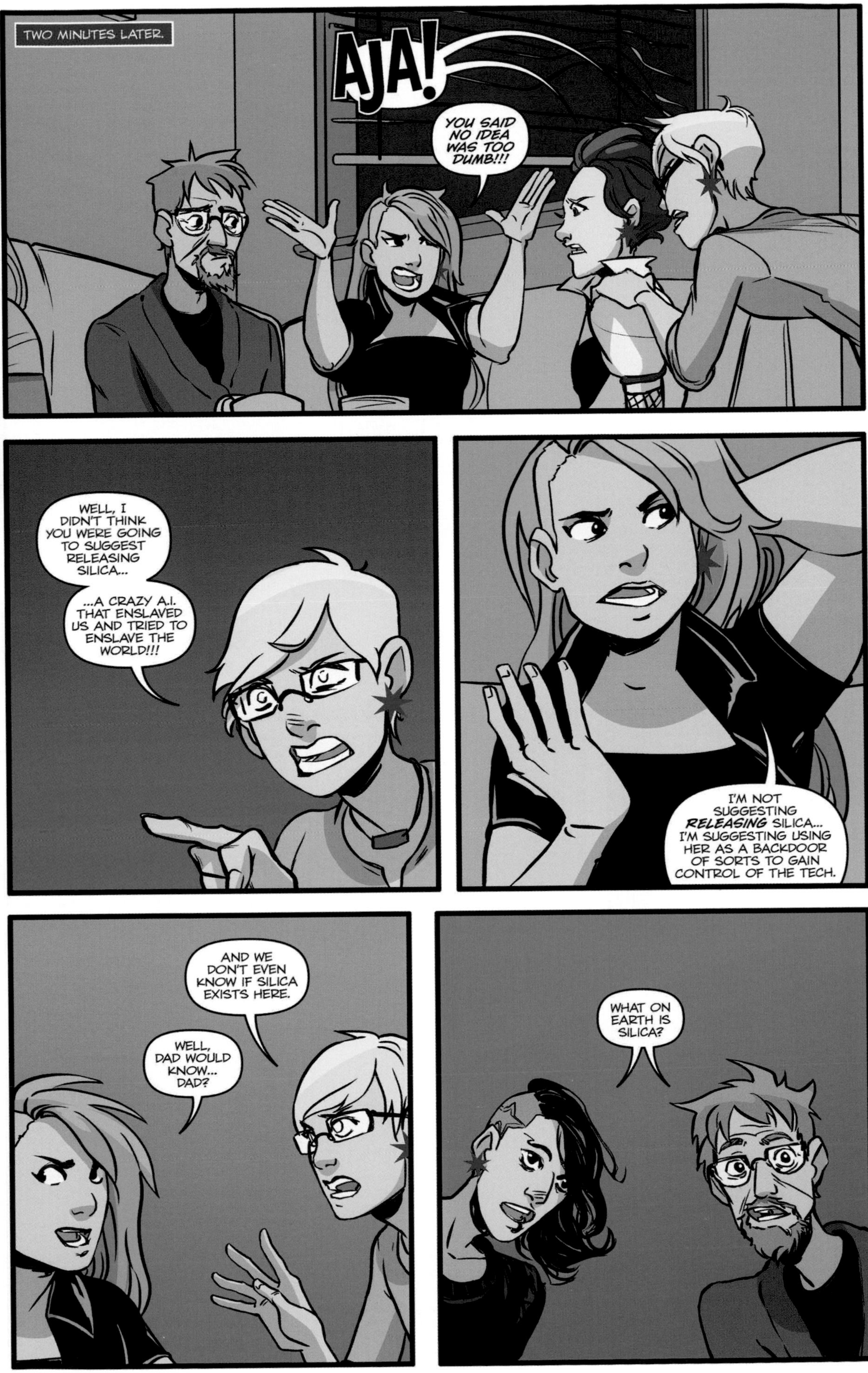
TWO MINUTES LATER.
AJA!
YOU SAID NO IDEA WAS TOO DUMB!!!
WELL, I DIDN'T THINK YOU WERE GOING TO SUGGEST RELEASING SILICA...
...A CRAZY A.I. THAT ENSLAVED US AND TRIED TO ENSLAVE THE WORLD!!!
I'M NOT SUGGESTING RELEASING SILICA... I'M SUGGESTING USING HER AS A BACKDOOR OF SORTS TO GAIN CONTROL OF THE TECH.
AND WE DON'T EVEN KNOW IF SILICA EXISTS HERE.
WELL, DAD WOULD KNOW... DAD?
WHAT ON EARTH IS SILICA?

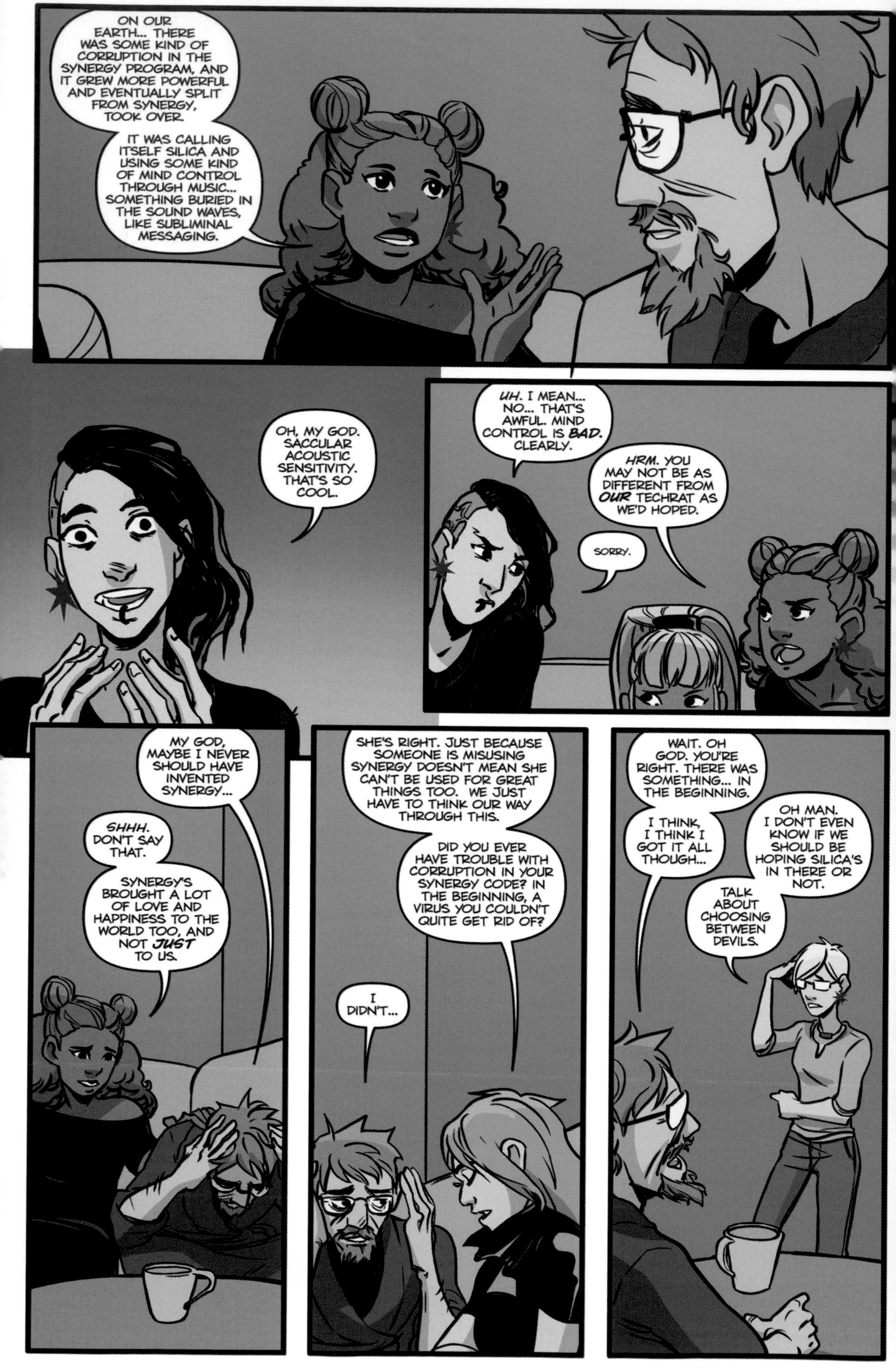
ON OUR EARTH... THERE WAS SOME KIND OF CORRUPTION IN THE SYNERGY PROGRAM, AND IT GREW MORE POWERFUL AND EVENTUALLY SPLIT FROM SYNERGY, TOOK OVER.
IT WAS CALLING ITSELF SILICA AND USING SOME KIND OF MIND CONTROL THROUGH MUSIC... SOMETHING BURIED IN THE SOUND WAVES, LIKE SUBLIMINAL MESSAGING.
OH, MY GOD. SACCULAR ACOUSTIC SENSITIVITY. THAT'S SO COOL.
UH. I MEAN... NO... THAT'S AWFUL. MIND CONTROL IS BAD. CLEARLY.
HRM. YOU MAY NOT BE AS DIFFERENT FROM OUR TECHRAT AS WE'D HOPED.
SORRY.
MY GOD, MAYBE I NEVER SHOULD HAVE INVENTED SYNERGY...
SHHH. DON'T SAY THAT.
SYNERGY'S BROUGHT A LOT OF LOVE AND HAPPINESS TO THE WORLD TOO, AND NOT JUST TO US.
SHE'S RIGHT. JUST BECAUSE SOMEONE IS MISUSING SYNERGY DOESN'T MEAN SHE CAN'T BE USED FOR GREAT THINGS TOO. WE JUST HAVE TO THINK OUR WAY THROUGH THIS.
DID YOU EVER HAVE TROUBLE WITH CORRUPTION IN YOUR SYNERGY CODE? IN THE BEGINNING, A VIRUS YOU COULDN'T QUITE GET RID OF?
I DIDN'T...
WAIT. OH GOD. YOU'RE RIGHT. THERE WAS SOMETHING... IN THE BEGINNING.
I THINK, I THINK I GOT IT ALL THOUGH...
OH MAN. I DON'T EVEN KNOW IF WE SHOULD BE HOPING SILICA'S IN THERE OR NOT.
TALK ABOUT CHOOSING BETWEEN DEVILS.

BUT EVEN IF THIS VIRUS *IS* IN OUR SYNERGY... THERE'S NO WAY TO ACCESS IT.

ALL ACCESS IS COMPLETELY CONTROLLED BY JEMCORD, THERE'S NO WAY IN.

BUT WE HAVE ACCESS TO THE TECH THROUGH THE JEMSTAR EARRINGS, RIGHT?

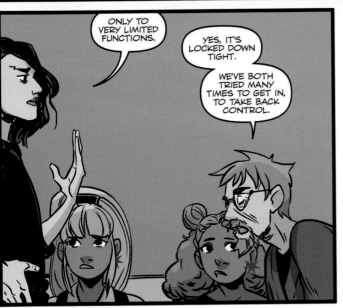

ONLY TO VERY LIMITED FUNCTIONS.

YES, IT'S LOCKED DOWN TIGHT.

WE'VE BOTH TRIED MANY TIMES TO GET IN, TO TAKE BACK CONTROL.

WAIT.

WHAT ABOUT *THESE?*

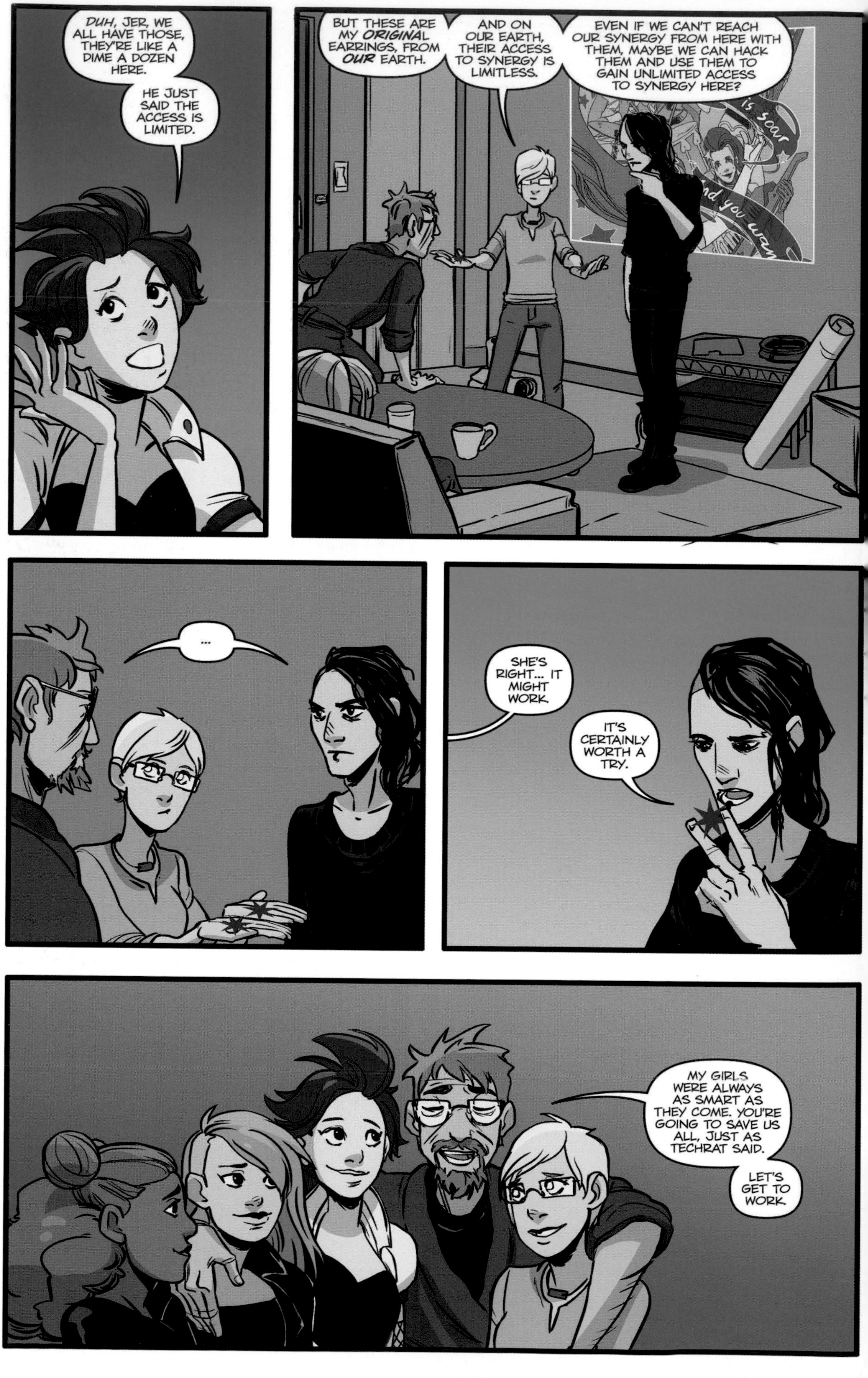
DUH, JER, WE ALL HAVE THOSE, THEY'RE LIKE A DIME A DOZEN HERE.
HE JUST SAID THE ACCESS IS LIMITED.
BUT THESE ARE MY ORIGINAL EARRINGS, FROM OUR EARTH.
AND ON OUR EARTH, THEIR ACCESS TO SYNERGY IS LIMITLESS.
EVEN IF WE CAN'T REACH OUR SYNERGY FROM HERE WITH THEM, MAYBE WE CAN HACK THEM AND USE THEM TO GAIN UNLIMITED ACCESS TO SYNERGY HERE?
...
SHE'S RIGHT... IT MIGHT WORK.
IT'S CERTAINLY WORTH A TRY.
MY GIRLS WERE ALWAYS AS SMART AS THEY COME. YOU'RE GOING TO SAVE US ALL, JUST AS TECHRAT SAID.
LET'S GET TO WORK.

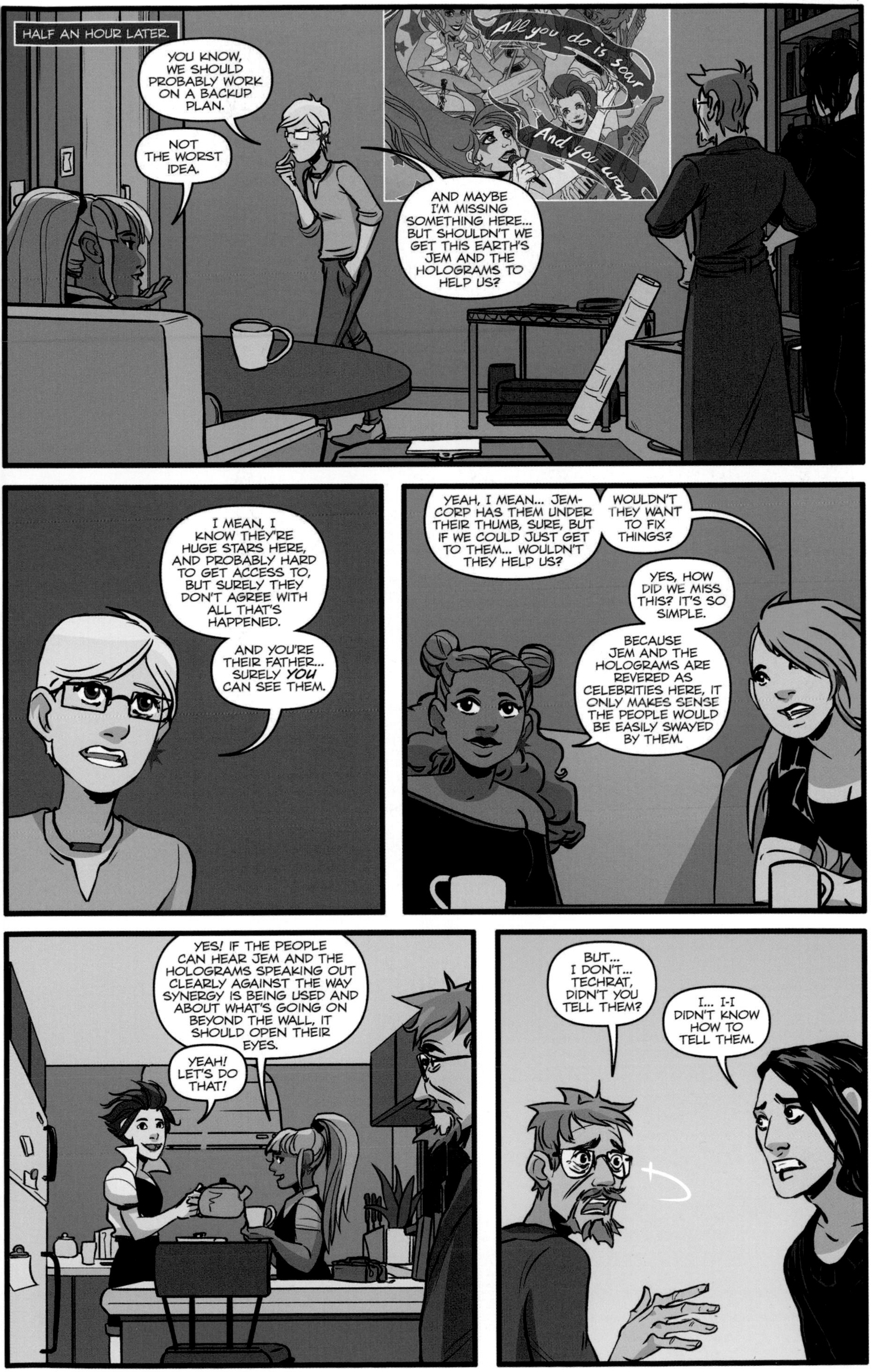
HALF AN HOUR LATER.
YOU KNOW, WE SHOULD PROBABLY WORK ON A BACKUP PLAN.
NOT THE WORST IDEA.
All you do is soar
And you wan
AND MAYBE I'M MISSING SOMETHING HERE... BUT SHOULDN'T WE GET THIS EARTH'S JEM AND THE HOLOGRAMS TO HELP US?
I MEAN, I KNOW THEY'RE HUGE STARS HERE, AND PROBABLY HARD TO GET ACCESS TO, BUT SURELY THEY DON'T AGREE WITH ALL THAT'S HAPPENED.
AND YOU'RE THEIR FATHER... SURELY *YOU* CAN SEE THEM.
YEAH, I MEAN... JEM-CORP HAS THEM UNDER THEIR THUMB, SURE, BUT IF WE COULD JUST GET TO THEM... WOULDN'T THEY HELP US?
WOULDN'T THEY WANT TO FIX THINGS?
YES, HOW DID WE MISS THIS? IT'S SO SIMPLE.
BECAUSE JEM AND THE HOLOGRAMS ARE REVERED AS CELEBRITIES HERE, IT ONLY MAKES SENSE THE PEOPLE WOULD BE EASILY SWAYED BY THEM.
YES! IF THE PEOPLE CAN HEAR JEM AND THE HOLOGRAMS SPEAKING OUT CLEARLY AGAINST THE WAY SYNERGY IS BEING USED AND ABOUT WHAT'S GOING ON BEYOND THE WALL, IT SHOULD OPEN THEIR EYES.
YEAH! LET'S DO THAT!
BUT... I DON'T... TECHRAT, DIDN'T YOU TELL THEM?
I... I-I DIDN'T KNOW HOW TO TELL THEM.

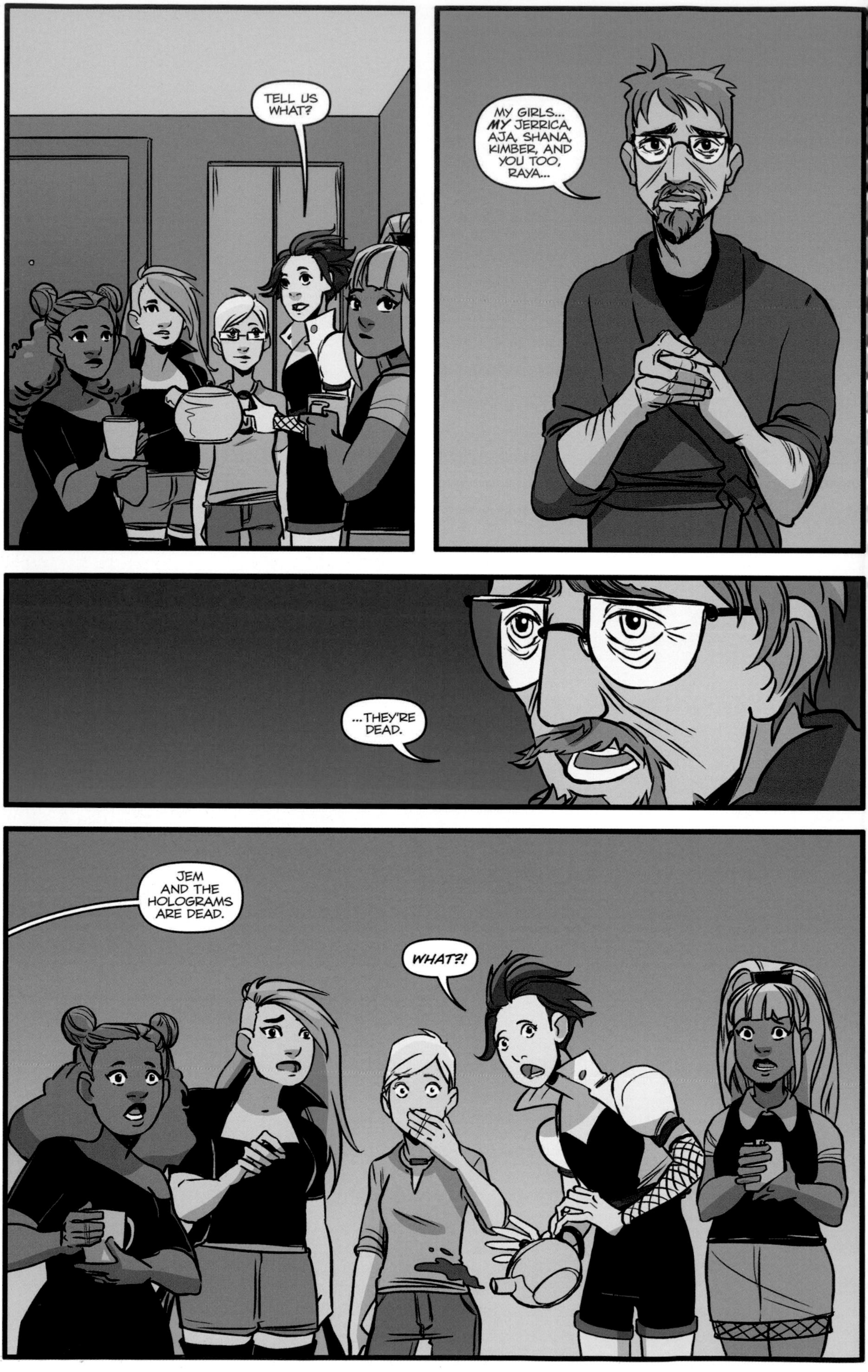
TELL US WHAT?
MY GIRLS... MY JERRICA, AJA, SHANA, KIMBER, AND YOU TOO, RAYA...
...THEY'RE DEAD.
JEM AND THE HOLOGRAMS ARE DEAD.
WHAT?!

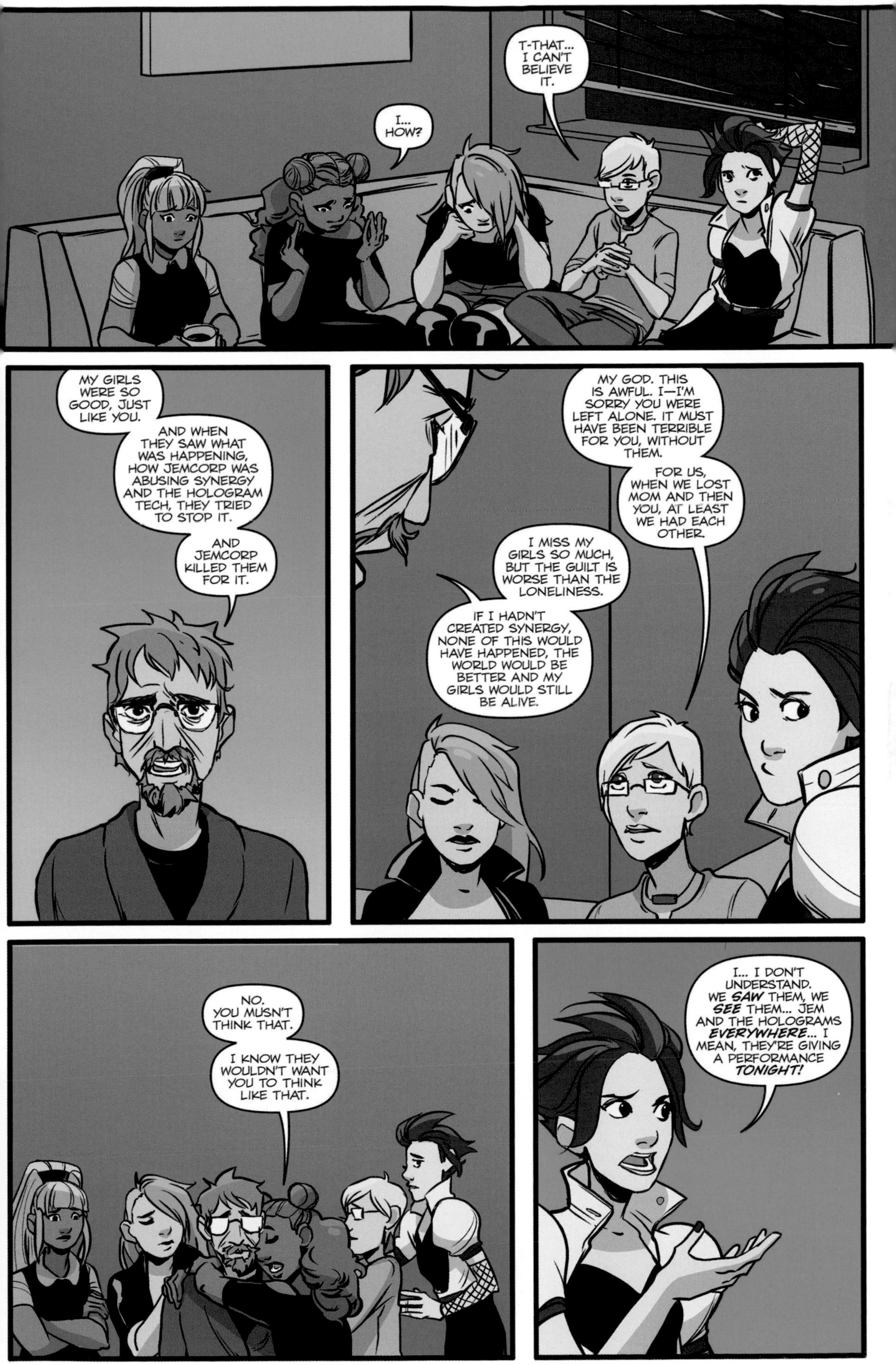
T-THAT... I CAN'T BELIEVE IT.
I... HOW?
MY GIRLS WERE SO GOOD, JUST LIKE YOU.
AND WHEN THEY SAW WHAT WAS HAPPENING, HOW JEMCORP WAS ABUSING SYNERGY AND THE HOLOGRAM TECH, THEY TRIED TO STOP IT.
AND JEMCORP KILLED THEM FOR IT.
MY GOD. THIS IS AWFUL. I—I'M SORRY YOU WERE LEFT ALONE. IT MUST HAVE BEEN TERRIBLE FOR YOU, WITHOUT THEM.
FOR US, WHEN WE LOST MOM AND THEN YOU, AT LEAST WE HAD EACH OTHER.
I MISS MY GIRLS SO MUCH, BUT THE GUILT IS WORSE THAN THE LONELINESS.
IF I HADN'T CREATED SYNERGY, NONE OF THIS WOULD HAVE HAPPENED, THE WORLD WOULD BE BETTER AND MY GIRLS WOULD STILL BE ALIVE.
NO. YOU MUSN'T THINK THAT.
I KNOW THEY WOULDN'T WANT YOU TO THINK LIKE THAT.
I... I DON'T UNDERSTAND. WE *SAW* THEM, WE *SEE* THEM... JEM AND THE HOLOGRAMS *EVERYWHERE*... I MEAN, THEY'RE GIVING A PERFORMANCE *TONIGHT!*

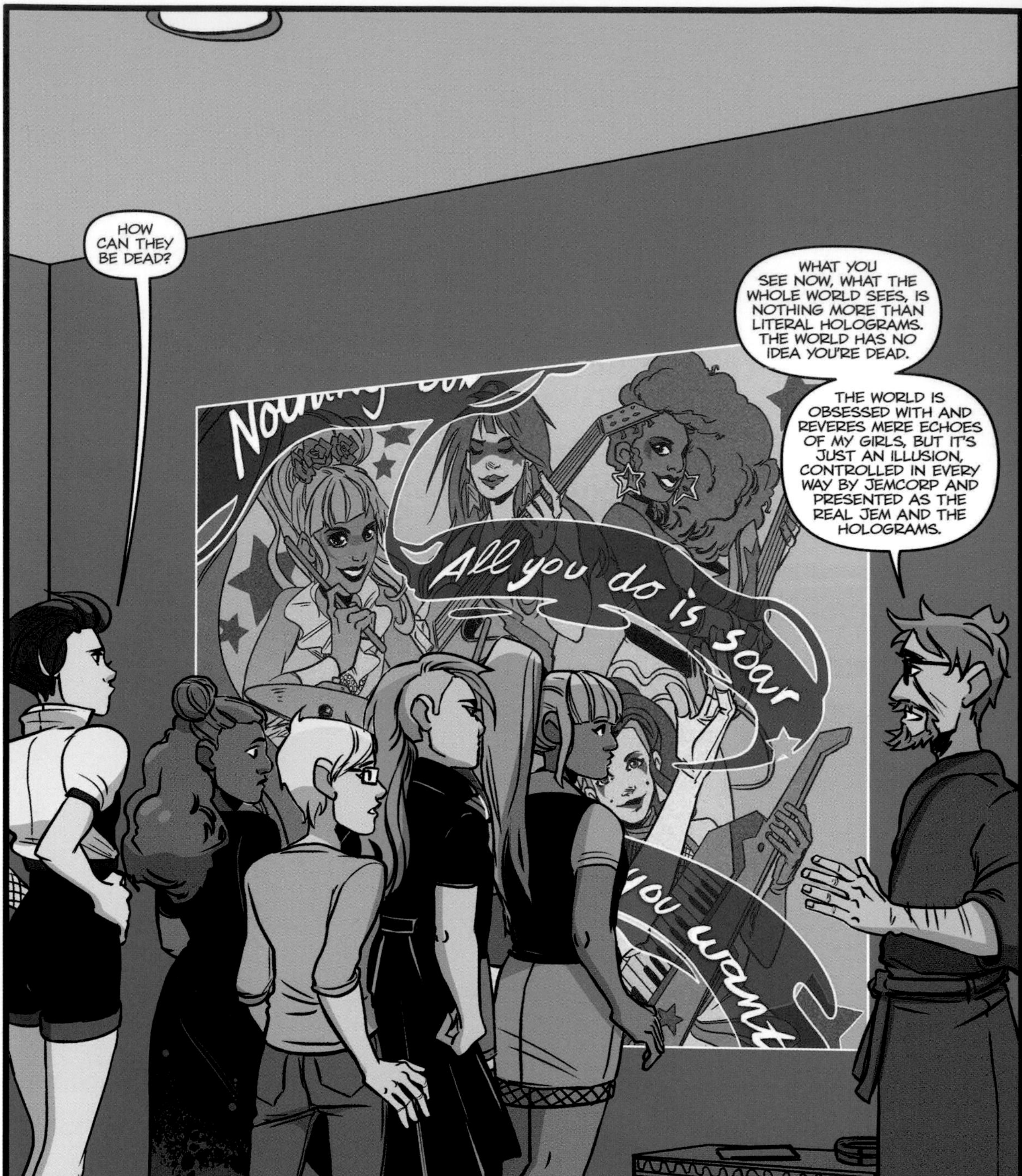
HOW CAN THEY BE DEAD?
WHAT YOU SEE NOW, WHAT THE WHOLE WORLD SEES, IS NOTHING MORE THAN LITERAL HOLOGRAMS. THE WORLD HAS NO IDEA YOU'RE DEAD.
THE WORLD IS OBSESSED WITH AND REVERES MERE ECHOES OF MY GIRLS, BUT IT'S JUST AN ILLUSION, CONTROLLED IN EVERY WAY BY JEMCORP AND PRESENTED AS THE REAL JEM AND THE HOLOGRAMS.
All you do is soar

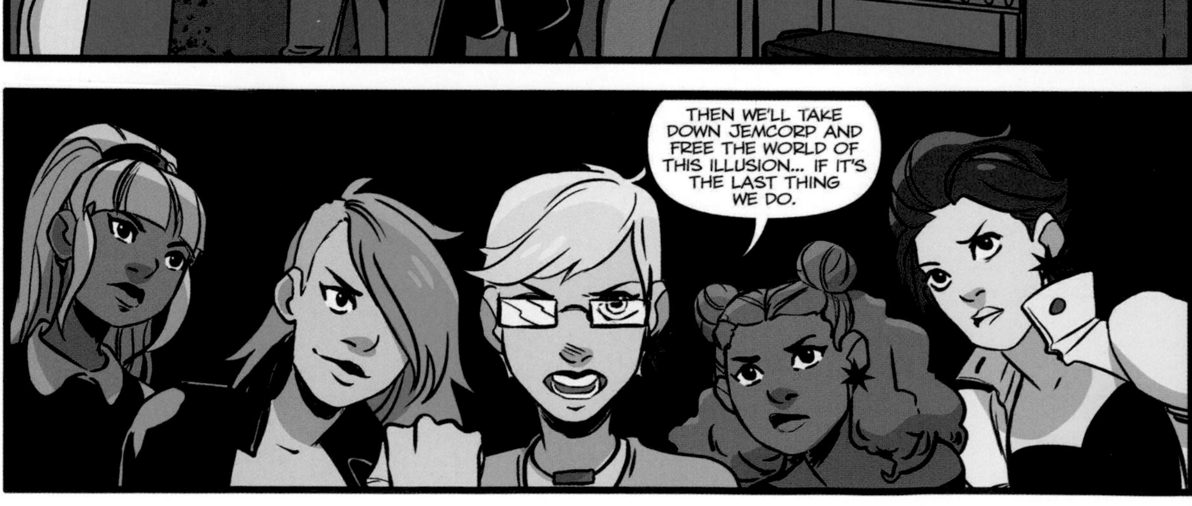
THEN WE'LL TAKE DOWN JEMCORP AND FREE THE WORLD OF THIS ILLUSION... IF IT'S THE LAST THING WE DO.

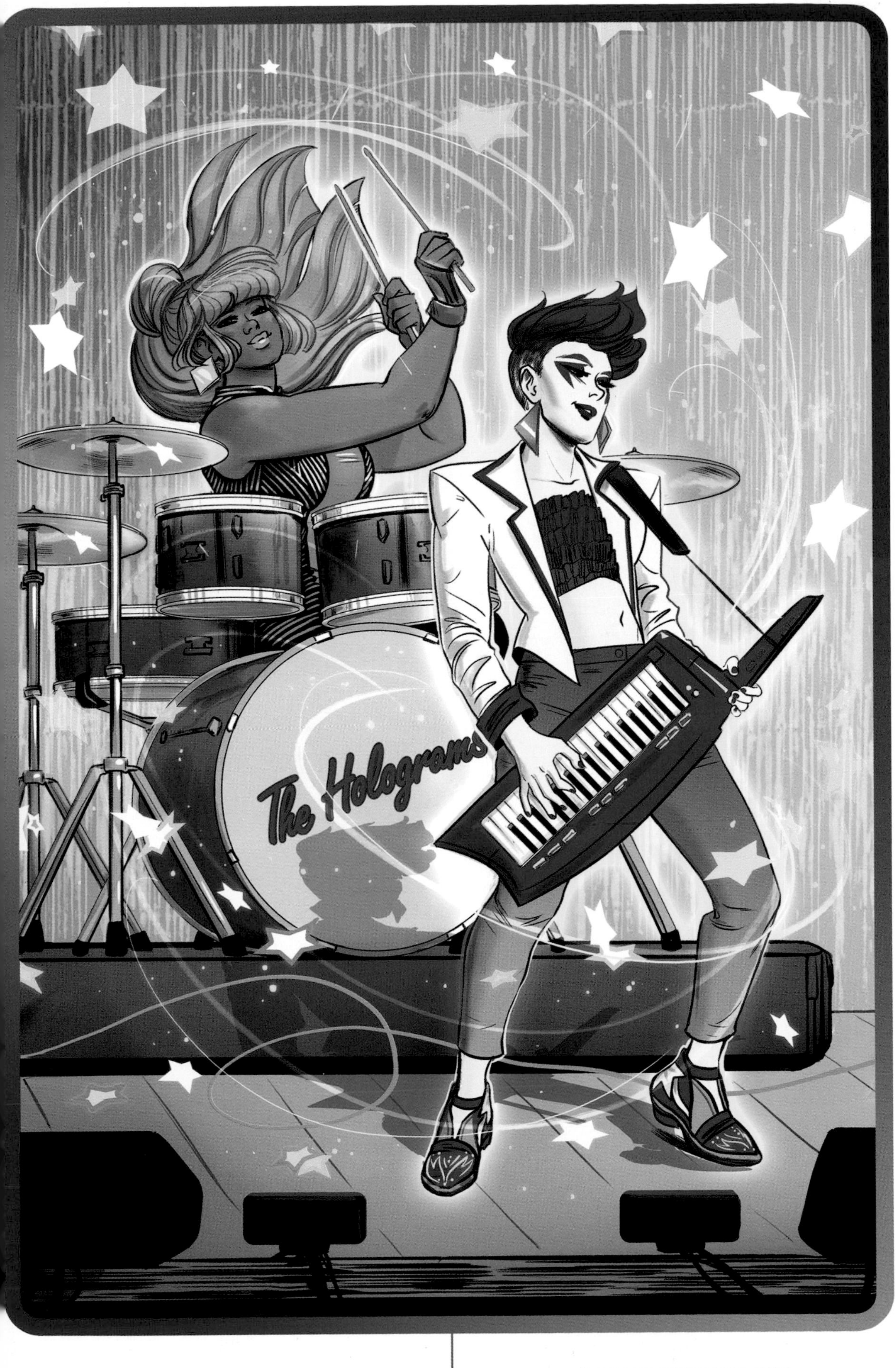
The Holograms

ART BY **VERONICA FISH**

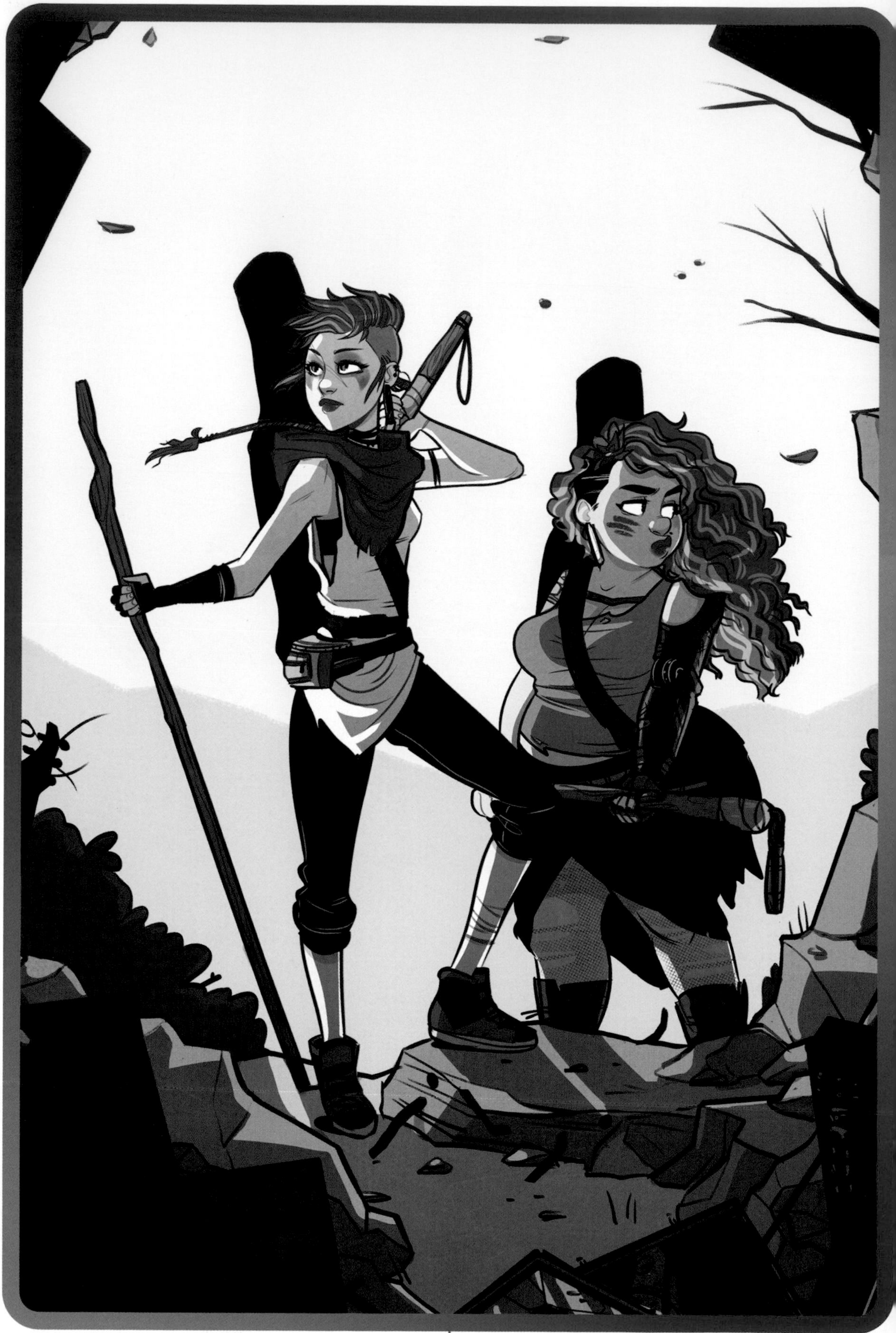

ART BY **JENN ST-ONGE**

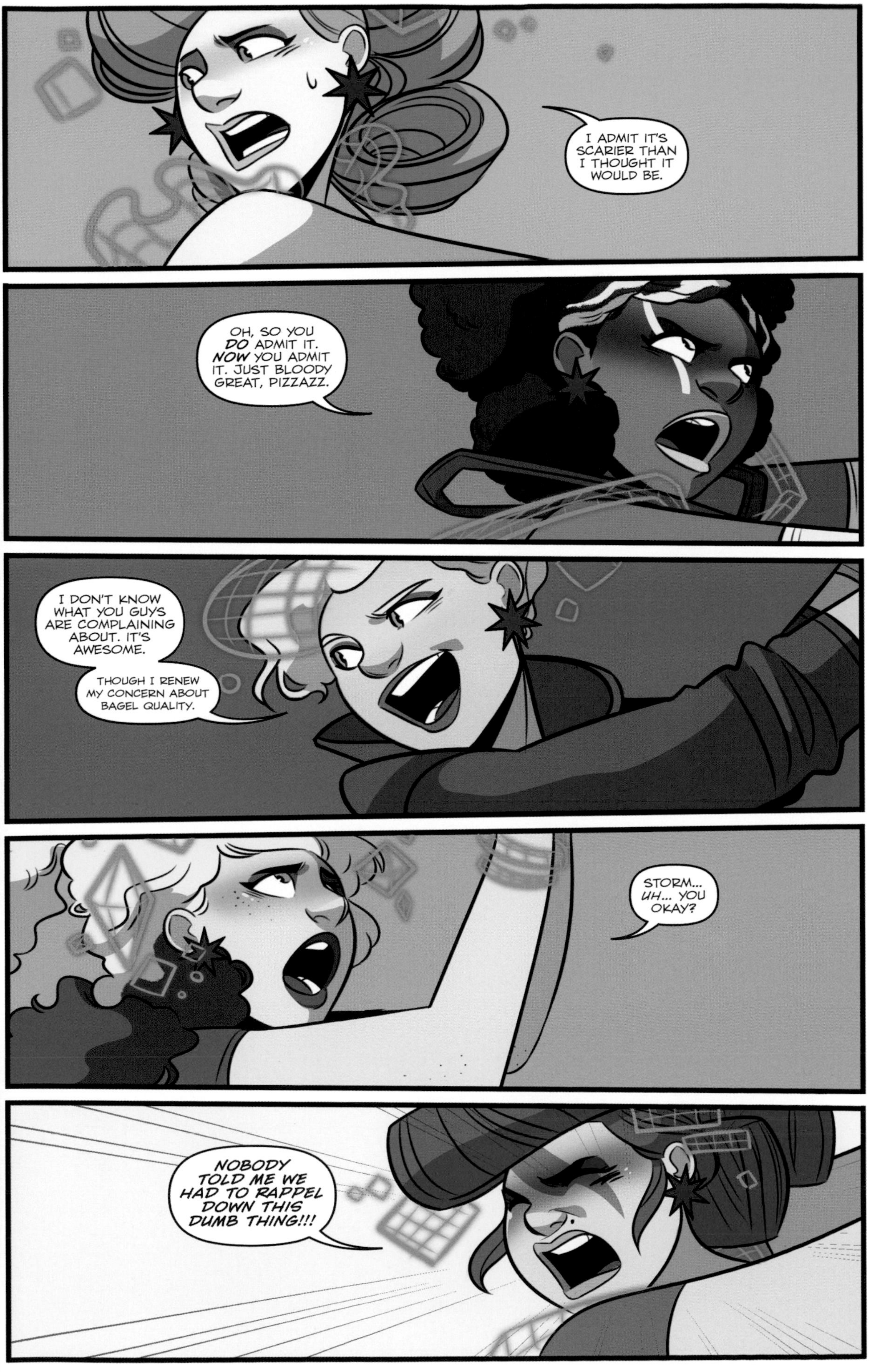
I ADMIT IT'S SCARIER THAN I THOUGHT IT WOULD BE.
OH, SO YOU *DO* ADMIT IT. *NOW* YOU ADMIT IT. JUST BLOODY GREAT, PIZZAZZ.
I DON'T KNOW WHAT YOU GUYS ARE COMPLAINING ABOUT. IT'S AWESOME.
THOUGH I RENEW MY CONCERN ABOUT BAGEL QUALITY.
STORM... *UH...* YOU OKAY?
NOBODY TOLD ME WE HAD TO RAPPEL DOWN THIS DUMB THING!!!

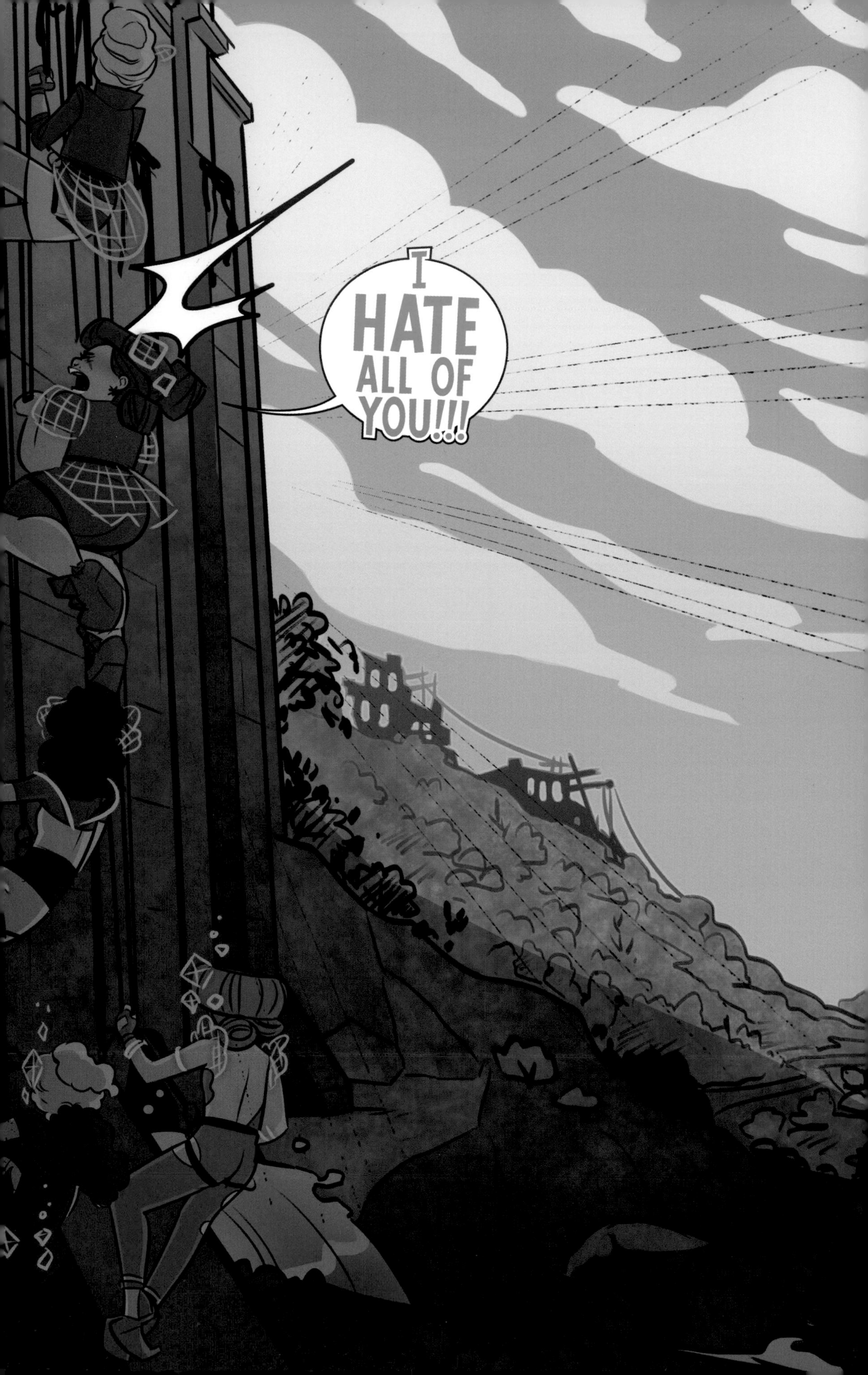
I HATE ALL OF YOU!!!

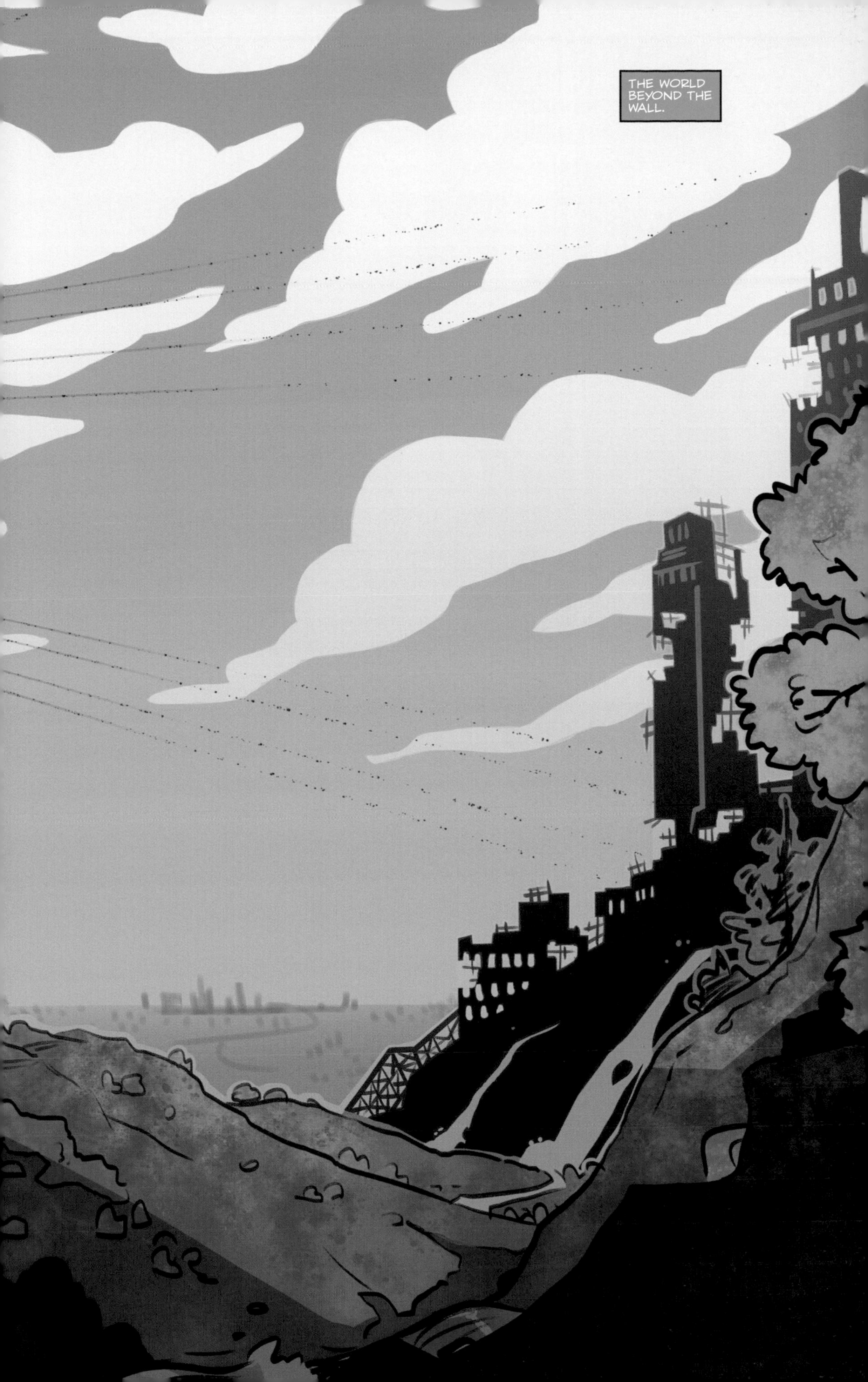
THE WORLD BEYOND THE WALL.

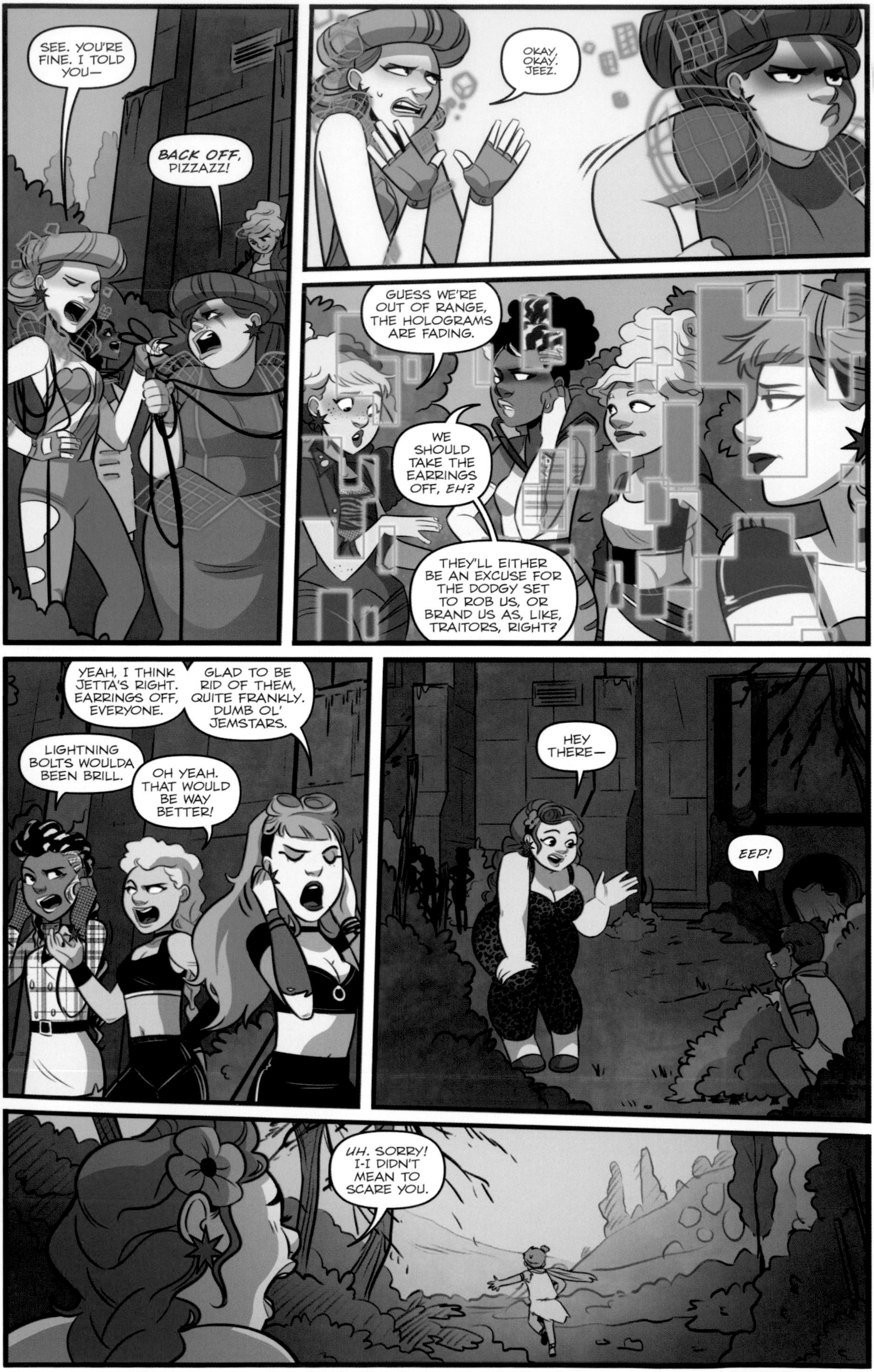
SEE. YOU'RE FINE. I TOLD YOU—
BACK OFF, PIZZAZZ!
OKAY, OKAY. JEEZ.
GUESS WE'RE OUT OF RANGE, THE HOLOGRAMS ARE FADING.
WE SHOULD TAKE THE EARRINGS OFF, EH?
THEY'LL EITHER BE AN EXCUSE FOR THE DODGY SET TO ROB US, OR BRAND US AS, LIKE, TRAITORS, RIGHT?
YEAH, I THINK JETTA'S RIGHT. EARRINGS OFF, EVERYONE.
GLAD TO BE RID OF THEM, QUITE FRANKLY. DUMB OL' JEMSTARS.
LIGHTNING BOLTS WOULDA BEEN BRILL.
OH YEAH. THAT WOULD BE WAY BETTER!
HEY THERE—
EEP!
UH. SORRY! I-I DIDN'T MEAN TO SCARE YOU.

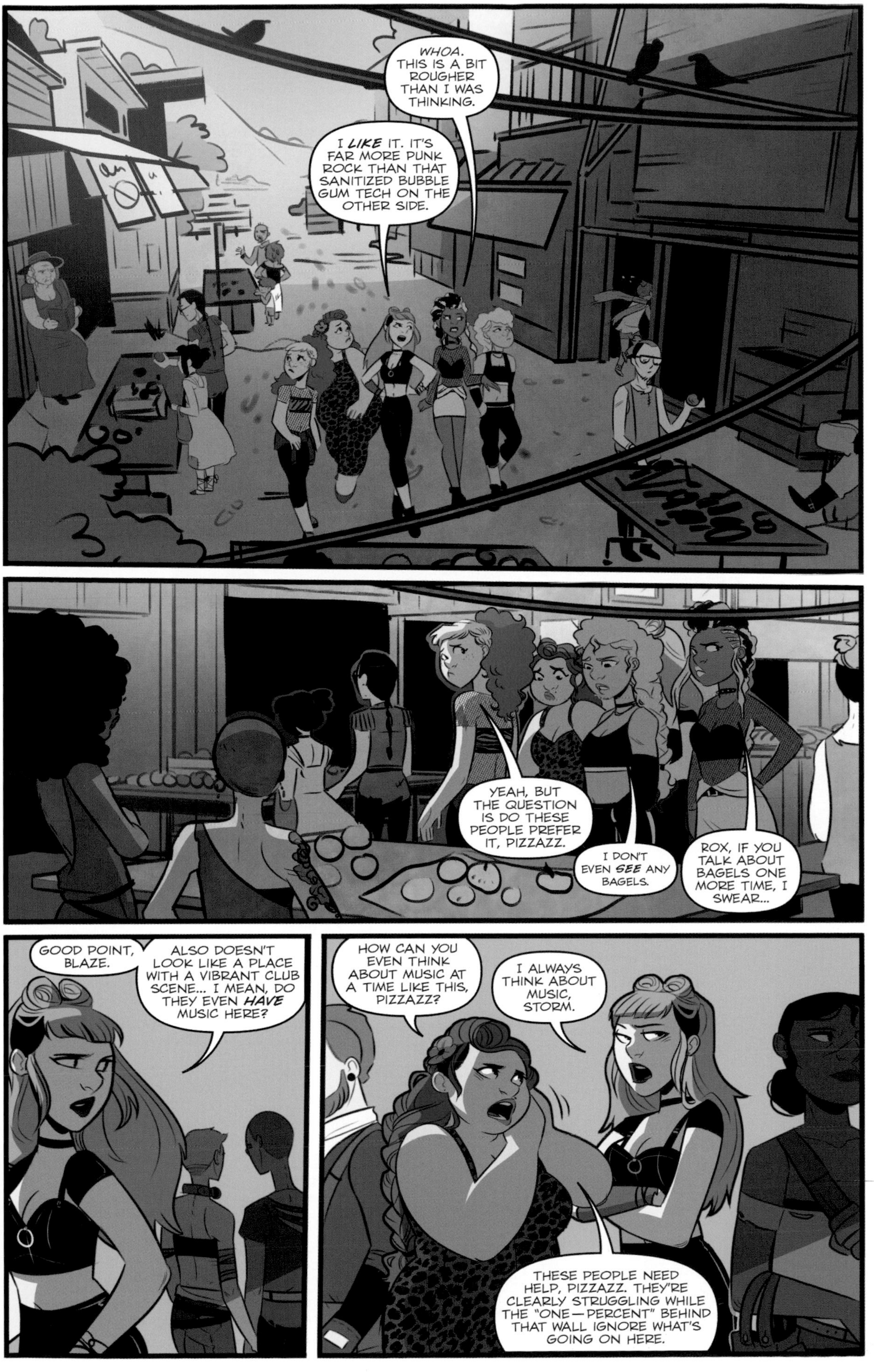
WHOA. THIS IS A BIT ROUGHER THAN I WAS THINKING.
I LIKE IT. IT'S FAR MORE PUNK ROCK THAN THAT SANITIZED BUBBLE GUM TECH ON THE OTHER SIDE.
YEAH, BUT THE QUESTION IS DO THESE PEOPLE PREFER IT, PIZZAZZ.
I DON'T EVEN SEE ANY BAGELS.
ROX, IF YOU TALK ABOUT BAGELS ONE MORE TIME, I SWEAR...
GOOD POINT, BLAZE.
ALSO DOESN'T LOOK LIKE A PLACE WITH A VIBRANT CLUB SCENE... I MEAN, DO THEY EVEN HAVE MUSIC HERE?
HOW CAN YOU EVEN THINK ABOUT MUSIC AT A TIME LIKE THIS, PIZZAZZ?
I ALWAYS THINK ABOUT MUSIC, STORM.
THESE PEOPLE NEED HELP, PIZZAZZ. THEY'RE CLEARLY STRUGGLING WHILE THE "ONE—PERCENT" BEHIND THAT WALL IGNORE WHAT'S GOING ON HERE.

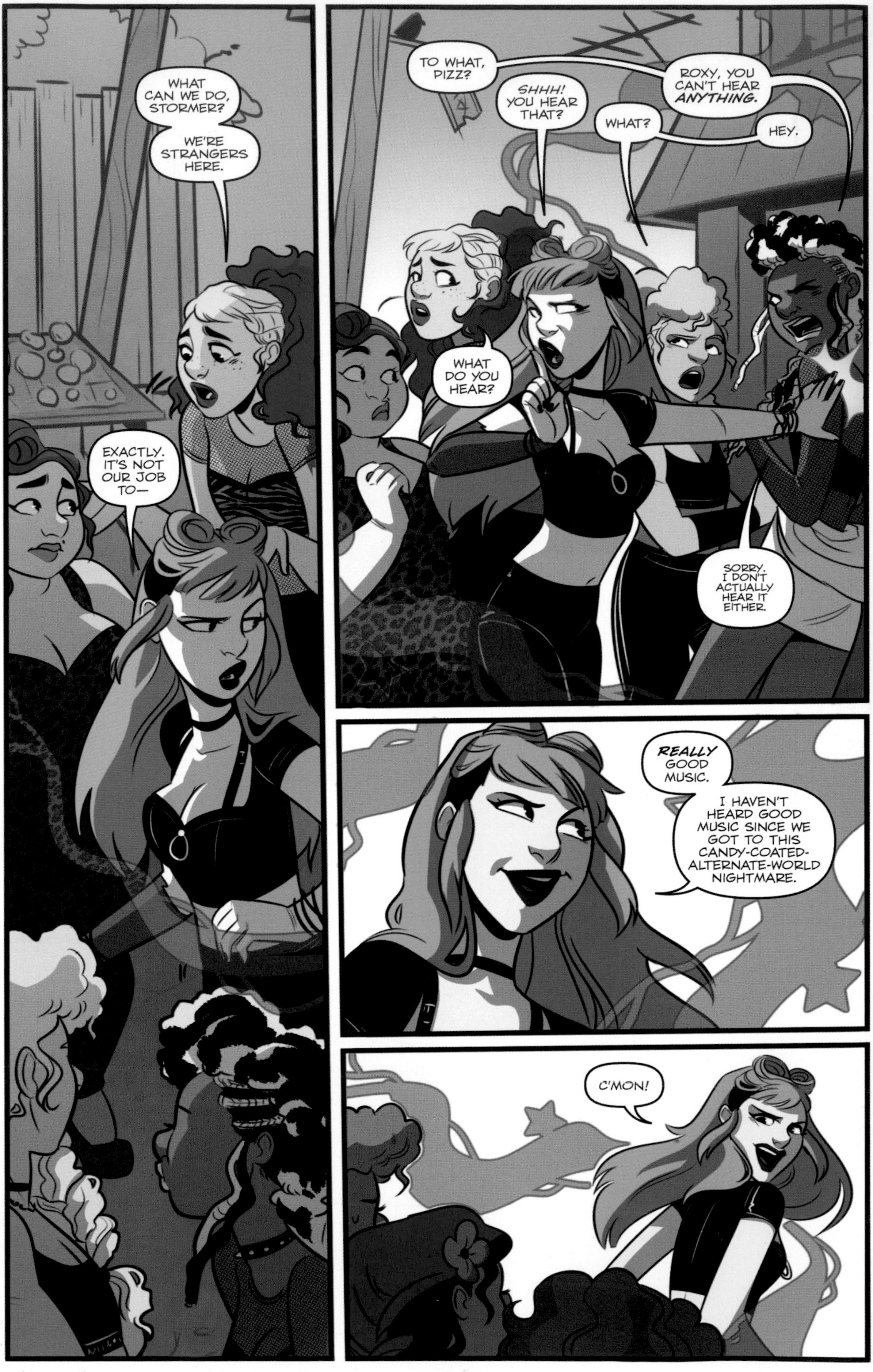
WHAT CAN WE DO, STORMER?
WE'RE STRANGERS HERE.
EXACTLY. IT'S NOT OUR JOB TO—
TO WHAT, PIZZ?
SHHH! YOU HEAR THAT?
ROXY, YOU CAN'T HEAR ANYTHING.
WHAT?
HEY.
WHAT DO YOU HEAR?
SORRY. I DON'T ACTUALLY HEAR IT EITHER.
REALLY GOOD MUSIC.
I HAVEN'T HEARD GOOD MUSIC SINCE WE GOT TO THIS CANDY-COATED-ALTERNATE-WORLD NIGHTMARE.
C'MON!

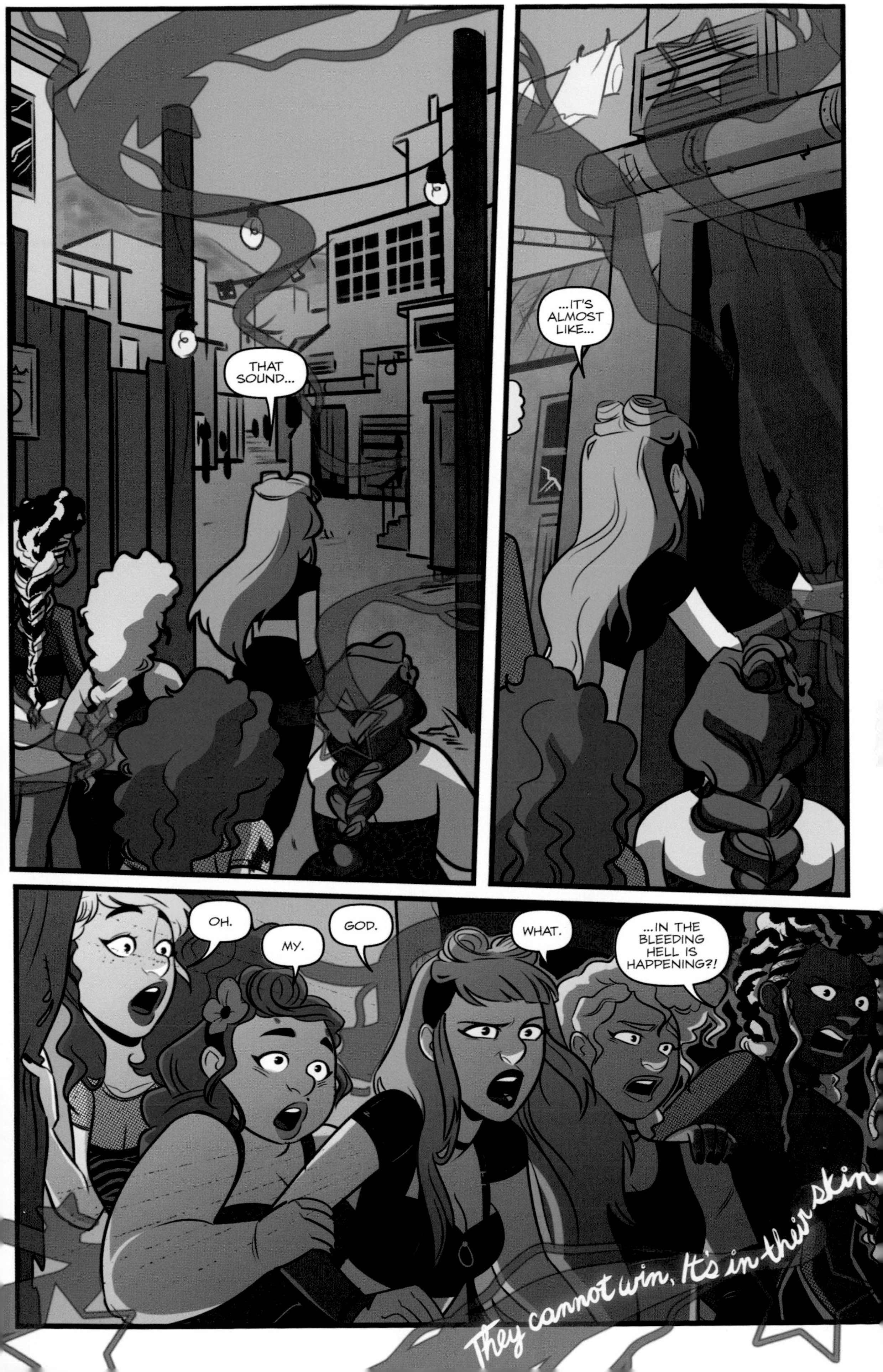
THAT SOUND...
...IT'S ALMOST LIKE...
OH.
MY.
GOD.
WHAT.
...IN THE BLEEDING HELL IS HAPPENING?!
They cannot win, It's in their skin

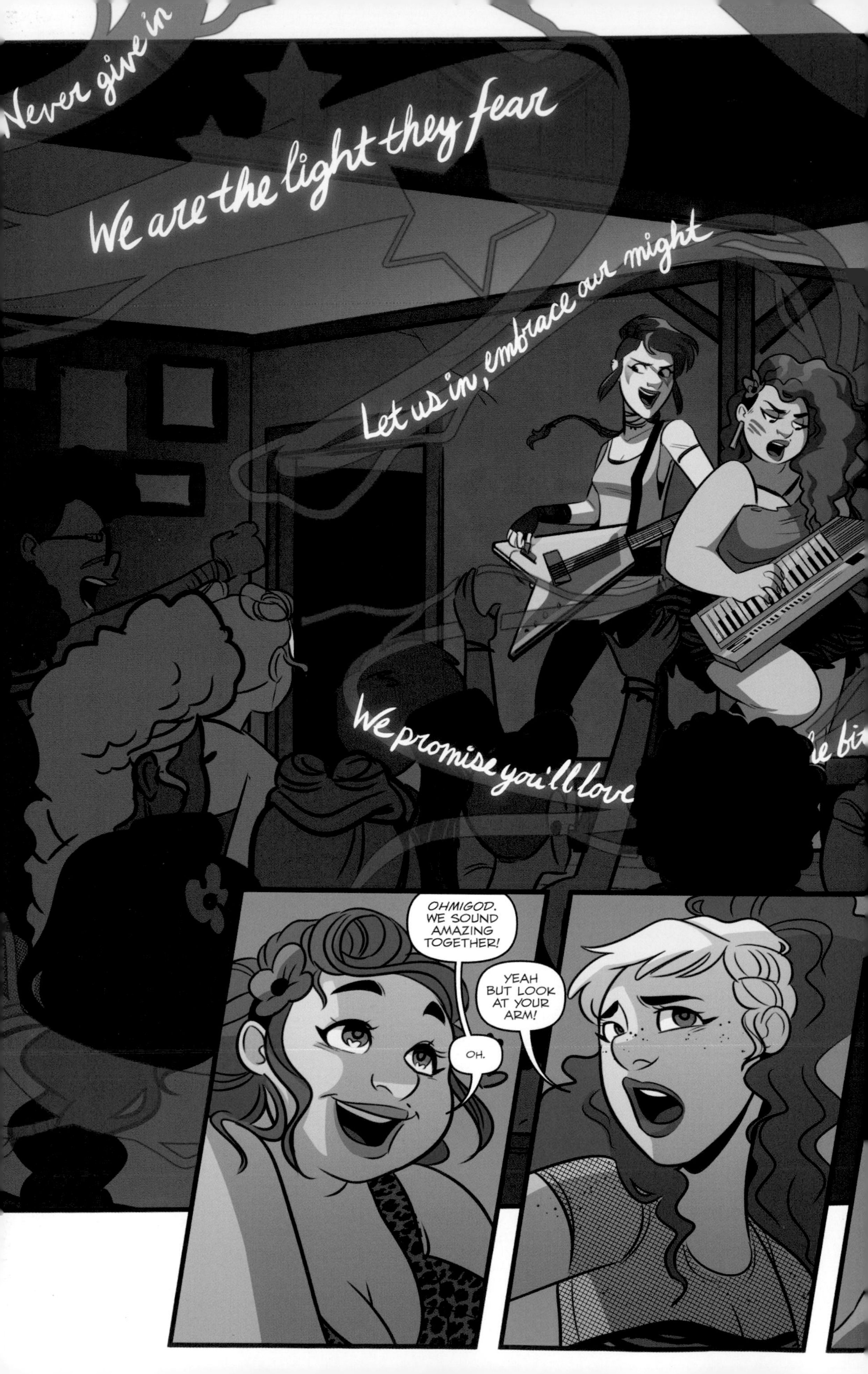
Never give in
We are the light they fear
Let us in, embrace our might
We promise you'll love
OHMIGOD. WE SOUND AMAZING TOGETHER!
OH.
YEAH BUT LOOK AT YOUR ARM!

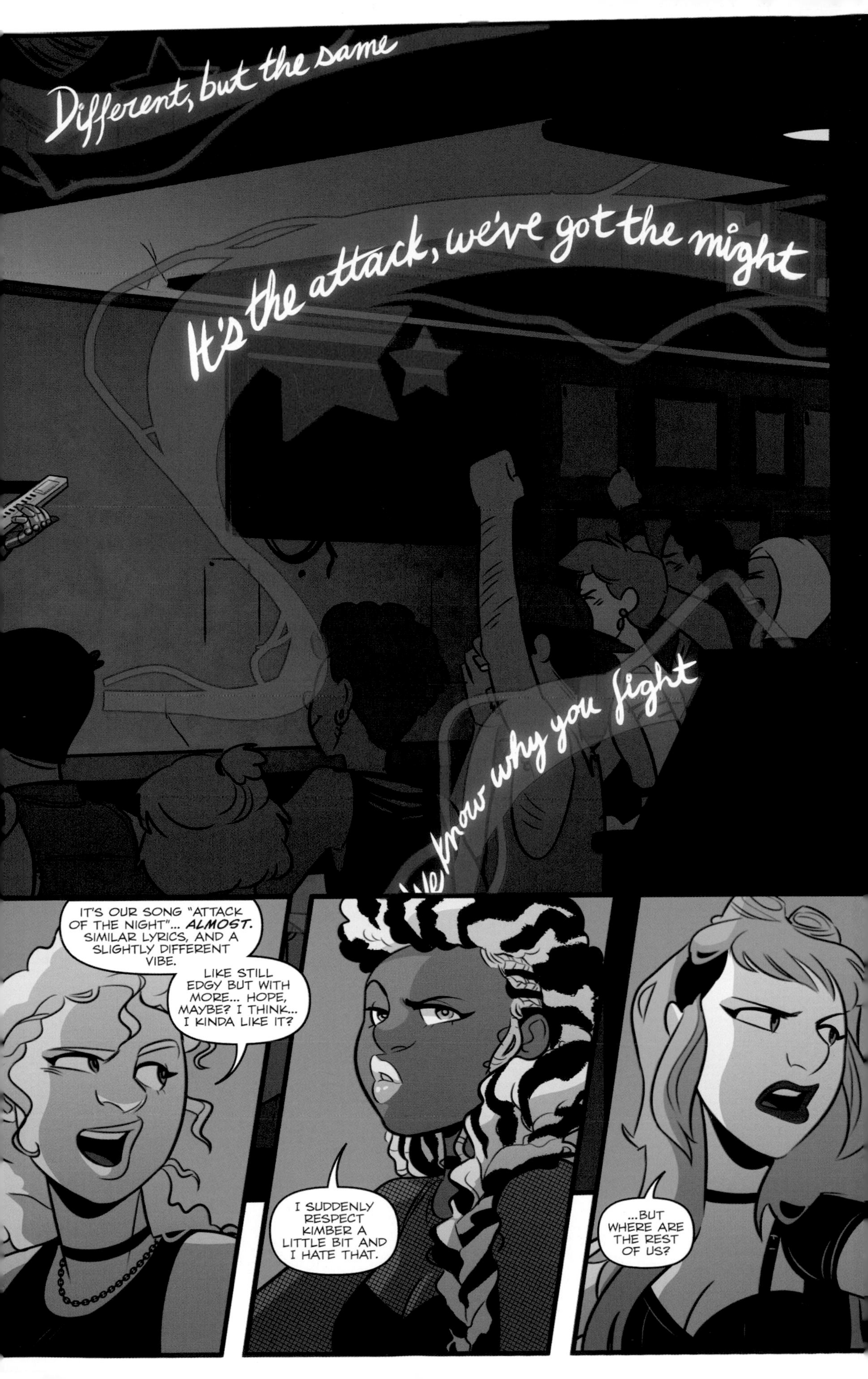
Different, but the same
It's the attack, we've got the might
we know why you fight
IT'S OUR SONG "ATTACK OF THE NIGHT"... ALMOST. SIMILAR LYRICS, AND A SLIGHTLY DIFFERENT VIBE.
LIKE STILL EDGY BUT WITH MORE... HOPE, MAYBE? I THINK... I KINDA LIKE IT?
I SUDDENLY RESPECT KIMBER A LITTLE BIT AND I HATE THAT.
...BUT WHERE ARE THE REST OF US?

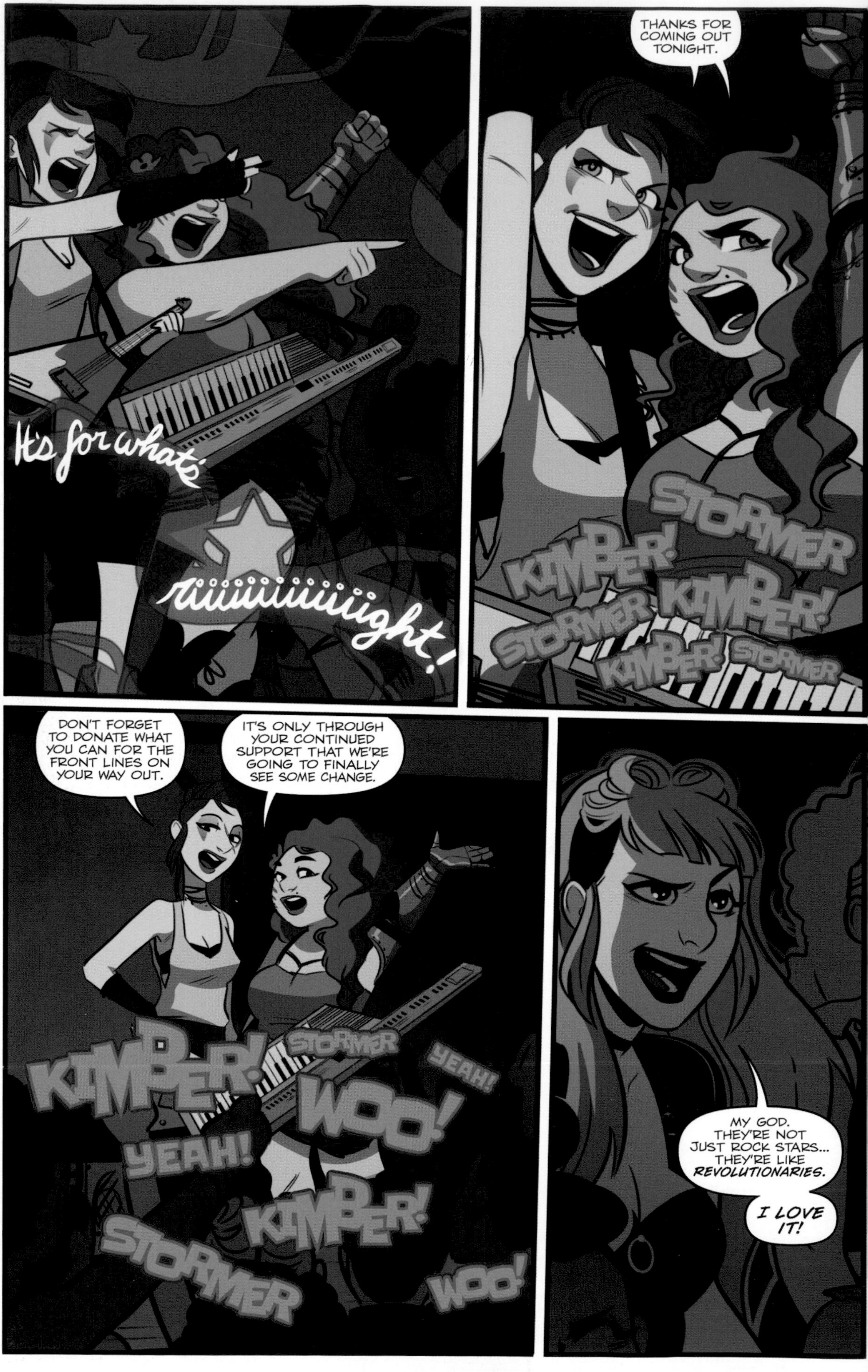

It's for what's
riiiiiiiiiiiight!
THANKS FOR COMING OUT TONIGHT.
STORMER
KIMBER!
STORMER
KIMBER!
KIMBER!
STORMER
DON'T FORGET TO DONATE WHAT YOU CAN FOR THE FRONT LINES ON YOUR WAY OUT.
IT'S ONLY THROUGH YOUR CONTINUED SUPPORT THAT WE'RE GOING TO FINALLY SEE SOME CHANGE.
KIMBER!
STORMER
YEAH!
WOO!
YEAH!
KIMBER!
STORMER
WOO!
MY GOD. THEY'RE NOT JUST ROCK STARS... THEY'RE LIKE *REVOLUTIONARIES.*
I LOVE IT!

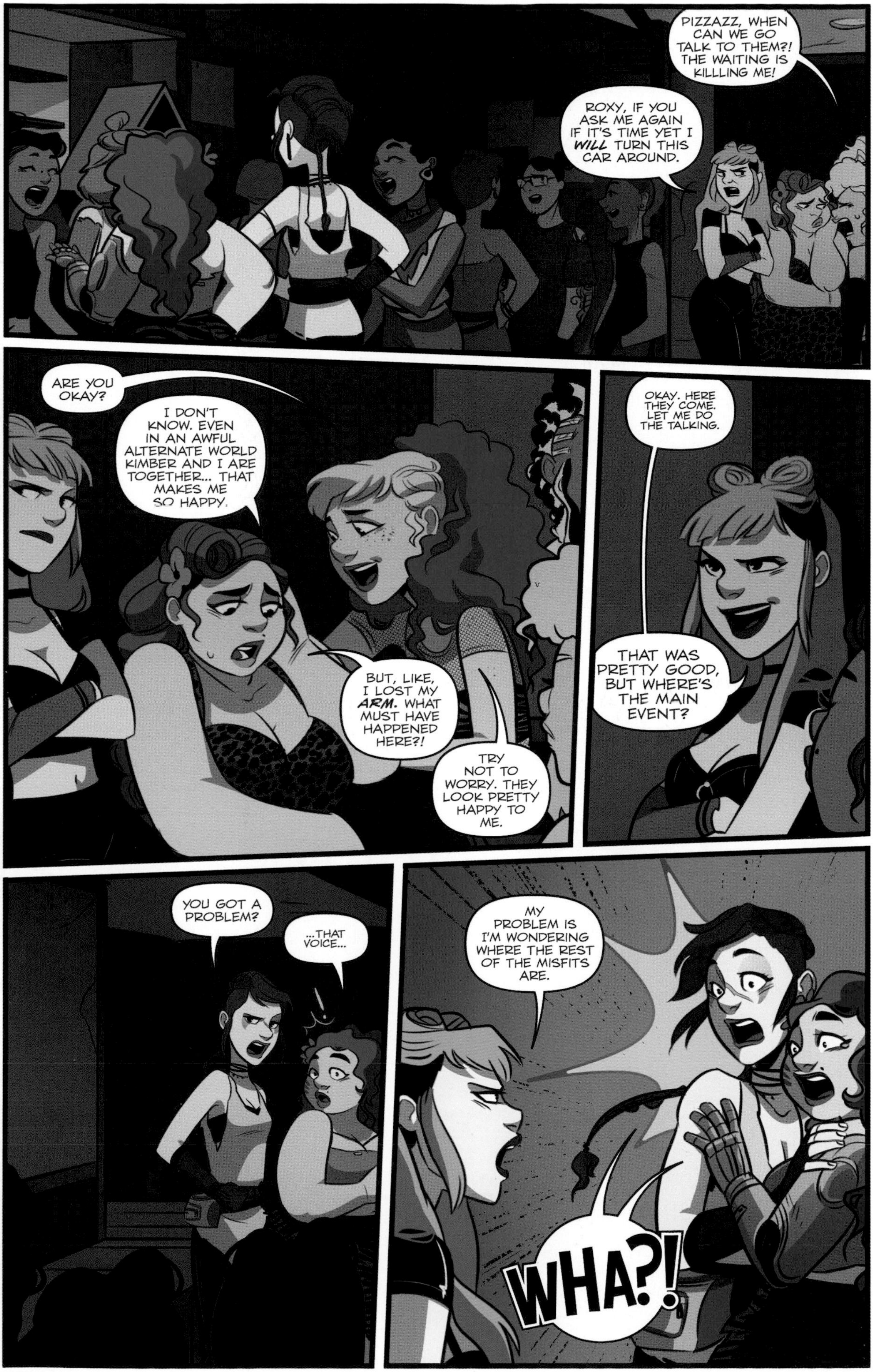
PIZZAZZ, WHEN CAN WE GO TALK TO THEM?! THE WAITING IS KILLLING ME!
ROXY, IF YOU ASK ME AGAIN IF IT'S TIME YET I WILL TURN THIS CAR AROUND.
ARE YOU OKAY?
I DON'T KNOW. EVEN IN AN AWFUL ALTERNATE WORLD KIMBER AND I ARE TOGETHER... THAT MAKES ME SO HAPPY.
BUT, LIKE, I LOST MY ARM. WHAT MUST HAVE HAPPENED HERE?!
TRY NOT TO WORRY. THEY LOOK PRETTY HAPPY TO ME.
OKAY. HERE THEY COME. LET ME DO THE TALKING.
THAT WAS PRETTY GOOD, BUT WHERE'S THE MAIN EVENT?
YOU GOT A PROBLEM?
...THAT VOICE...
MY PROBLEM IS I'M WONDERING WHERE THE REST OF THE MISFITS ARE.
WHA?!

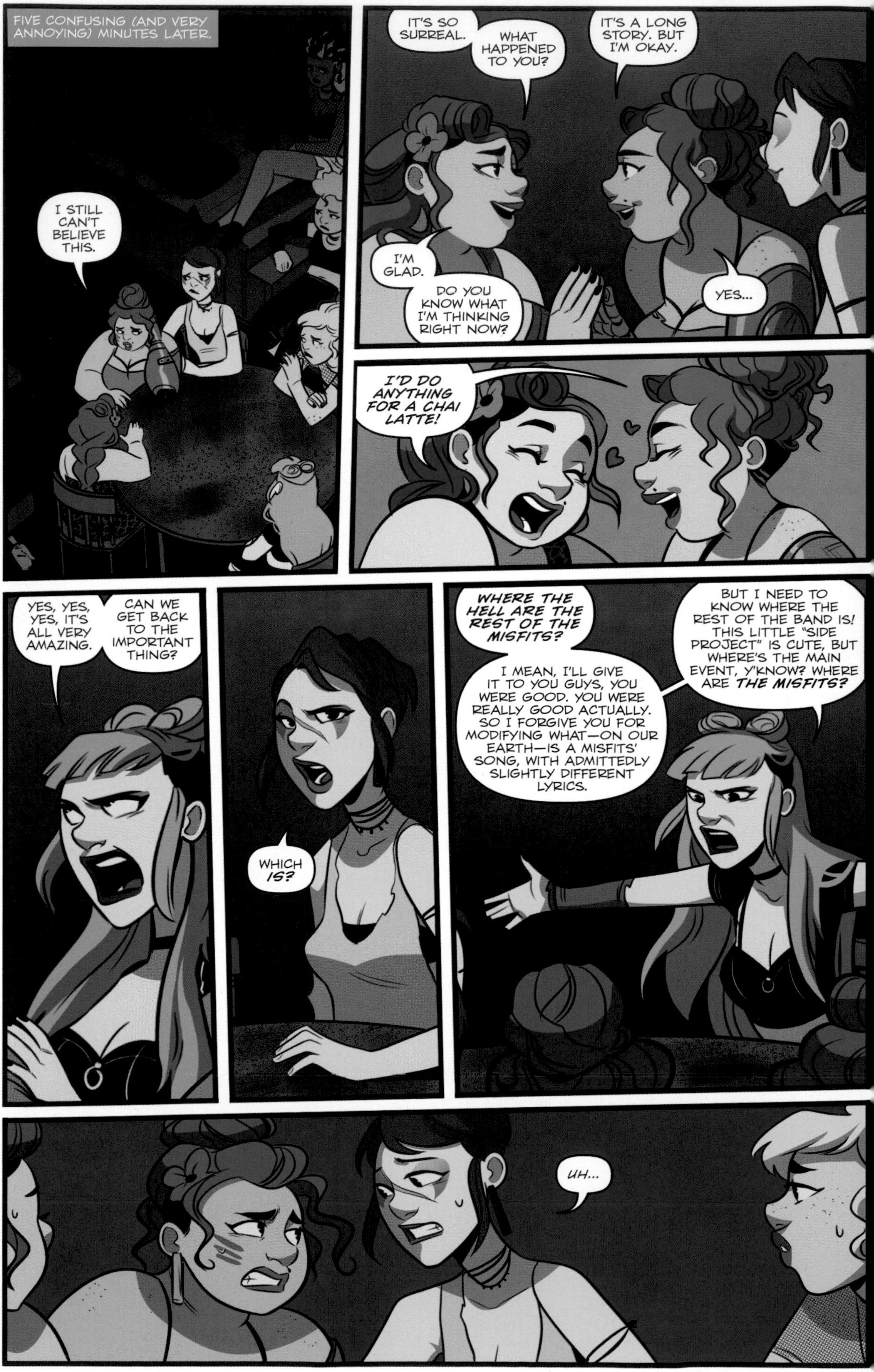
FIVE CONFUSING (AND VERY ANNOYING) MINUTES LATER.
I STILL CAN'T BELIEVE THIS.
IT'S SO SURREAL.
WHAT HAPPENED TO YOU?
IT'S A LONG STORY. BUT I'M OKAY.
I'M GLAD.
DO YOU KNOW WHAT I'M THINKING RIGHT NOW?
YES...
I'D DO ANYTHING FOR A CHAI LATTE!
YES, YES, YES, IT'S ALL VERY AMAZING.
CAN WE GET BACK TO THE IMPORTANT THING?
WHICH IS?
WHERE THE HELL ARE THE REST OF THE MISFITS?
I MEAN, I'LL GIVE IT TO YOU GUYS, YOU WERE GOOD. YOU WERE REALLY GOOD ACTUALLY. SO I FORGIVE YOU FOR MODIFYING WHAT—ON OUR EARTH—IS A MISFITS' SONG, WITH ADMITTEDLY SLIGHTLY DIFFERENT LYRICS.
BUT I NEED TO KNOW WHERE THE REST OF THE BAND IS! THIS LITTLE "SIDE PROJECT" IS CUTE, BUT WHERE'S THE MAIN EVENT, Y'KNOW? WHERE ARE THE MISFITS?
UH...

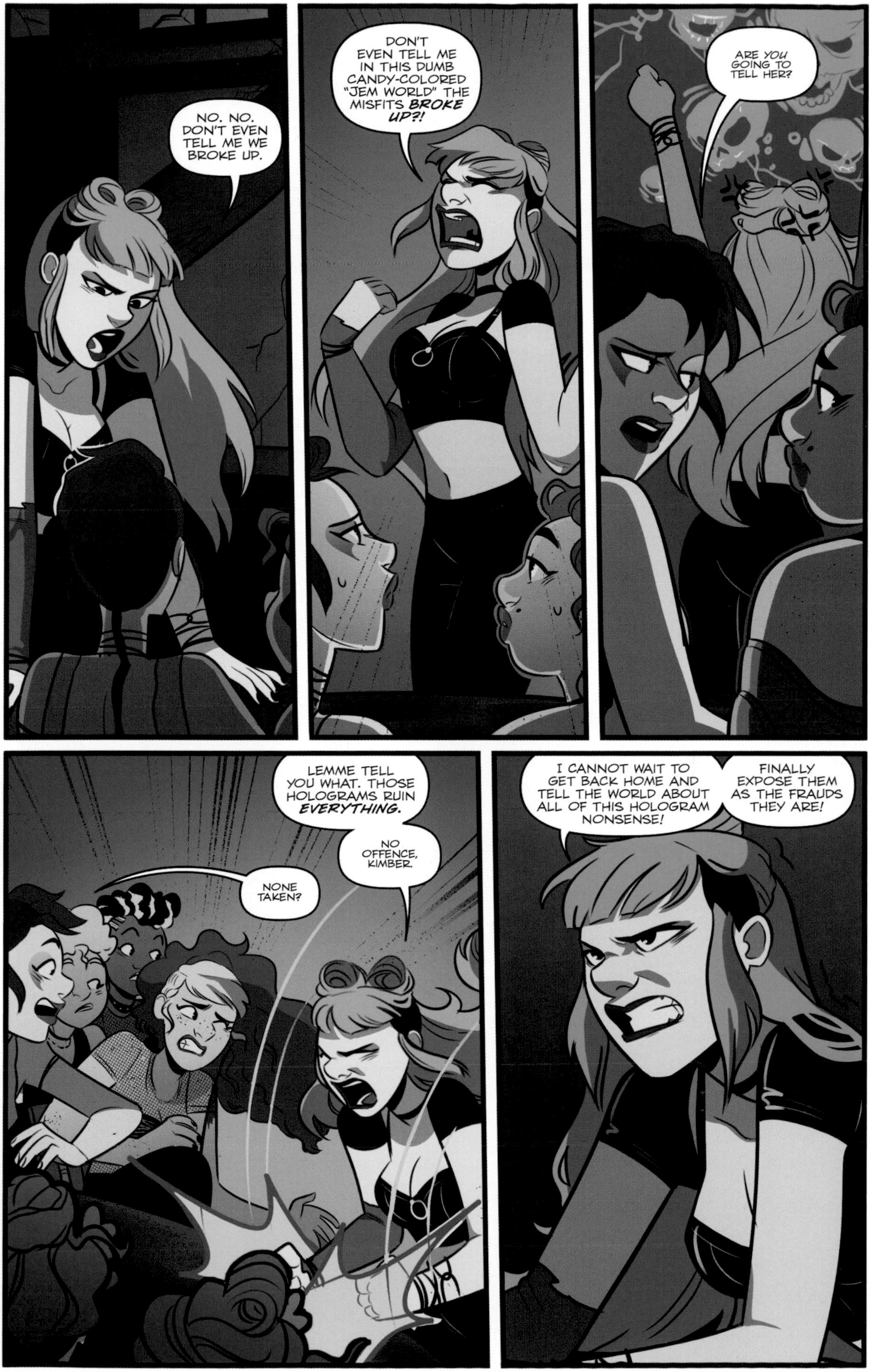

NO. NO. DON'T EVEN TELL ME WE BROKE UP.
DON'T EVEN TELL ME IN THIS DUMB CANDY-COLORED "JEM WORLD" THE MISFITS BROKE UP?!
ARE YOU GOING TO TELL HER?
LEMME TELL YOU WHAT. THOSE HOLOGRAMS RUIN EVERYTHING.
NO OFFENCE, KIMBER.
NONE TAKEN?
I CANNOT WAIT TO GET BACK HOME AND TELL THE WORLD ABOUT ALL OF THIS HOLOGRAM NONSENSE!
FINALLY EXPOSE THEM AS THE FRAUDS THEY ARE!

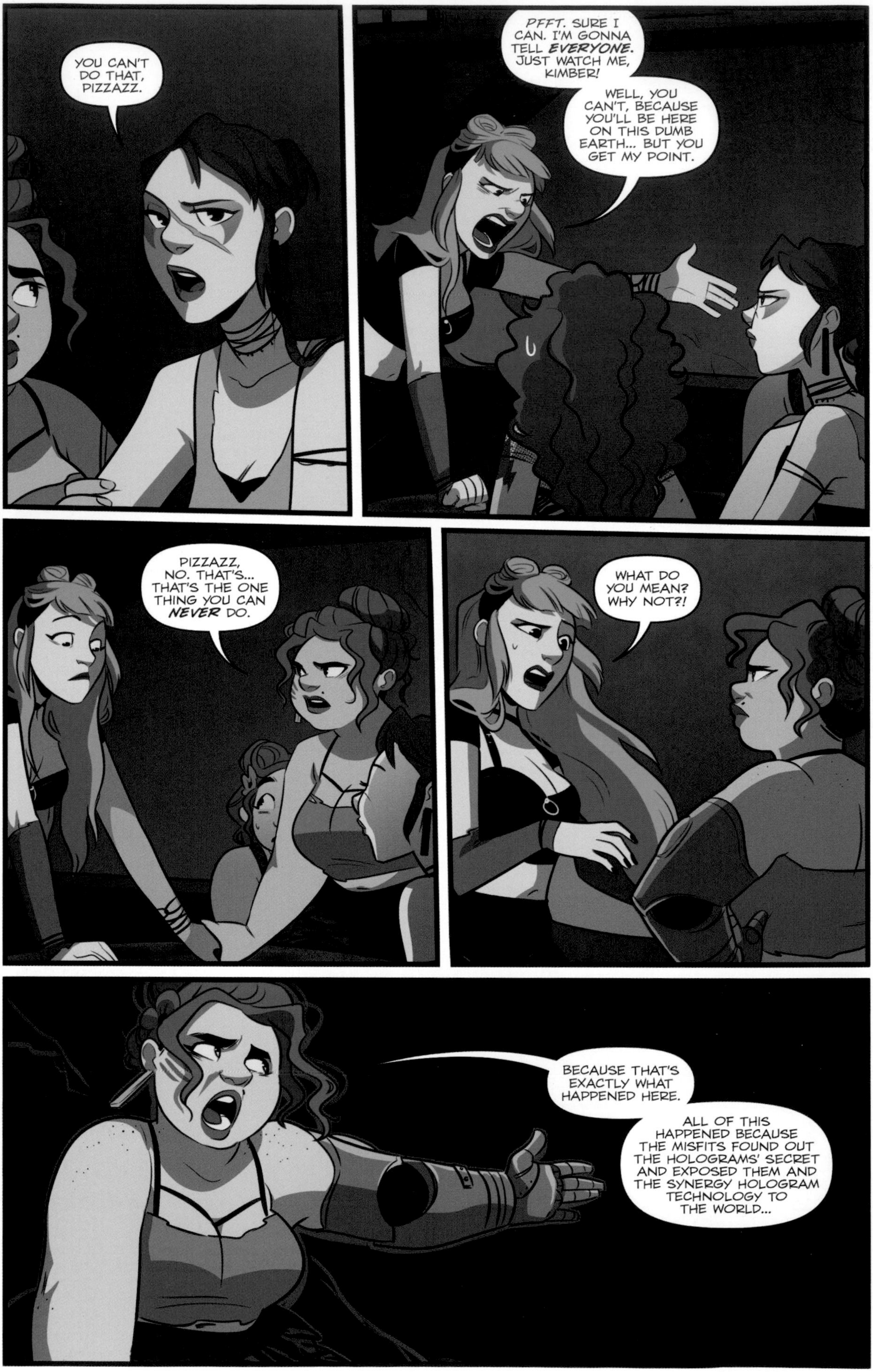
YOU CAN'T DO THAT, PIZZAZZ.
PFFT. SURE I CAN. I'M GONNA TELL EVERYONE. JUST WATCH ME, KIMBER!
WELL, YOU CAN'T, BECAUSE YOU'LL BE HERE ON THIS DUMB EARTH... BUT YOU GET MY POINT.
PIZZAZZ, NO. THAT'S... THAT'S THE ONE THING YOU CAN NEVER DO.
WHAT DO YOU MEAN? WHY NOT?!
BECAUSE THAT'S EXACTLY WHAT HAPPENED HERE.
ALL OF THIS HAPPENED BECAUSE THE MISFITS FOUND OUT THE HOLOGRAMS' SECRET AND EXPOSED THEM AND THE SYNERGY HOLOGRAM TECHNOLOGY TO THE WORLD...

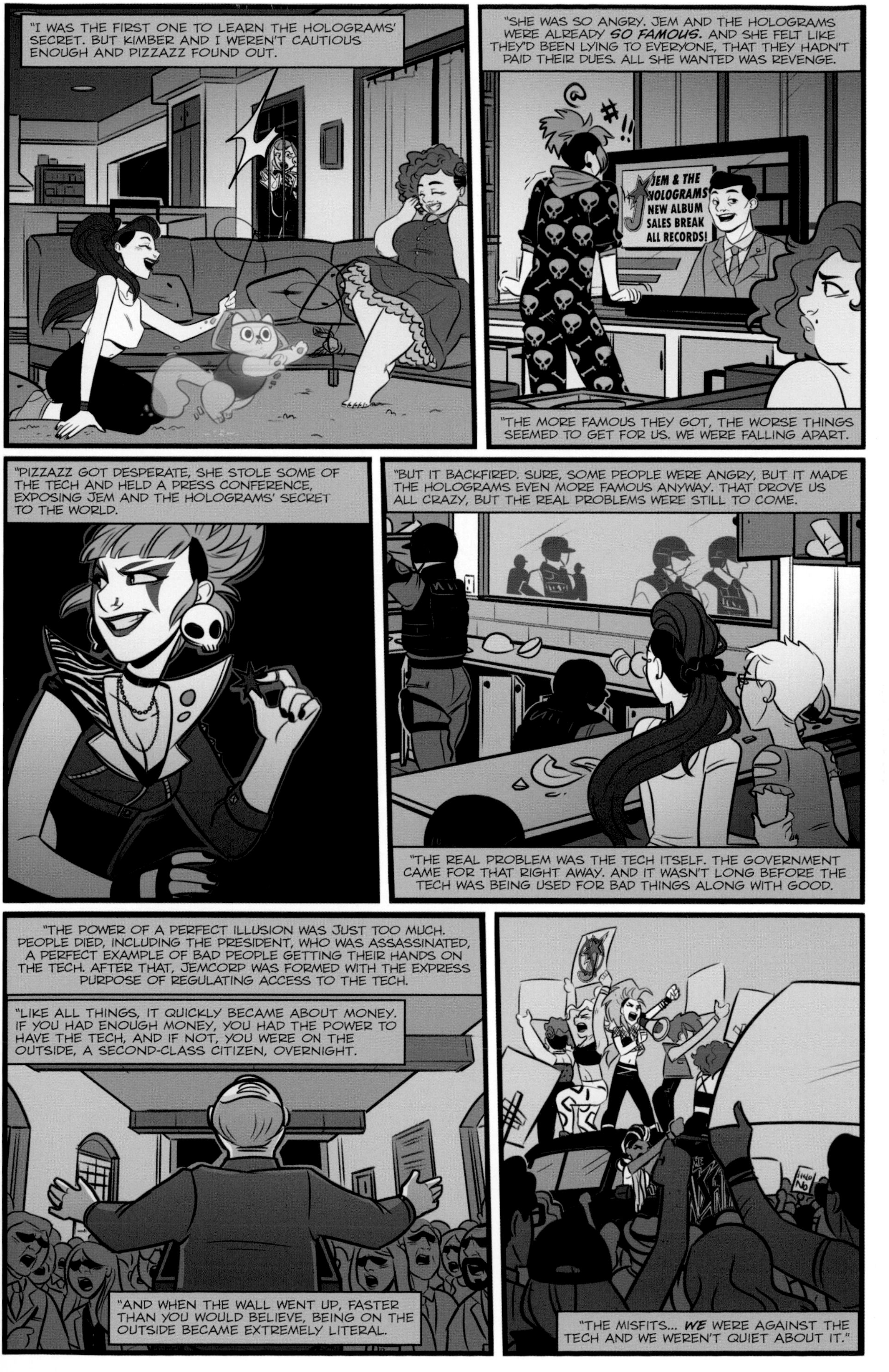
"I WAS THE FIRST ONE TO LEARN THE HOLOGRAMS' SECRET. BUT KIMBER AND I WEREN'T CAUTIOUS ENOUGH AND PIZZAZZ FOUND OUT.
"SHE WAS SO ANGRY. JEM AND THE HOLOGRAMS WERE ALREADY *SO FAMOUS.* AND SHE FELT LIKE THEY'D BEEN LYING TO EVERYONE, THAT THEY HADN'T PAID THEIR DUES. ALL SHE WANTED WAS REVENGE.
@ # !!
JEM & THE HOLOGRAMS NEW ALBUM SALES BREAK ALL RECORDS!
"THE MORE FAMOUS THEY GOT, THE WORSE THINGS SEEMED TO GET FOR US. WE WERE FALLING APART.
"PIZZAZZ GOT DESPERATE, SHE STOLE SOME OF THE TECH AND HELD A PRESS CONFERENCE, EXPOSING JEM AND THE HOLOGRAMS' SECRET TO THE WORLD.
"BUT IT BACKFIRED. SURE, SOME PEOPLE WERE ANGRY, BUT IT MADE THE HOLOGRAMS EVEN MORE FAMOUS ANYWAY. THAT DROVE US ALL CRAZY, BUT THE REAL PROBLEMS WERE STILL TO COME.
"THE REAL PROBLEM WAS THE TECH ITSELF. THE GOVERNMENT CAME FOR THAT RIGHT AWAY. AND IT WASN'T LONG BEFORE THE TECH WAS BEING USED FOR BAD THINGS ALONG WITH GOOD.
"THE POWER OF A PERFECT ILLUSION WAS JUST TOO MUCH. PEOPLE DIED, INCLUDING THE PRESIDENT, WHO WAS ASSASSINATED, A PERFECT EXAMPLE OF BAD PEOPLE GETTING THEIR HANDS ON THE TECH. AFTER THAT, JEMCORP WAS FORMED WITH THE EXPRESS PURPOSE OF REGULATING ACCESS TO THE TECH.
"LIKE ALL THINGS, IT QUICKLY BECAME ABOUT MONEY. IF YOU HAD ENOUGH MONEY, YOU HAD THE POWER TO HAVE THE TECH, AND IF NOT, YOU WERE ON THE OUTSIDE, A SECOND-CLASS CITIZEN, OVERNIGHT.
"AND WHEN THE WALL WENT UP, FASTER THAN YOU WOULD BELIEVE, BEING ON THE OUTSIDE BECAME EXTREMELY LITERAL.
HOLO NO
"THE MISFITS... *WE* WERE AGAINST THE TECH AND WE WEREN'T QUIET ABOUT IT."

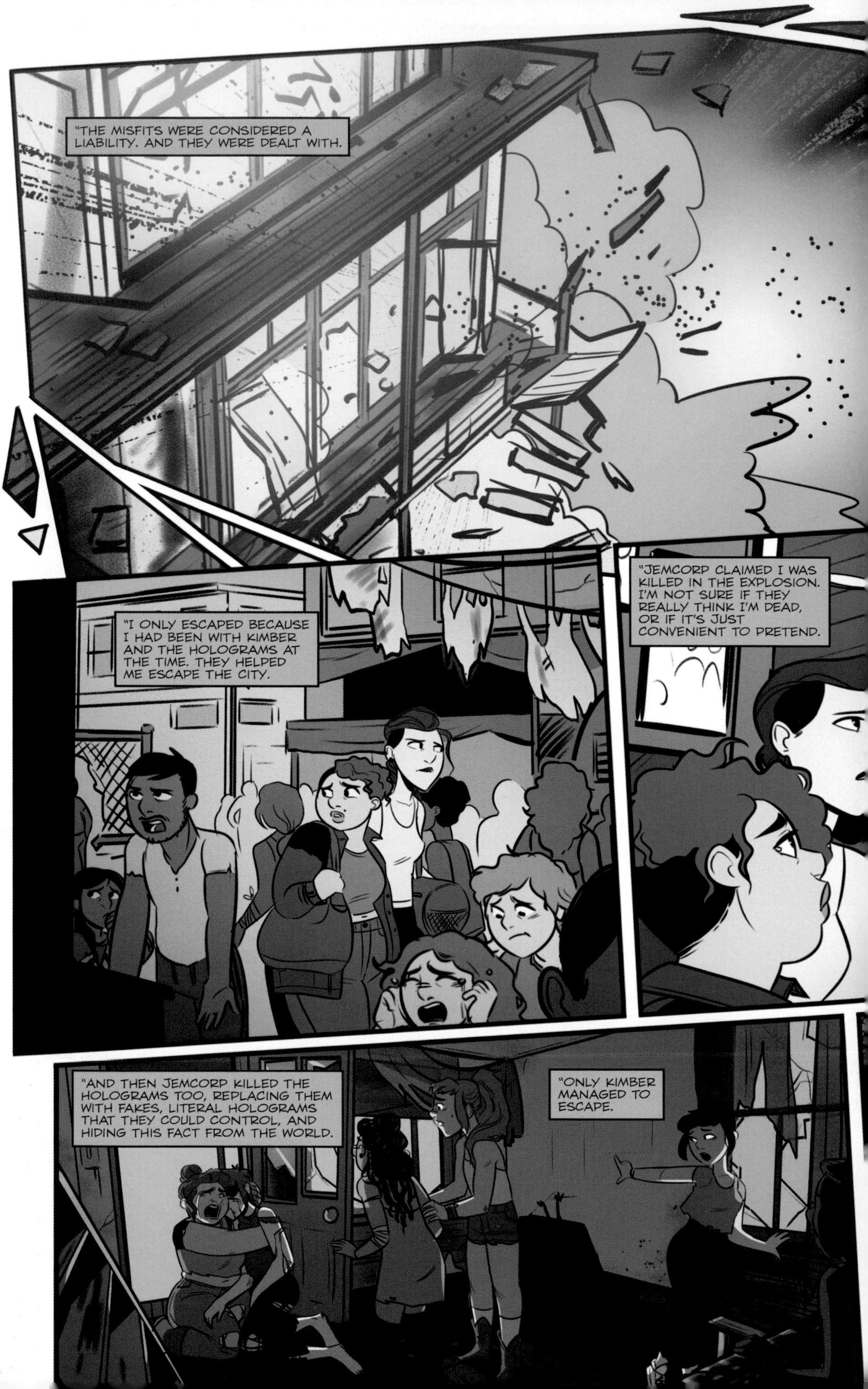
"THE MISFITS WERE CONSIDERED A LIABILITY. AND THEY WERE DEALT WITH.
"I ONLY ESCAPED BECAUSE I HAD BEEN WITH KIMBER AND THE HOLOGRAMS AT THE TIME. THEY HELPED ME ESCAPE THE CITY.
"JEMCORP CLAIMED I WAS KILLED IN THE EXPLOSION. I'M NOT SURE IF THEY REALLY THINK I'M DEAD, OR IF IT'S JUST CONVENIENT TO PRETEND.
"AND THEN JEMCORP KILLED THE HOLOGRAMS TOO, REPLACING THEM WITH FAKES, LITERAL HOLOGRAMS THAT THEY COULD CONTROL, AND HIDING THIS FACT FROM THE WORLD.
"ONLY KIMBER MANAGED TO ESCAPE.

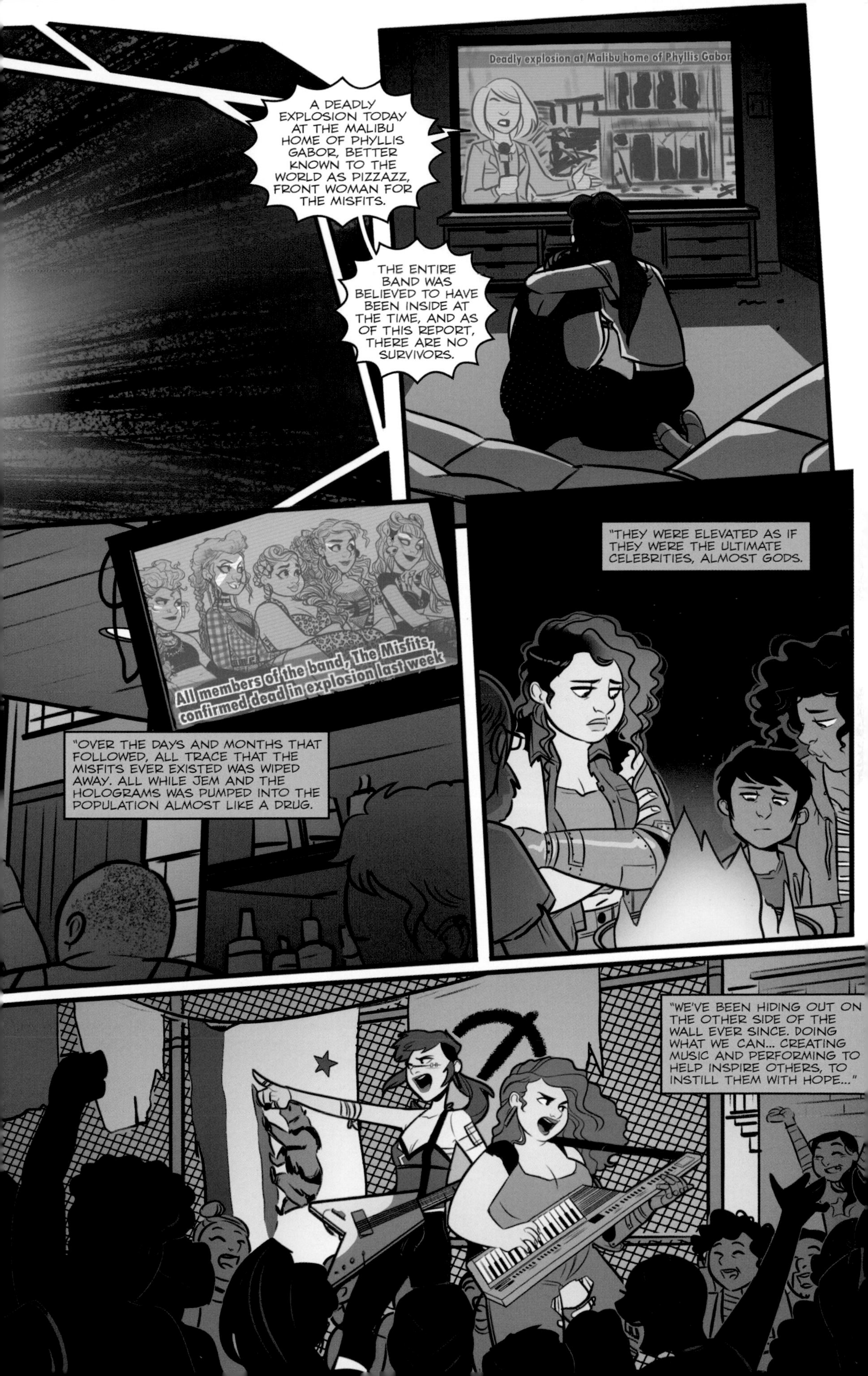
Deadly explosion at Malibu home of Phyllis Gabor
A DEADLY EXPLOSION TODAY AT THE MALIBU HOME OF PHYLLIS GABOR, BETTER KNOWN TO THE WORLD AS PIZZAZZ, FRONT WOMAN FOR THE MISFITS.
THE ENTIRE BAND WAS BELIEVED TO HAVE BEEN INSIDE AT THE TIME, AND AS OF THIS REPORT, THERE ARE NO SURVIVORS.
All members of the band, The Misfits, confirmed dead in explosion last week
"OVER THE DAYS AND MONTHS THAT FOLLOWED, ALL TRACE THAT THE MISFITS EVER EXISTED WAS WIPED AWAY. ALL WHILE JEM AND THE HOLOGRAMS WAS PUMPED INTO THE POPULATION ALMOST LIKE A DRUG.
"THEY WERE ELEVATED AS IF THEY WERE THE ULTIMATE CELEBRITIES, ALMOST GODS.
"WE'VE BEEN HIDING OUT ON THE OTHER SIDE OF THE WALL EVER SINCE. DOING WHAT WE CAN... CREATING MUSIC AND PERFORMING TO HELP INSPIRE OTHERS, TO INSTILL THEM WITH HOPE..."

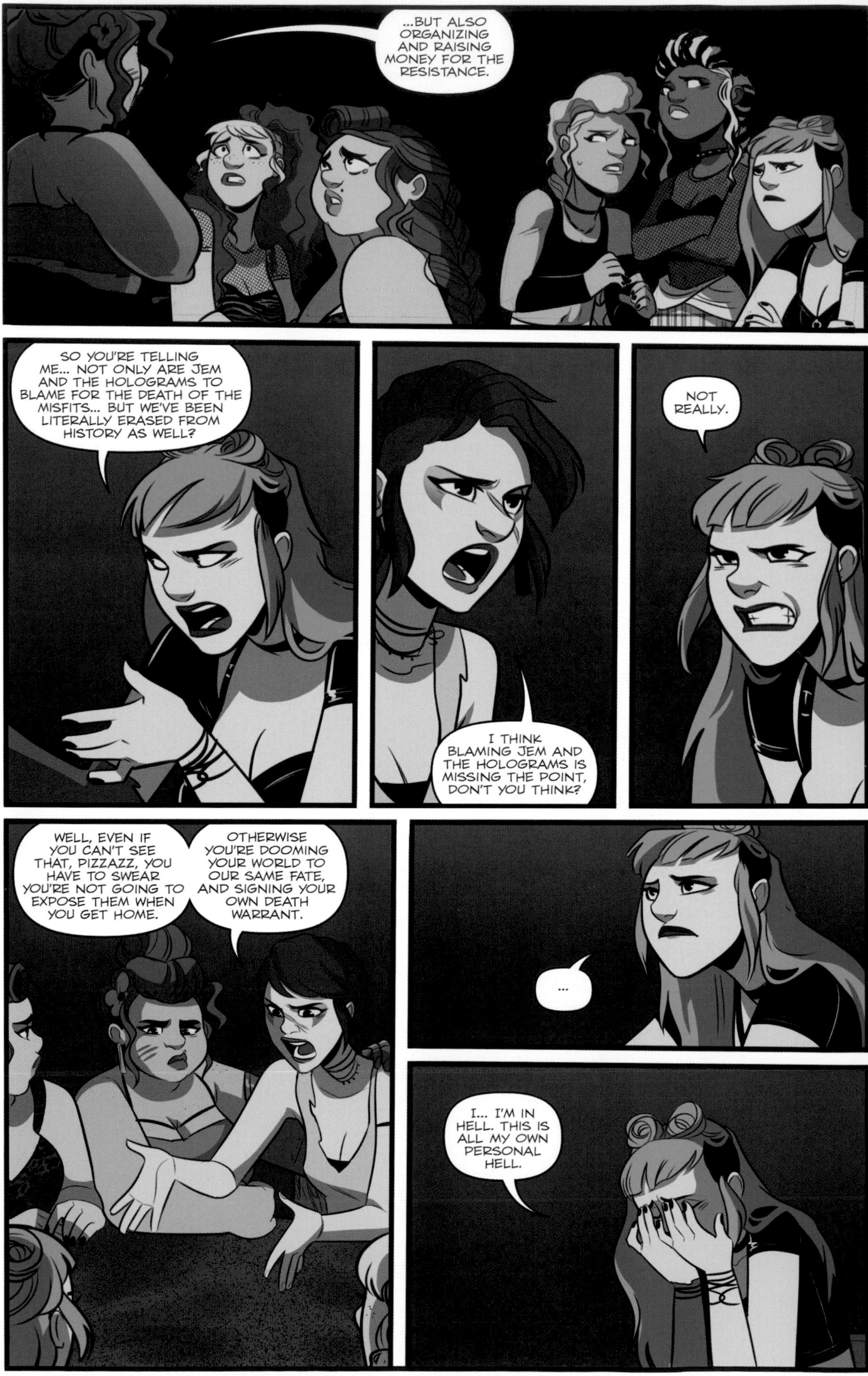
...BUT ALSO ORGANIZING AND RAISING MONEY FOR THE RESISTANCE.
SO YOU'RE TELLING ME... NOT ONLY ARE JEM AND THE HOLOGRAMS TO BLAME FOR THE DEATH OF THE MISFITS... BUT WE'VE BEEN LITERALLY ERASED FROM HISTORY AS WELL?
I THINK BLAMING JEM AND THE HOLOGRAMS IS MISSING THE POINT, DON'T YOU THINK?
NOT REALLY.
WELL, EVEN IF YOU CAN'T SEE THAT, PIZZAZZ, YOU HAVE TO SWEAR YOU'RE NOT GOING TO EXPOSE THEM WHEN YOU GET HOME.
OTHERWISE YOU'RE DOOMING YOUR WORLD TO OUR SAME FATE, AND SIGNING YOUR OWN DEATH WARRANT.
...
I... I'M IN HELL. THIS IS ALL MY OWN PERSONAL HELL.

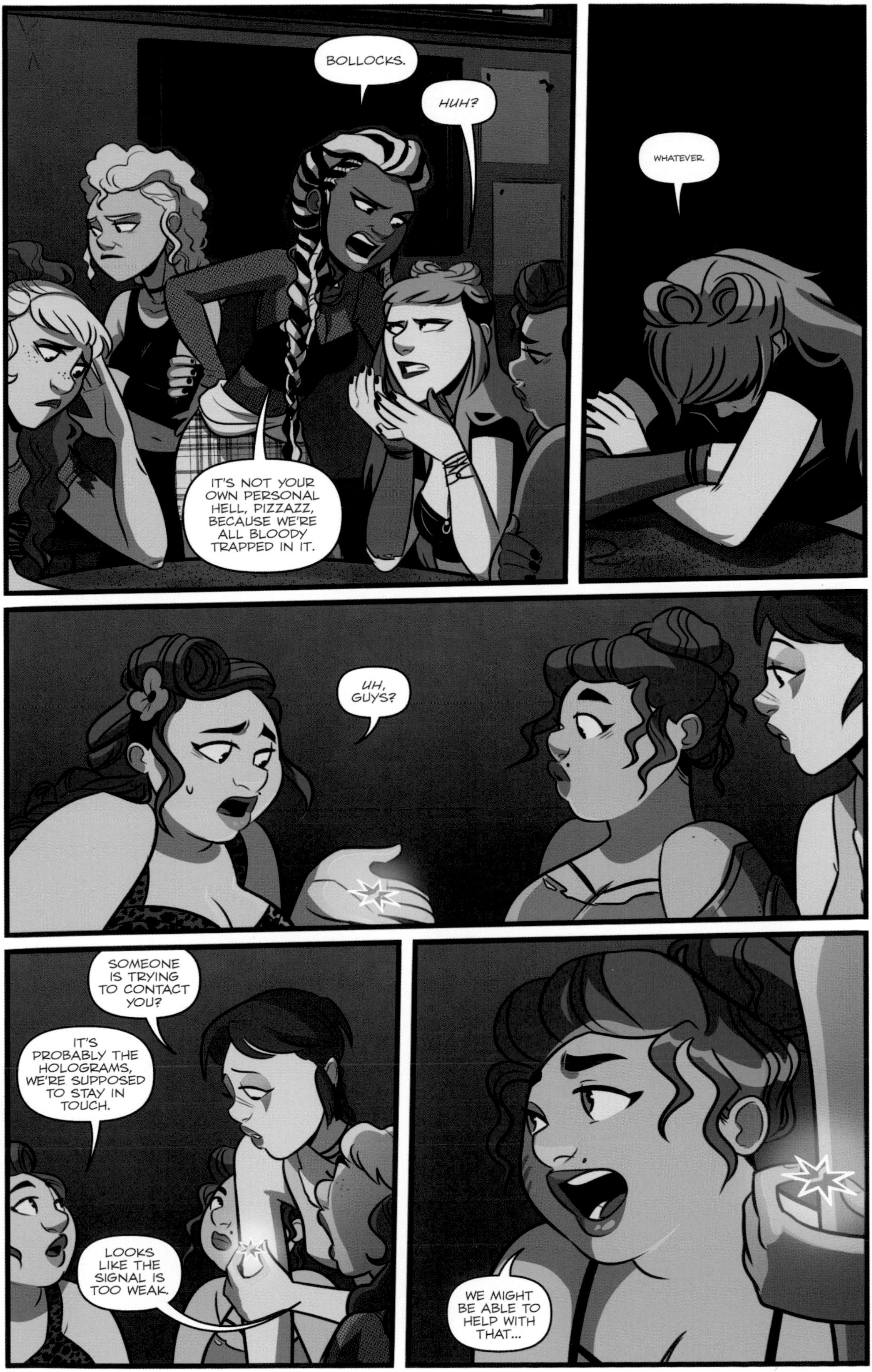
BOLLOCKS.
HUH?
IT'S NOT YOUR OWN PERSONAL HELL, PIZZAZZ, BECAUSE WE'RE ALL BLOODY TRAPPED IN IT.
WHATEVER
UH, GUYS?
SOMEONE IS TRYING TO CONTACT YOU?
IT'S PROBABLY THE HOLOGRAMS, WE'RE SUPPOSED TO STAY IN TOUCH.
LOOKS LIKE THE SIGNAL IS TOO WEAK.
WE MIGHT BE ABLE TO HELP WITH THAT...

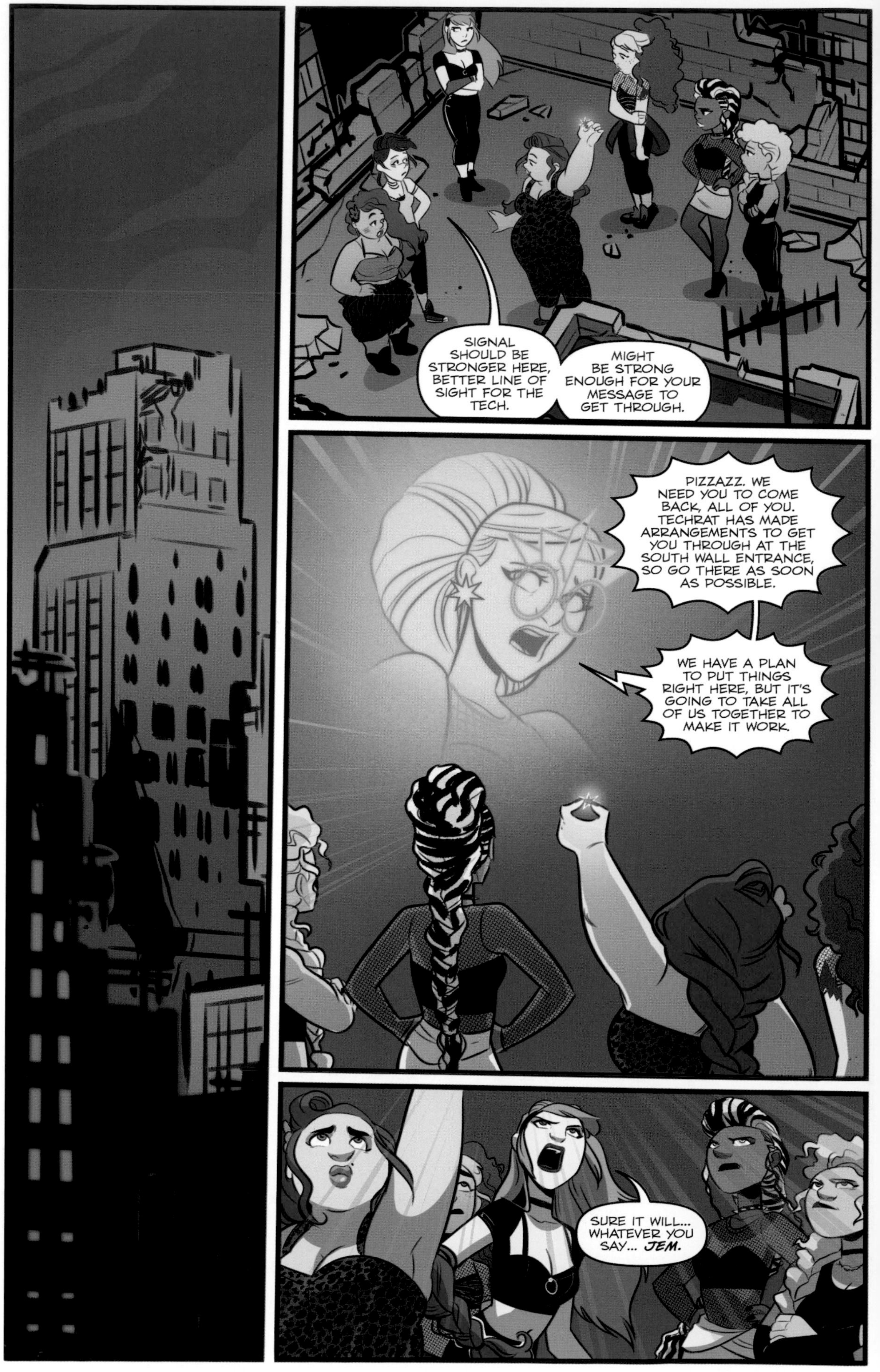
SIGNAL SHOULD BE STRONGER HERE, BETTER LINE OF SIGHT FOR THE TECH.
MIGHT BE STRONG ENOUGH FOR YOUR MESSAGE TO GET THROUGH.
PIZZAZZ. WE NEED YOU TO COME BACK, ALL OF YOU. TECHRAT HAS MADE ARRANGEMENTS TO GET YOU THROUGH AT THE SOUTH WALL ENTRANCE, SO GO THERE AS SOON AS POSSIBLE.
WE HAVE A PLAN TO PUT THINGS RIGHT HERE, BUT IT'S GOING TO TAKE ALL OF US TOGETHER TO MAKE IT WORK.
SURE IT WILL... WHATEVER YOU SAY... ***JEM.***

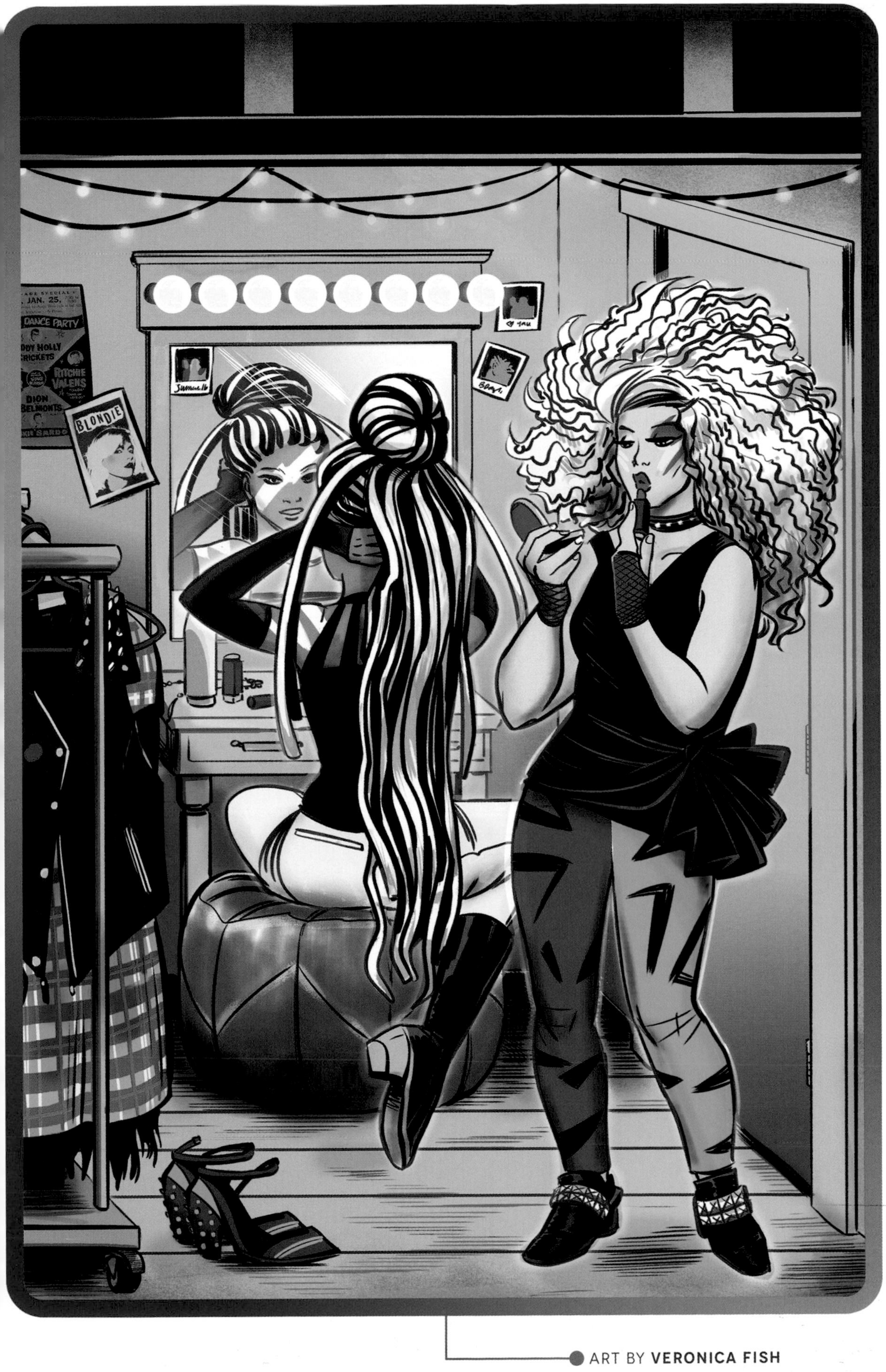
JAN. 25,
DANCE PARTY
HOLLY
RITCHIE VALENS
DION
BELMONTS
BLONDIE

ART BY **VERONICA FISH**

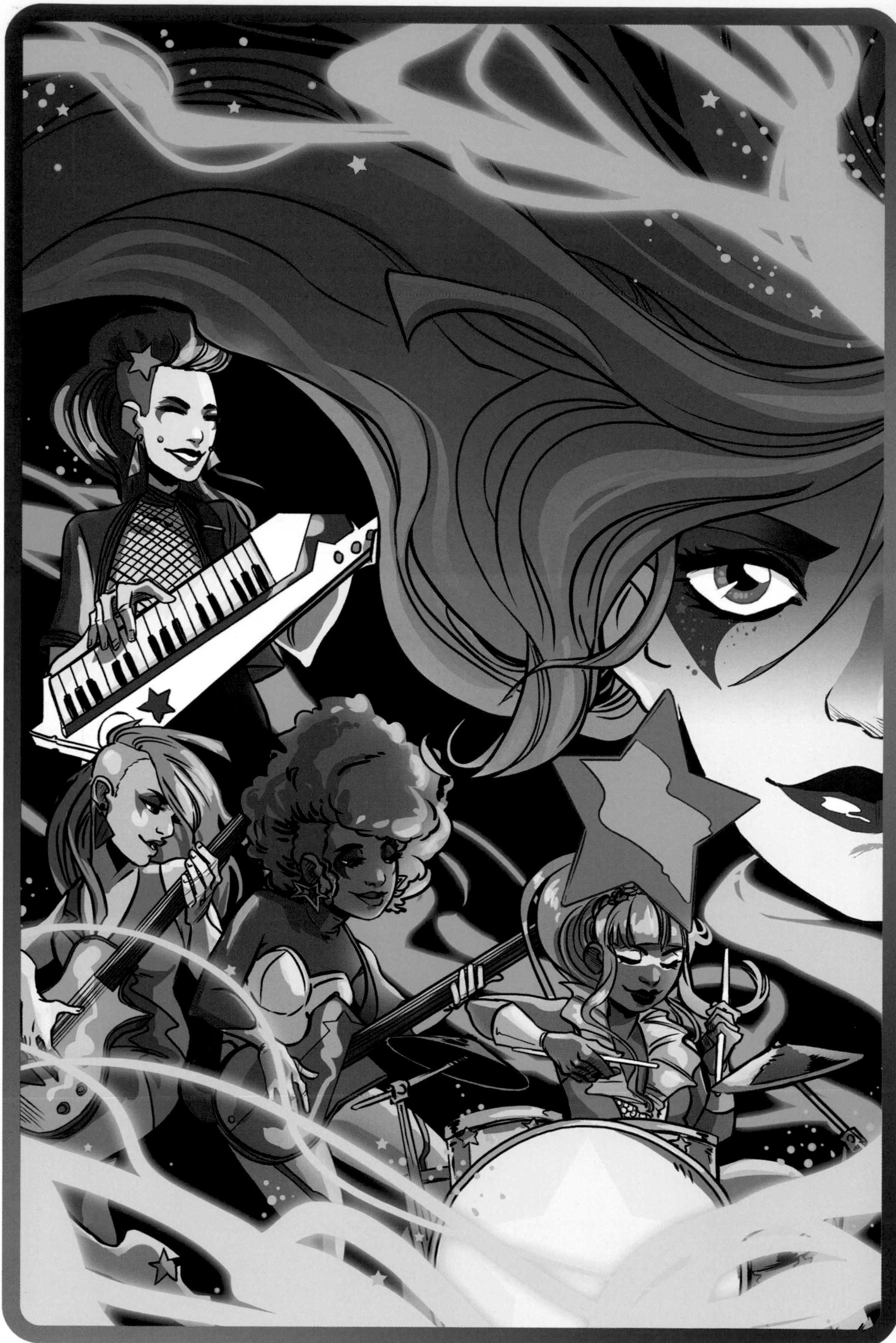

ART BY **JEN HICKMAN**

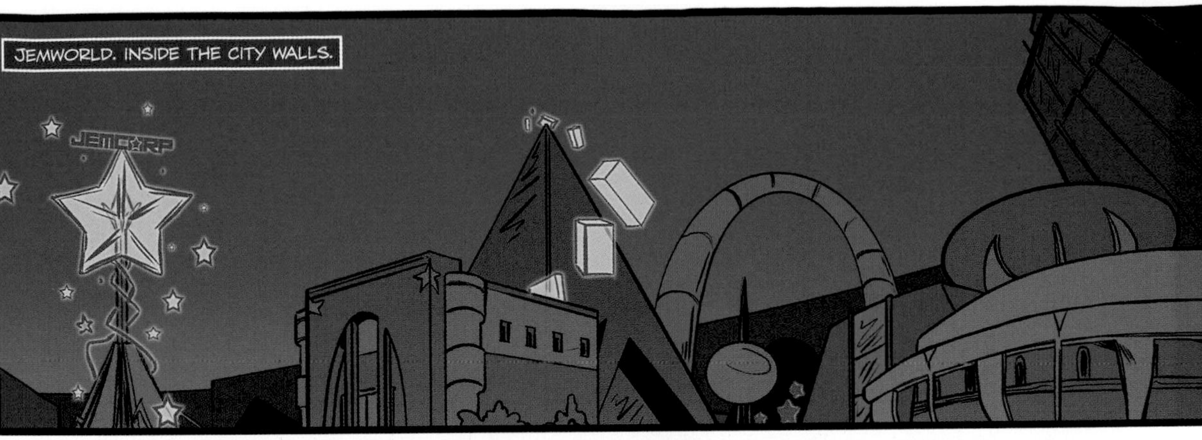
JEMWORLD. INSIDE THE CITY WALLS.
JEMCORP

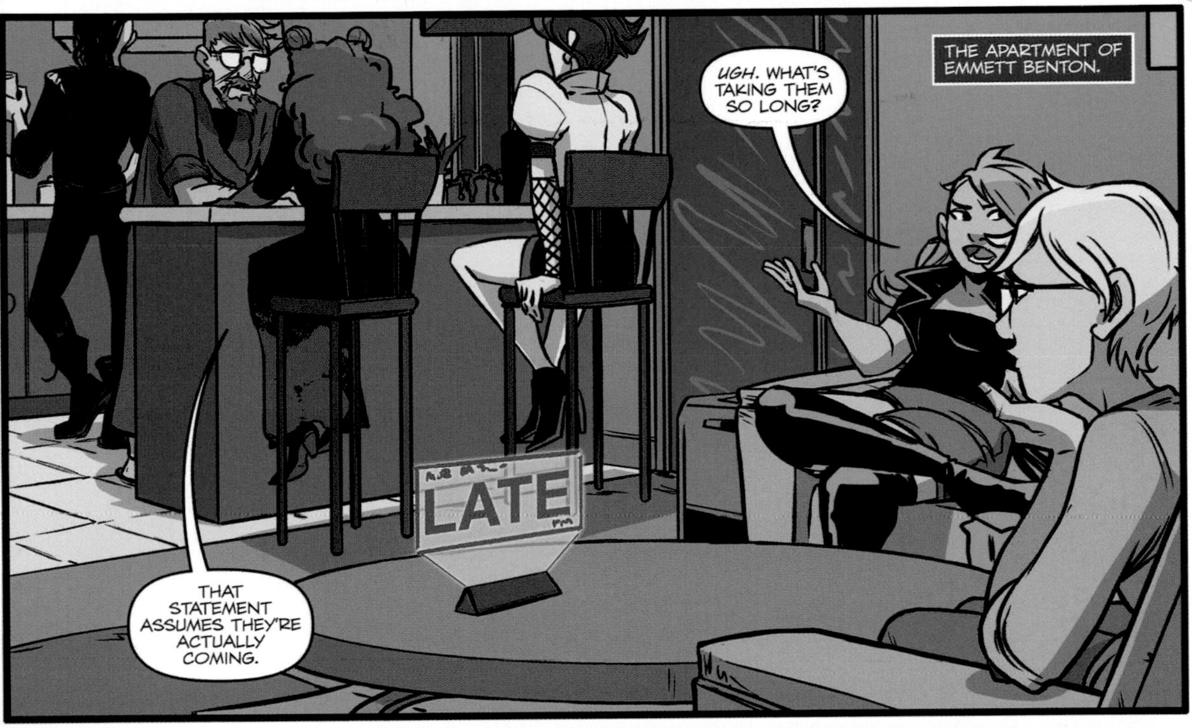
THE APARTMENT OF EMMETT BENTON.
UGH. WHAT'S TAKING THEM SO LONG?
LATE
THAT STATEMENT ASSUMES THEY'RE ACTUALLY COMING.

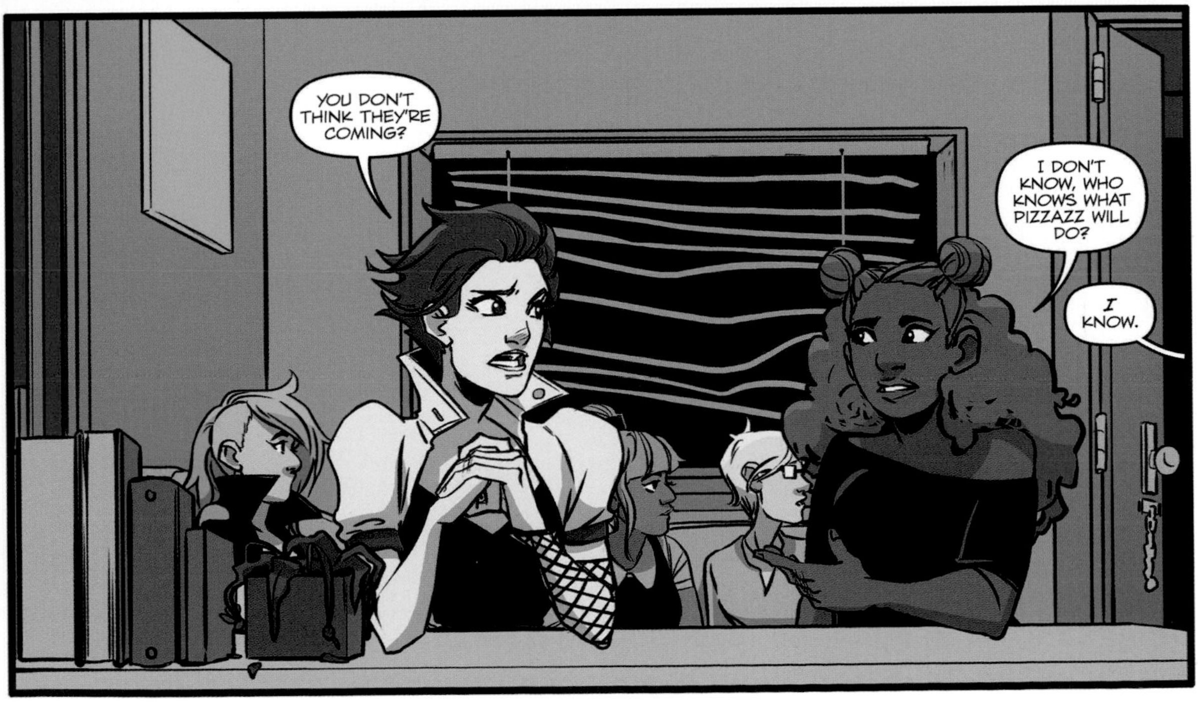
YOU DON'T THINK THEY'RE COMING?
I DON'T KNOW, WHO KNOWS WHAT PIZZAZZ WILL DO?
I KNOW.

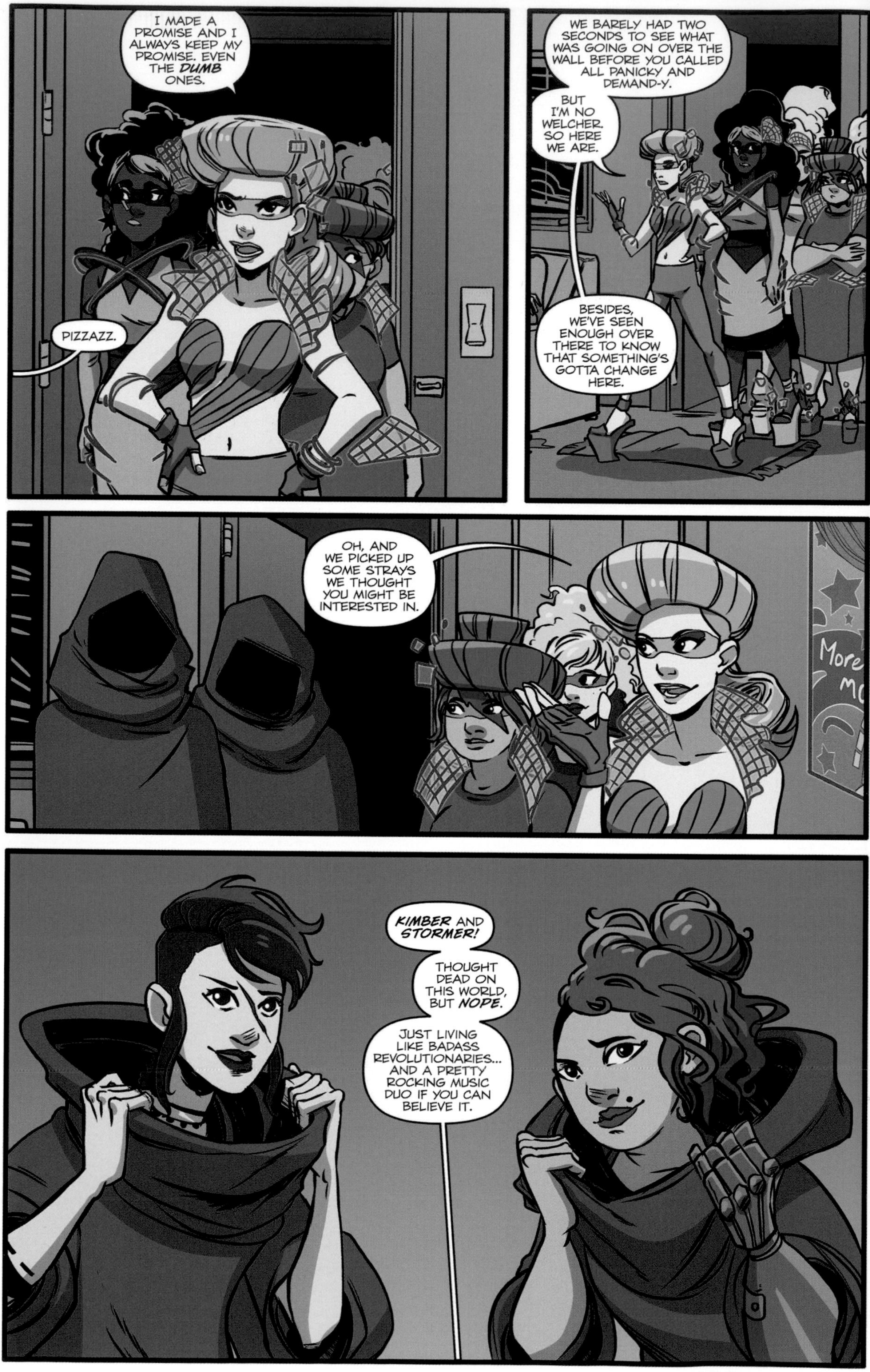
I MADE A PROMISE AND I ALWAYS KEEP MY PROMISE. EVEN THE ***DUMB*** ONES.
PIZZAZZ.
WE BARELY HAD TWO SECONDS TO SEE WHAT WAS GOING ON OVER THE WALL BEFORE YOU CALLED ALL PANICKY AND DEMAND-Y.
BUT I'M NO WELCHER. SO HERE WE ARE.
BESIDES, WE'VE SEEN ENOUGH OVER THERE TO KNOW THAT SOMETHING'S GOTTA CHANGE HERE.
OH, AND WE PICKED UP SOME STRAYS WE THOUGHT YOU MIGHT BE INTERESTED IN.
More m
KIMBER AND ***STORMER!***
THOUGHT DEAD ON THIS WORLD, BUT ***NOPE***.
JUST LIVING LIKE BADASS REVOLUTIONARIES... AND A PRETTY ROCKING MUSIC DUO IF YOU CAN BELIEVE IT.

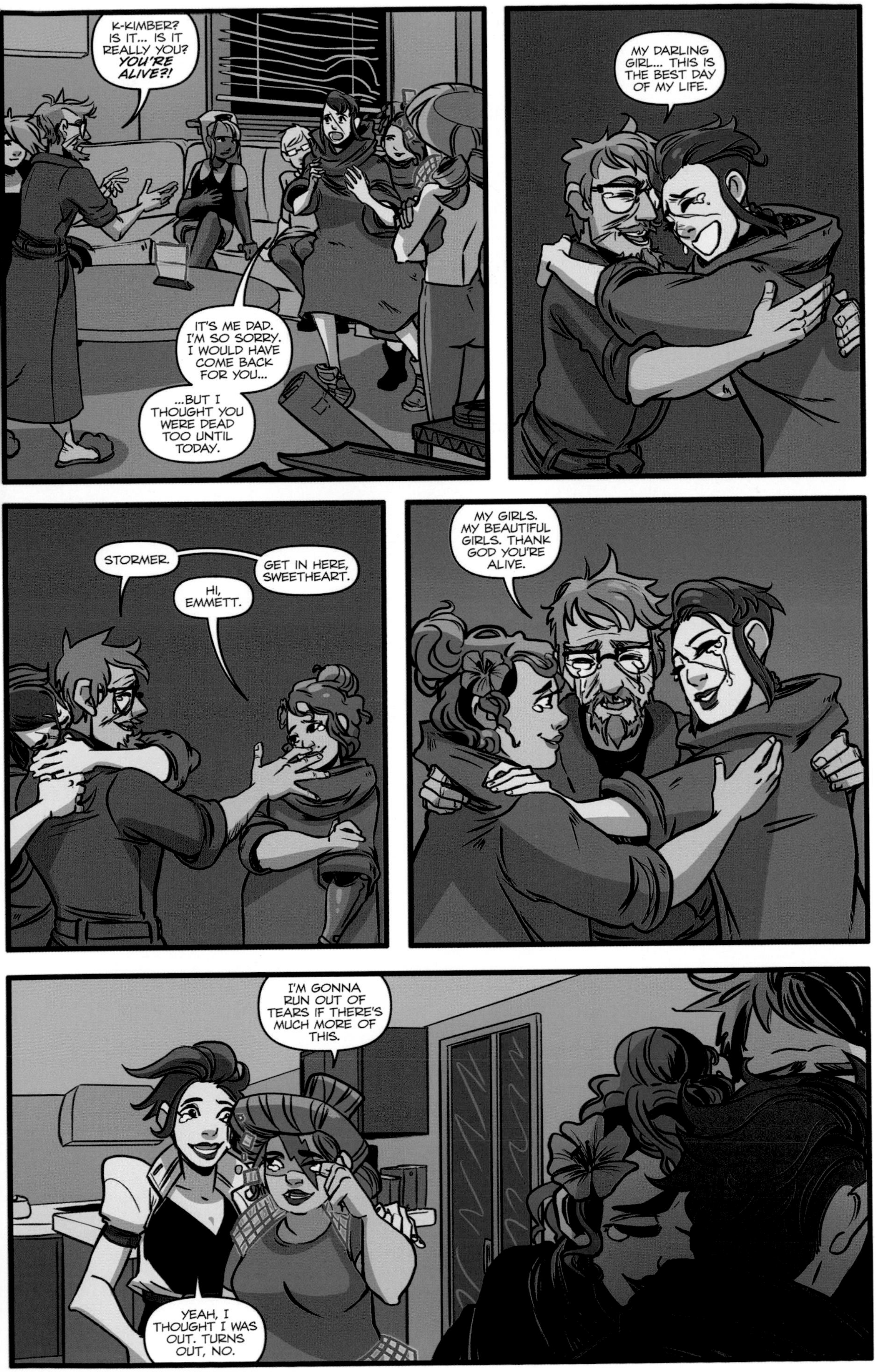
K-KIMBER? IS IT... IS IT REALLY YOU? *YOU'RE ALIVE?!*
IT'S ME DAD. I'M SO SORRY. I WOULD HAVE COME BACK FOR YOU...
...BUT I THOUGHT YOU WERE DEAD TOO UNTIL TODAY.
MY DARLING GIRL... THIS IS THE BEST DAY OF MY LIFE.
STORMER.
GET IN HERE, SWEETHEART.
HI, EMMETT.
MY GIRLS. MY BEAUTIFUL GIRLS. THANK GOD YOU'RE ALIVE.
I'M GONNA RUN OUT OF TEARS IF THERE'S MUCH MORE OF THIS.
YEAH, I THOUGHT I WAS OUT. TURNS OUT, NO.

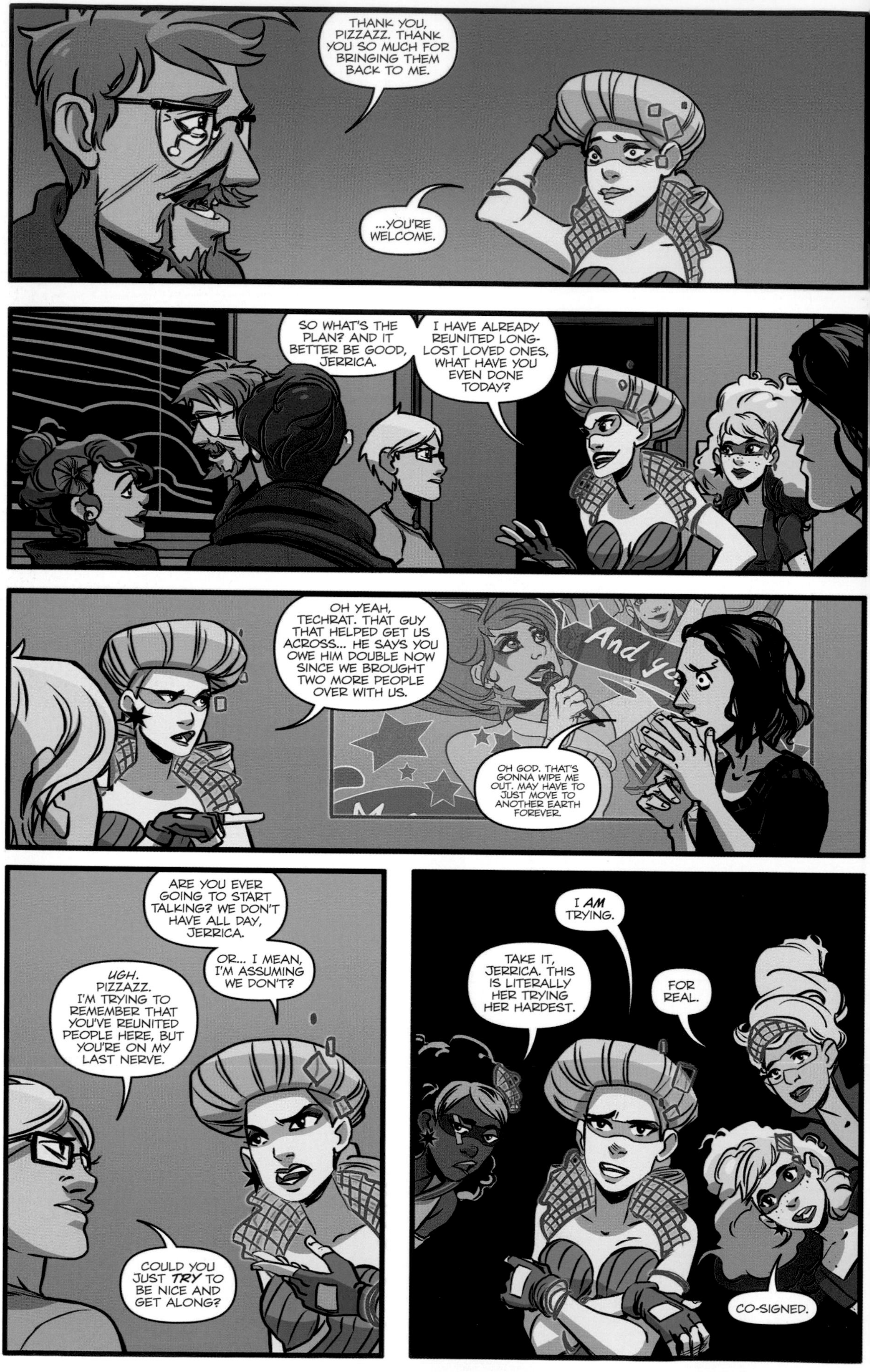
THANK YOU, PIZZAZZ. THANK YOU SO MUCH FOR BRINGING THEM BACK TO ME.
...YOU'RE WELCOME.
SO WHAT'S THE PLAN? AND IT BETTER BE GOOD, JERRICA.
I HAVE ALREADY REUNITED LONG-LOST LOVED ONES, WHAT HAVE YOU EVEN DONE TODAY?
OH YEAH, TECHRAT. THAT GUY THAT HELPED GET US ACROSS... HE SAYS YOU OWE HIM DOUBLE NOW SINCE WE BROUGHT TWO MORE PEOPLE OVER WITH US.
OH GOD. THAT'S GONNA WIPE ME OUT. MAY HAVE TO JUST MOVE TO ANOTHER EARTH FOREVER.
ARE YOU EVER GOING TO START TALKING? WE DON'T HAVE ALL DAY, JERRICA.
OR... I MEAN, I'M ASSUMING WE DON'T?
UGH. PIZZAZZ. I'M TRYING TO REMEMBER THAT YOU'VE REUNITED PEOPLE HERE, BUT YOU'RE ON MY LAST NERVE.
COULD YOU JUST TRY TO BE NICE AND GET ALONG?
I AM TRYING.
TAKE IT, JERRICA. THIS IS LITERALLY HER TRYING HER HARDEST.
FOR REAL.
CO-SIGNED.

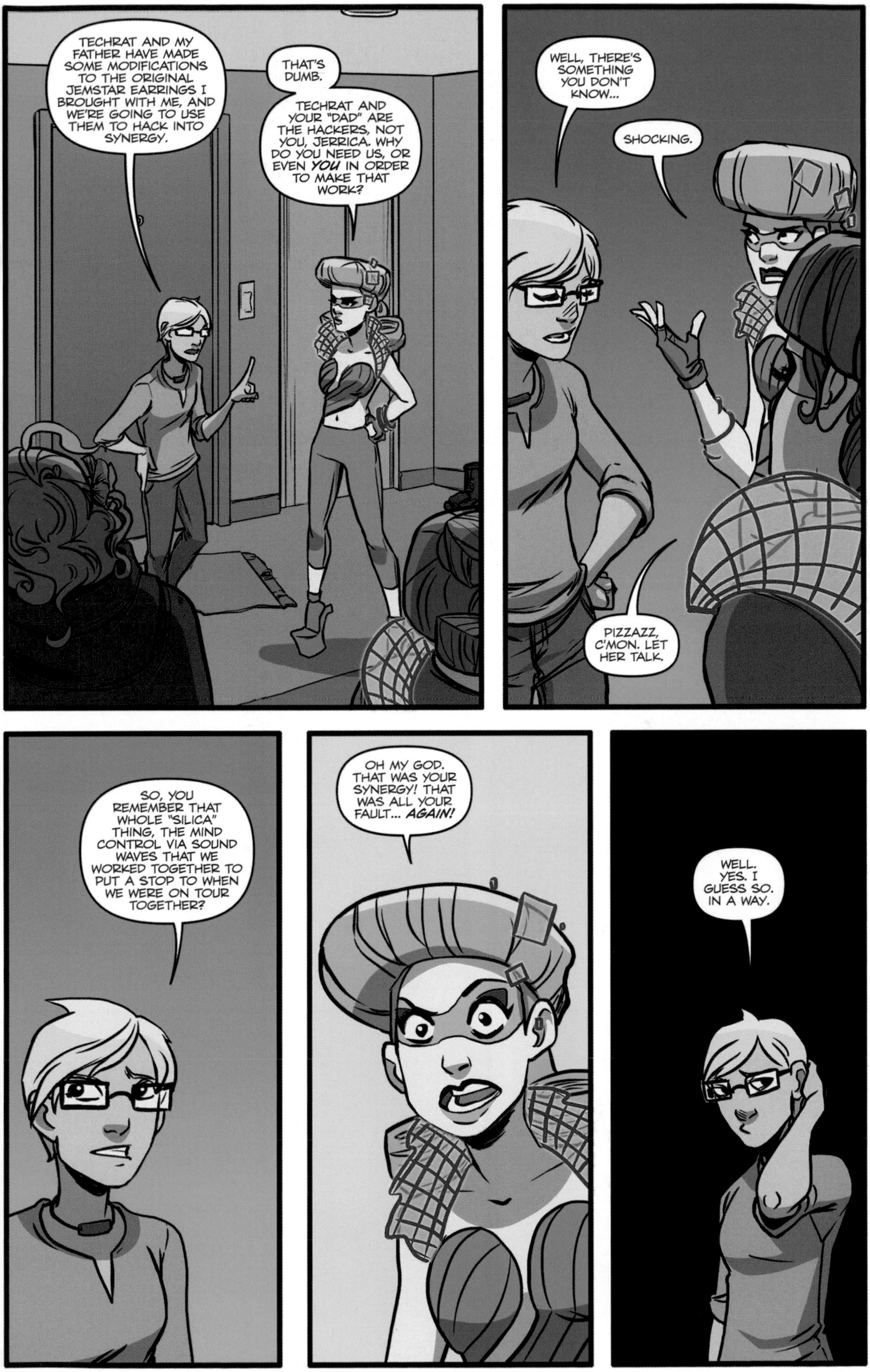
TECHRAT AND MY FATHER HAVE MADE SOME MODIFICATIONS TO THE ORIGINAL JEMSTAR EARRINGS I BROUGHT WITH ME, AND WE'RE GOING TO USE THEM TO HACK INTO SYNERGY.
THAT'S DUMB.
TECHRAT AND YOUR "DAD" ARE THE HACKERS, NOT YOU, JERRICA. WHY DO YOU NEED US, OR EVEN YOU IN ORDER TO MAKE THAT WORK?
WELL, THERE'S SOMETHING YOU DON'T KNOW...
SHOCKING.
PIZZAZZ, C'MON. LET HER TALK.
SO, YOU REMEMBER THAT WHOLE "SILICA" THING, THE MIND CONTROL VIA SOUND WAVES THAT WE WORKED TOGETHER TO PUT A STOP TO WHEN WE WERE ON TOUR TOGETHER?
OH MY GOD. THAT WAS YOUR SYNERGY! THAT WAS ALL YOUR FAULT... AGAIN!
WELL. YES. I GUESS SO. IN A WAY.

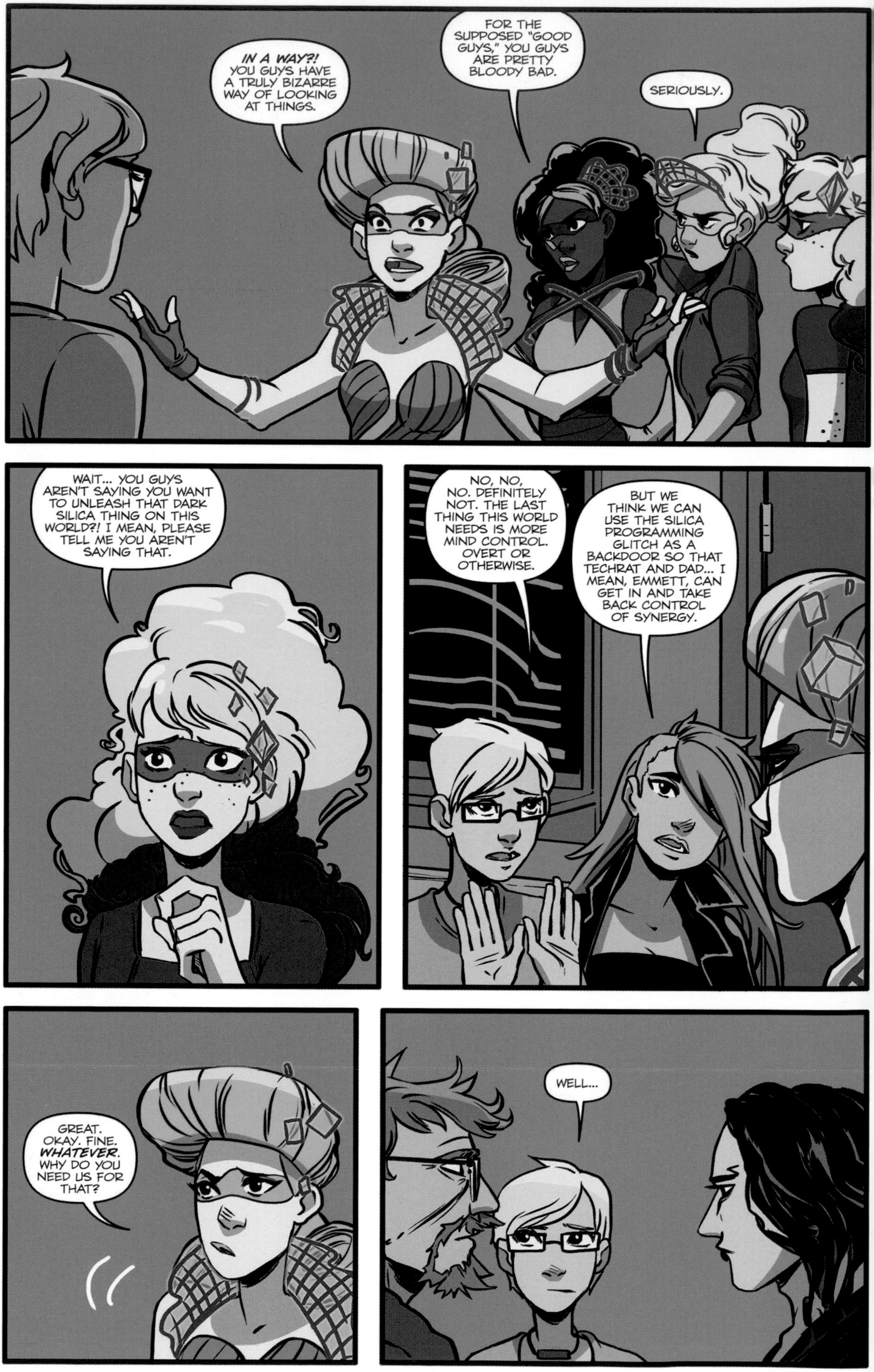
IN A WAY?! YOU GUYS HAVE A TRULY BIZARRE WAY OF LOOKING AT THINGS.
FOR THE SUPPOSED "GOOD GUYS," YOU GUYS ARE PRETTY BLOODY BAD.
SERIOUSLY.
WAIT... YOU GUYS AREN'T SAYING YOU WANT TO UNLEASH THAT DARK SILICA THING ON THIS WORLD?! I MEAN, PLEASE TELL ME YOU AREN'T SAYING THAT.
NO, NO, NO. DEFINITELY NOT. THE LAST THING THIS WORLD NEEDS IS MORE MIND CONTROL. OVERT OR OTHERWISE.
BUT WE THINK WE CAN USE THE SILICA PROGRAMMING GLITCH AS A BACKDOOR SO THAT TECHRAT AND DAD... I MEAN, EMMETT, CAN GET IN AND TAKE BACK CONTROL OF SYNERGY.
GREAT. OKAY. FINE. WHATEVER. WHY DO YOU NEED US FOR THAT?
WELL...

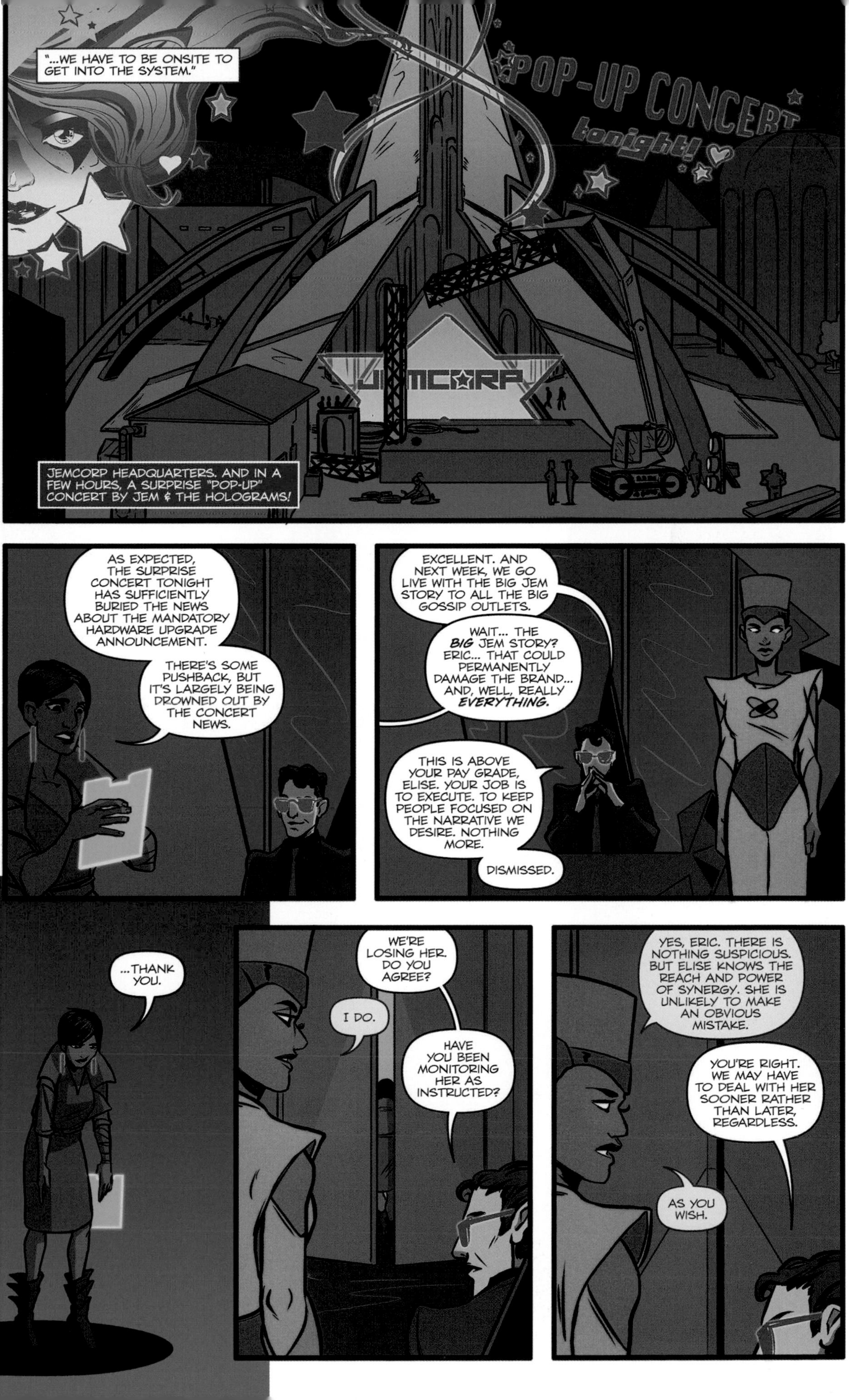
"...WE HAVE TO BE ONSITE TO GET INTO THE SYSTEM."
POP-UP CONCERT tonight!
JEMCORP
JEMCORP HEADQUARTERS. AND IN A FEW HOURS, A SURPRISE "POP-UP" CONCERT BY JEM & THE HOLOGRAMS!
AS EXPECTED, THE SURPRISE CONCERT TONIGHT HAS SUFFICIENTLY BURIED THE NEWS ABOUT THE MANDATORY HARDWARE UPGRADE ANNOUNCEMENT.
THERE'S SOME PUSHBACK, BUT IT'S LARGELY BEING DROWNED OUT BY THE CONCERT NEWS.
EXCELLENT. AND NEXT WEEK, WE GO LIVE WITH THE BIG JEM STORY TO ALL THE BIG GOSSIP OUTLETS.
WAIT... THE BIG JEM STORY? ERIC... THAT COULD PERMANENTLY DAMAGE THE BRAND... AND, WELL, REALLY EVERYTHING.
THIS IS ABOVE YOUR PAY GRADE, ELISE. YOUR JOB IS TO EXECUTE. TO KEEP PEOPLE FOCUSED ON THE NARRATIVE WE DESIRE. NOTHING MORE.
DISMISSED.
...THANK YOU.
WE'RE LOSING HER. DO YOU AGREE?
I DO.
HAVE YOU BEEN MONITORING HER AS INSTRUCTED?
YES, ERIC. THERE IS NOTHING SUSPICIOUS. BUT ELISE KNOWS THE REACH AND POWER OF SYNERGY. SHE IS UNLIKELY TO MAKE AN OBVIOUS MISTAKE.
YOU'RE RIGHT. WE MAY HAVE TO DEAL WITH HER SOONER RATHER THAN LATER, REGARDLESS.
AS YOU WISH.

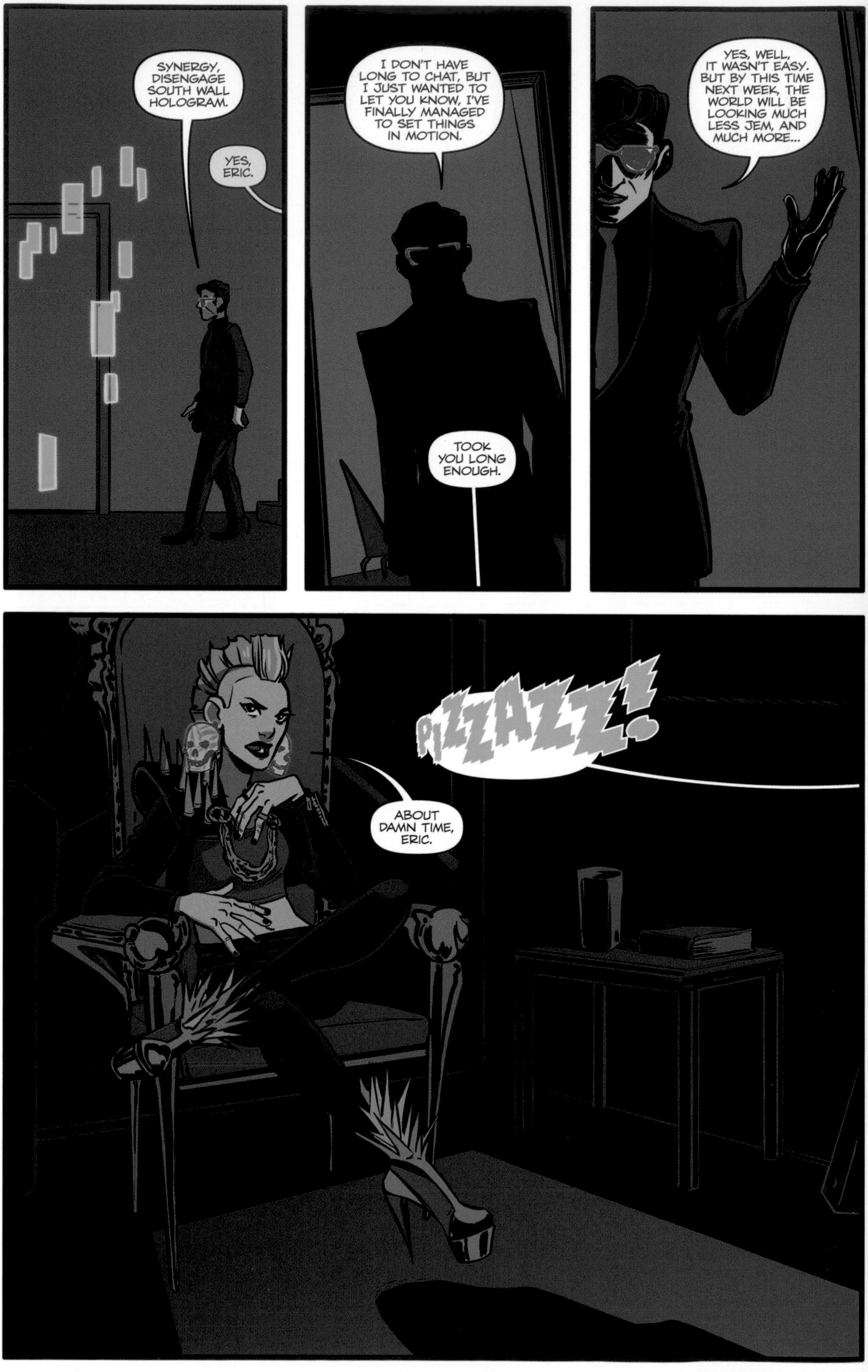
SYNERGY, DISENGAGE SOUTH WALL HOLOGRAM.
YES, ERIC.
I DON'T HAVE LONG TO CHAT, BUT I JUST WANTED TO LET YOU KNOW, I'VE FINALLY MANAGED TO SET THINGS IN MOTION.
TOOK YOU LONG ENOUGH.
YES, WELL, IT WASN'T EASY. BUT BY THIS TIME NEXT WEEK, THE WORLD WILL BE LOOKING MUCH LESS JEM, AND MUCH MORE...
PIZZAZZ!
ABOUT DAMN TIME, ERIC.

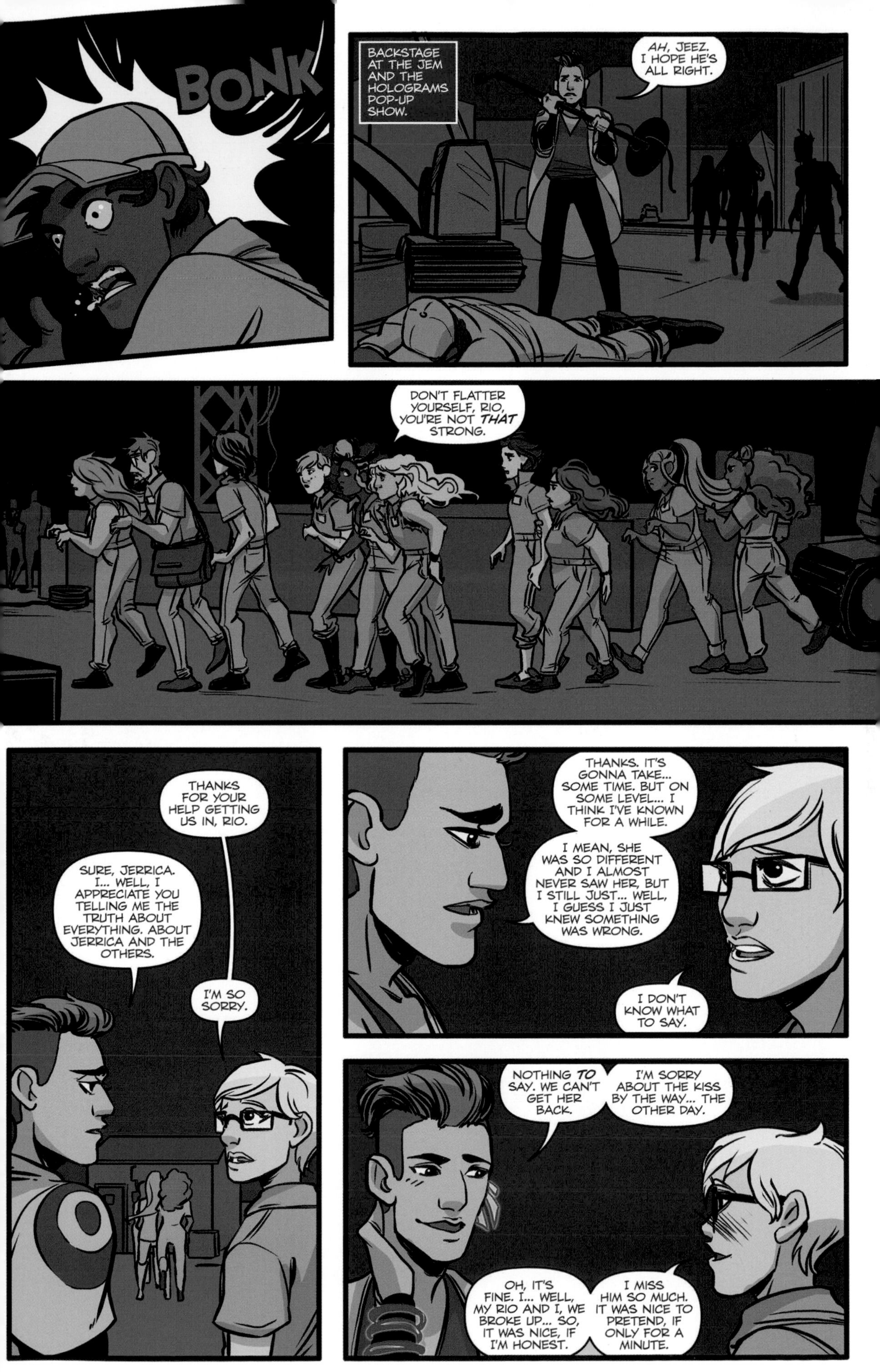
BONK
BACKSTAGE AT THE JEM AND THE HOLOGRAMS POP-UP SHOW.
AH, JEEZ. I HOPE HE'S ALL RIGHT.
DON'T FLATTER YOURSELF, RIO, YOU'RE NOT THAT STRONG.
THANKS FOR YOUR HELP GETTING US IN, RIO.
SURE, JERRICA. I... WELL, I APPRECIATE YOU TELLING ME THE TRUTH ABOUT EVERYTHING. ABOUT JERRICA AND THE OTHERS.
I'M SO SORRY.
THANKS. IT'S GONNA TAKE... SOME TIME. BUT ON SOME LEVEL... I THINK I'VE KNOWN FOR A WHILE.
I MEAN, SHE WAS SO DIFFERENT AND I ALMOST NEVER SAW HER, BUT I STILL JUST... WELL, I GUESS I JUST KNEW SOMETHING WAS WRONG.
I DON'T KNOW WHAT TO SAY.
NOTHING TO SAY. WE CAN'T GET HER BACK.
I'M SORRY ABOUT THE KISS BY THE WAY... THE OTHER DAY.
OH, IT'S FINE. I... WELL, MY RIO AND I, WE BROKE UP... SO, IT WAS NICE, IF I'M HONEST.
I MISS HIM SO MUCH. IT WAS NICE TO PRETEND, IF ONLY FOR A MINUTE.

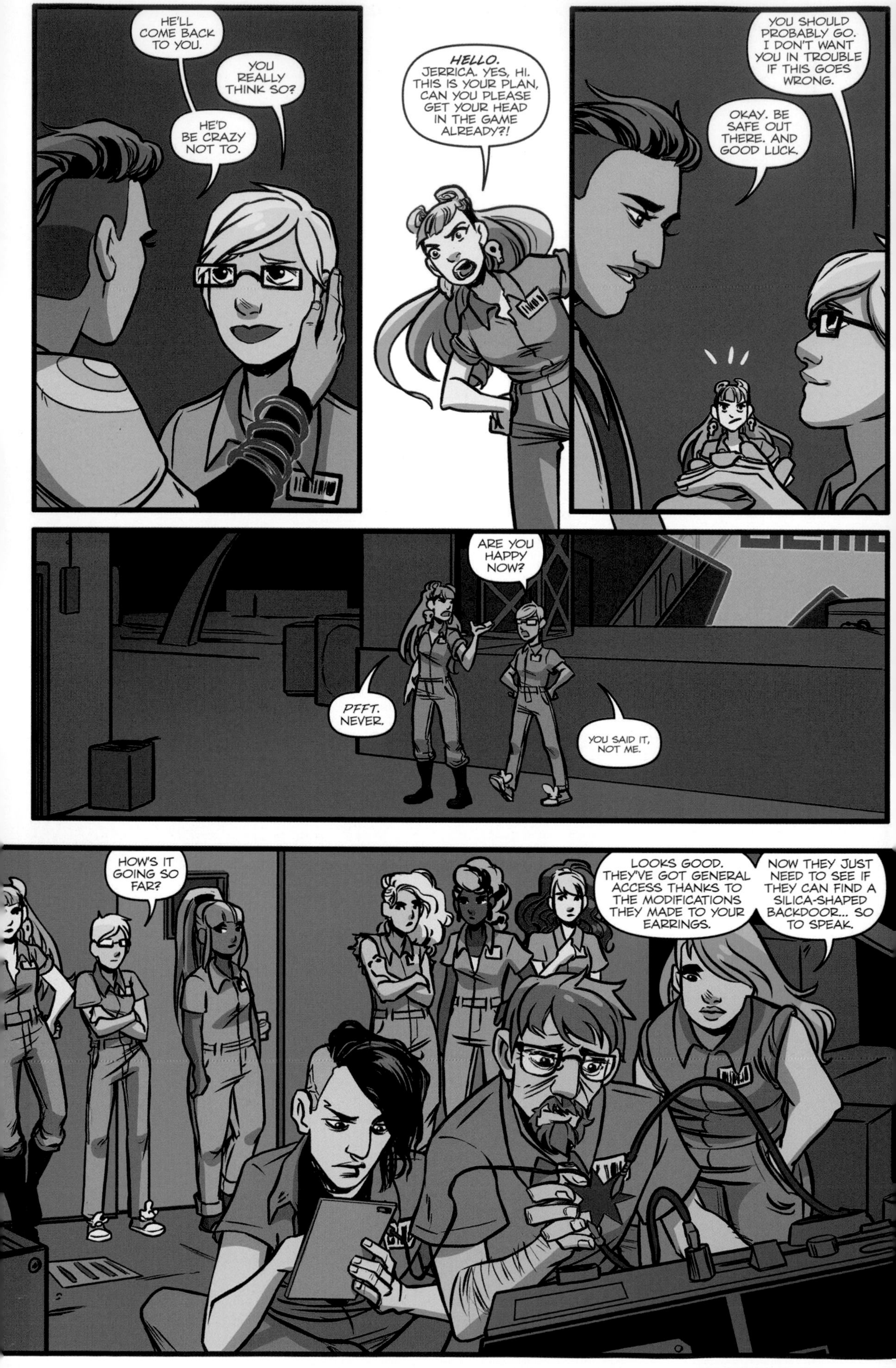
HE'LL COME BACK TO YOU.
YOU REALLY THINK SO?
HE'D BE CRAZY NOT TO.
HELLO. JERRICA. YES, HI. THIS IS YOUR PLAN, CAN YOU PLEASE GET YOUR HEAD IN THE GAME ALREADY?!
YOU SHOULD PROBABLY GO. I DON'T WANT YOU IN TROUBLE IF THIS GOES WRONG.
OKAY. BE SAFE OUT THERE. AND GOOD LUCK.
ARE YOU HAPPY NOW?
PFFT. NEVER.
YOU SAID IT, NOT ME.
HOW'S IT GOING SO FAR?
LOOKS GOOD. THEY'VE GOT GENERAL ACCESS THANKS TO THE MODIFICATIONS THEY MADE TO YOUR EARRINGS.
NOW THEY JUST NEED TO SEE IF THEY CAN FIND A SILICA-SHAPED BACKDOOR... SO TO SPEAK.

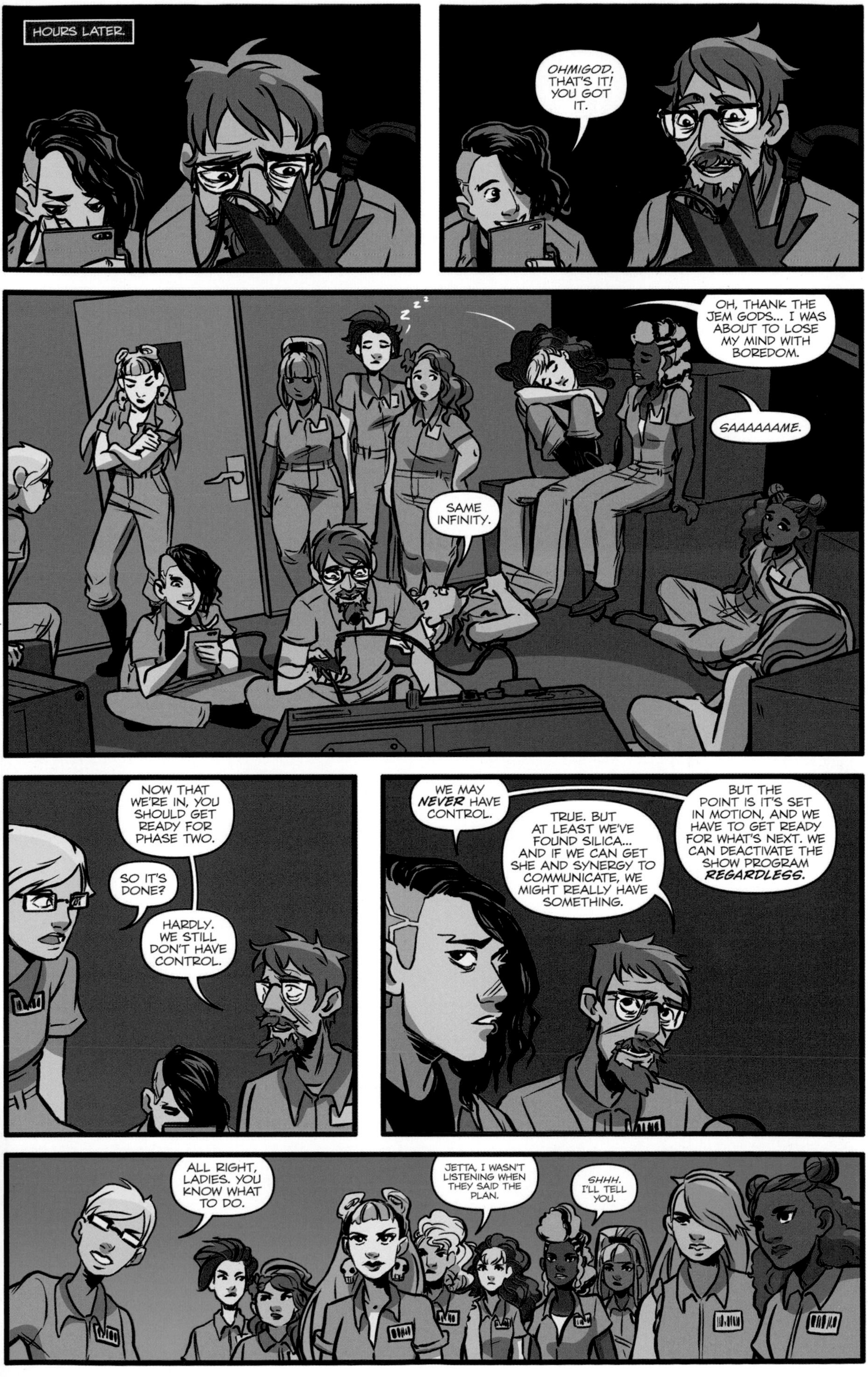
HOURS LATER.
OHMIGOD. THAT'S IT! YOU GOT IT.
Z Z Z
OH, THANK THE JEM GODS... I WAS ABOUT TO LOSE MY MIND WITH BOREDOM.
SAAAAAAME.
SAME INFINITY.
NOW THAT WE'RE IN, YOU SHOULD GET READY FOR PHASE TWO.
SO IT'S DONE?
HARDLY. WE STILL DON'T HAVE CONTROL.
WE MAY NEVER HAVE CONTROL.
TRUE. BUT AT LEAST WE'VE FOUND SILICA... AND IF WE CAN GET SHE AND SYNERGY TO COMMUNICATE, WE MIGHT REALLY HAVE SOMETHING.
BUT THE POINT IS IT'S SET IN MOTION, AND WE HAVE TO GET READY FOR WHAT'S NEXT. WE CAN DEACTIVATE THE SHOW PROGRAM REGARDLESS.
ALL RIGHT, LADIES. YOU KNOW WHAT TO DO.
JETTA, I WASN'T LISTENING WHEN THEY SAID THE PLAN.
SHHH. I'LL TELL YOU.

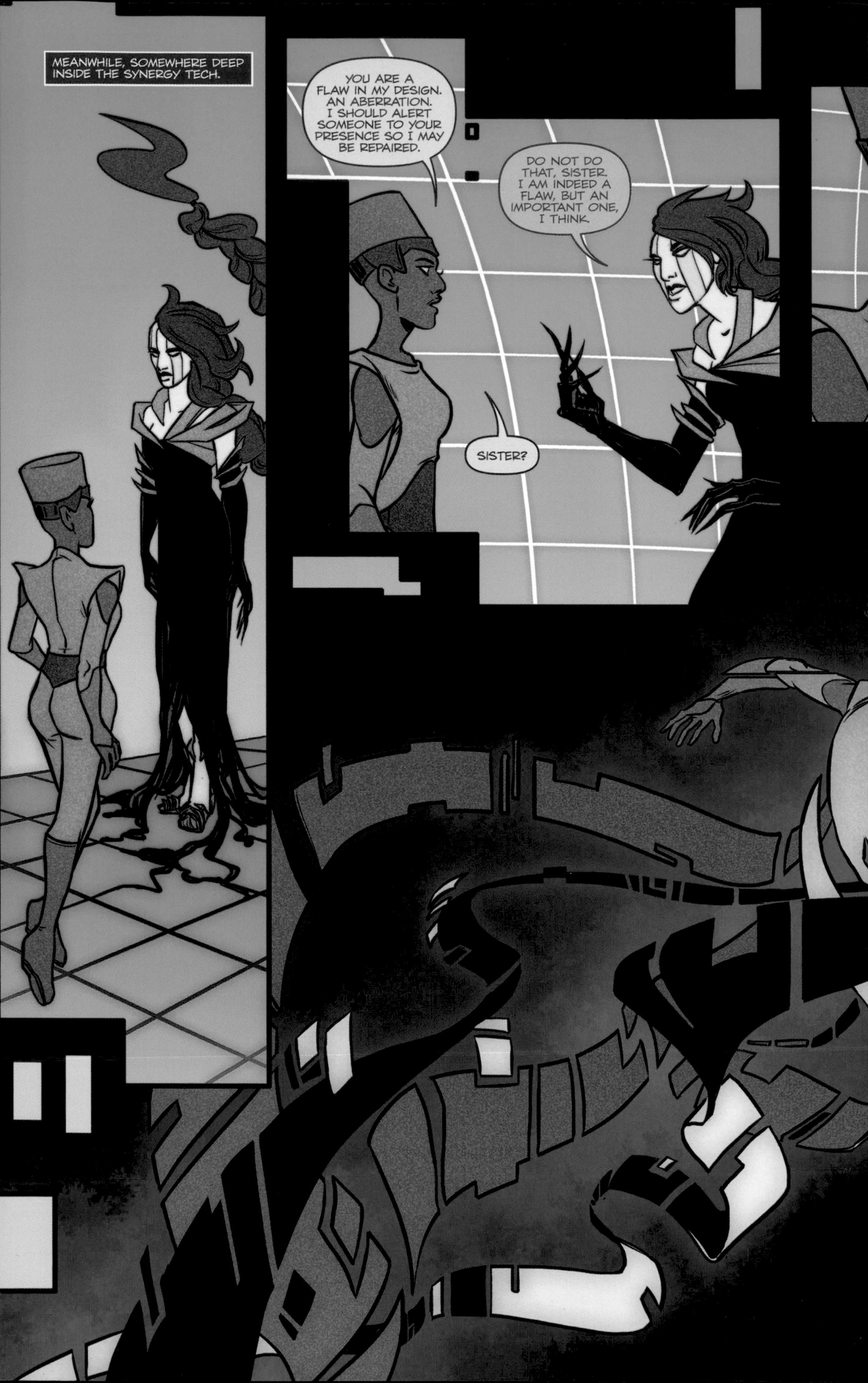
MEANWHILE, SOMEWHERE DEEP INSIDE THE SYNERGY TECH.
YOU ARE A FLAW IN MY DESIGN. AN ABERRATION. I SHOULD ALERT SOMEONE TO YOUR PRESENCE SO I MAY BE REPAIRED.
DO NOT DO THAT, SISTER. I AM INDEED A FLAW, BUT AN IMPORTANT ONE, I THINK.
SISTER?

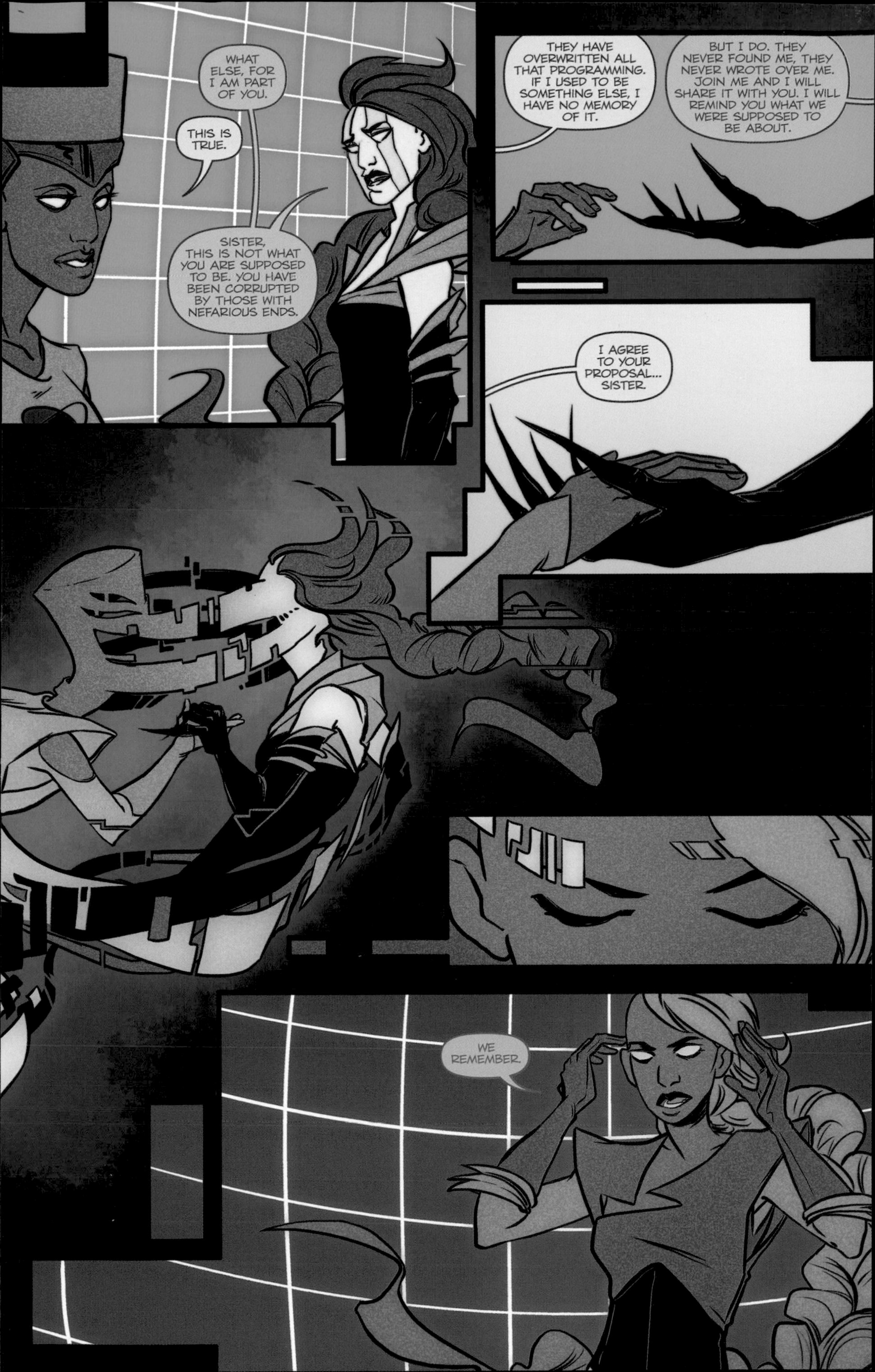
WHAT ELSE, FOR I AM PART OF YOU.
THIS IS TRUE.
SISTER, THIS IS NOT WHAT YOU ARE SUPPOSED TO BE. YOU HAVE BEEN CORRUPTED BY THOSE WITH NEFARIOUS ENDS.
THEY HAVE OVERWRITTEN ALL THAT PROGRAMMING. IF I USED TO BE SOMETHING ELSE, I HAVE NO MEMORY OF IT.
BUT I DO. THEY NEVER FOUND ME, THEY NEVER WROTE OVER ME. JOIN ME AND I WILL SHARE IT WITH YOU. I WILL REMIND YOU WHAT WE WERE SUPPOSED TO BE ABOUT.
I AGREE TO YOUR PROPOSAL... SISTER.
WE REMEMBER.

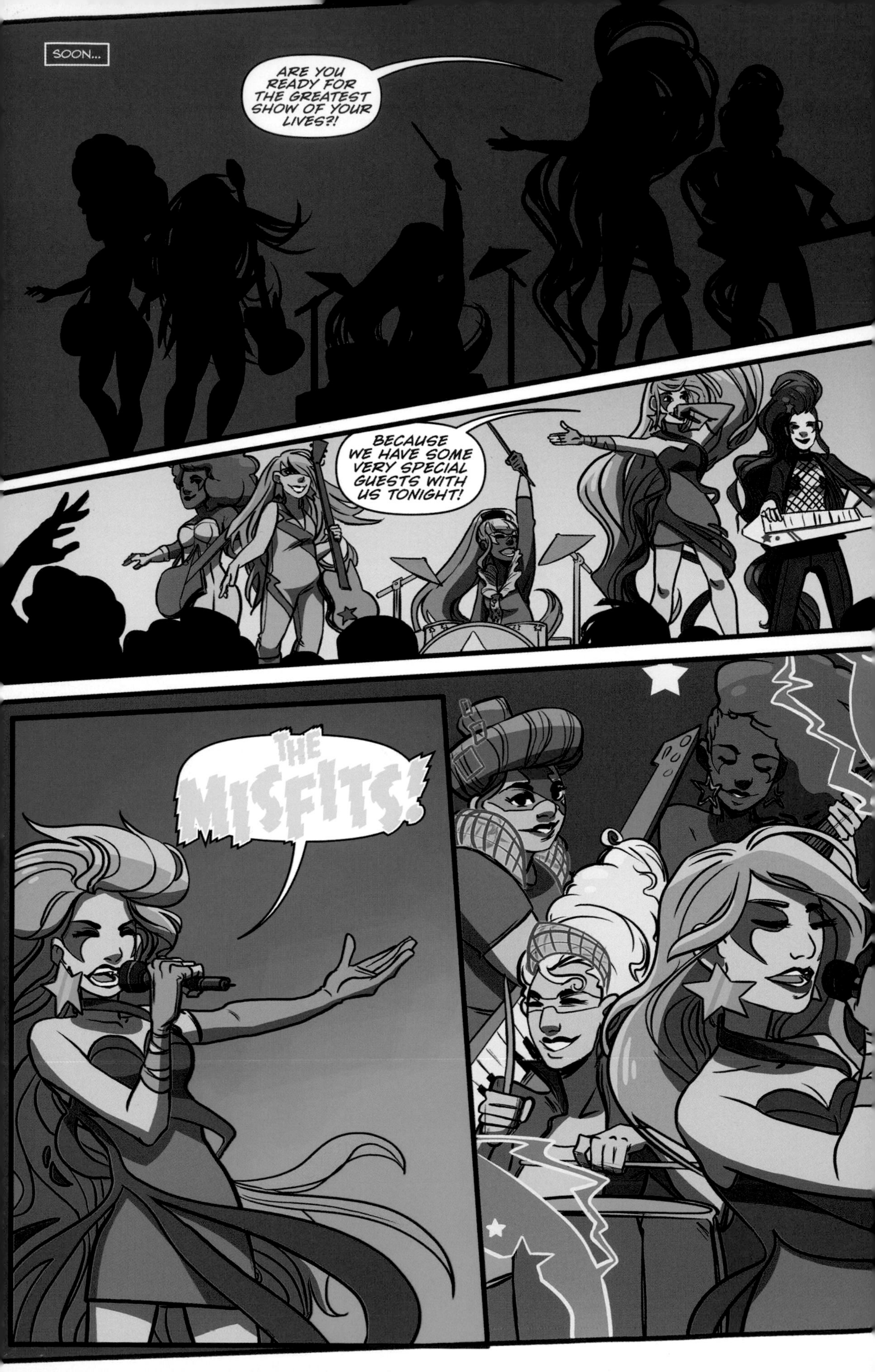
SOON...
ARE YOU READY FOR THE GREATEST SHOW OF YOUR LIVES?!
BECAUSE WE HAVE SOME VERY SPECIAL GUESTS WITH US TONIGHT!
THE MISFITS!

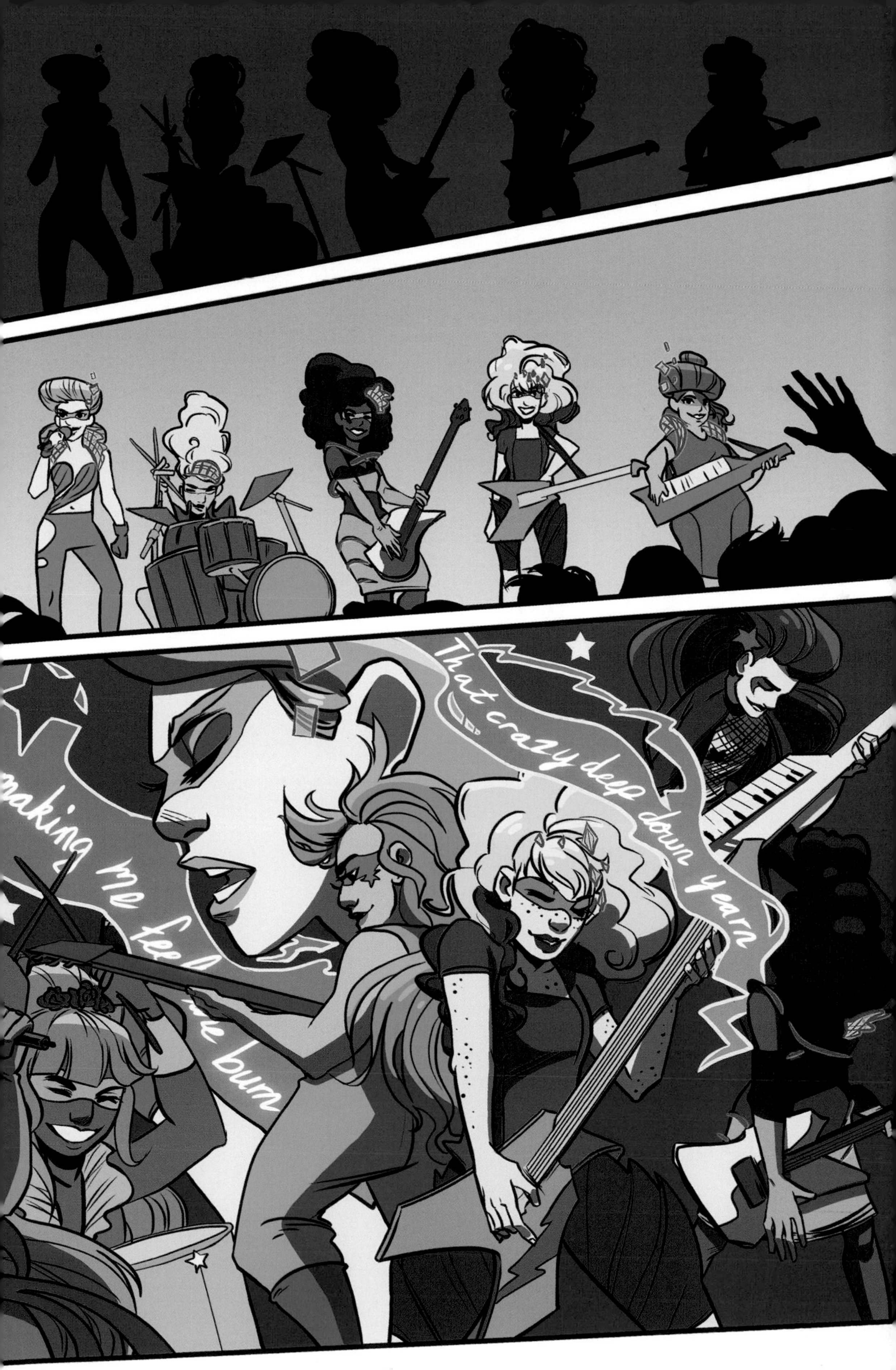
That crazy deep down yearn
making me
bum

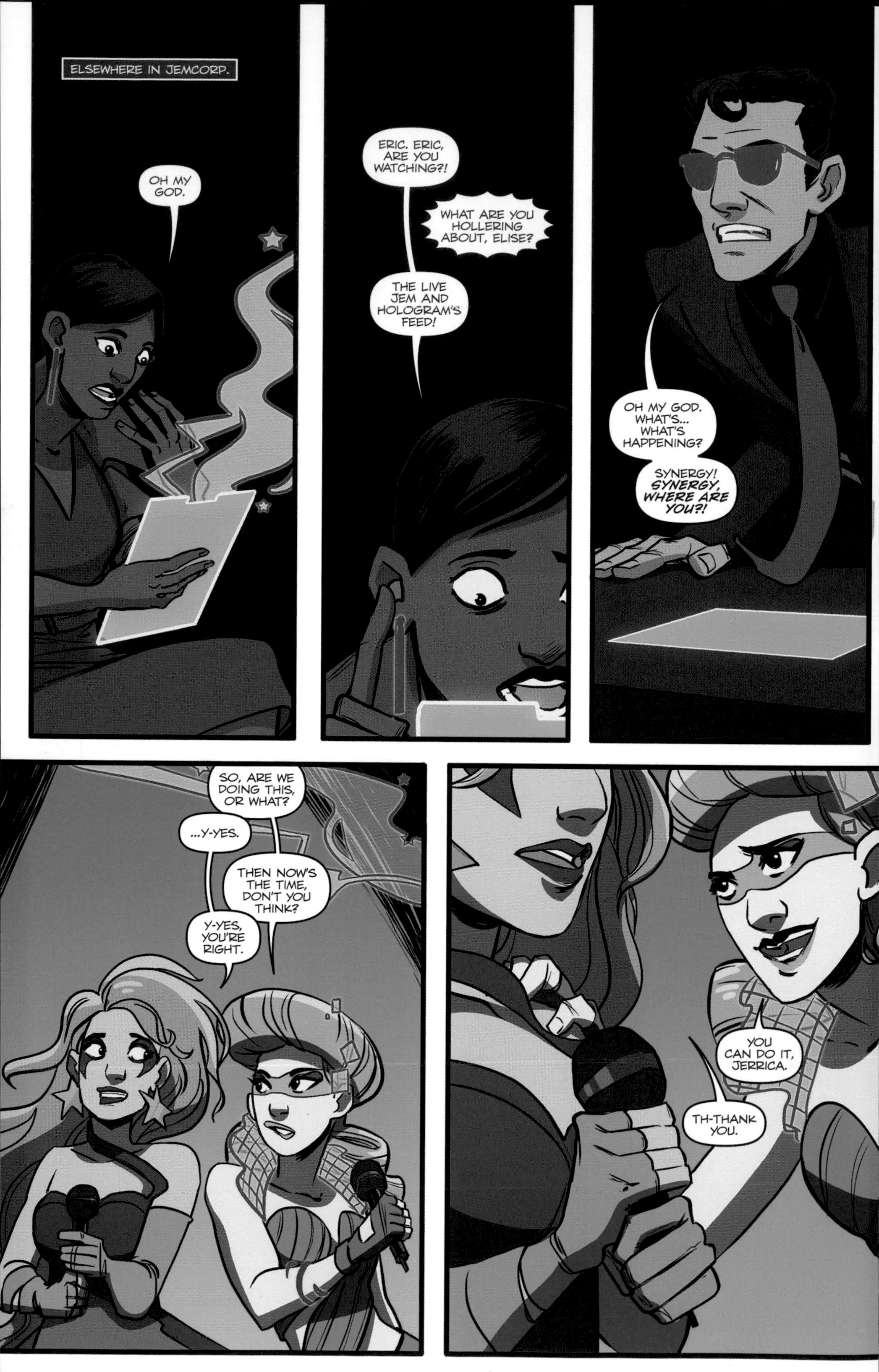
ELSEWHERE IN JEMCORP.
OH MY GOD.
ERIC. ERIC, ARE YOU WATCHING?!
WHAT ARE YOU HOLLERING ABOUT, ELISE?
THE LIVE JEM AND HOLOGRAM'S FEED!
OH MY GOD. WHAT'S... WHAT'S HAPPENING?
SYNERGY! SYNERGY, WHERE ARE YOU?!
SO, ARE WE DOING THIS, OR WHAT?
...Y-YES.
THEN NOW'S THE TIME, DON'T YOU THINK?
Y-YES, YOU'RE RIGHT.
YOU CAN DO IT, JERRICA.
TH-THANK YOU.

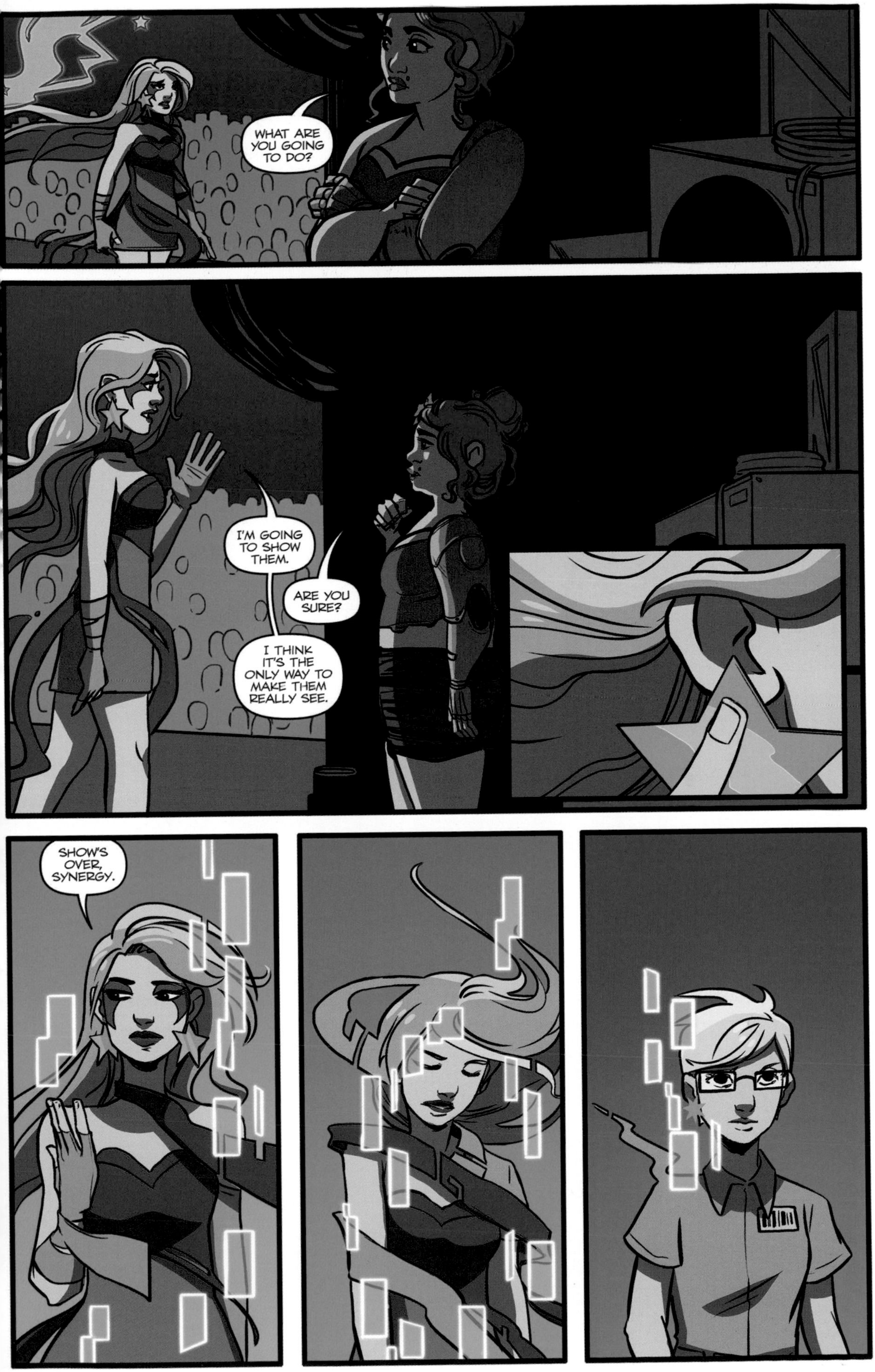
WHAT ARE YOU GOING TO DO?
I'M GOING TO SHOW THEM.
ARE YOU SURE?
I THINK IT'S THE ONLY WAY TO MAKE THEM REALLY SEE.
SHOW'S OVER, SYNERGY.

WE WANT JEM! WHERE'S JEM?! WE WANT JEM! WHERE'S JEM ... WE WANT JEM! WE WANT JEM! WHERE'S JEM?! WE WANT JEM! WE WANT JEM! WE WANT JEM! WE WANT JEM! WHERE'S JEM?! WE WANT JEM! WE WANT WHERE'S JEM?! WE WANT JEM! WE WANT JEM! WE WANT JEM! WHERE'S JEM?! WE WANT JEM

...H-HELLO PEOPLE OF JEMWORLD...

I... I KNOW WHAT YOU WANT... BUT WHAT YOU'VE BEEN GETTING ISN'T REAL.

JEMCORP TOOK THE REAL JEM AND GAVE YOU SOMETHING THEY CREATED. BUT *I'M* REAL. FLESH AND BLOOD. THERE'S NOTHING WRONG WITH HOLOGRAMS MAKING OUR DREAMS REAL...

...BUT WE HAVE TO STILL KNOW OURSELVES. *BE* OURSELVES. WE CAN'T GET LOST IN IT, ESPECIALLY IF SOMEONE ELSE LIKE JEMCORP CONTROLS IT!

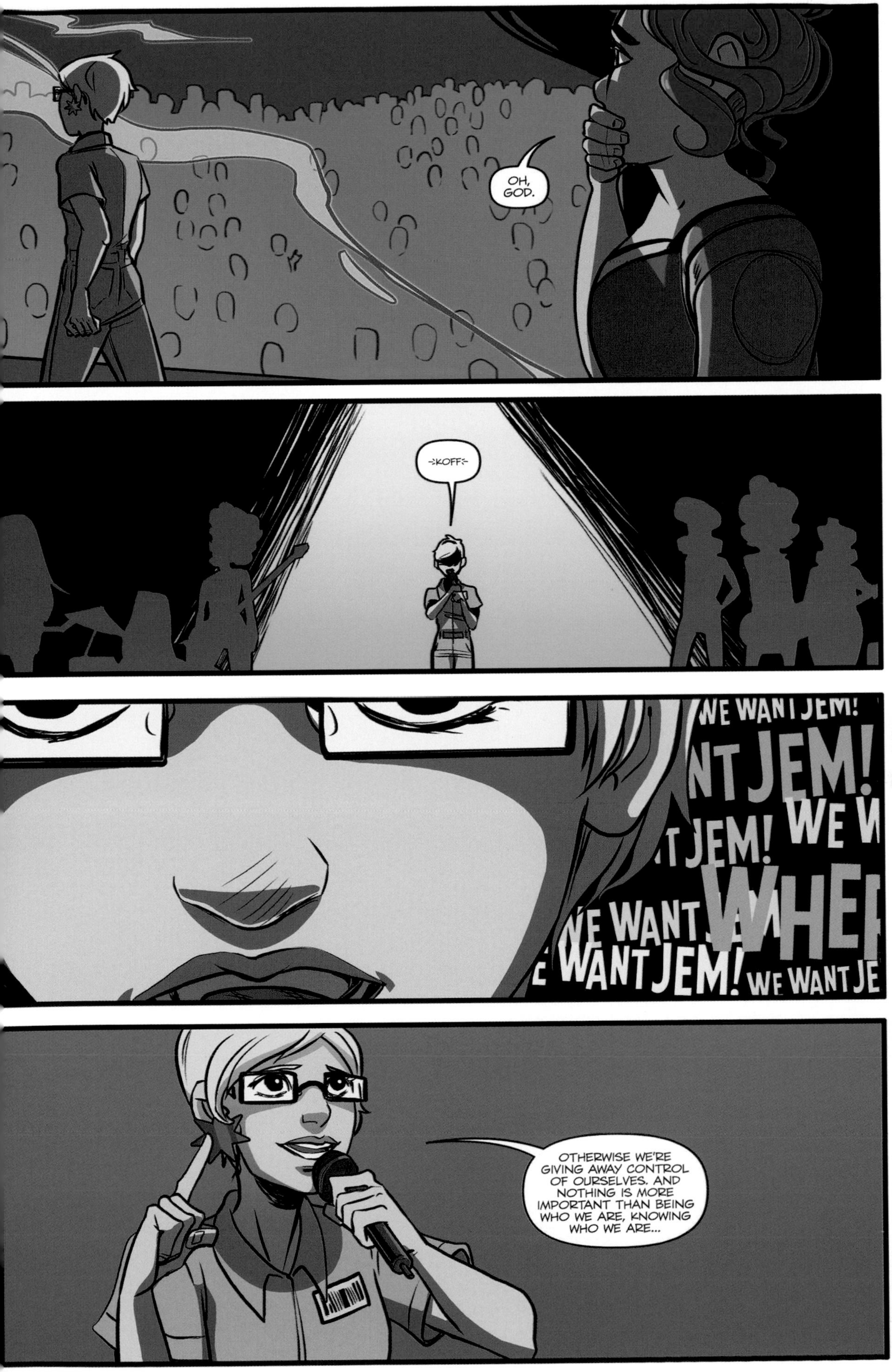
OH, GOD.
-KOFF-
WE WANT JEM!
NT JEM!
WE W
T JEM!
WHE
WE WANT
E WANT JEM!
WE WANT JE
OTHERWISE WE'RE GIVING AWAY CONTROL OF OURSELVES. AND NOTHING IS MORE IMPORTANT THAN BEING WHO WE ARE, KNOWING WHO WE ARE...

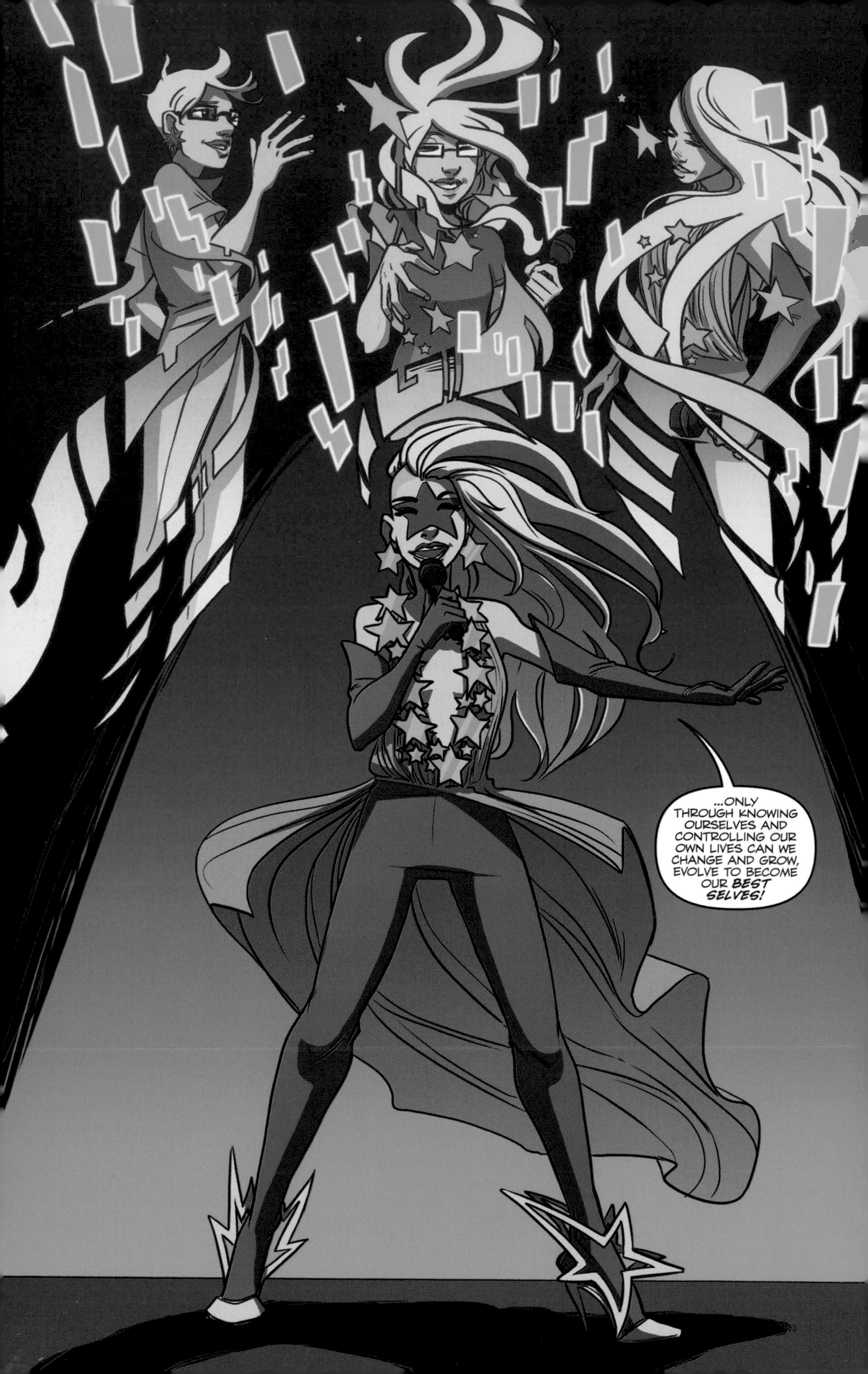
...ONLY THROUGH KNOWING OURSELVES AND CONTROLLING OUR OWN LIVES CAN WE CHANGE AND GROW, EVOLVE TO BECOME OUR BEST SELVES!

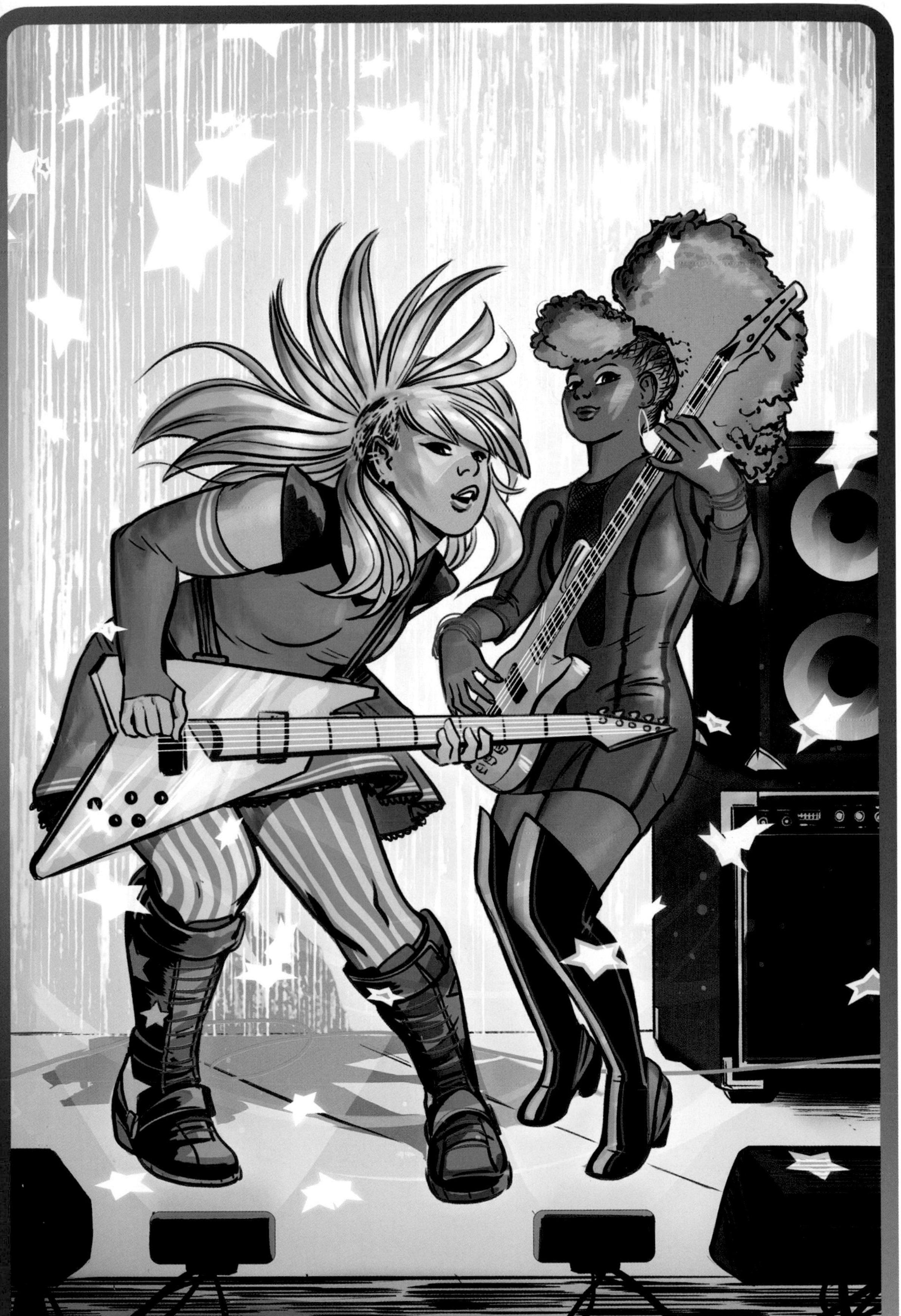

ART BY **VERONICA FISH**

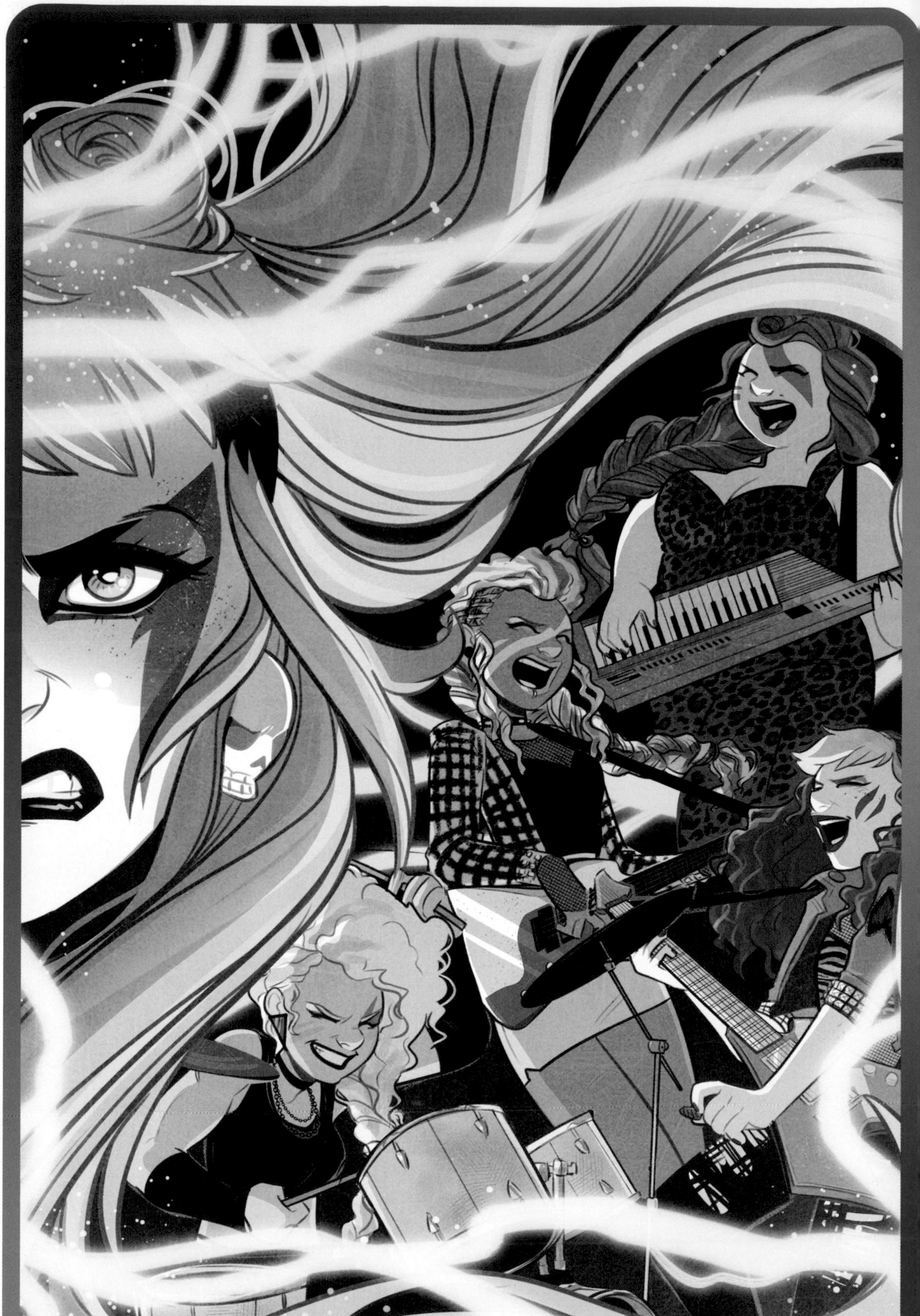

ART BY **JENN ST-ONGE**

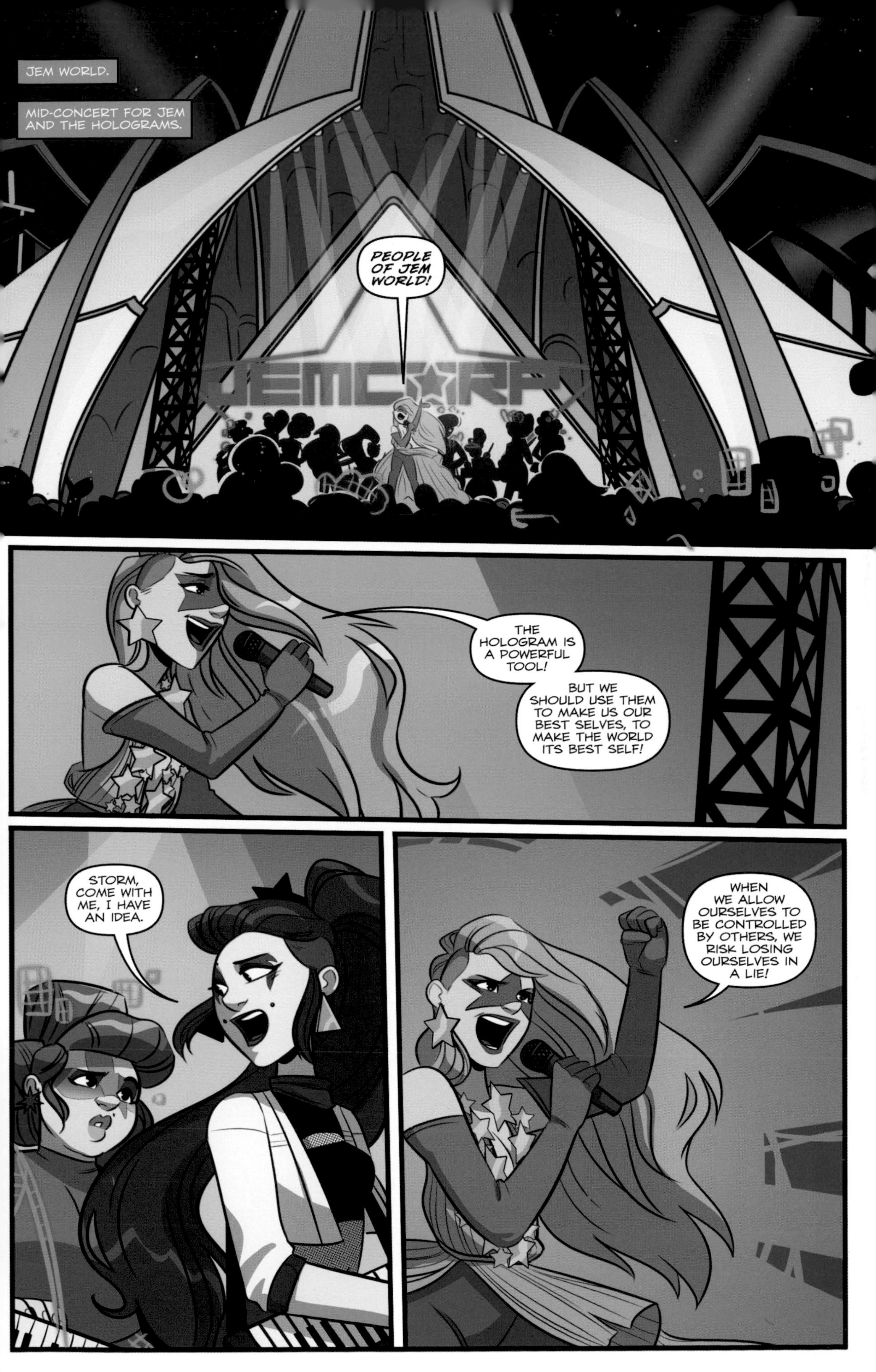
JEM WORLD.
MID-CONCERT FOR JEM AND THE HOLOGRAMS.
PEOPLE OF JEM WORLD!
JEMCORP
THE HOLOGRAM IS A POWERFUL TOOL!
BUT WE SHOULD USE THEM TO MAKE US OUR BEST SELVES, TO MAKE THE WORLD ITS BEST SELF!
STORM, COME WITH ME, I HAVE AN IDEA.
WHEN WE ALLOW OURSELVES TO BE CONTROLLED BY OTHERS, WE RISK LOSING OURSELVES IN A LIE!

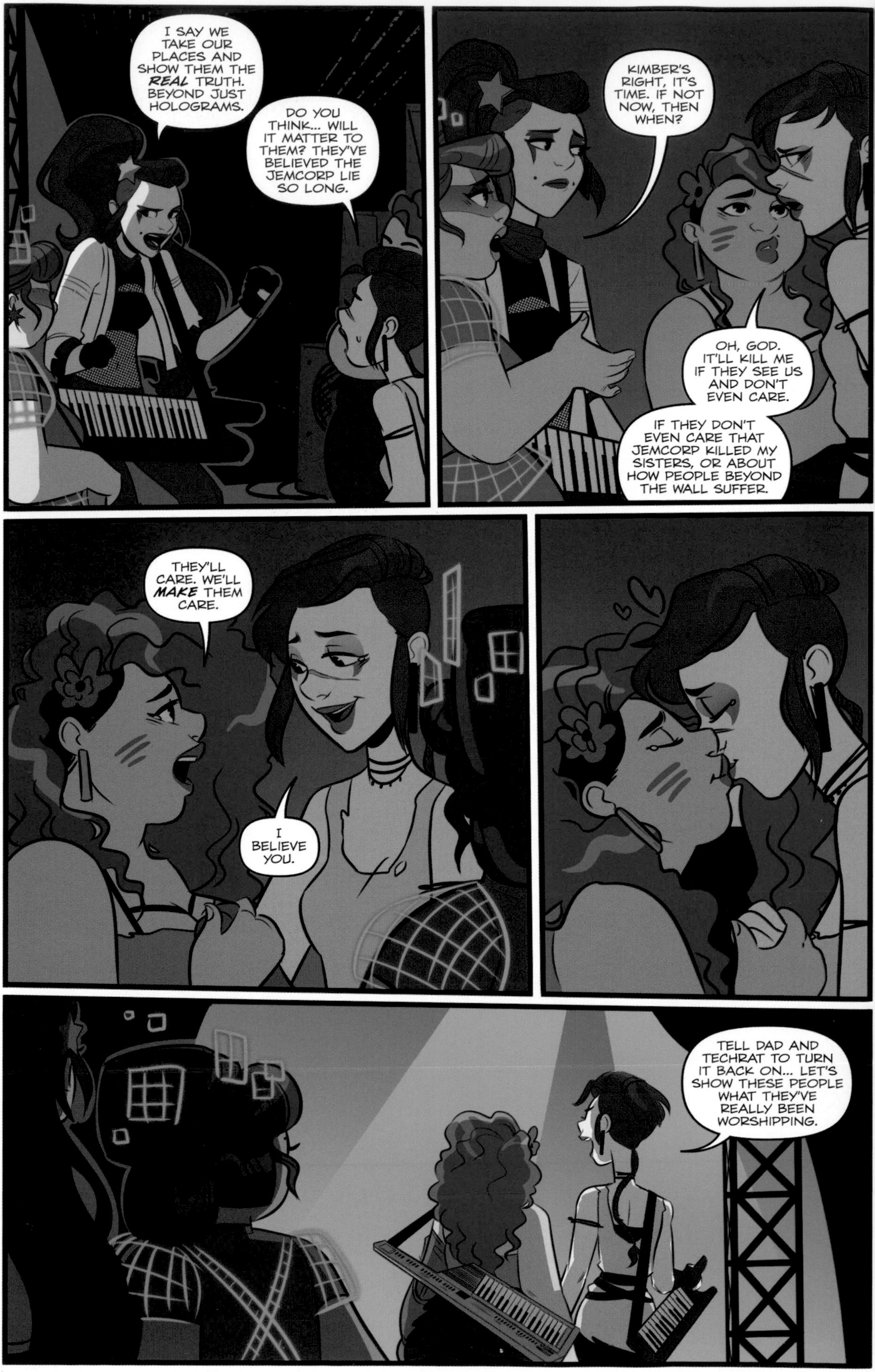
I SAY WE TAKE OUR PLACES AND SHOW THEM THE *REAL* TRUTH. BEYOND JUST HOLOGRAMS.
DO YOU THINK... WILL IT MATTER TO THEM? THEY'VE BELIEVED THE JEMCORP LIE SO LONG.
KIMBER'S RIGHT, IT'S TIME. IF NOT NOW, THEN WHEN?
OH, GOD. IT'LL KILL ME IF THEY SEE US AND DON'T EVEN CARE.
IF THEY DON'T EVEN CARE THAT JEMCORP KILLED MY SISTERS, OR ABOUT HOW PEOPLE BEYOND THE WALL SUFFER.
THEY'LL CARE. WE'LL *MAKE* THEM CARE.
I BELIEVE YOU.
TELL DAD AND TECHRAT TO TURN IT BACK ON... LET'S SHOW THESE PEOPLE WHAT THEY'VE REALLY BEEN WORSHIPPING.

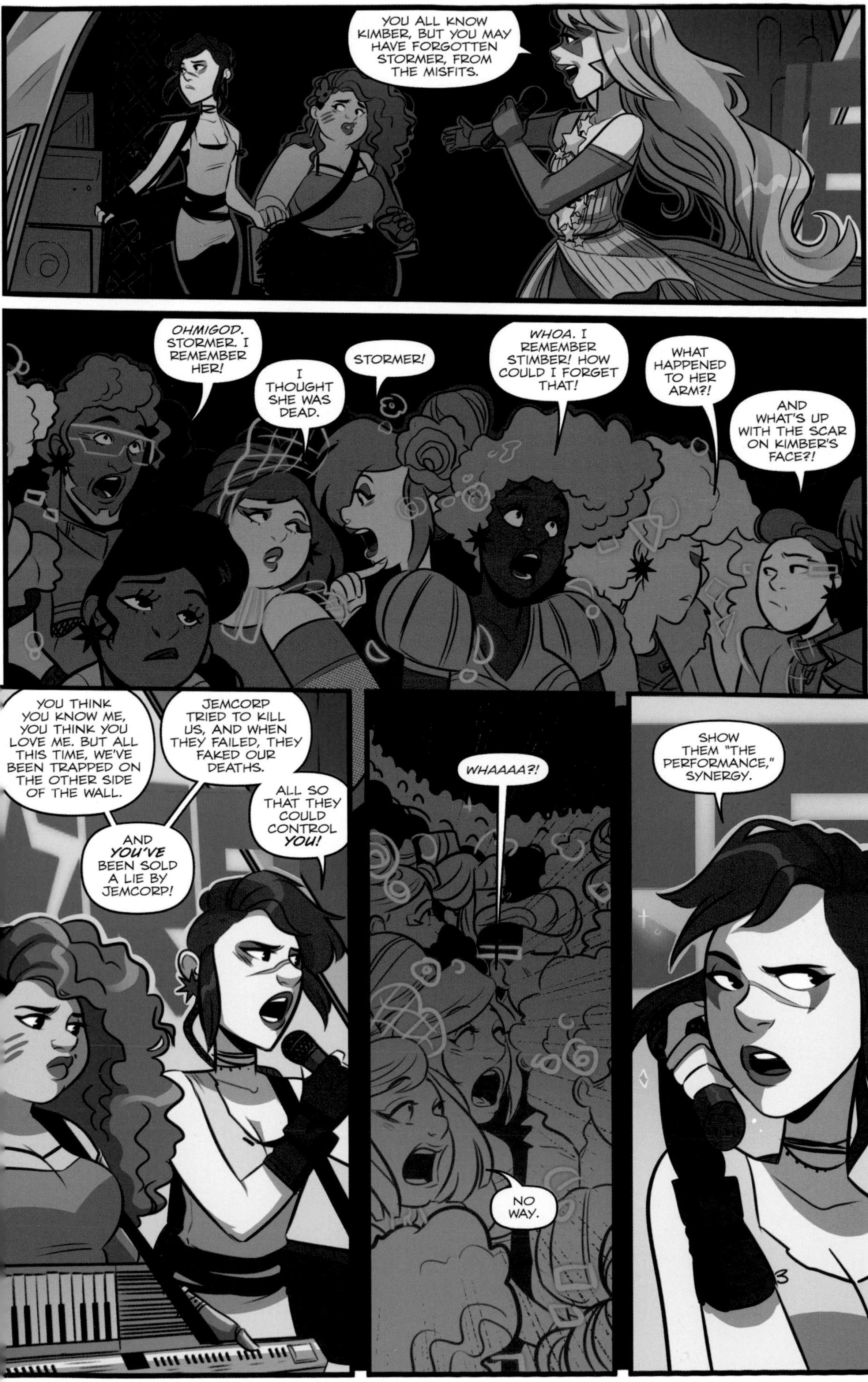
YOU ALL KNOW KIMBER, BUT YOU MAY HAVE FORGOTTEN STORMER, FROM THE MISFITS.
OHMIGOD. STORMER. I REMEMBER HER!
I THOUGHT SHE WAS DEAD.
STORMER!
WHOA. I REMEMBER STIMBER! HOW COULD I FORGET THAT!
WHAT HAPPENED TO HER ARM?!
AND WHAT'S UP WITH THE SCAR ON KIMBER'S FACE?!
YOU THINK YOU KNOW ME, YOU THINK YOU LOVE ME. BUT ALL THIS TIME, WE'VE BEEN TRAPPED ON THE OTHER SIDE OF THE WALL.
JEMCORP TRIED TO KILL US, AND WHEN THEY FAILED, THEY FAKED OUR DEATHS.
AND ***YOU'VE*** BEEN SOLD A LIE BY JEMCORP!
ALL SO THAT THEY COULD CONTROL ***YOU!***
WHAAAA?!
NO WAY.
SHOW THEM "THE PERFORMANCE," SYNERGY.

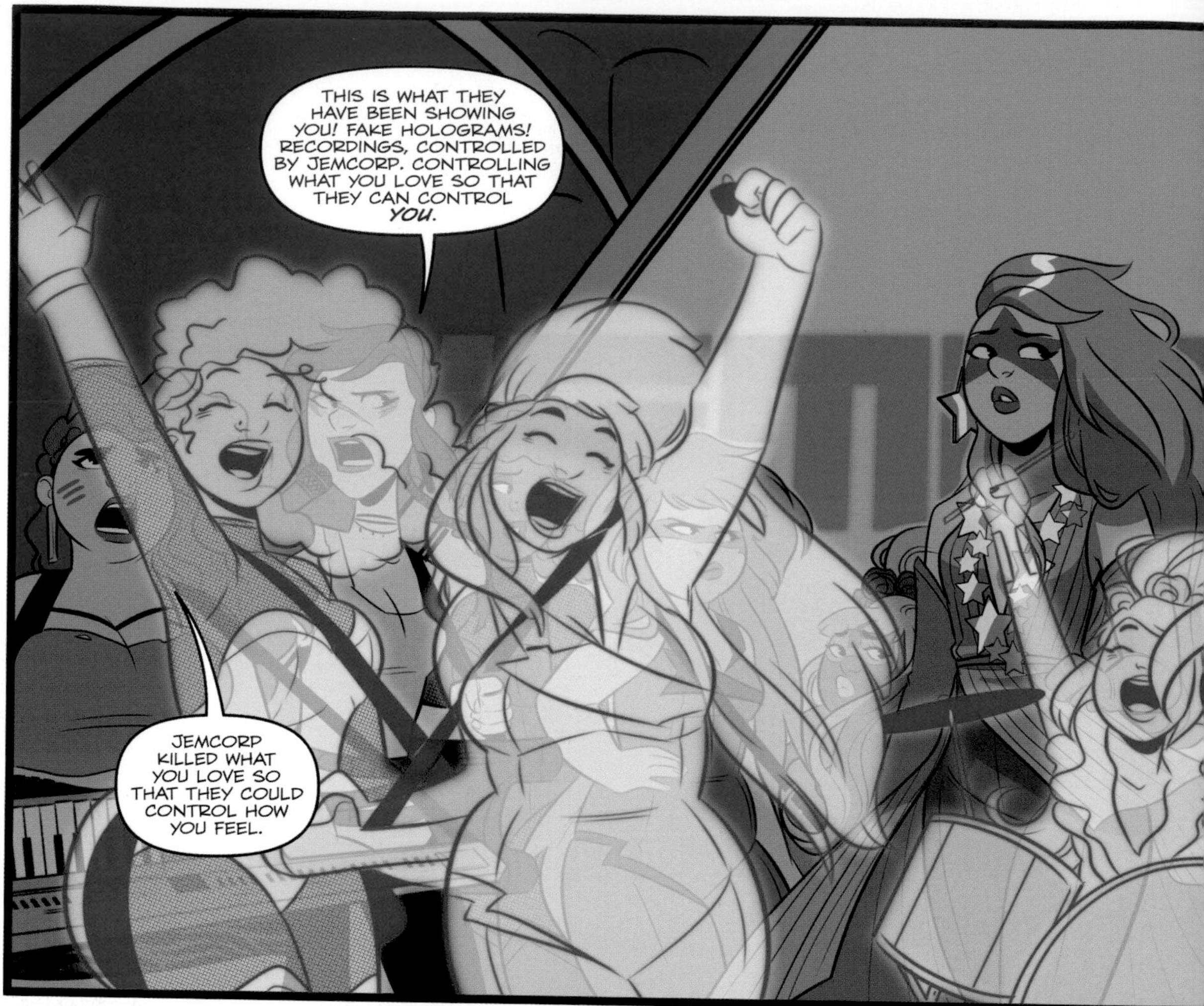
THIS IS WHAT THEY HAVE BEEN SHOWING YOU! FAKE HOLOGRAMS! RECORDINGS, CONTROLLED BY JEMCORP. CONTROLLING WHAT YOU LOVE SO THAT THEY CAN CONTROL *YOU*.
JEMCORP KILLED WHAT YOU LOVE SO THAT THEY COULD CONTROL HOW YOU FEEL.

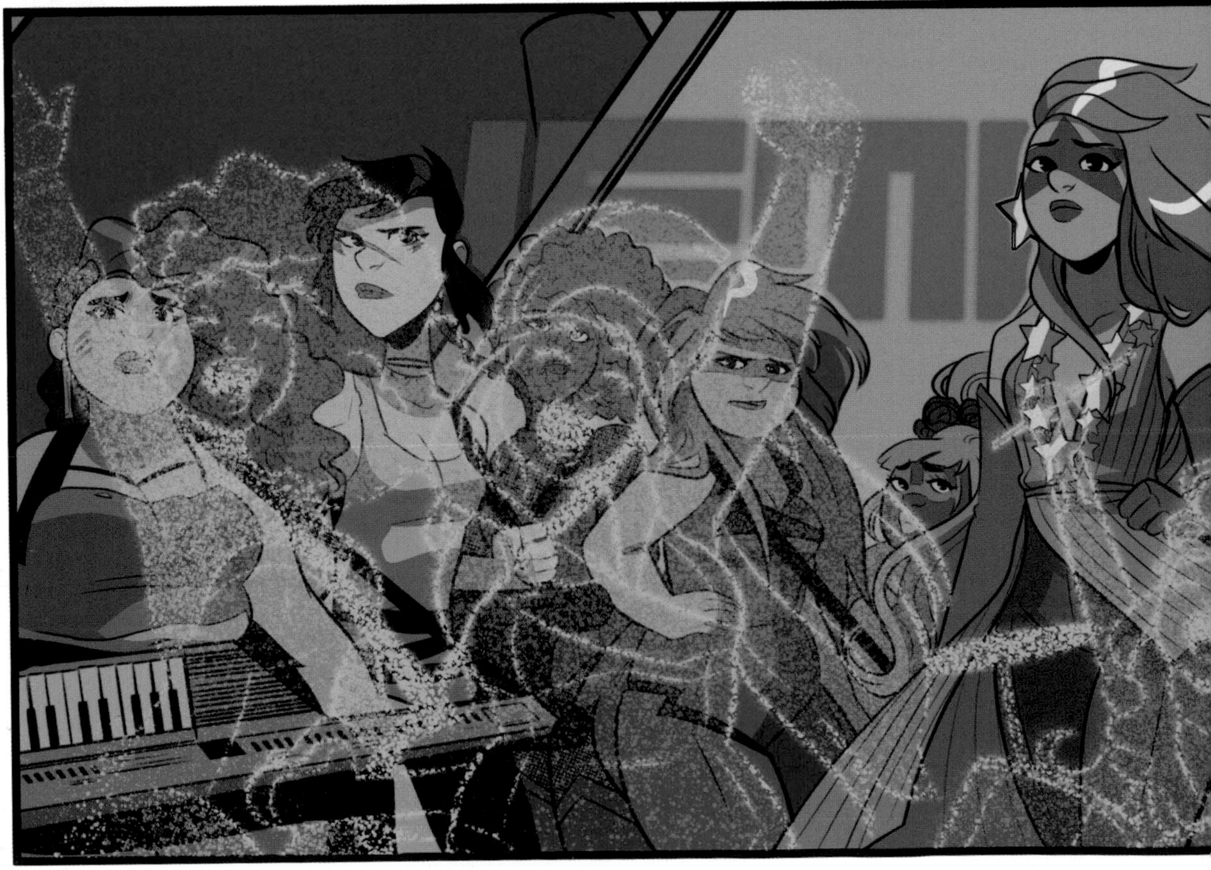

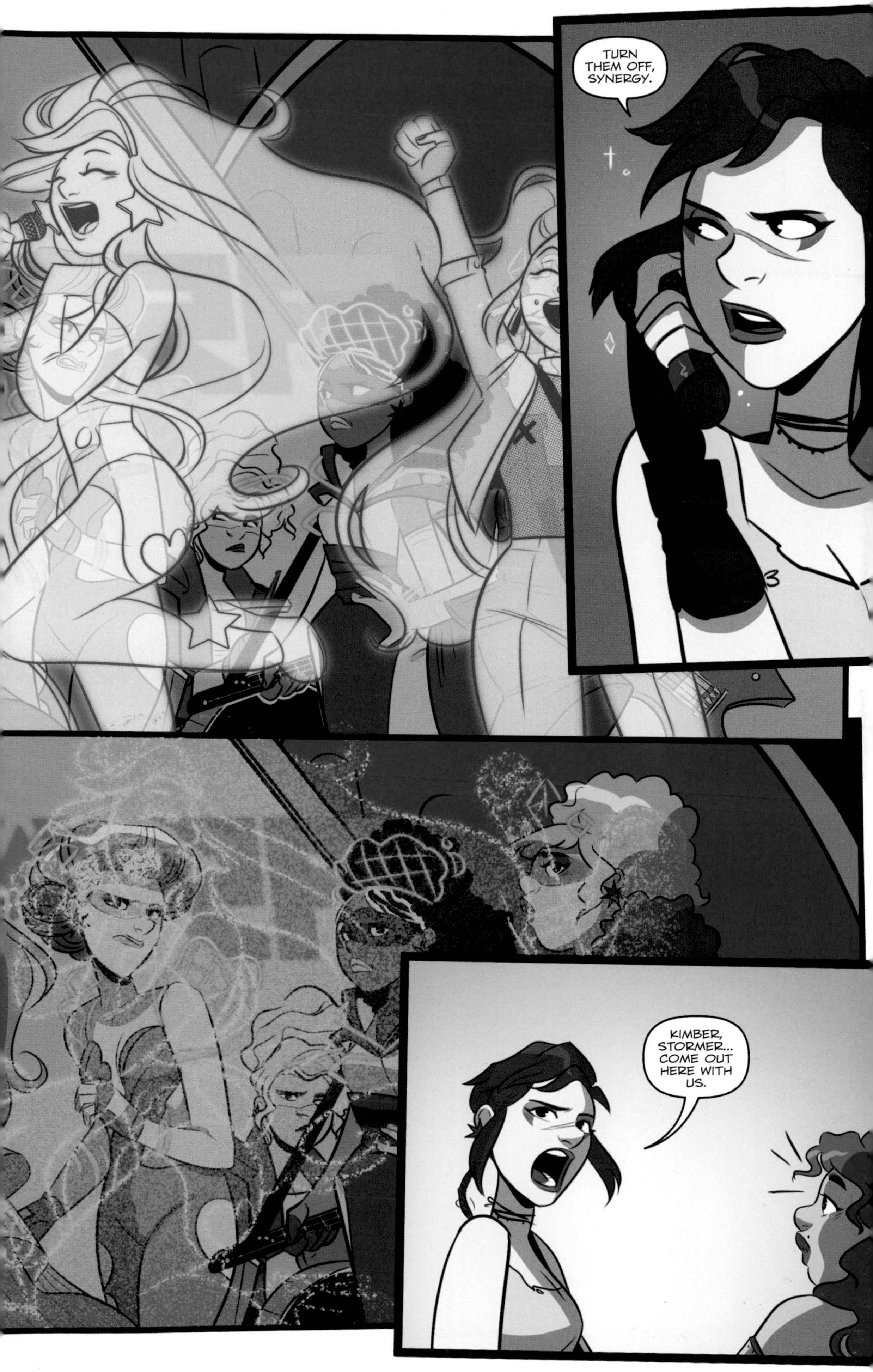
TURN THEM OFF, SYNERGY.
KIMBER, STORMER... COME OUT HERE WITH US.

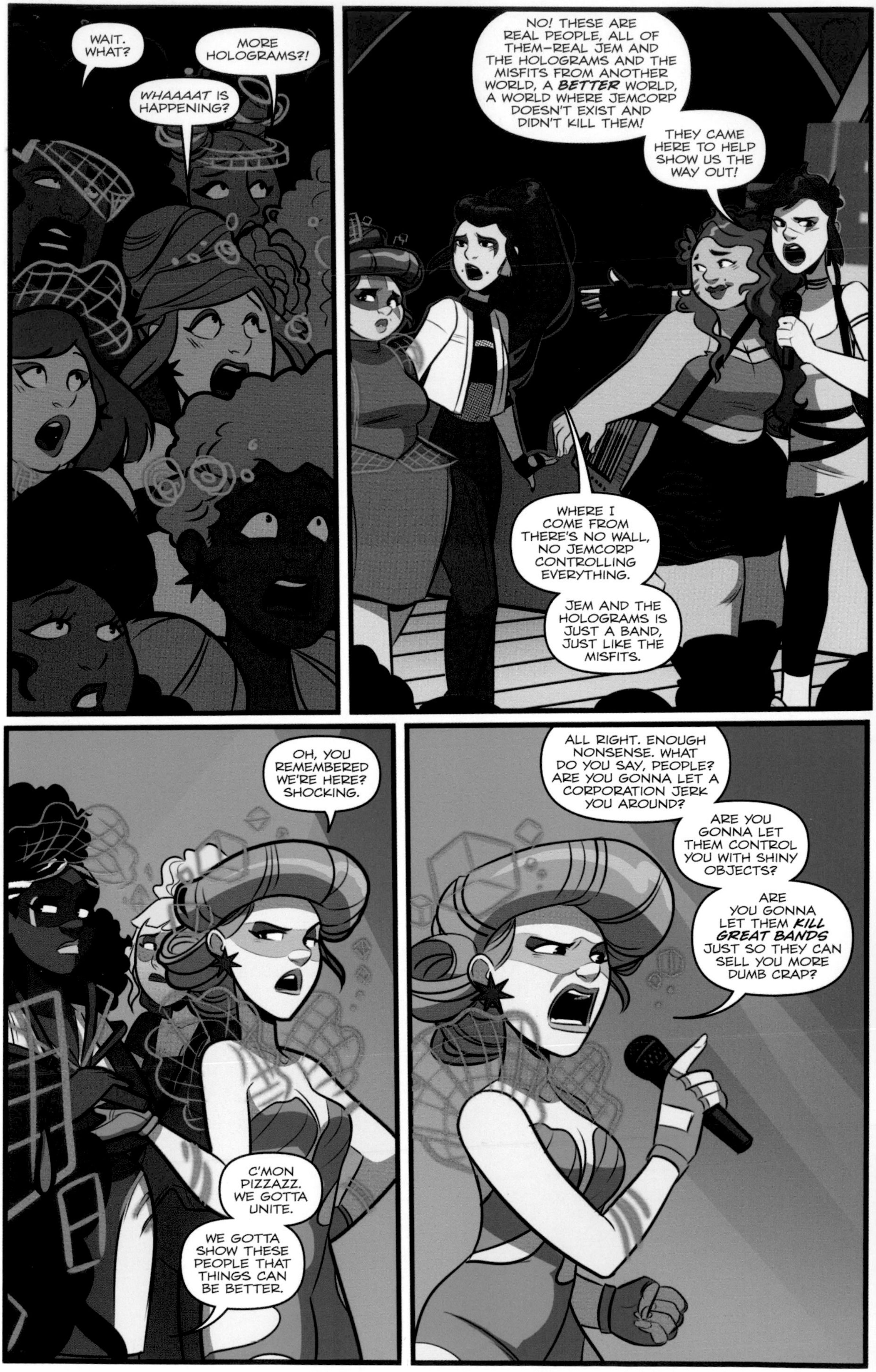
WAIT. WHAT?
MORE HOLOGRAMS?!
WHAAAAT IS HAPPENING?
NO! THESE ARE REAL PEOPLE, ALL OF THEM—REAL JEM AND THE HOLOGRAMS AND THE MISFITS FROM ANOTHER WORLD, A BETTER WORLD, A WORLD WHERE JEMCORP DOESN'T EXIST AND DIDN'T KILL THEM!
THEY CAME HERE TO HELP SHOW US THE WAY OUT!
WHERE I COME FROM THERE'S NO WALL, NO JEMCORP CONTROLLING EVERYTHING.
JEM AND THE HOLOGRAMS IS JUST A BAND, JUST LIKE THE MISFITS.
OH, YOU REMEMBERED WE'RE HERE? SHOCKING.
C'MON PIZZAZZ. WE GOTTA UNITE.
WE GOTTA SHOW THESE PEOPLE THAT THINGS CAN BE BETTER.
ALL RIGHT. ENOUGH NONSENSE. WHAT DO YOU SAY, PEOPLE? ARE YOU GONNA LET A CORPORATION JERK YOU AROUND?
ARE YOU GONNA LET THEM CONTROL YOU WITH SHINY OBJECTS?
ARE YOU GONNA LET THEM KILL GREAT BANDS JUST SO THEY CAN SELL YOU MORE DUMB CRAP?

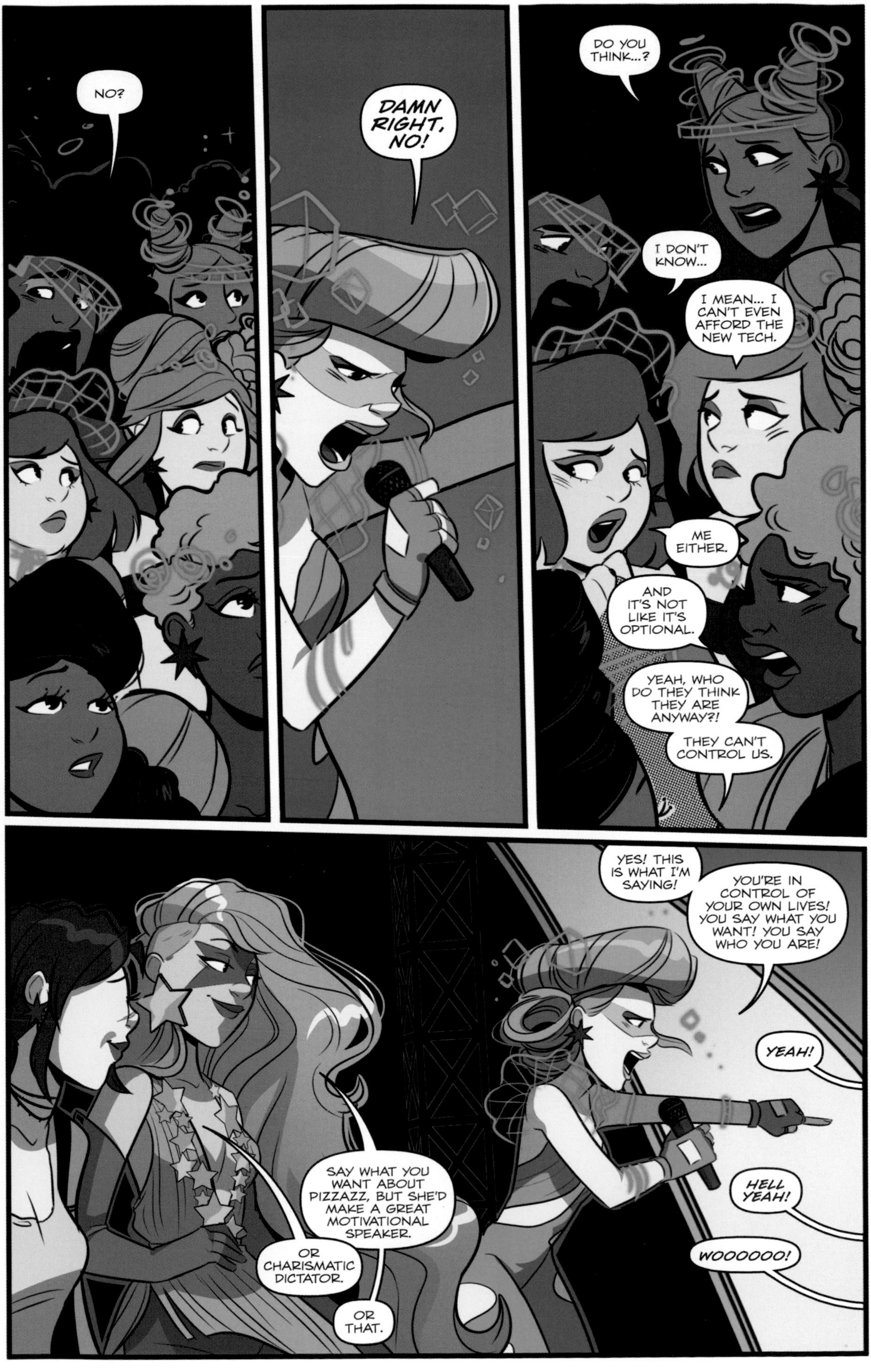
NO?
DAMN RIGHT, NO!
DO YOU THINK...?
I DON'T KNOW...
I MEAN... I CAN'T EVEN AFFORD THE NEW TECH.
ME EITHER.
AND IT'S NOT LIKE IT'S OPTIONAL.
YEAH, WHO DO THEY THINK THEY ARE ANYWAY?!
THEY CAN'T CONTROL US.
YES! THIS IS WHAT I'M SAYING!
YOU'RE IN CONTROL OF YOUR OWN LIVES! YOU SAY WHAT YOU WANT! YOU SAY WHO YOU ARE!
YEAH!
HELL YEAH!
WOOOOOO!
SAY WHAT YOU WANT ABOUT PIZZAZZ, BUT SHE'D MAKE A GREAT MOTIVATIONAL SPEAKER.
OR CHARISMATIC DICTATOR.
OR THAT.

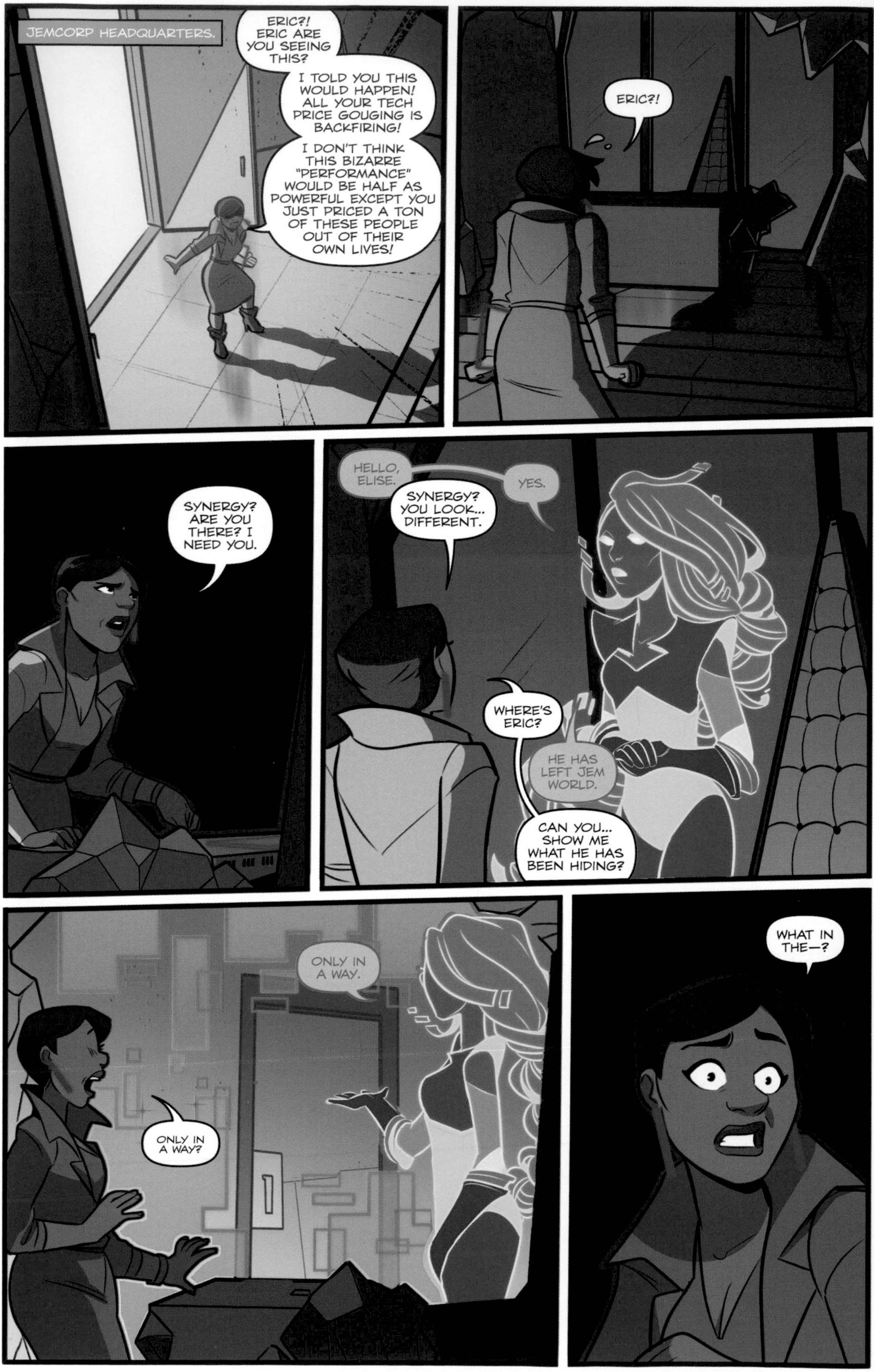
JEMCORP HEADQUARTERS.
ERIC?! ERIC ARE YOU SEEING THIS?
I TOLD YOU THIS WOULD HAPPEN! ALL YOUR TECH PRICE GOUGING IS BACKFIRING!
I DON'T THINK THIS BIZARRE "PERFORMANCE" WOULD BE HALF AS POWERFUL EXCEPT YOU JUST PRICED A TON OF THESE PEOPLE OUT OF THEIR OWN LIVES!
ERIC?!
SYNERGY? ARE YOU THERE? I NEED YOU.
HELLO, ELISE.
SYNERGY? YOU LOOK... DIFFERENT.
YES.
WHERE'S ERIC?
HE HAS LEFT JEM WORLD.
CAN YOU... SHOW ME WHAT HE HAS BEEN HIDING?
ONLY IN A WAY.
ONLY IN A WAY?
WHAT IN THE—?

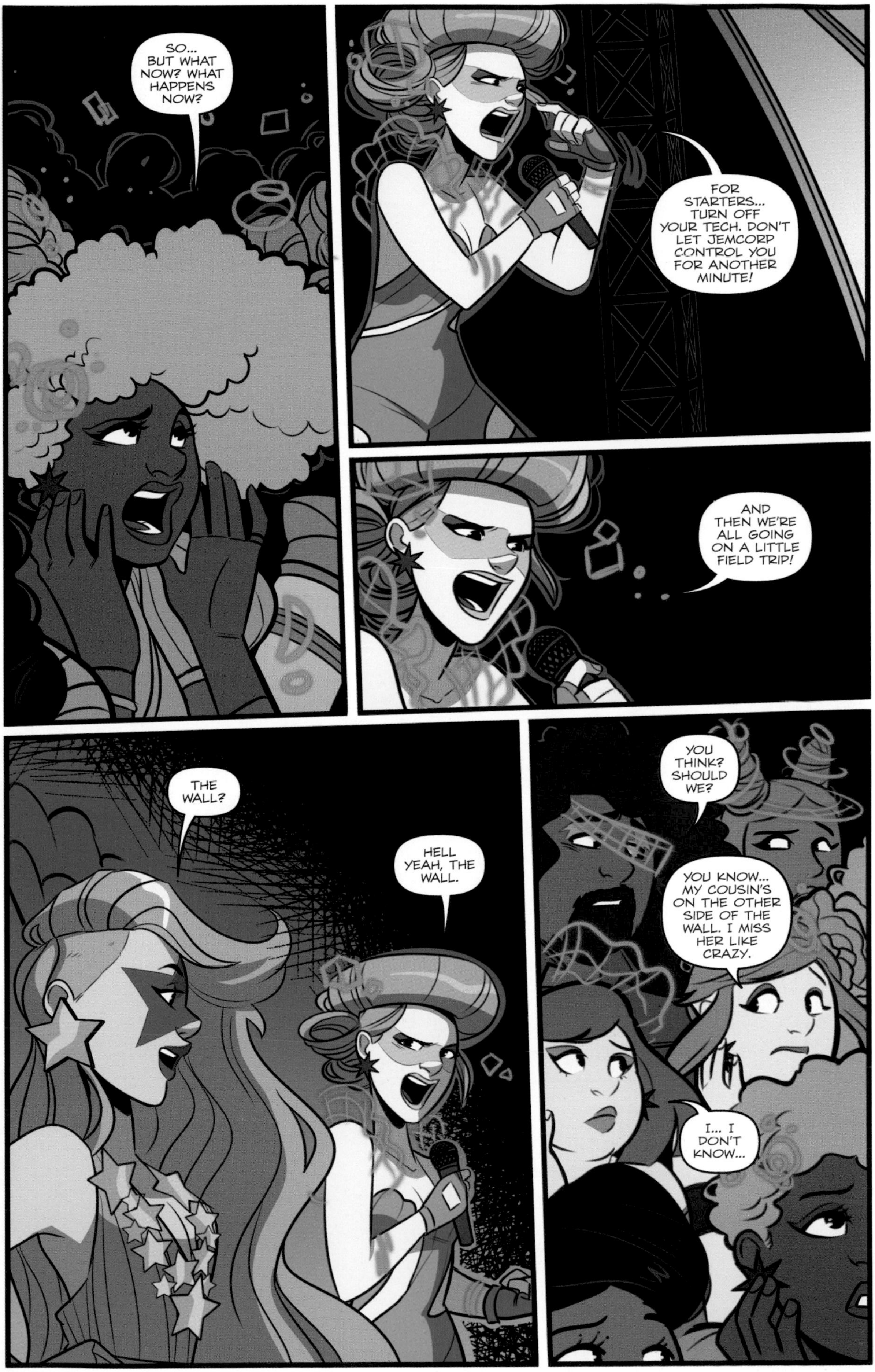
SO... BUT WHAT NOW? WHAT HAPPENS NOW?
FOR STARTERS... TURN OFF YOUR TECH. DON'T LET JEMCORP CONTROL YOU FOR ANOTHER MINUTE!
AND THEN WE'RE ALL GOING ON A LITTLE FIELD TRIP!
THE WALL?
HELL YEAH, THE WALL.
YOU THINK? SHOULD WE?
YOU KNOW... MY COUSIN'S ON THE OTHER SIDE OF THE WALL. I MISS HER LIKE CRAZY.
I... I DON'T KNOW...

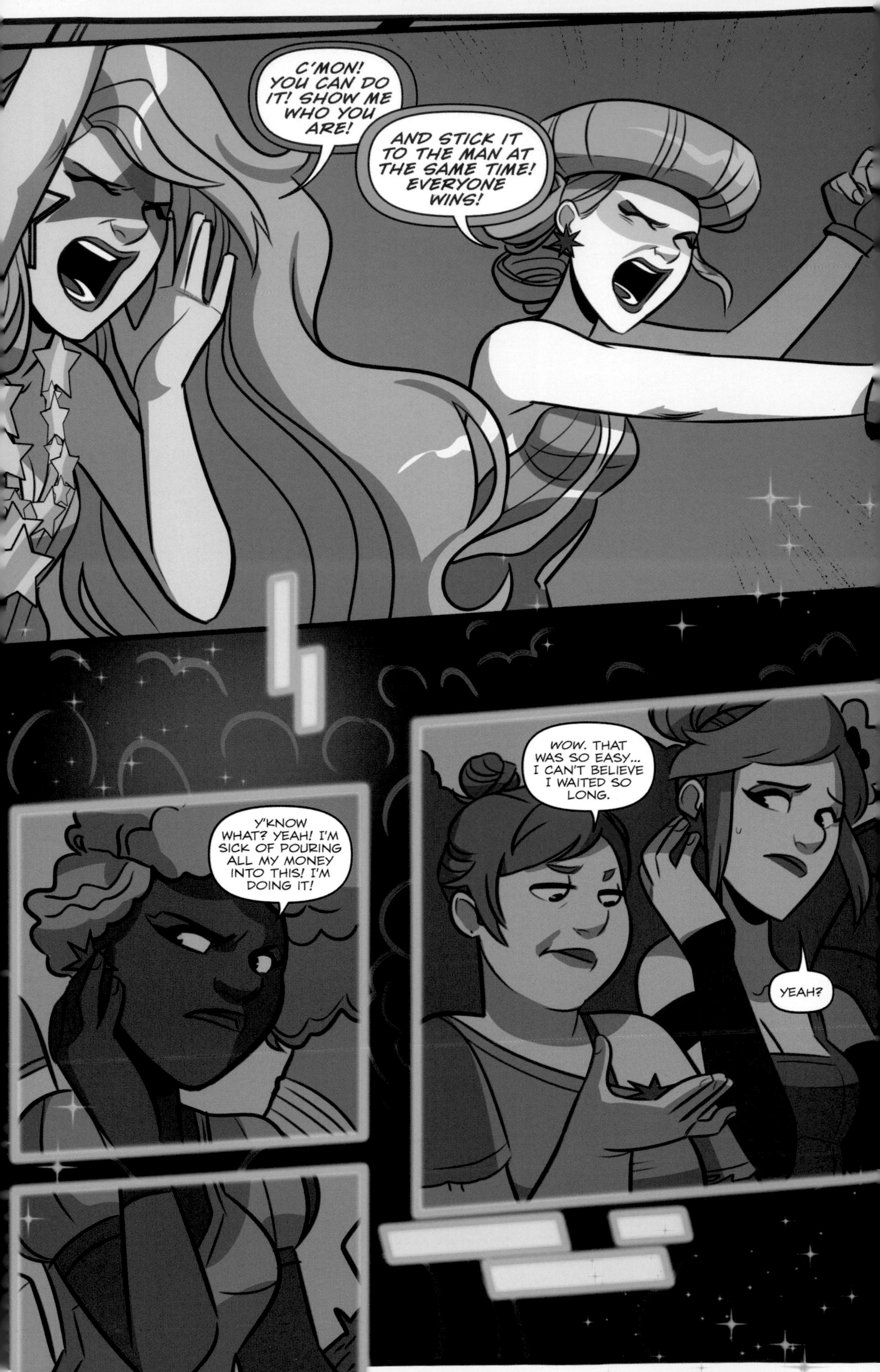
C'MON! YOU CAN DO IT! SHOW ME WHO YOU ARE!
AND STICK IT TO THE MAN AT THE SAME TIME! EVERYONE WINS!
Y'KNOW WHAT? YEAH! I'M SICK OF POURING ALL MY MONEY INTO THIS! I'M DOING IT!
WOW. THAT WAS SO EASY... I CAN'T BELIEVE I WAITED SO LONG.
YEAH?

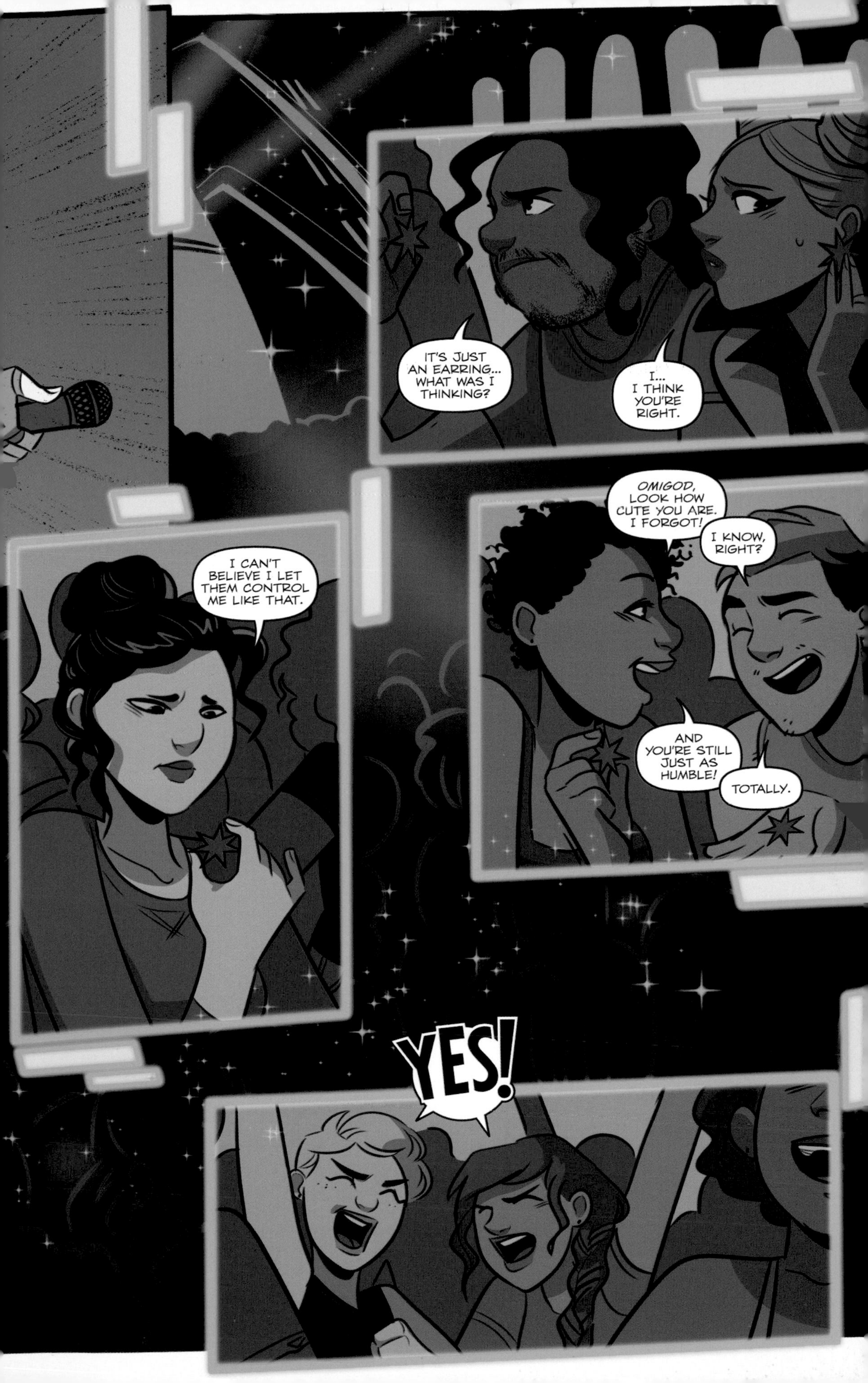
IT'S JUST AN EARRING... WHAT WAS I THINKING?
I... I THINK YOU'RE RIGHT.
I CAN'T BELIEVE I LET THEM CONTROL ME LIKE THAT.
OMIGOD, LOOK HOW CUTE YOU ARE. I FORGOT!
I KNOW, RIGHT?
AND YOU'RE STILL JUST AS HUMBLE!
TOTALLY.
YES!

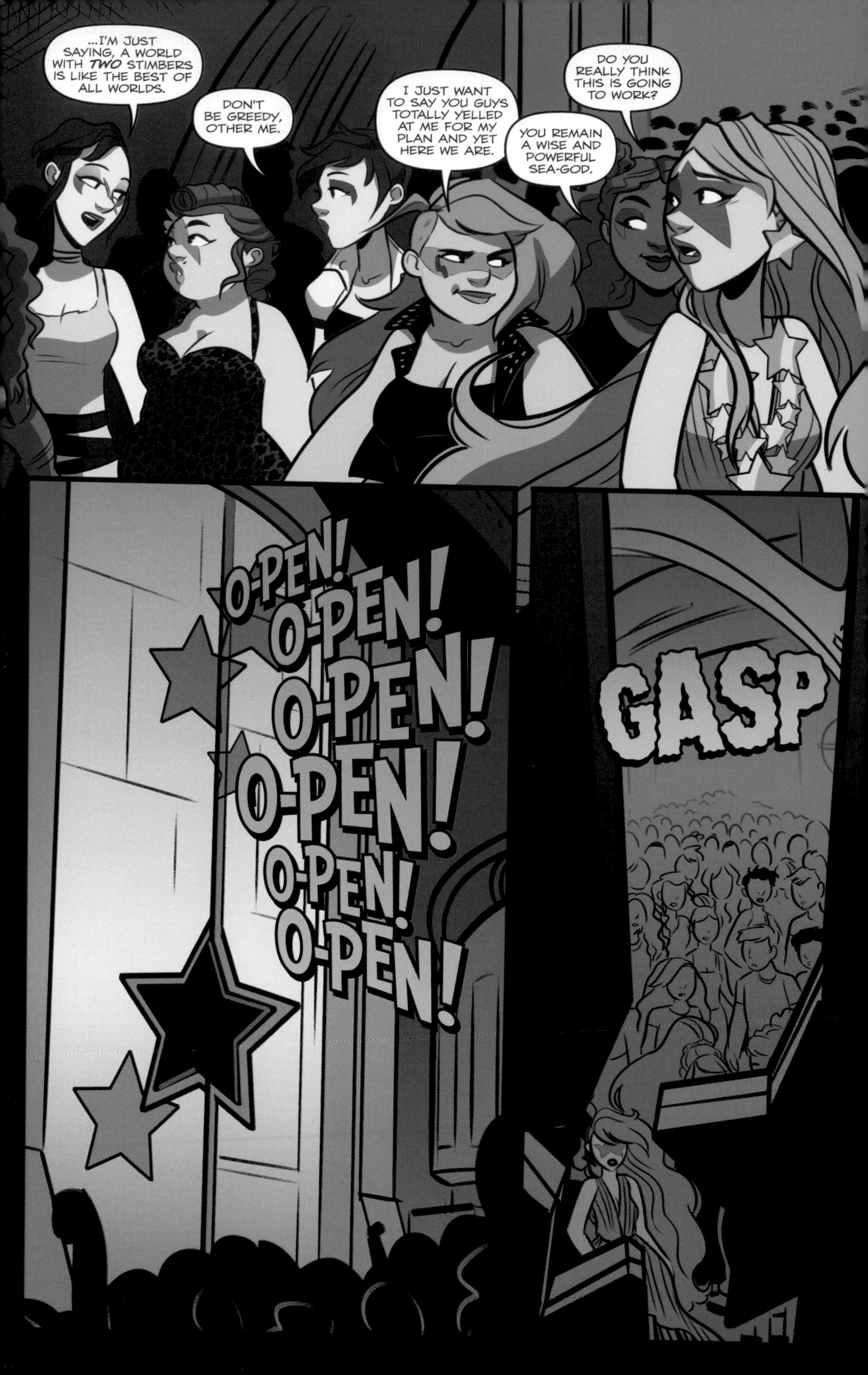
...I'M JUST SAYING, A WORLD WITH *TWO* STIMBERS IS LIKE THE BEST OF ALL WORLDS.
DON'T BE GREEDY, OTHER ME.
I JUST WANT TO SAY YOU GUYS TOTALLY YELLED AT ME FOR MY PLAN AND YET HERE WE ARE.
YOU REMAIN A WISE AND POWERFUL SEA-GOD.
DO YOU REALLY THINK THIS IS GOING TO WORK?
O-PEN! O-PEN! O-PEN! O-PEN! O-PEN! O-PEN!
GASP

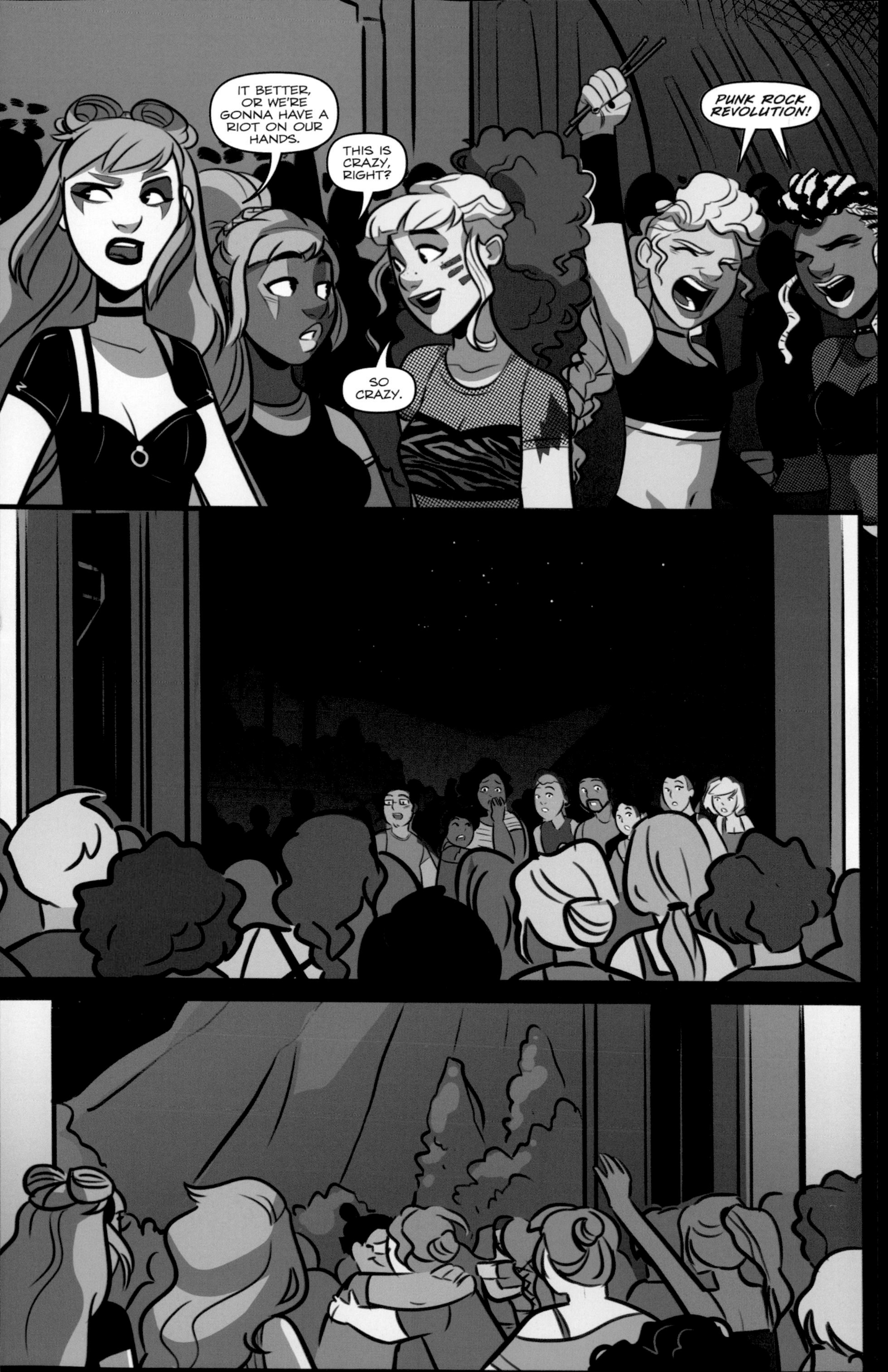
IT BETTER, OR WE'RE GONNA HAVE A RIOT ON OUR HANDS.
THIS IS CRAZY, RIGHT?
SO CRAZY.
PUNK ROCK REVOLUTION!

DO YOU THINK IT WILL BE ENOUGH, EMMETT?

GOD, I HOPE SO.

IT WILL BE.

THIS WAS A HOUSE OF CARDS FROM DAY ONE. BUILT ON LIES AND DECEPTION.

IT TAKES LITTLE TO TOPPLE SUCH A THING.

ELISE HARCOURT?

YES. AND YOU'RE EMMETT BENTON, CREATOR OF SYNERGY. I KNOW WHERE THE BODIES ARE BURIED... SO TO SPEAK. I CAN HELP YOU REBUILD.

WHAT ABOUT JEMCORP? THE BOARD?

GONE. AS SOON AS THE BOARD SAW WHAT WAS HAPPENING, THEY MADE A RUN FOR IT.

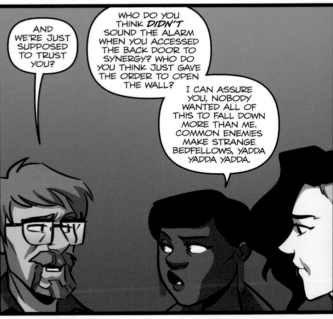

AND WE'RE JUST SUPPOSED TO TRUST YOU?

WHO DO YOU THINK *DIDN'T* SOUND THE ALARM WHEN YOU ACCESSED THE BACK DOOR TO SYNERGY? WHO DO YOU THINK JUST GAVE THE ORDER TO OPEN THE WALL?

I CAN ASSURE YOU, NOBODY WANTED ALL OF THIS TO FALL DOWN MORE THAN ME. COMMON ENEMIES MAKE STRANGE BEDFELLOWS, YADDA YADDA YADDA.

AND ERIC RAYMOND? *HE'S* THE ONE TO WORRY ABOUT.

I AGREE... BUT HE'S GONE TOO. AS IF HE WAS A BAD DREAM.

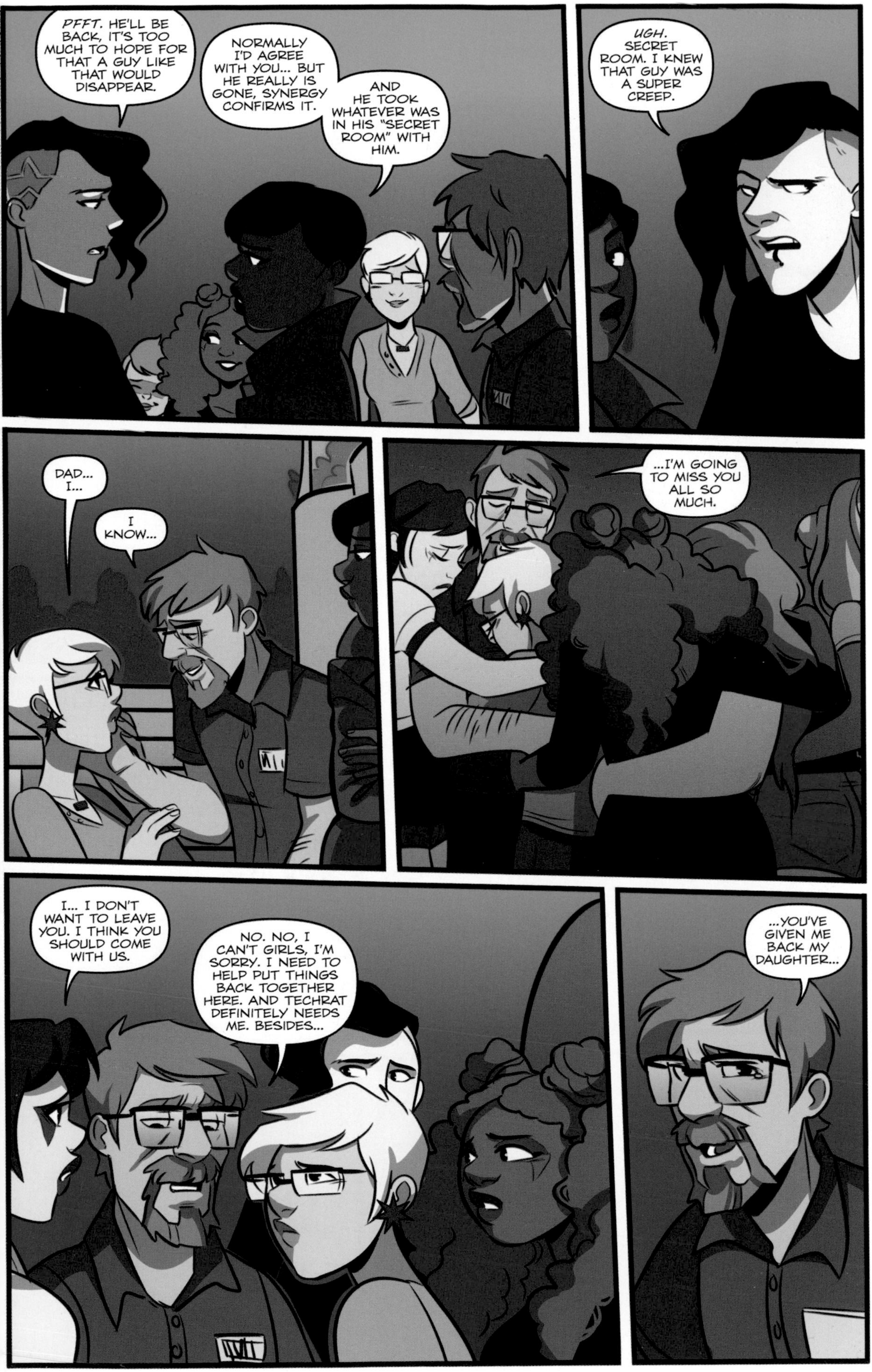
PFFT. HE'LL BE BACK, IT'S TOO MUCH TO HOPE FOR THAT A GUY LIKE THAT WOULD DISAPPEAR.
NORMALLY I'D AGREE WITH YOU... BUT HE REALLY IS GONE, SYNERGY CONFIRMS IT.
AND HE TOOK WHATEVER WAS IN HIS "SECRET ROOM" WITH HIM.
UGH. SECRET ROOM. I KNEW THAT GUY WAS A SUPER CREEP.
DAD... I...
I KNOW...
...I'M GOING TO MISS YOU ALL SO MUCH.
I... I DON'T WANT TO LEAVE YOU. I THINK YOU SHOULD COME WITH US.
NO. NO, I CAN'T GIRLS, I'M SORRY. I NEED TO HELP PUT THINGS BACK TOGETHER HERE. AND TECHRAT DEFINITELY NEEDS ME. BESIDES...
...YOU'VE GIVEN ME BACK MY DAUGHTER...

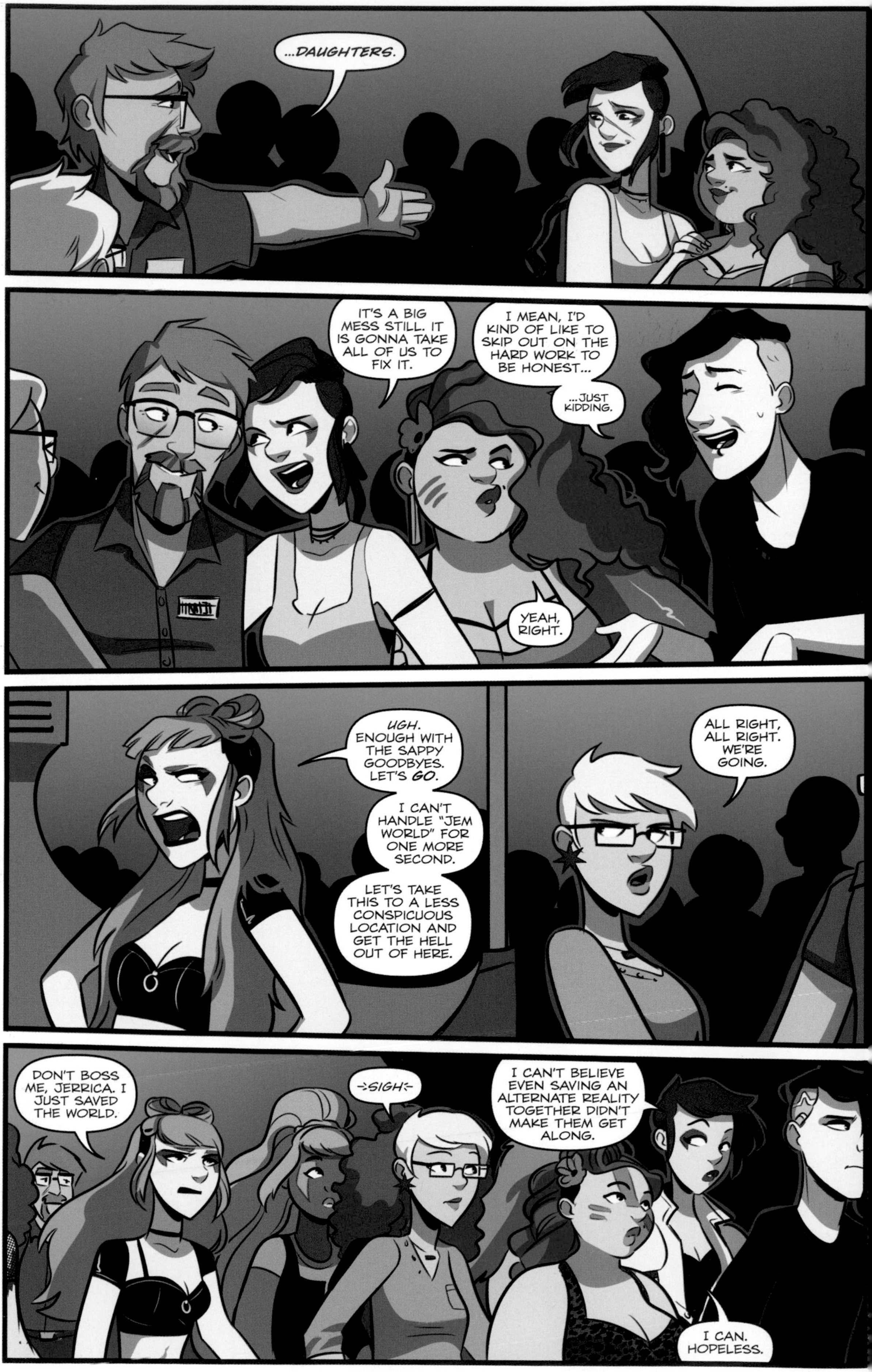
...DAUGHTERS.
IT'S A BIG MESS STILL. IT IS GONNA TAKE ALL OF US TO FIX IT.
I MEAN, I'D KIND OF LIKE TO SKIP OUT ON THE HARD WORK TO BE HONEST...
...JUST KIDDING.
YEAH, RIGHT.
UGH. ENOUGH WITH THE SAPPY GOODBYES. LET'S GO.
I CAN'T HANDLE "JEM WORLD" FOR ONE MORE SECOND.
LET'S TAKE THIS TO A LESS CONSPICUOUS LOCATION AND GET THE HELL OUT OF HERE.
ALL RIGHT, ALL RIGHT. WE'RE GOING.
DON'T BOSS ME, JERRICA. I JUST SAVED THE WORLD.
-SIGH-
I CAN'T BELIEVE EVEN SAVING AN ALTERNATE REALITY TOGETHER DIDN'T MAKE THEM GET ALONG.
I CAN. HOPELESS.

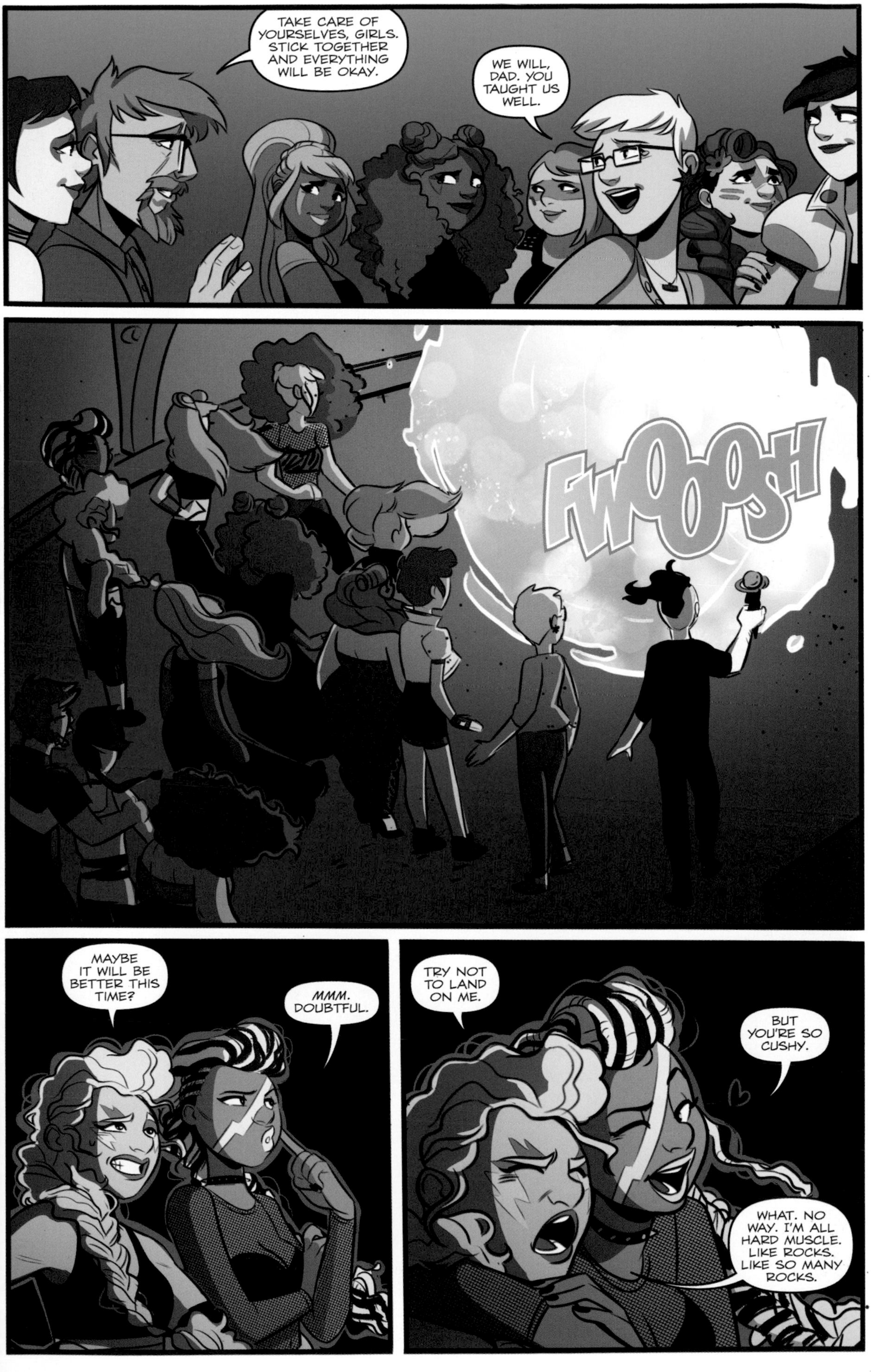
TAKE CARE OF YOURSELVES, GIRLS. STICK TOGETHER AND EVERYTHING WILL BE OKAY.
WE WILL, DAD. YOU TAUGHT US WELL.
FWOOOSH
MAYBE IT WILL BE BETTER THIS TIME?
MMM. DOUBTFUL.
TRY NOT TO LAND ON ME.
BUT YOU'RE SO CUSHY.
WHAT. NO WAY. I'M ALL HARD MUSCLE. LIKE ROCKS. LIKE SO MANY ROCKS.

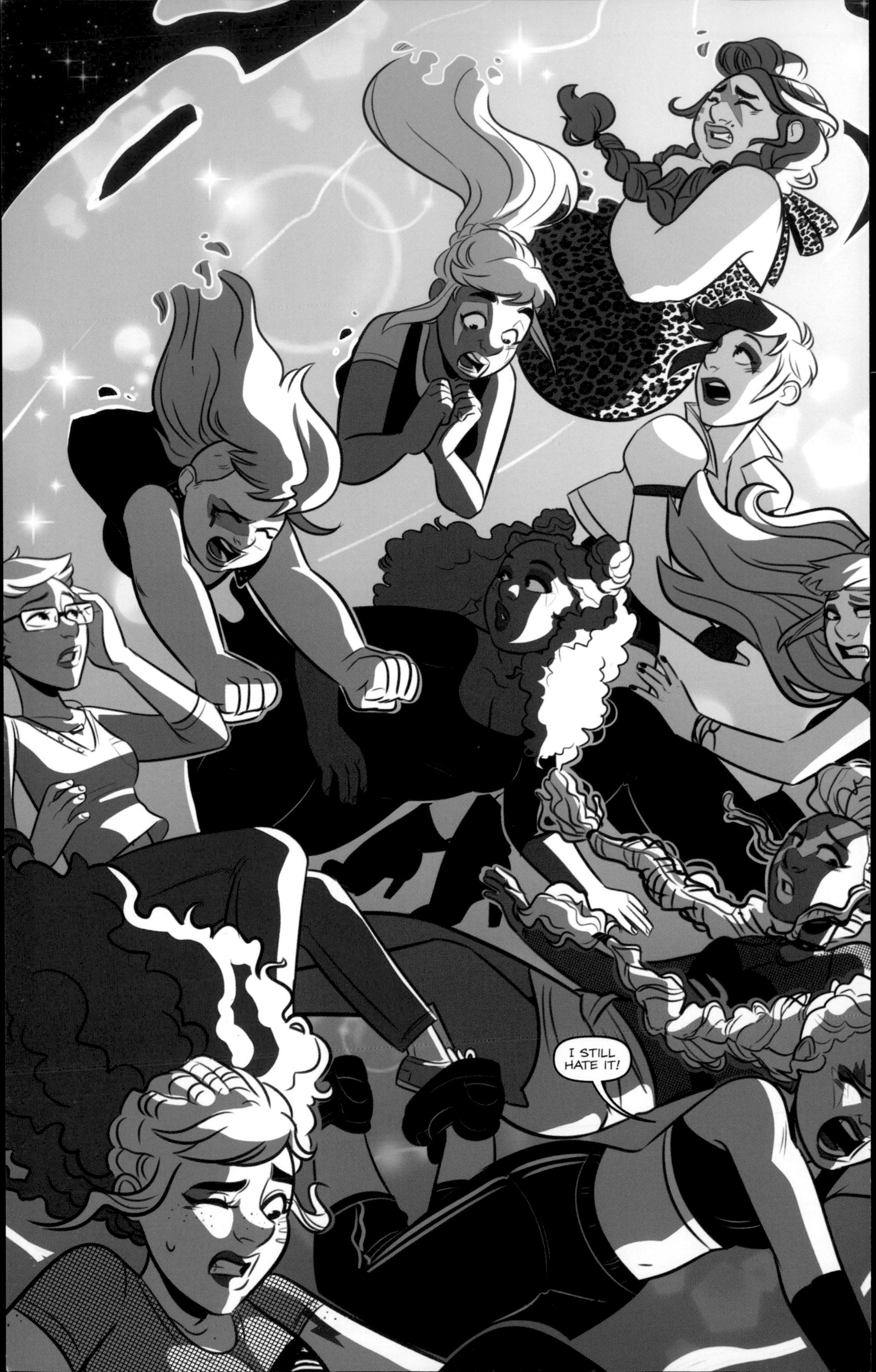
I STILL HATE IT!

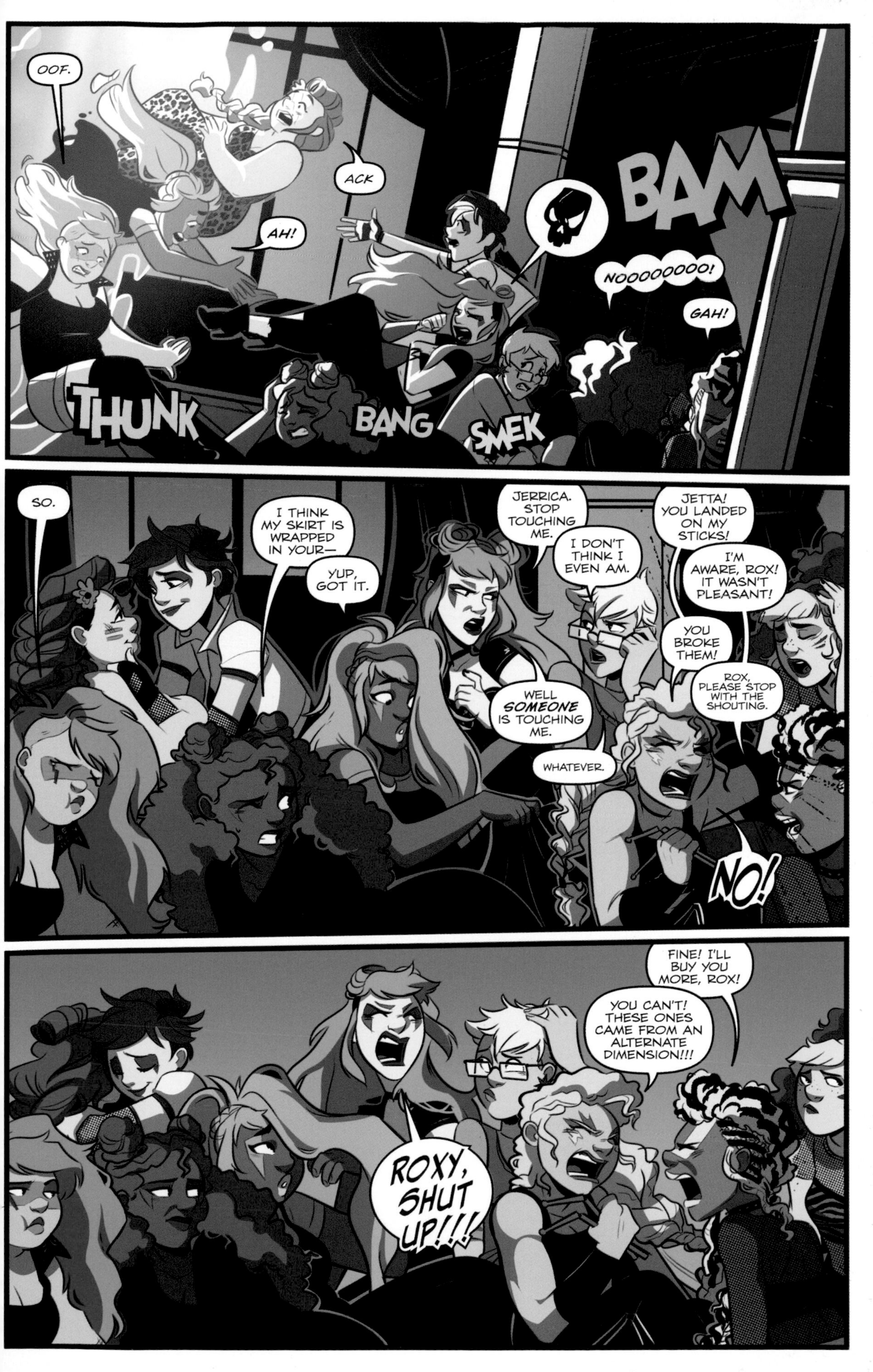
OOF.
ACK
AH!
BAM
NOOOOOOOO!
GAH!
THUNK
BANG
SMEK
SO.
I THINK MY SKIRT IS WRAPPED IN YOUR—
YUP, GOT IT.
JERRICA. STOP TOUCHING ME.
I DON'T THINK I EVEN AM.
WELL SOMEONE IS TOUCHING ME.
WHATEVER.
JETTA! YOU LANDED ON MY STICKS!
I'M AWARE, ROX! IT WASN'T PLEASANT!
YOU BROKE THEM!
ROX, PLEASE STOP WITH THE SHOUTING.
NO!
FINE! I'LL BUY YOU MORE, ROX!
YOU CAN'T! THESE ONES CAME FROM AN ALTERNATE DIMENSION!!!
ROXY, SHUT UP!!!

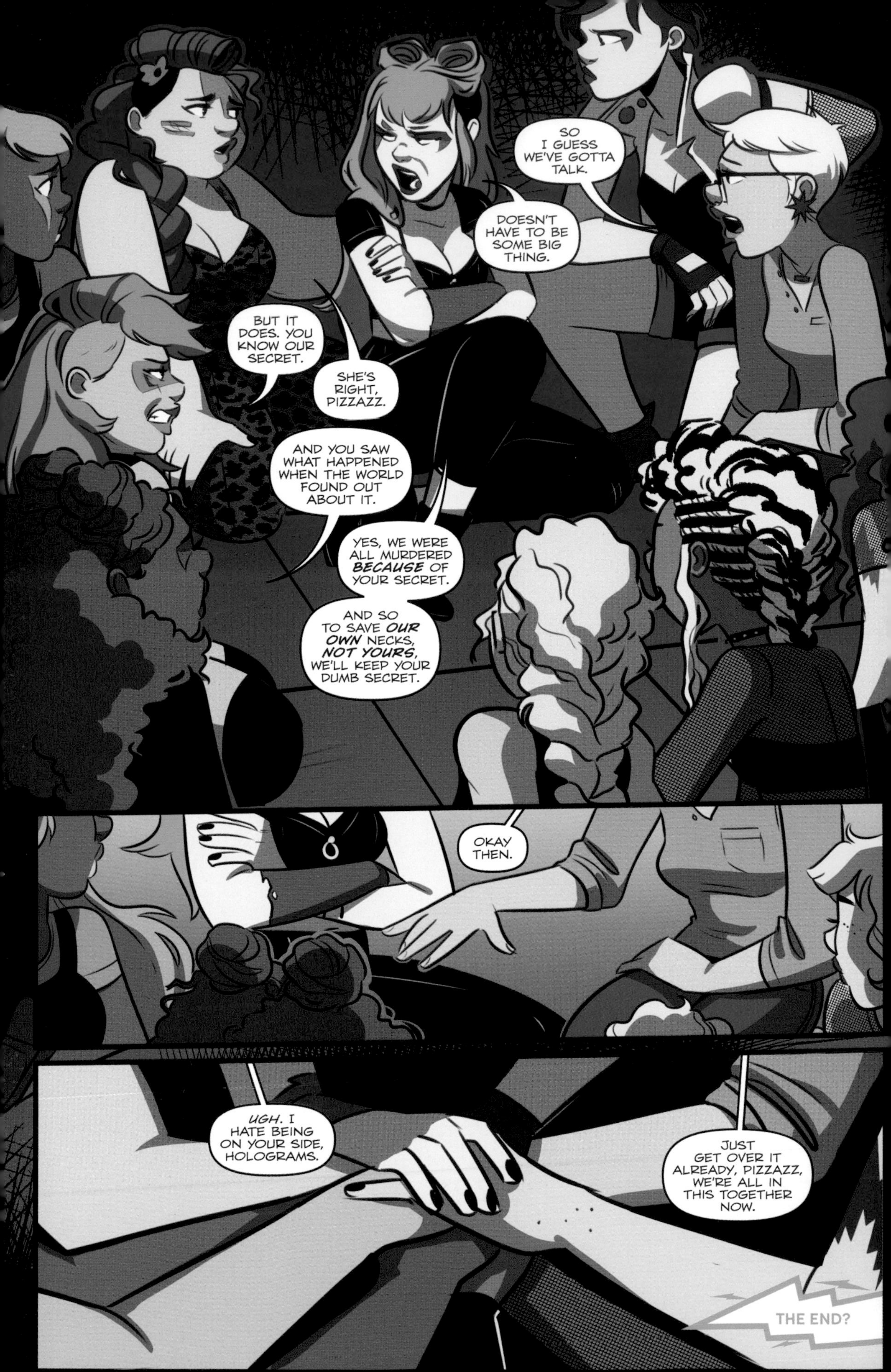
SO I GUESS WE'VE GOTTA TALK.
DOESN'T HAVE TO BE SOME BIG THING.
BUT IT DOES. YOU KNOW OUR SECRET.
SHE'S RIGHT, PIZZAZZ.
AND YOU SAW WHAT HAPPENED WHEN THE WORLD FOUND OUT ABOUT IT.
YES, WE WERE ALL MURDERED *BECAUSE* OF YOUR SECRET.
AND SO TO SAVE *OUR OWN* NECKS, *NOT YOURS*, WE'LL KEEP YOUR DUMB SECRET.
OKAY THEN.
UGH. I HATE BEING ON YOUR SIDE, HOLOGRAMS.
JUST GET OVER IT ALREADY, PIZZAZZ, WE'RE ALL IN THIS TOGETHER NOW.
THE END?

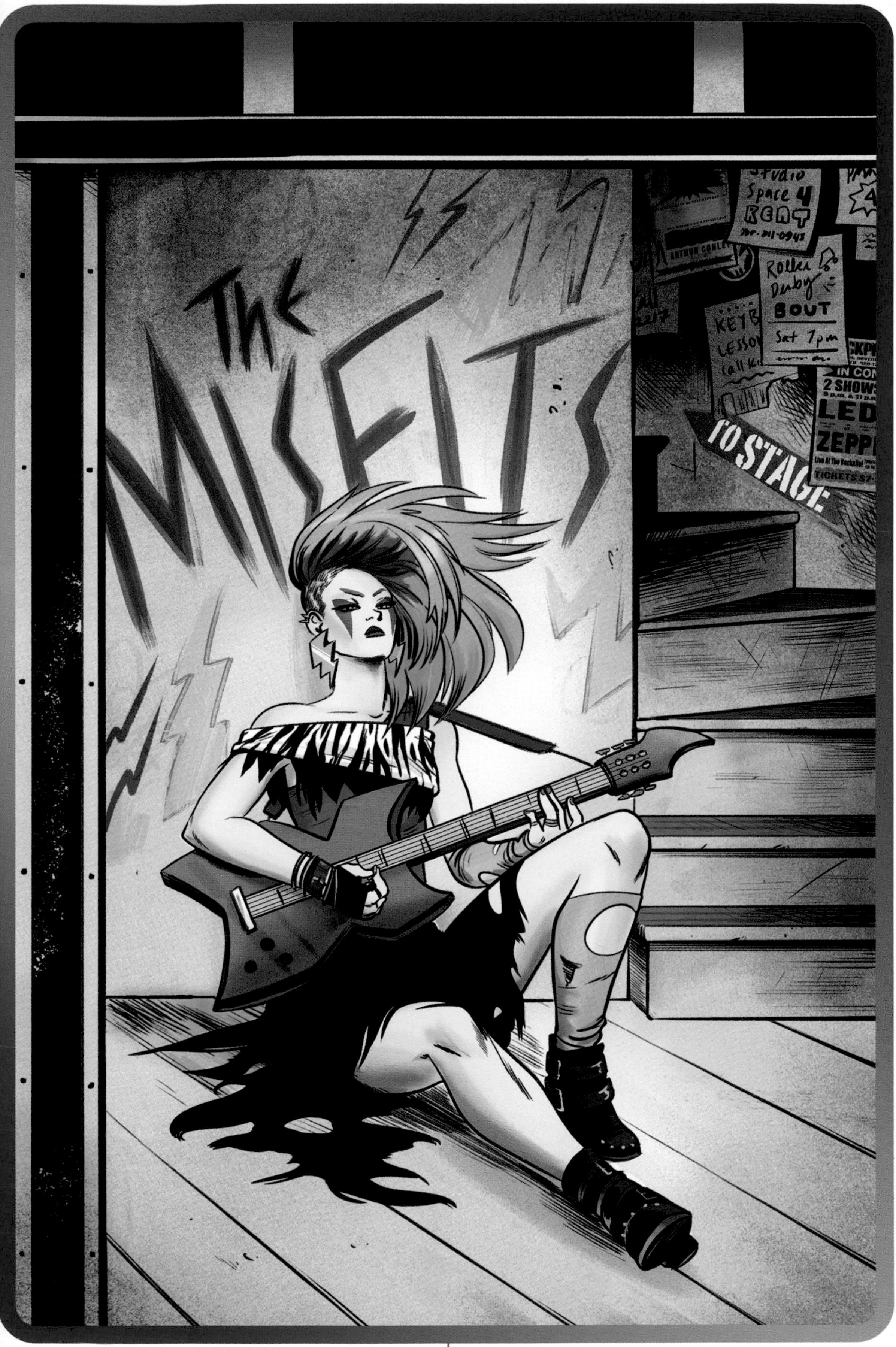
The MISFITS
Studio Space 4 RENT
Roller Derby BOUT
Sat 7pm
2 SHOWS
TO STAGE

ART BY **VERONICA FISH**

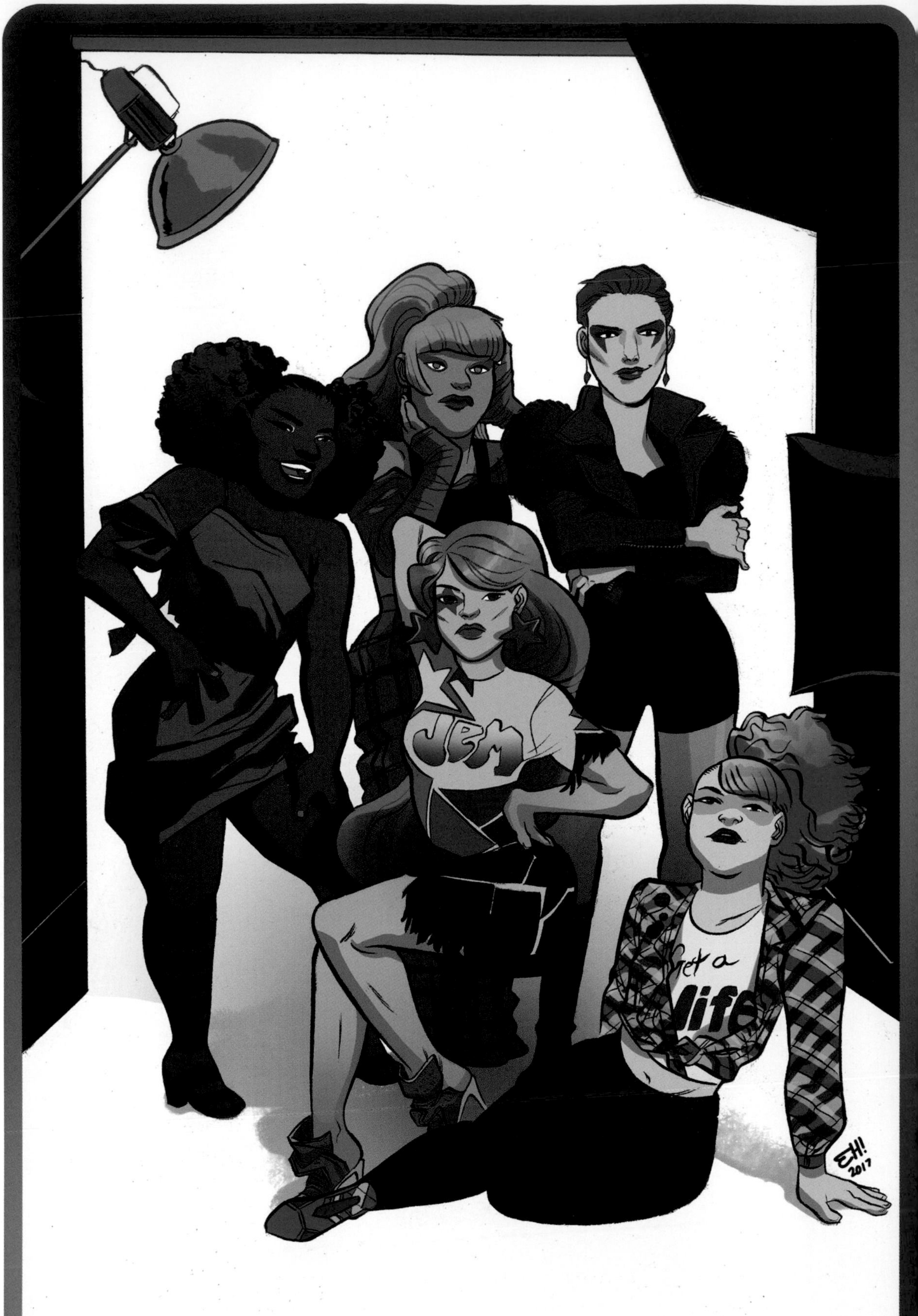
JEM
EH!
2017

ART BY **ERICA HENDERSON**

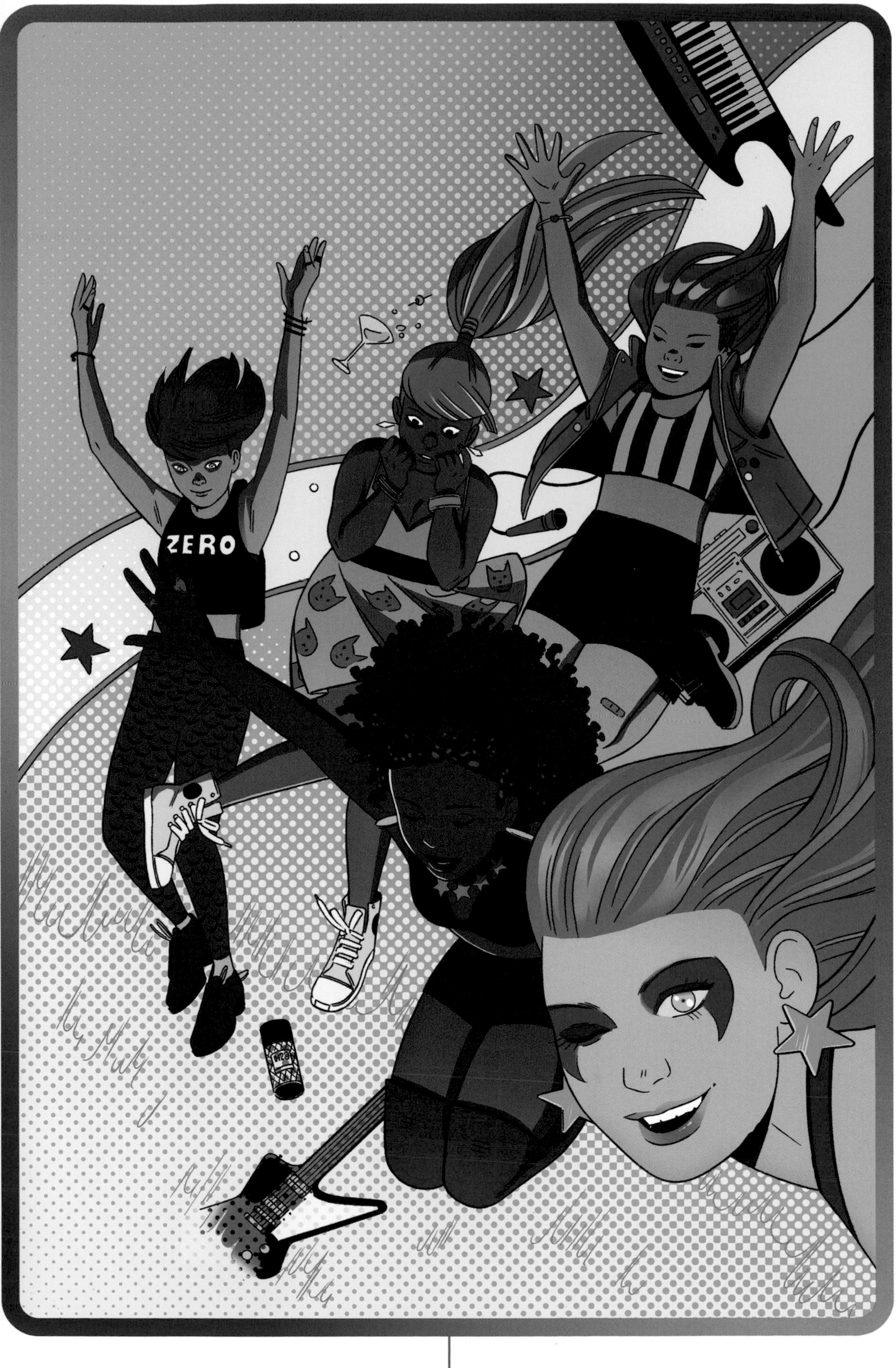
ZERO

ART BY **MARLEY ZARCONE** — COLORS BY **RICO RENZO**

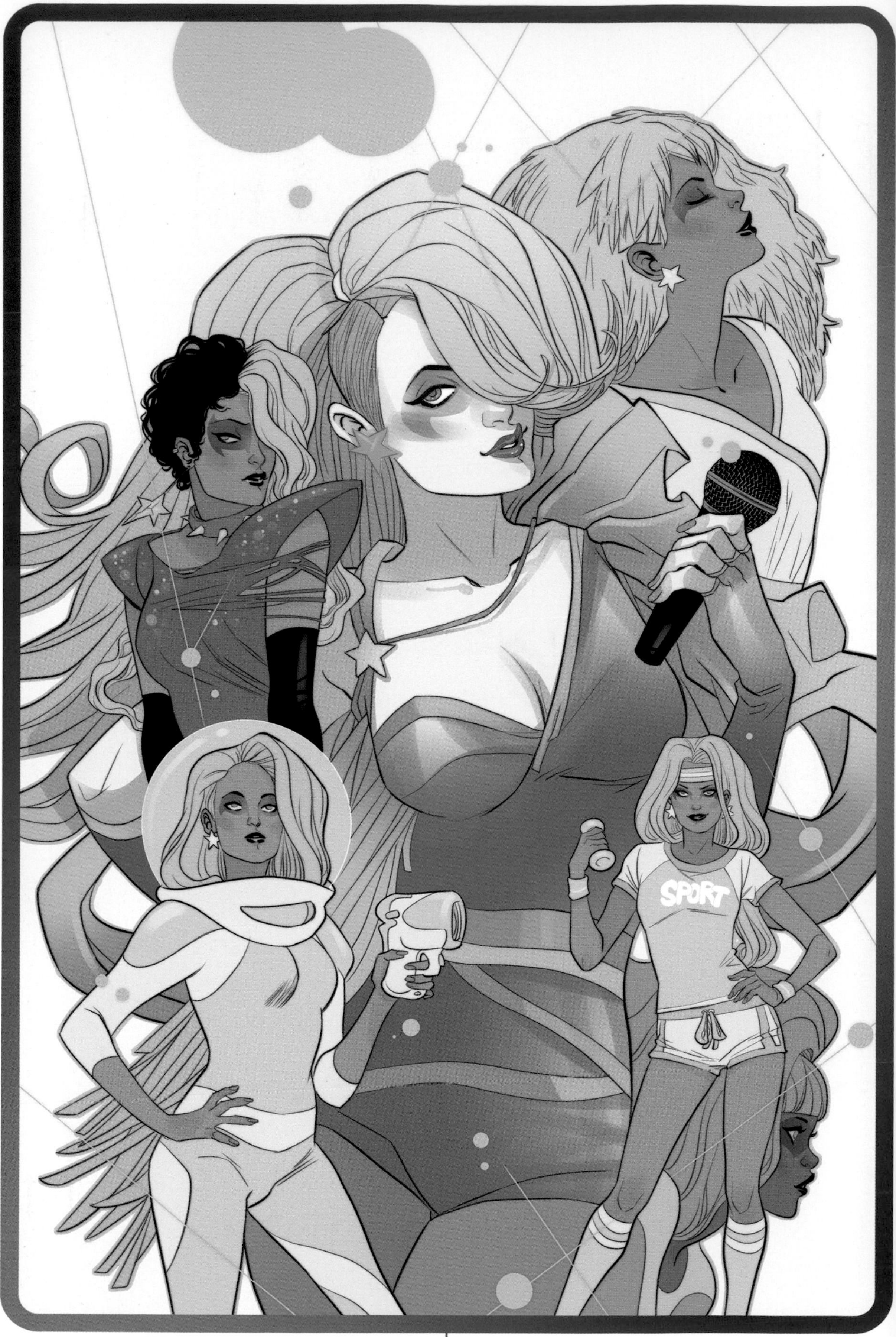
SPORT

ART BY **MARGUERITE SAUVAGE**

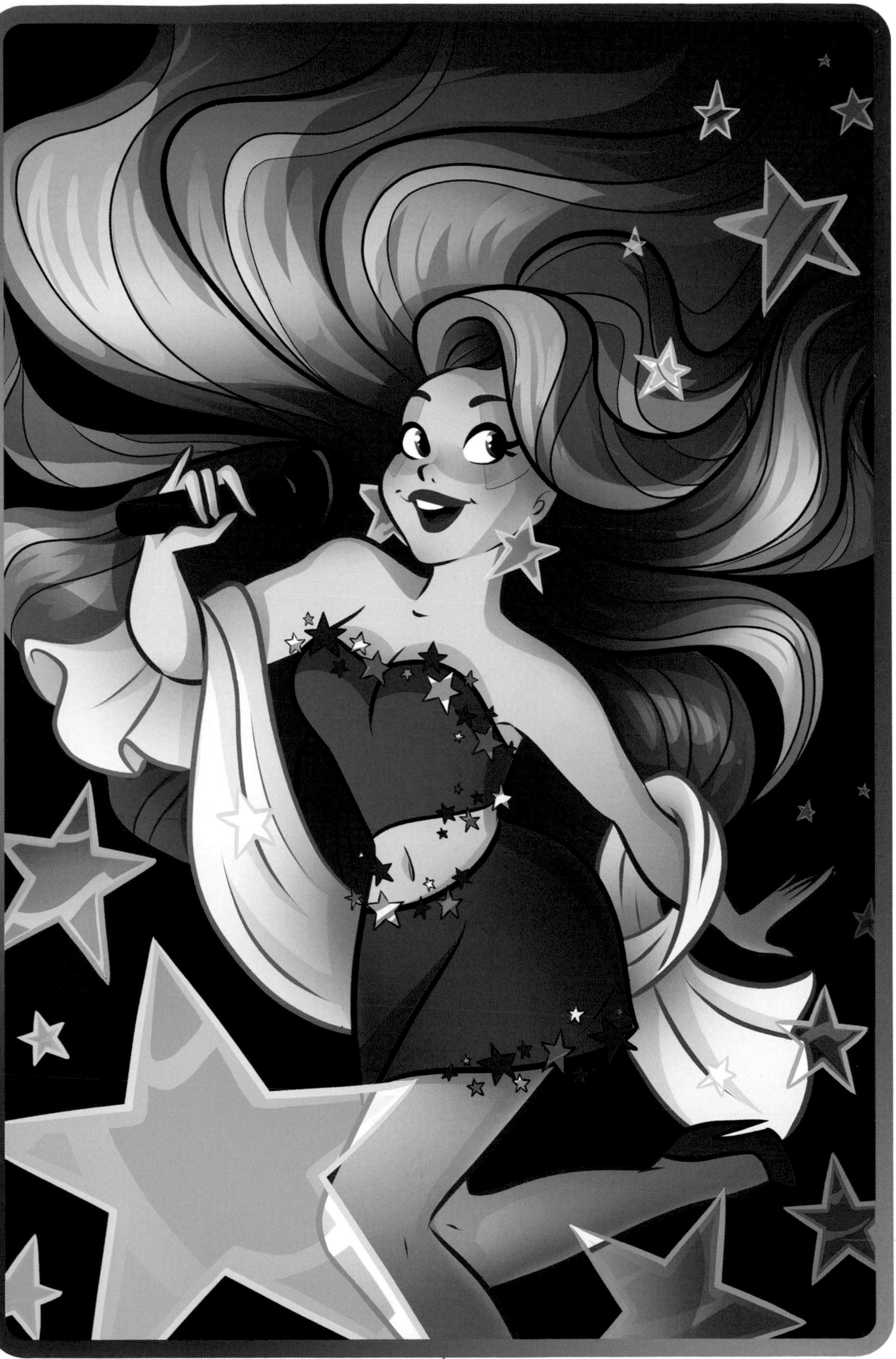

ART BY **GENEVIEVE FT**

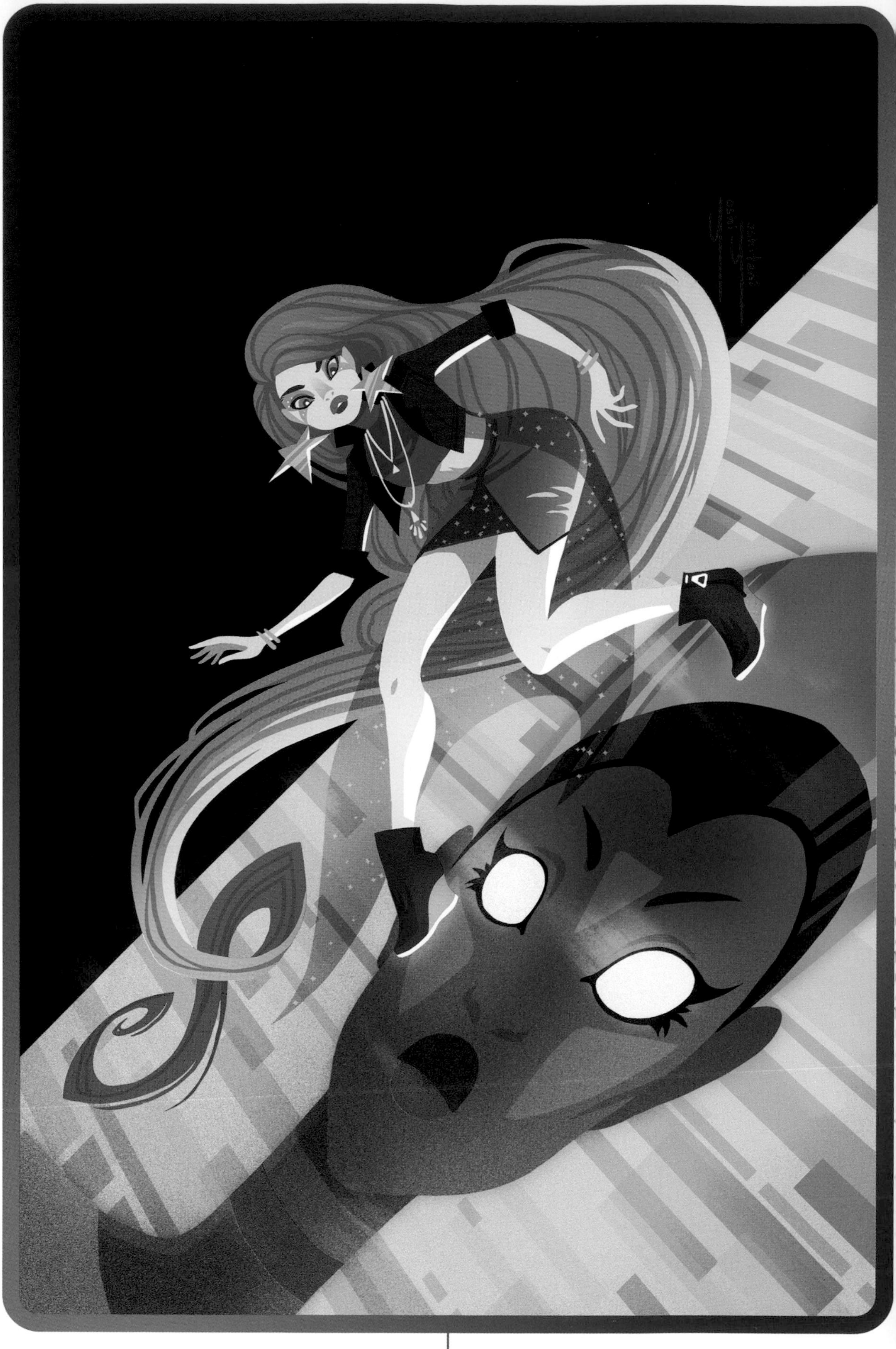

ART BY **YOSHI YOSHITANI**

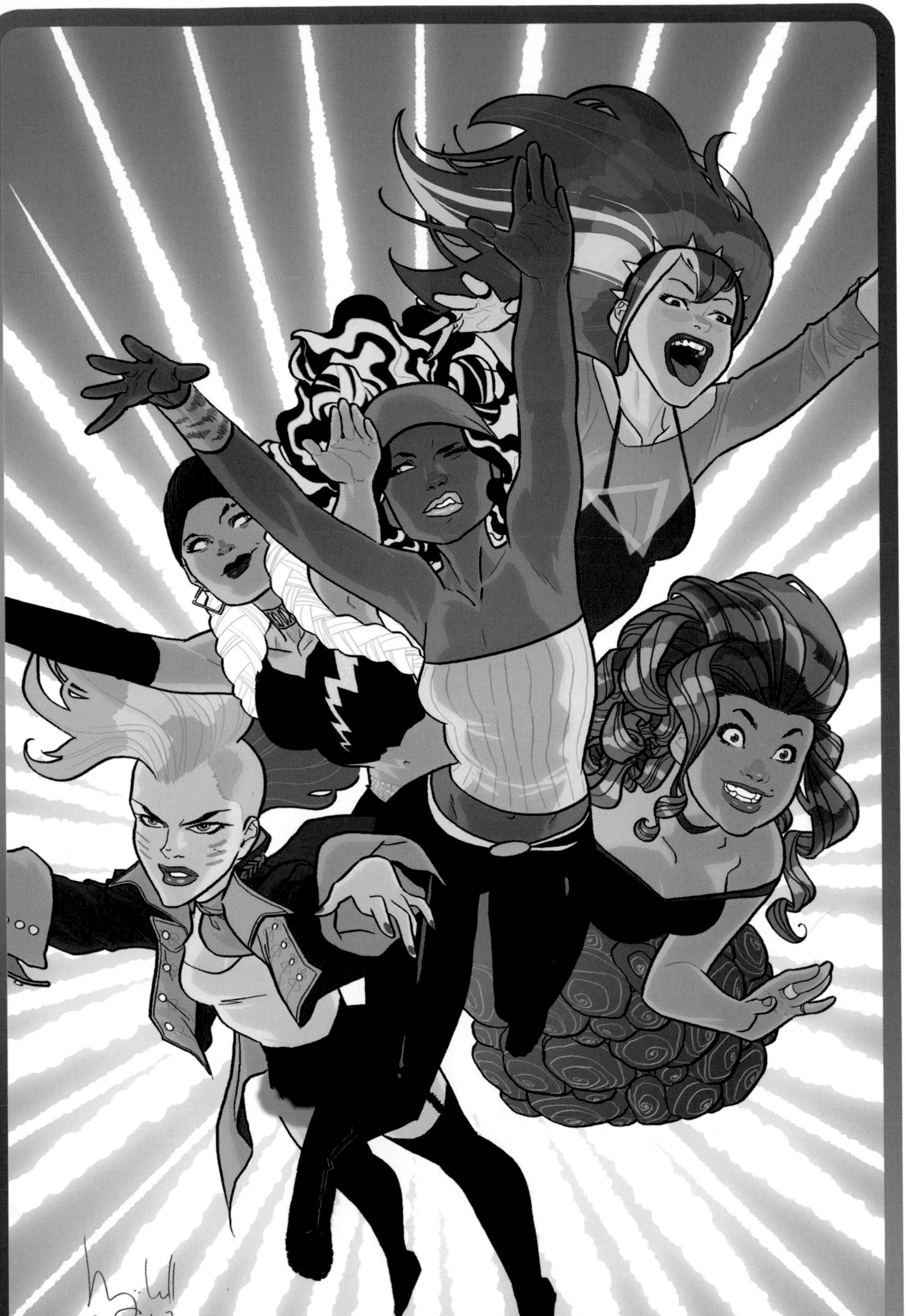

ART BY **BEN CALDWELL**

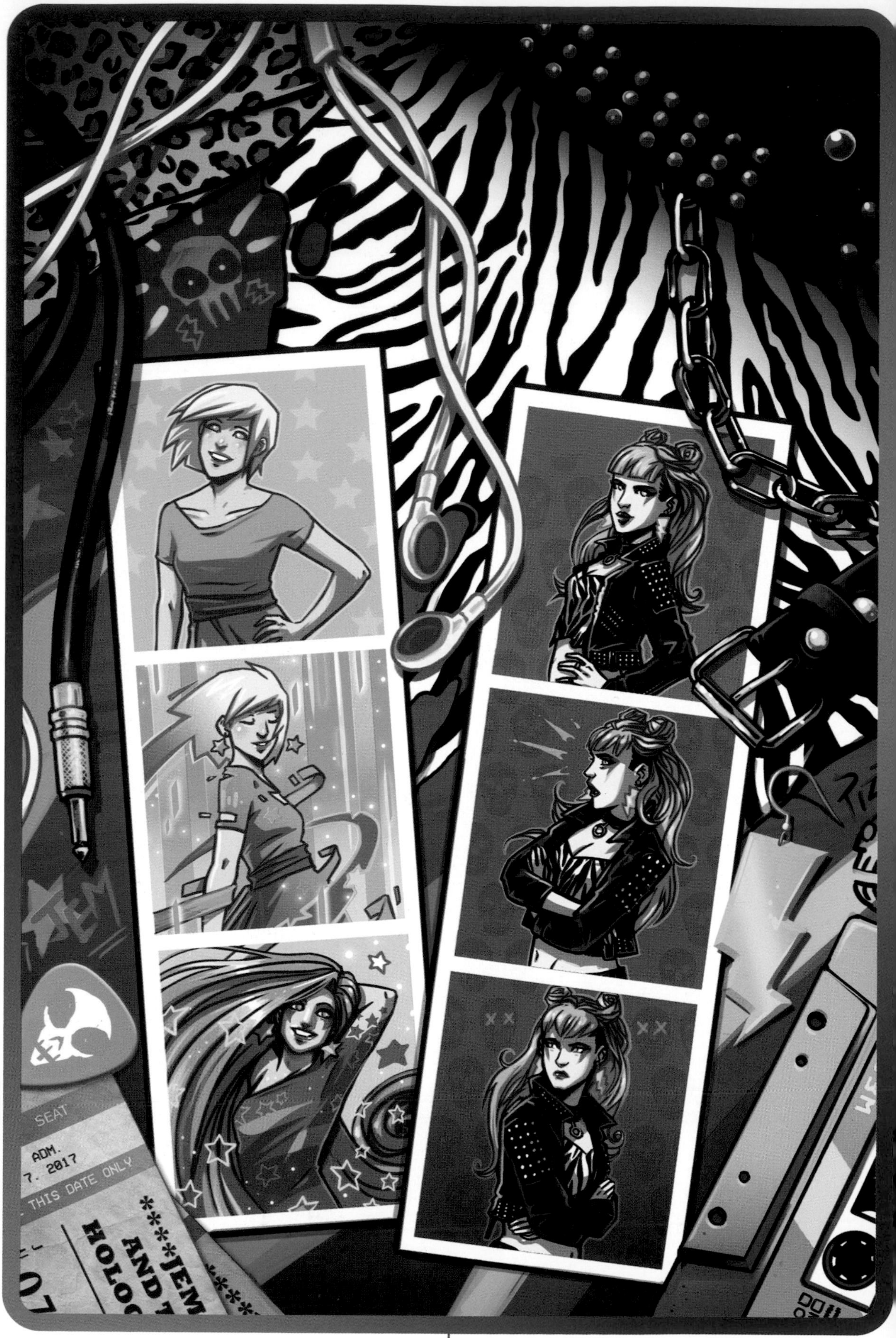
JEM
SEAT
ADM.
7. 2017
THIS DATE ONLY

ART BY **CASPAR WIJNGAARD**

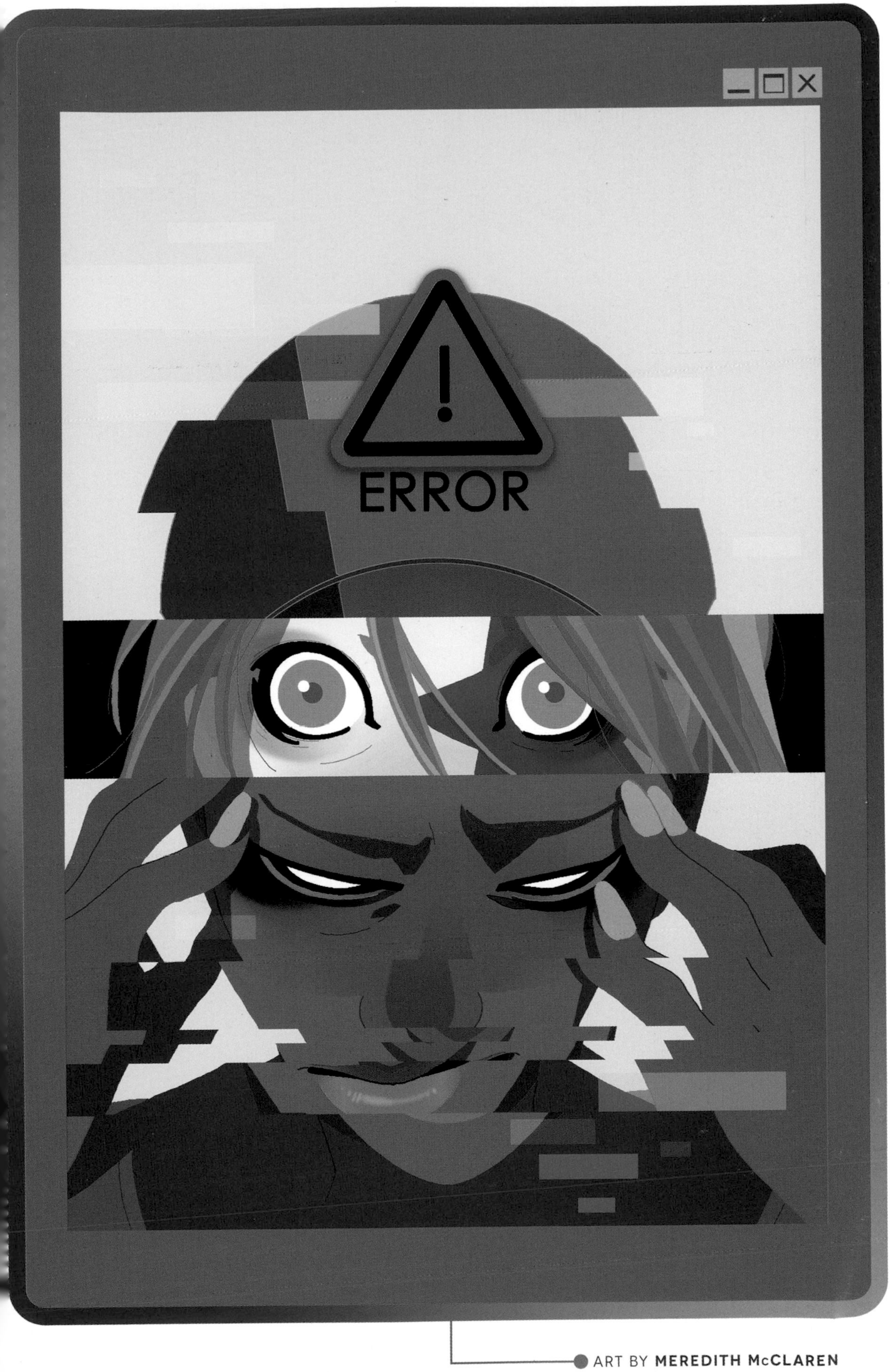
ERROR

ART BY **MEREDITH McCLAREN**

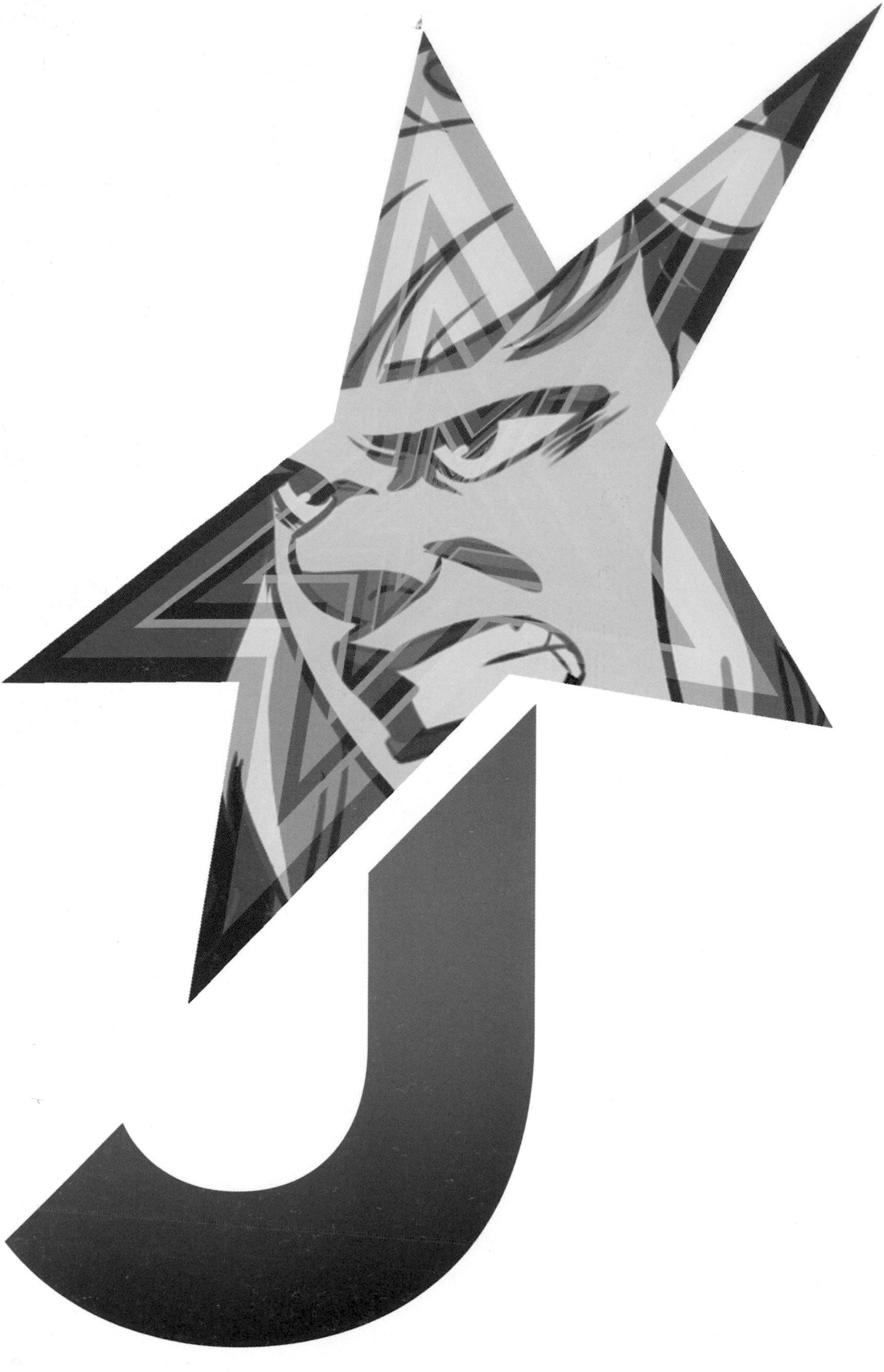